SHRED**GUITAR** **SOLOING**COLLECTION

Three Comprehensive Shred Guitar Soloing Books in One Definitive Edition

CHRIS**ZOUPA**

FUNDAMENTAL**CHANGES**

Shred Guitar Soloing Compilation

Three Comprehensive Shred Guitar Soloing Books in One Definitive Edition

ISBN: 978-1-78933-197-4

Published by www.fundamental-changes.com

Copyright © 2019 Joseph Alexander

The moral right of this author has been asserted.

All rights reserved. No part of this publication may be reproduced, stored in a retrieval system, or transmitted in any form or by any means, without the prior permission in writing from the publisher.

The publisher is not responsible for websites (or their content) that are not owned by the publisher.

www.fundamental-changes.com

Twitter: @guitar_joseph

Over 10,000 fans on Facebook: **FundamentalChangesInGuitar**

Instagram: **FundamentalChanges**

For over 350 Free Guitar Lessons with Videos Check Out

www.fundamental-changes.com

Special thanks to Ben of *Artwork by Electric Bears* for the cover art.

Foreword

Howdy all and welcome to my book trilogy compilation... WOW! A Trilogy... Let that word sink in... TRI-LO-GY. It's crazy to think some chump with a YouTube channel who hadn't done proper academic writing since high school has three books out now... but the world is a hilarious place. I mean, look at the platypus: a duck-billed mammal that lays eggs. Crazy right? So really, anything is possible.

This trilogy contains *Ultimate Shred Machine, Rock Guitar Mode Mastery* and *Shred Guitar Improvisation*. With their powers combined, this compilation contains hundreds of exercises to build your technique and mechanics, as well as theoretical explanations that allow you to navigate the world of modes and improvisation confidently.

I can't thank Fundamental Changes and the YouTube guitar community enough for all of the combined support I've received over the last couple of years. I've thoroughly enjoyed not having a "real job", and with everyone's help, I can continue to do what I love, with the added bonus of somehow being able to support my family with toasted savoury croissants.

There is no specific order in which you need to read these books, so dive in where you want. I think MC Hammer summed it up best in his 1994 masterpiece *It's All Good* by saying "Heeeeey... Itz all gooood!"

Without further ado, pick up that guitar, get reading and start playing!

Your boy,

Chris Z

Contents

Ultimate Shred Machine

Introduction	02
Chapter One: Shredding Tips, Tricks 'n' Lick	04
Chapter Two: Legato and the Secrets of Smooth Erotic Playing	40
Chapter Three: Tappin' Like A Boss!	64
Chapter Four: Sweeping Arpeggio Tips and Exercises (Unleash your Inner Janitor!)	87
Secrets of a Janitor and Bringing it All Together	109
Epilogue and Acknowledgements	110

Rock Guitar Mode Mastery

An Introduction to Modes	114
Chapter 1: Owning your Ionian	116
Chapter 2: Deciphering Dorian	130
Chapter 3: Phabulous Phrygian	144
Chapter 4: Luscious Lydian	157
Chapter 5: The Magic of Mixolydian	171
Chapter 6: Astonishing Aeolian	184
Chapter 7: Elusive Locrian	198
Epilogue & Acknowledgements	210

Shred Guitar Improvisation

Introduction	212
Chapter 1 – Chord Tones and Chord Numbers	214
Chapter 2 – The I Chord (G Major)	221
Chapter 3 – The ii chord (A minor)	227
Chapter 4 – The iii chord (B minor)	232
Chapter 5 – IV chord (C Major)	237
Chapter 6 – The V chord (D Major)	242
Chapter 7 – The vi chord (E minor)	248
Chapter 8 – The vii chord (F#m7b5)	254
Chapter 9 – Handling Non-Diatonic Chords	262
Chapter 10 – Soloing Using Chords & Breaking Out of the Single Note Box	281
Chapter 11 – Varying Scales & Shred Sequences	289
Chapter 12 – Adding Even More Flair, Sass & Pizazz	302
Chapter 13 – Writing a Solo and Bringing it all Together	309
Full Solo	313
A Gentleman's Conclusion	315

ULTIMATE SHRED MACHINE

Shred guitar: The ultimate guide to picking, tapping and sweeping

CHRIS **ZOUPA**

FUNDAMENTAL**CHANGES**

Introduction

For as long as I can remember, students and passing YouTube fans have asked me, "Is there a book you would recommend to help me shred?" or "Is there a book with some cool exercises that you know of?" So one day I thought, "It's time, Chris… it's time to write the great Australian Romance novel!"

The original plot was about a young woman called Josie who grew up in the country. She's beautiful, independent, strong and not afraid to get her hands dirty, which is exactly what her dad Darryl loved about her. He passed over the family farm to her just before he died.

Josie ends up falling in love with not one, but two of the local farm boys who regularly get sweaty and topless around her, presumably after a big day of hard work. Who will she choose? Can she have it all?

It was then that I realised I wasn't cut out for writing romance novels and decided to write a book about effective shredding! My aim was to make the book action packed and full of advice, exercises and the kind of ironic and questionably dated references you will only find in conversations (and the written word) with yours truly.

Without further ado, sit back, relax, read and shred. We'll be looking at improving alternate picking, swept and non-swept arpeggios, legato, tapping and the dreaded string-skipping technique. By the end of this book, I hope you'll all be Ultimate Shred Machines!

Get The Audio

The audio files for this book are available to download for *free* from **www.fundamental-changes.com** and the link is in the top right corner. Simply select this book title from the drop-down menu and follow the instructions to get the audio.

We recommend that you download the files directly to your computer, not to your tablet and extract them there before adding them to your media library. You can then put them on your tablet, iPod or burn them to CD. On the download page there is a help PDF and *we also provide technical support through the form on the download page.*

We spend a long time getting the audio just right and you will benefit greatly from listening to these examples as you work through the book. They're free, so what are you waiting for?!

Head over to **www.fundamental-changes.com** and grab the audio files now.

There are also over 250 free guitar lessons to get your teeth into.

Chapter One: Shredding Tips, Tricks 'n' Licks

Since the dawn of time, man has yearned for speed. This desire unquestionably influenced the invention of the wheel, jetpacks, roller-skates and laxatives. Since the '70s, the speed of one's guitar playing has been a crucial part of the rock and metal guitarist's mentality. The quest for speed often becomes the *be all and end all* of some guitarist's playing – as if it were a life and death situation. Recent findings also show that guitar playing speed directly corresponds with the length and breadth of a man's genitalia!

Many of my students and YouTube fans have asked me, "How do I get faster? What are the secrets to playing fast?" I used to give them the following advice:

"Stand in front of the mirror with a glass of tomato juice. Close your eyes and say, 'Christopher Lambert' 10 times. He will appear in full *Highlander* attire and sprinkle you with magic dust, immediately giving you the speed and skill to play like Yngwie Malmsteen in a few short minutes."

As funny as I found giving this advice, it was too time consuming, so I shortened that spiel to, "Just practise real hard with a metronome and build up your speed slowly."

Unfortunately, both answers were too vague. People continued to ask the same question, over and over again. So, in this book I want to give you my two cents on shredding speed and efficiency with a couple of tips and tricks. In the process, we'll also lay to rest a few misconceptions.

Pick Choice

This tip may seem obvious, but it's likely that you'll have a specific pick you prefer to use with scale practice – one which is entirely related to your comfort and preference as a guitarist. You'll need to mess around with the variables of size and thickness to find what suits you. Let's look at a few options and discuss the pros and cons of each.

THIN (.40mm to .60mm): These picks have a lighter sound, a flimsy feeling, and a less aggressive attack than medium and thick picks. This can make it harder to play rhythm guitar with the aggression and precision needed in rock and metal. Thin picks are ideal for delicate playing and for those who like a pick with a lot of give.

MEDIUM (.60mm to .80mm): This is the most common pick choice among guitarists. You get some of the flimsiness of the thin pick and some of the thickness of the heavy pick, which makes them suitable for both rhythm and lead playing. I would highly recommend this pick for beginner players.

HEAVY: (.80mm to 1.2mm): Heavy or "thick" picks will give you the most control. The lack of flimsiness of the heavy pick means that it's less likely to "fall" from one string to another as it's harder to fall through the strings unintentionally. The heavy pick generally provides a fat rhythm sound, has a pronounced attack and is great for playing aggressive leads!

JAZZ: These stubby little fellas are great for speed and precision picking. However, their lack of protrusion from your hand can make it feel like you're too close to the strings, and this can create complications for certain riffs and heavy rhythm playing. These are absolutely *not* for beginners and are an acquired taste!

NAIL: If you're a rare breed like me and it works for you, you can always file a fingernail into a pick. This means that you can feel the string on your hand and there's nothing in between you and the guitar. This requires enormous maintenance as your nail growth will change the shape of your nail pick every few days.

Plus, if you happen to break a nail, it's a nightmare waiting for it to grow back whilst living with a hazardous HANGNAIL! I thoroughly advise against this approach, even though I do it myself, as there are so many things that can go wrong. Chris Broderick has a range of picks that simulate the "fingernail pick" experience if the idea appeals to you.

Effects: Distortion or Clean?

Over my 5 years on YouTube, and occasionally at the gigs I've played since I was a wee tot, people have asked me about the kinds of pedals I use. What amps, software, what kinds of distortion? The list goes on. I'll keep it simple here and just talk about a clean versus distorted tone and how this affects your practice. I've heard a lot of terrible advice over the years, and I'm sure you have too, so I'd like to clear a few things up.

Many advise players to, "Always practise scales and runs with a clean tone." The thought behind this notion is that many people will play fast, but not cleanly, and with the help of distortion, disguise their sloppiness and lack of articulation. This advice has some merit, but I would suggest you get a feel for practising with both clean *and* distorted tones.

Your effects and amp settings should be fitting for the genre and context you're playing in. If you're trying to play an aggressive technical metal solo, for example, and the original recording is drenched in distortion, then you're going to want to emulate that player's obnoxious tone in order to get as close to the original sound as possible. In this instance, practising the solo with a clean tone would be counter-productive. (I should point out here that it is, of course, important for you to tidy up any excess noise and sloppiness when playing with distortion).

It all comes down to context. There's a reason I never practise jazz with distortion! If I'm listening to a player with mild overdrive or a clean reverb setting, I'll try to emulate that sound to be stylistically accurate to the piece I'm learning. Having the right tone won't necessarily grant you magic speed, but it's a more accurate way to build towards the speed and sound you desire.

Befriending the Metronome and Finding a Pulse When Practising

It has been foretold for centuries that an aspiring shred guitarist's rite of passage begins at a very early stage of their shred quest. They will most likely approach a role model, elder or oracle of shred and request either a meeting, phone call or just send them long, rambling, boring emails. Upon their eventual meeting they will be told by this bastion of wisdom to "practise with a metronome". In essence, this is great advice, however it's incredibly vague and fails to go into detail about the fruits of metronome usage and the value that will come with its inclusion in your practice regime.

BORING DISCLAIMER/CALL TO ACTION: Get a metronome, because you'll need it to play through all the exercises in this book at the pace I recommend (or slower if you're struggling). If you haven't got a physical metronome, there are heaps of metronome apps available to download on your smartphone and almost all of them are free.

Regularly practising to a metronome will not only make you a better player, it will help you monitor your speed progress. For example, you might practise an exercise at 85bpm, then gradually, week by week increase the tempo to 100bpm (while, of course, making sure you can play comfortably, cleanly and with control).

Metronome practise can include multiple varying speeds, pulses and emphases, depending on the speed and feel (straight notes or triplets) of the exercise you're working on. In other words, you could have three different exercises, all played at the same bpm, but with varying notes per second. Confused yet? You should be! Don't worry, I'll explain all of this in thorough detail as we go on.

Let's start by playing simple dead notes with a *straight* pulse over an 80bpm metronome setting. We're going to be looking at three different straight pulses using varying note lengths. We'll start with a 1/4 note pulse (AKA crotchets) then work into 1/8 notes (AKA quavers) and finally end on 1/16 notes (AKA semiquavers). Make sure that you play several repeats of each bar before you move on, to ensure you get the right feel and are able to "lock in" with the click.

Example 1a: Straight dead note pulses: 1/4 + 1/8 + 1/16th @ 80bpm

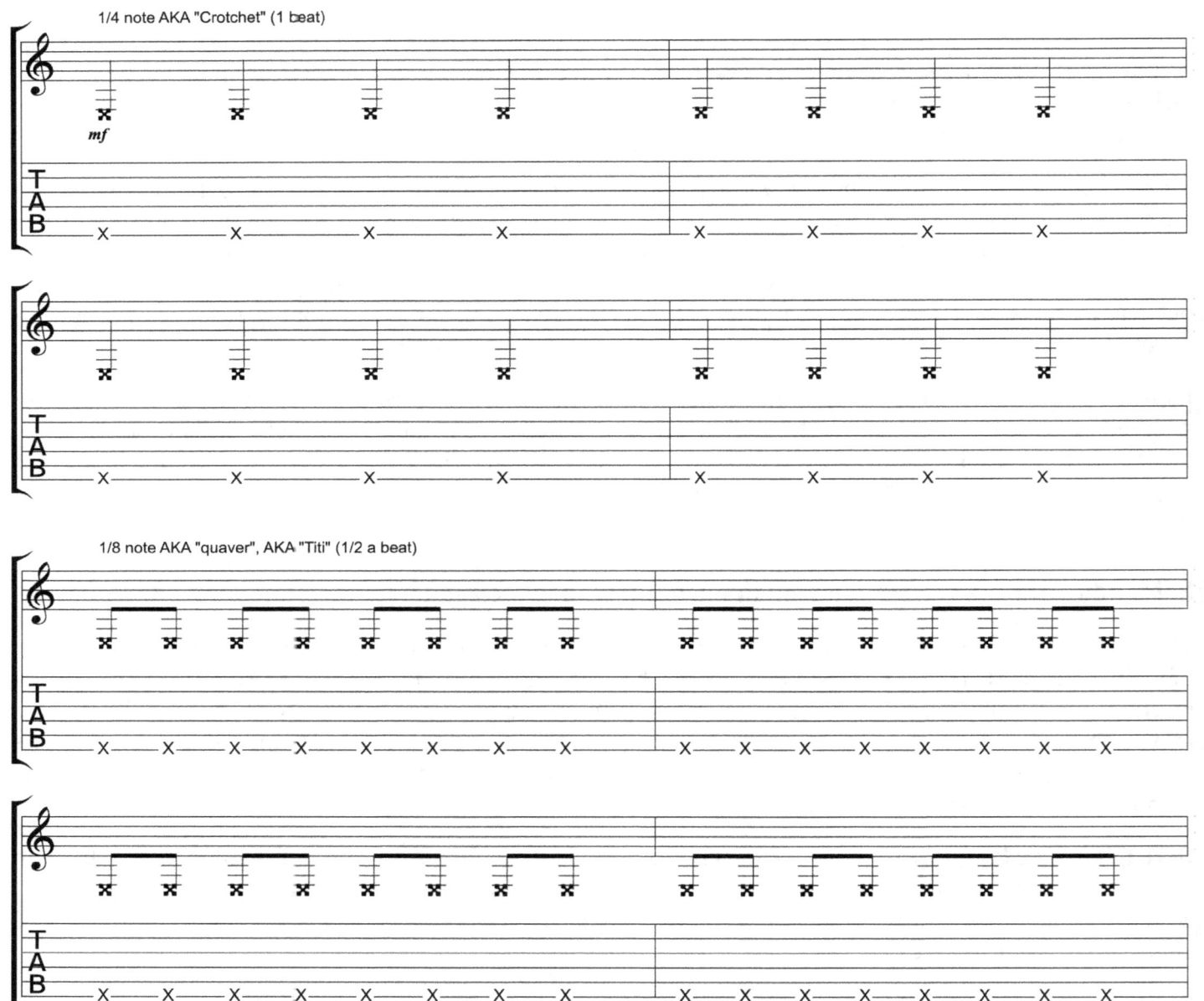

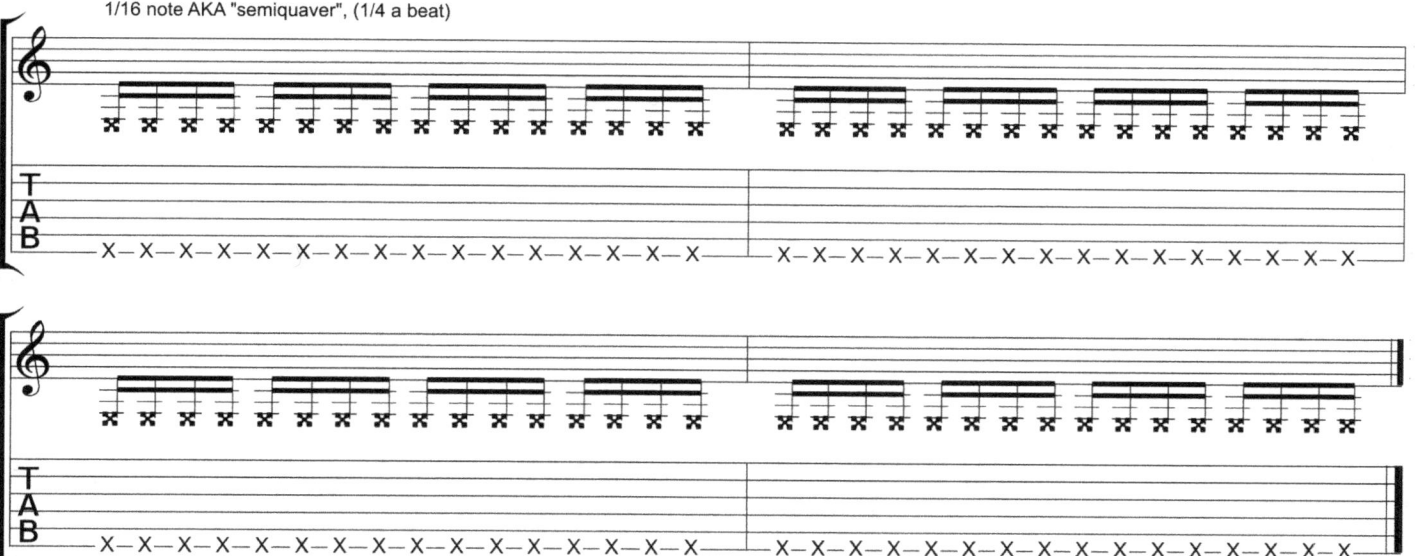

1/16 note AKA "semiquaver", (1/4 a beat)

We're now going to delve into the slightly more complicated *triplet* pulse. Once again, we'll play dead notes over an 80bpm metronome setting. As with the previous example, we're going to be looking at three different pulses, but this time using a triplet 1/4 note pulse (AKA triplet crotchets), then triplet 1/8 notes (AKA triplet quavers) and finally ending on triplet 1/16th notes (AKA triplet semiquavers). This will be slightly more complicated than Example 1a, so it will require multiple repeats before you move on to the next section of the book.

If you have difficulty with finding or "feeling" the triplet pulse, think of it like this: Picture a pirate shanty and wag your elbow from side to side. The other secret weapon I have is the word PINE-AP-PLE…

I know, I sound crazy, but hear me out!

We can use this three-syllable word to help us feel an *odd number of notes* over an *even number of beats*.

1/4 note triplet pulse = 1 x PINE-AP-PLE over two beats

1/8 note triplet pulse = 1 x PINE-AP-PLE over every beat

1/16th note triplet pulse = 2 x PINE-AP-PLE over every beat

Example 1b: Triplet dead note pulses: 1/4 + 1/8 + 1/16th @ 80bpm

1/4 note triplets AKA triplet crotchets

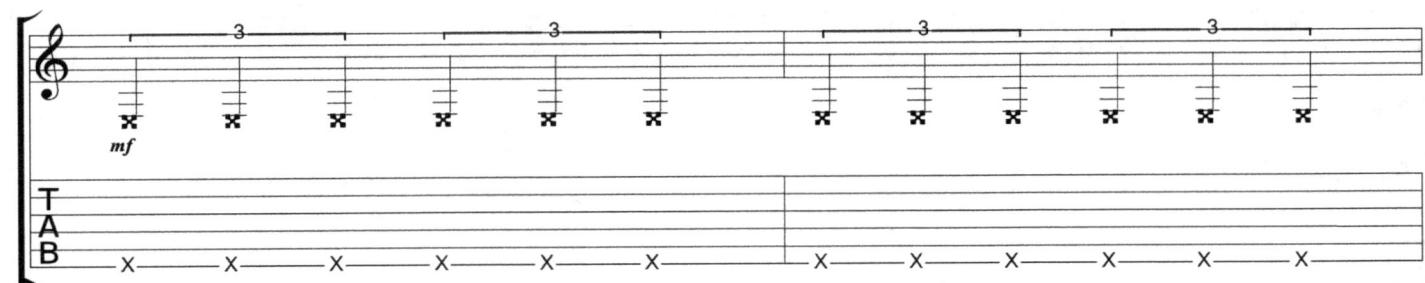

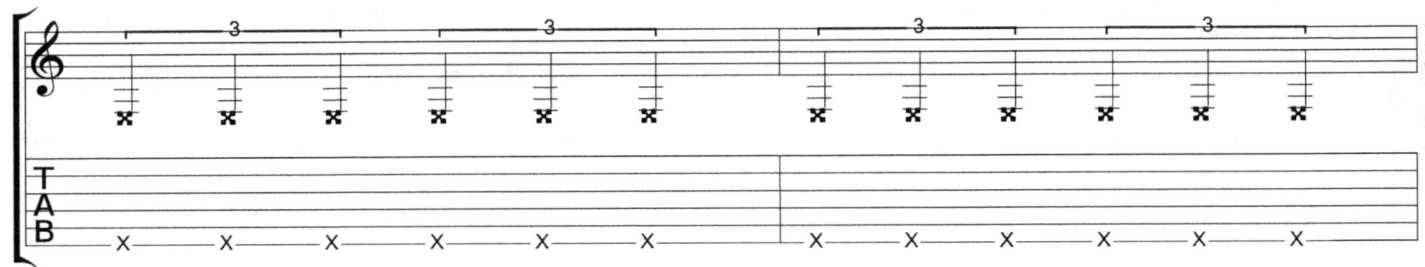

1/8 note triplets AKA triplet quavers

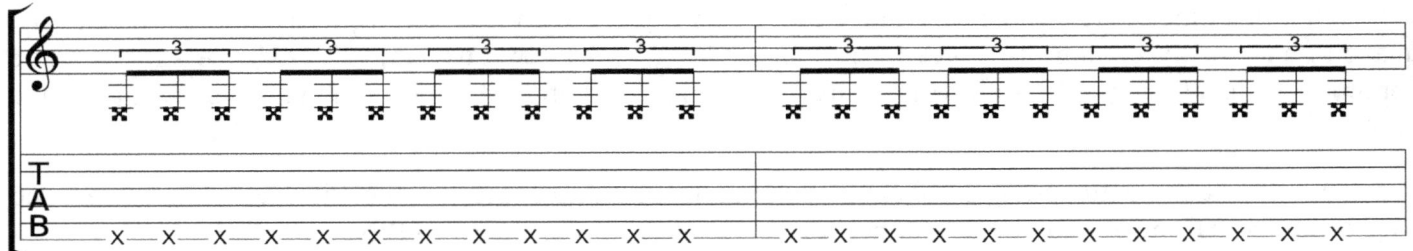

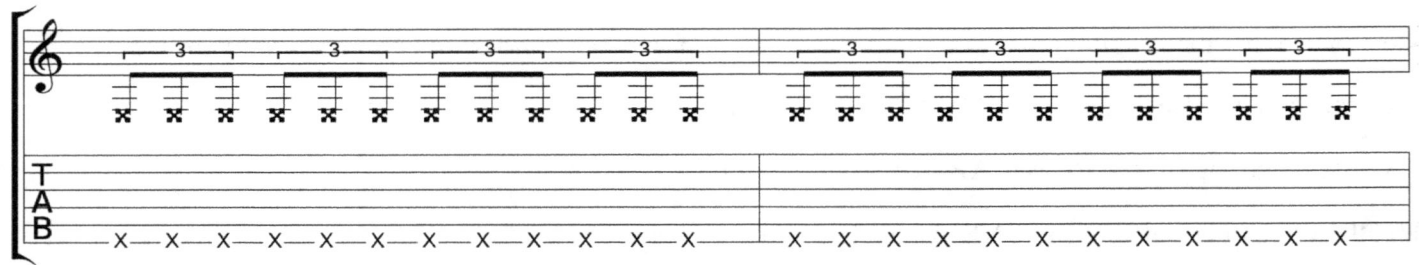

1/16 note triplets AKA triplet semiquavers

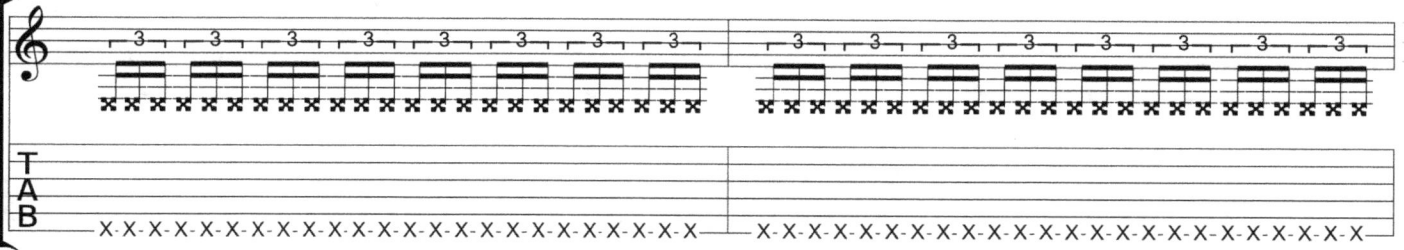

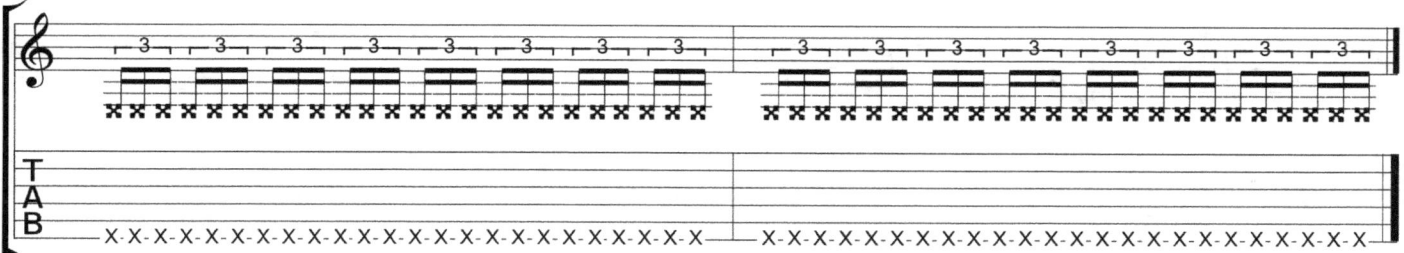

To summarise quickly, it's pointless trying to become an amazing shredder if you can't stay in time or play with consistency. As boring and rudimentary as these early exercises may seem, they will bear much fruit on your shred journey, I promise!

Now that I've bored you with all this pulse stuff, we can look at some exercises with actual notes! The first exercise is an ascending A Minor Pentatonic pattern with a 1/8th note pulse, to be played at 80bpm.

Example 1c: A Minor Pentatonic exercise with 1/8th note pulse @ 80bpm

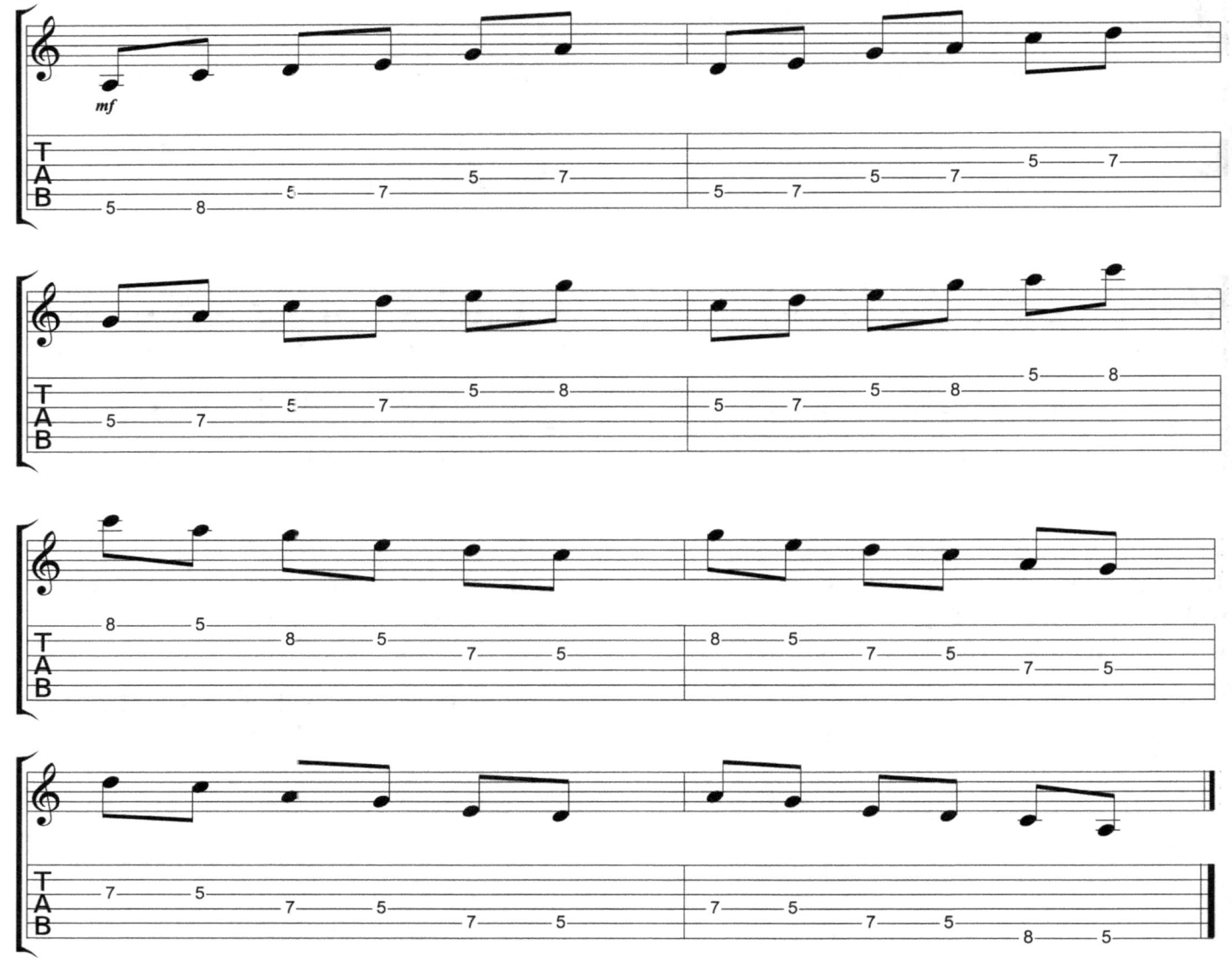

Keep the metronome at 80bpm or slower. For each click play two notes (two 1/8th notes per click). The key word here is PULSE. Make sure you are locking in with it and playing the appropriate number of notes per click.

Now practise a 1/16th note pulse over a chromatic descending and ascending scale. Set your metronome to 65bpm and try playing four notes per click.

Example 1d: E Chromatic Scale with 1/16th note pulse @ 65bpm

If you're struggling to play this exercise at 65bpm, slow it down. Once again, make sure that you are locking in with the pulse and playing the appropriate number of notes per click.

Finally, we'll tackle a common rock pentatonic lick with a triplet 1/8th note pulse. We are now going to play three notes per click. Keep in mind that this is the trickiest pulse to get your head around; counting in threes can feel a bit strange. If you're having trouble making sense of it, put down your guitar, turn on the metronome and say "Pine-ap-ple" over each click. Alternatively, play dead notes until you lock in with the metronome.

Example 1e: A Minor Pentatonic with triplet 1/8th note pulse @ 80bpm

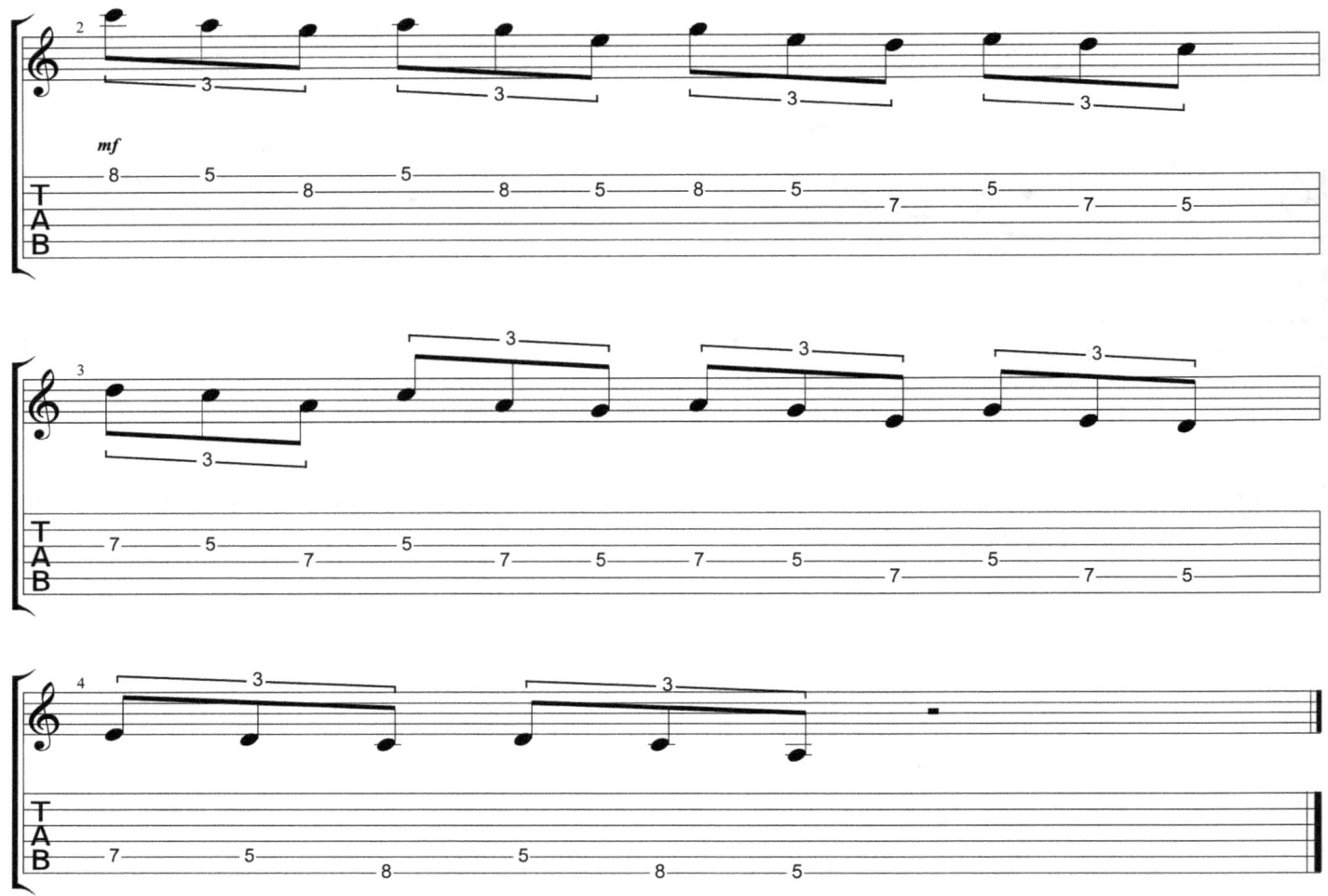

If 80bpm is too tricky to "pineapple" over, slow your metronome down by a couple of bpm's. Once you get used to evenly distributing the three-syllable word PINE-AP-PLE over every click, you're ready to start playing licks and scales with a triplet pulse. Yet another reason to be thankful for the awesome power of this sweet and delicious summer fruit!

The Radius of Your Picking Motion and Left- and Right-Hand Synchronisation

The *radius motion* refers to how far your pick swings back and forth between alternate picking. Put simply, the larger the radius of this pendulum-like movement, the more time will elapse between pick strokes and the less quick and efficient your picking action will be.

A simple way to begin a well-controlled picking motion, alongside general fretting and picking hand synchronisation, is to do simple shredding licks and exercises that only use one string. The main reason I say this is that I've often found aspiring shredders will have difficulty reaching higher speeds in the early stages of their shredding journey. Then major spanners are thrown into the works when string changes are added into the equation.

Let's look at a simple E Minor lick that descends then ascends, using only the high E string.

Example 1f: One-string E Minor exercise with 1/16th note pulse @ 80bpm

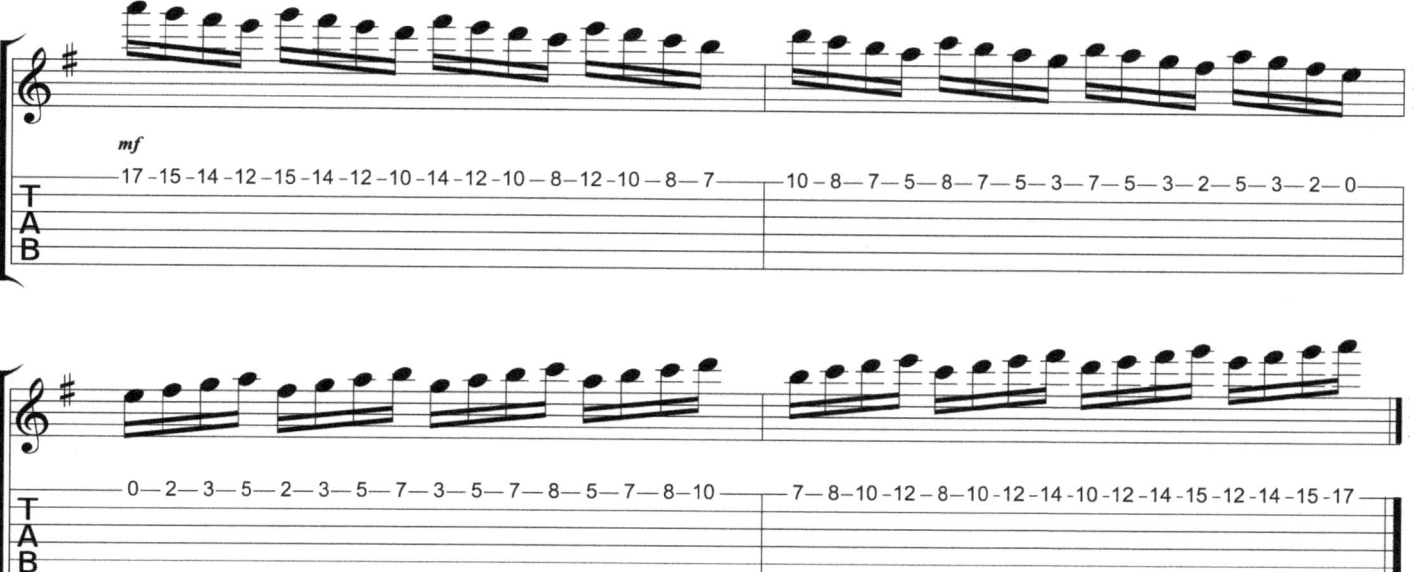

As a starting point, practise this lick at 80bpm to your metronome. If you find it hard to keep up with 80bpm, drop down by increments of 5bpm until you find a manageable tempo. Within a few days or weeks of practise, you'll have built up enough speed to play any of the exercises in this book at faster tempos!

To take hand synchronicity and pick radius further we'll need to get comfortable shredding on multiple strings, but let's start with something simple. Play this 10-note shred lick in A Minor, making sure you alternate pick all of it.

Example 1g: Two-string 10 note A Minor lick with 1/8th note pulse @ 100bpm

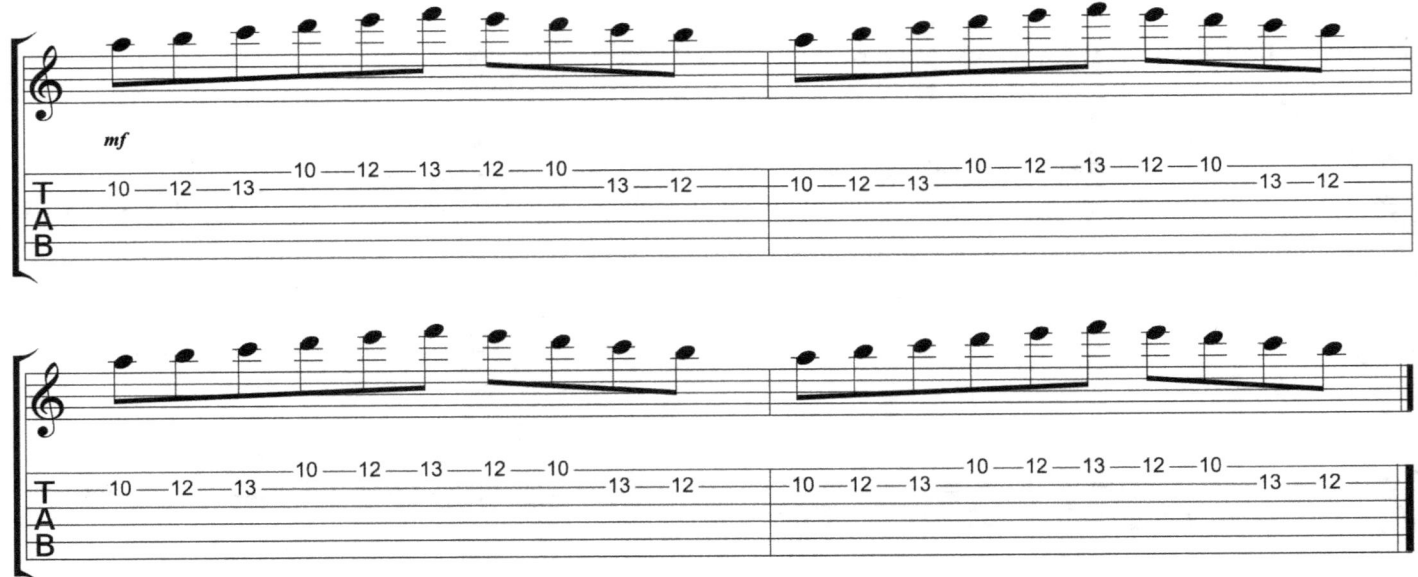

This isn't a particularly complex shred lick, but if your picking hand is doing lengthy, superfluous movements, this will greatly decrease your chances of shredding like a mofo. Try looping this 10-note lick multiple times. Pay special attention to how far your pick is going back and forth between notes and how far past the string you are picking in both directions. You may find it useful to look at your picking hand the whole time.

Once you get the hang of this simple concept, move onto the next exercise. It will reinforce the fundamentals of string changing across the neck and over a longer period. This exercise uses the A Harmonic Minor scale.

Example 1h: Two-string extended 10 note A Minor lick with 1/16th note pulse @ 85bpm

Shredding Pentatonics and Chromatics

In the early stages of your shredding and speed building journey, I recommend you practise two-note-per-string pentatonics and four-note-per-string chromatic scales. The reason being, pentatonics are commonly two-note-per-string scales and chromatics, four-note-per-string. This means that every string will be picked an even number of times in either a descending or ascending direction. To simplify things further, every string will always be picked starting with a down stroke, regardless of how many string changes you make. Let's take a look at a simple pentatonic run in A Minor.

Example 1i: Alternate pick-building A Minor Pentatonic lick with 1/8th note pulse @ 95bpm

Having played through the A Minor pentatonic run in Example 1i, you'll notice that an even number of picks per string is relatively simple to deal with, compared with trying to shred an odd number of notes per string, whether in triplets or groups of five (or seven if you're a madman).

The great thing about starting each string change with a down stroke is that every string is attacked in the same way. I daresay this would've been Zakk Wylde's method to building speed in his early years. Even now he shreds pretty hard using two-note-per-string pentatonic licks.

Given that he is the King of fast pentatonic licks, I wanted to try a few Zakk Wylde-inspired shred licks to help you build speed and deal with a variety of different pulses. This first exercise uses a two-note-per-string pentatonic idea with a triplet pulse in the key of A Minor. The exercise was heavily inspired by one of the licks Zakk plays in the climax to the solo of the Ozzy Osbourne classic *No More Tears*.

Example 1j: Zakk Wylde-style two-string grouping A Minor Pentatonic lick with triplet 1/8th note pulse @ 100bpm

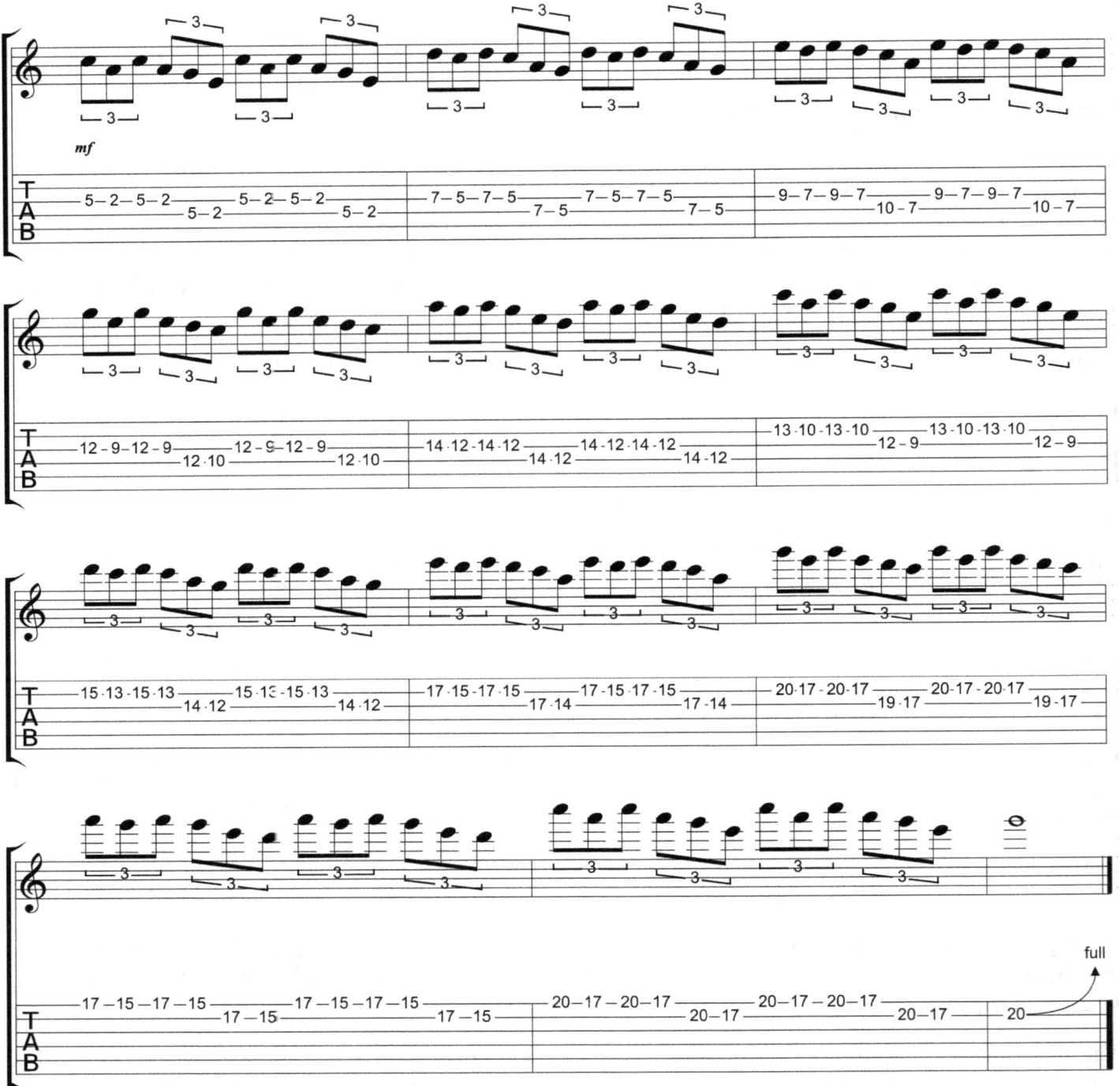

Make sure when you're practising this exercise that you play with a triplet pulse. If feeling the triplet pulse is too difficult in the early stages, most metronome apps will have a "three-note-per-beat" option, which will give you that nice triplet, pirate shanty, type pulse.

Now that we've addressed a pentatonic lick with a triplet 1/8th note pulse, let's attempt a faster 1/16th note pulse running through all five positions of the E Minor Pentatonic scale, using ascending and descending patterns.

Example 1k: E Minor Pentatonic speedball lick with 1/16th note pulse @ 90bpm

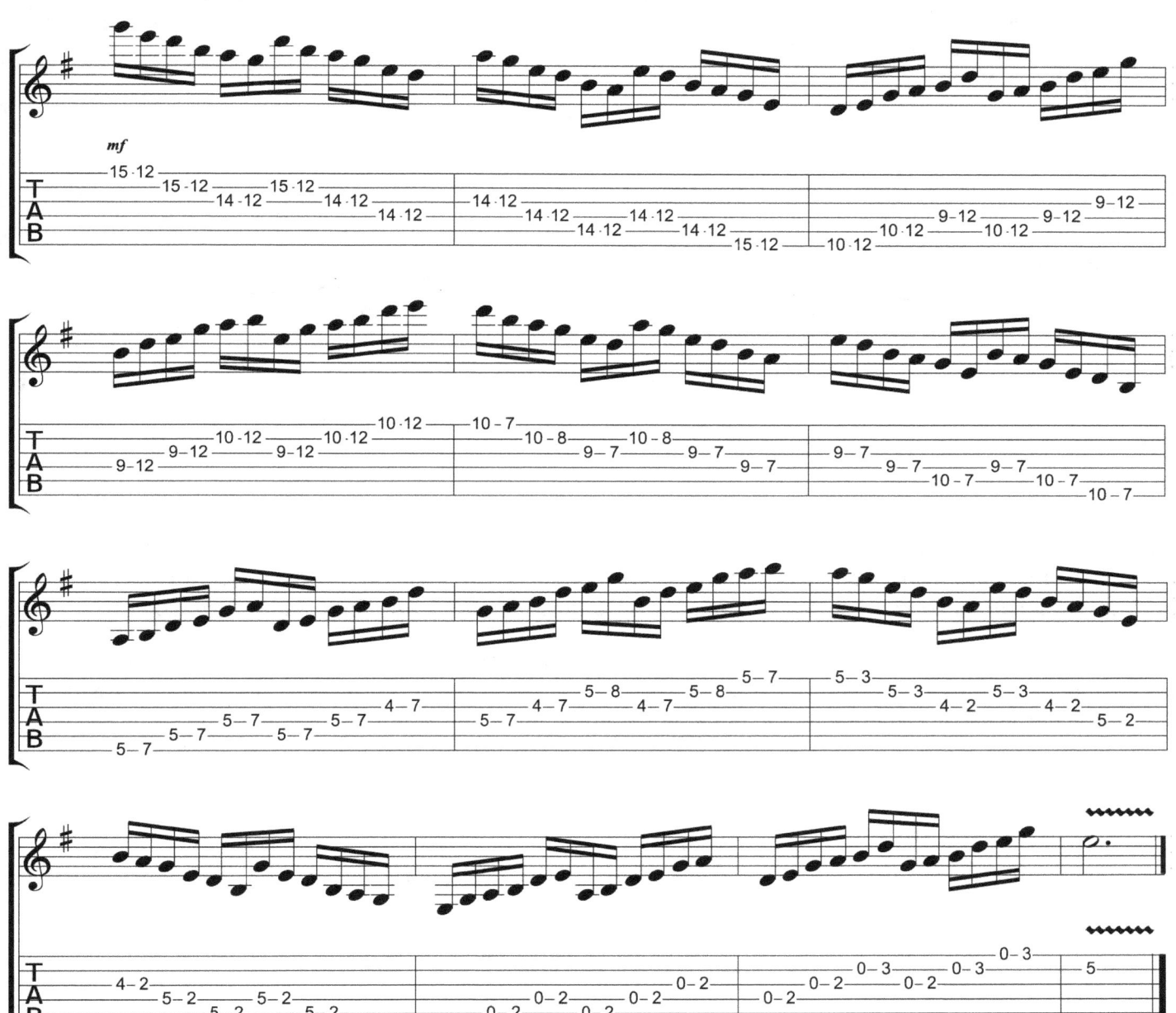

Keep in mind that this exercise uses 1/16th notes and NOT triplets. In other words, there's one more note for every beat. To compensate for this extra note per beat, you will need to begin at a lower bpm.

Now we've had some fun with two-note-per-string pentatonics, let's take a plunge into the zany world of four-note-per-string chromatics. We will start with a "meat and veg" ascending and descending exercise. Pay close attention to the picking direction on the first four 1/16th notes and carry that through to every group of four notes throughout the duration of the exercise.

Example 1l: Four-note-per-string chromatic ascending and descending exercise with 1/16th note pulse @ 90bpm

Although this is a great way to build speed and hand synchronicity, I'd like to mention that I'm aware this is as enchanting and melodically captivating as bat excrement! One plus of this exercise, however, is that it demands you build a stronger comradery and response time between your Ring and Pinky fingers.

To make things more interesting, let's mix up the order of our fingers. Instead of rolling from Pointer to Pinky on ascends and Pinky to Pointer on descends, this exercise uses Pointer-Pinky-Middle-Ring on ascends and Pinky-Pointer-Middle-Ring on descends.

Example 1m: Four-note-per-string chromatic ascending and descending 1 4 2 3 exercise with 1/16th note pulse @ 90bpm

Not every pattern you learn, or compose with, will consist of linear, predictable fingerings. It's best to be prepared for as many complex and unorthodox situations as possible. This will reduce the possibility of getting egg on one's face or falling into the trap of composing solos and runs in a bland, linear, diatonic fashion (cough, cough… every *Bullet For My Valentine* solo, ever).

We can also take this whacky, messed up, chromatic concept one step further by using chromatic four-finger patterns, but crossing strings in a less linear, four-note-per-string fashion. Let's have a look at a few diagonal spider crawl exercises. (FYI, they're called that because when you play them fast, apparently your hand looks like a spider. I apologise in advance to any arachnophobic readers I may have triggered).

The first spider pattern descends then ascends. Pay close attention to the picking in this exercise. I'm using a technique called "outside picking". In other words, I'm picking from the *outside in*. It's easier to get a more fluid and intuitive shred speed if we start the sequence on an *up* pick on the 1st string and a *down* pick on the immediate jump to the 2nd string.

Example 1n: Four-finger spider crawl descending into ascending with 1/8th note pulse @ 100bpm

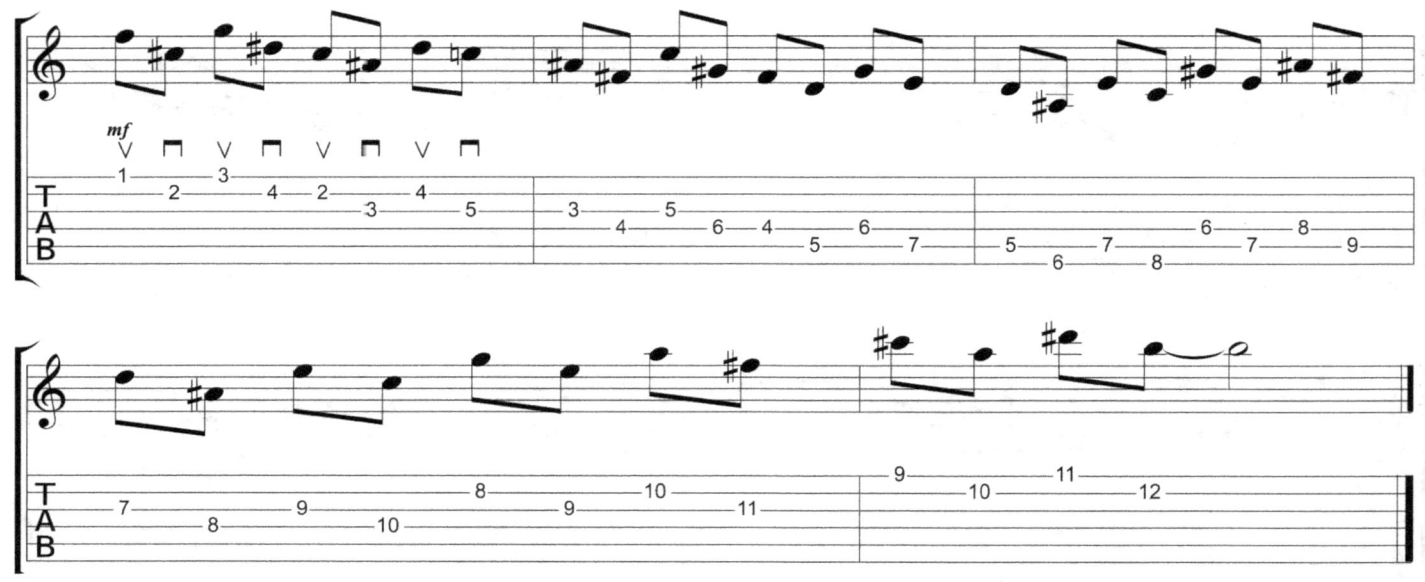

The next pattern inverts the first spider crawl and begins with an ascending sequence, descending to finish. You can hear this kind of "spider chromatic" crawling scale in the Mastodon song *Bladecatcher*. Notice this sequence starts on a down pick, so we can just use our regular alternate picking technique.

Example 1o: Four-finger spider crawl ascending into descending with 1/8th note pulse @ 100bpm

The final chromatic exercise we'll look at uses waves of twelve notes at a time. The first time I heard this type of sequence was Dave Mustaine's solo in *Sweating Bullets*. Pay close attention to your picking direction.

Example 1p: Chromatic waves descending and ascending with 1/16th note pulse @ 90bpm

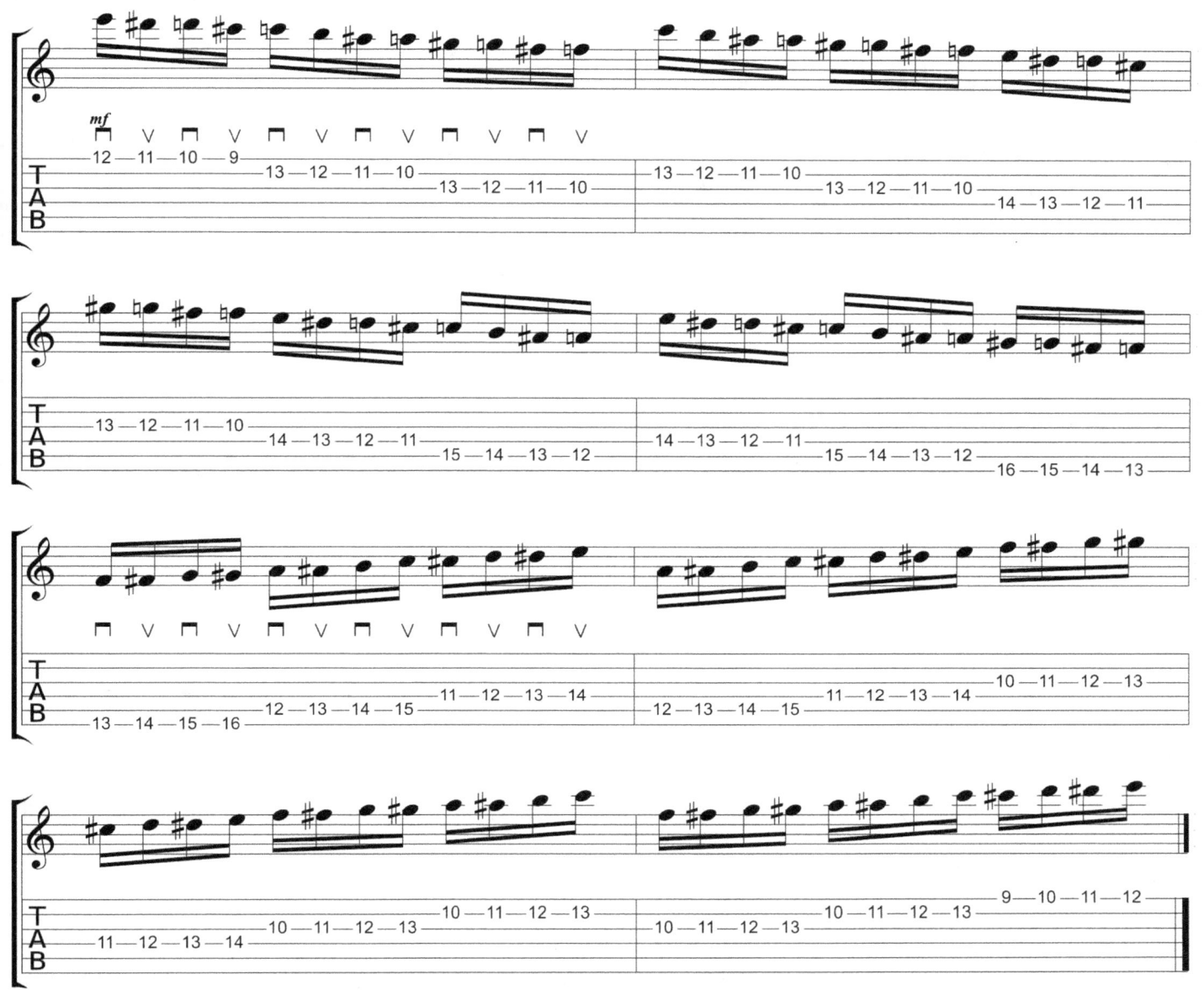

Once again, each string change starts with a down stroke. There are an even number of picks per string before we change to a new one. This is absolutely killer for hand synchronicity and building up that sweet, sweet shred speed.

Keep practising both pentatonic and chromatic scales as tools to help you build to a deadly fast picking pace. Befriending these scales and exercises will be a crucial part of your shredding journey.

Shredding Diatonics and Three-Note-Per-String Patterns

In the early stages of a shredder's journey, most will have problems trying to shred diatonic three-note-per-string scales and patterns, often attempting to play them immediately at lightning speed. The challenge with this type of shred pattern is that it often involves triplets and changing pick direction on string changes.

Let's begin our three-note-per-string journey by drilling the three most common scale shapes. We'll address all of them with alternate picking. Practise the next exercise to get used to those quick string changes beginning with an *up* pick.

Example 1q: Three common three-note per string shapes:

I know this sounds incredibly bland, but with enough practise and attention to all three of these common diatonic shapes, you'll be more confident and prepared for changing strings beginning with an up pick. This kind of shred drill is very similar to Paul Gilbert's shredding style. I can only assume he must have put many hours into practising concepts like these to get to his magnificent, god-like shred-ability!

Now that we're acquainted with our three diatonic shapes, let's look at a typical three-note-per-string alternate picked scale pattern in A Minor. Pay close attention to the picking directions.

Example 1r: Three-note-per-string A Aeolian scale with triplet 1/8th note pulse @ 95bpm

You'll notice that there are triplet 1/8th notes on every string, and on each string change we also change picking direction. In the rudimentary stages of alternate picking (which will one day turn into shredding) this can cause a lot of problems. You will need to get used to the feeling of addressing a string change with an *up* pick, rather than the incorrect technique of a big slow down mid-shred, to execute a shabby economy pick. (If you're unfamiliar with this term, *economy picking* will be explained later in this chapter). Please stick with the alternate picking pattern for triplet passages like this one and the other examples that follow.

The next exercise is going to focus on triplets with a fast string change, going back and forth between the 1st and 2nd string. This exercise was heavily inspired by the warm-ups and practice routines of Skwisgaar Skwigelf. Pay close attention to the picking pattern in the first measure and carry it through the whole exercise.

Example 1s: Two-string Skwisgaar-style warm-up shred with triplet 1/8th note pulse @ 110bpm

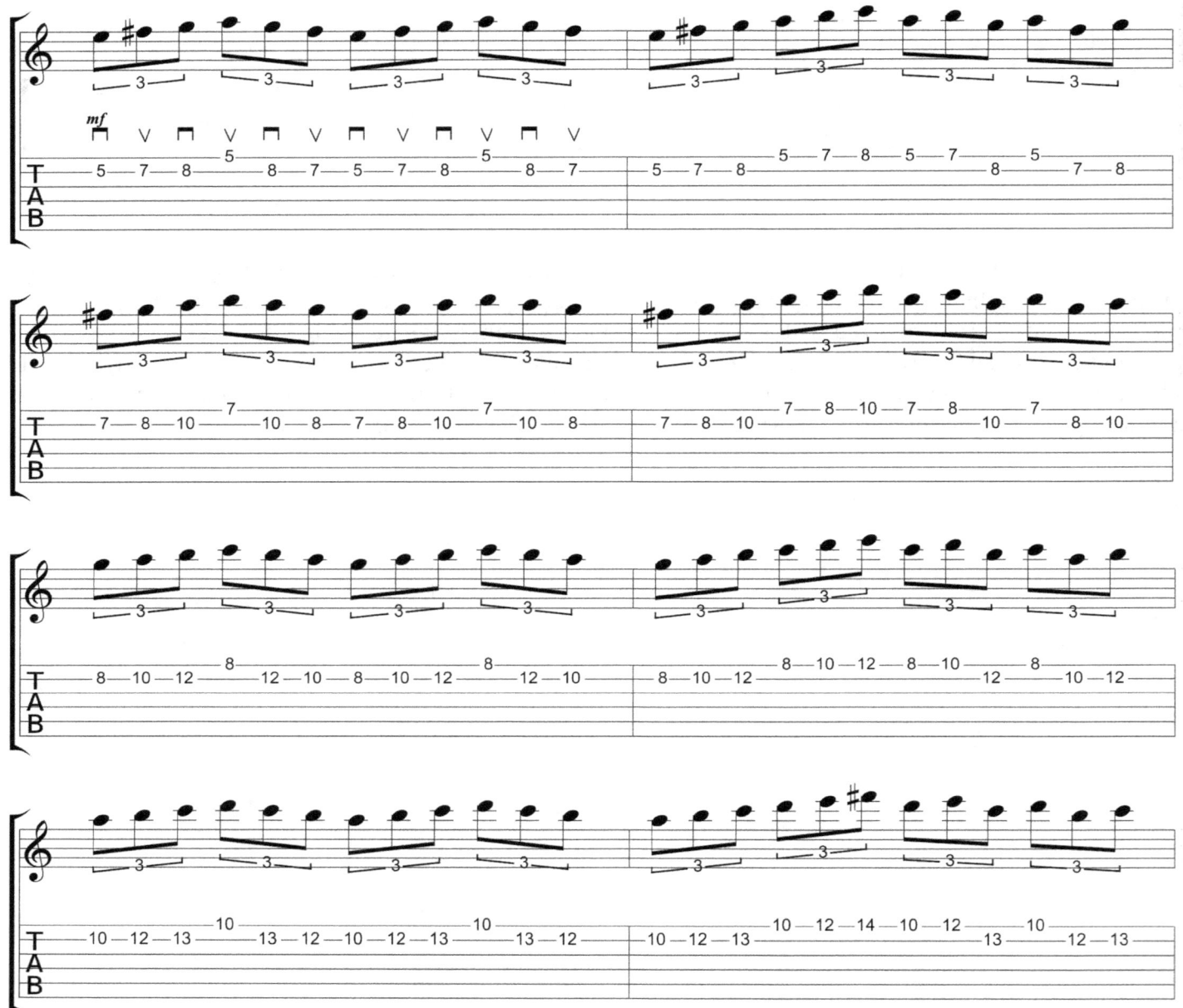

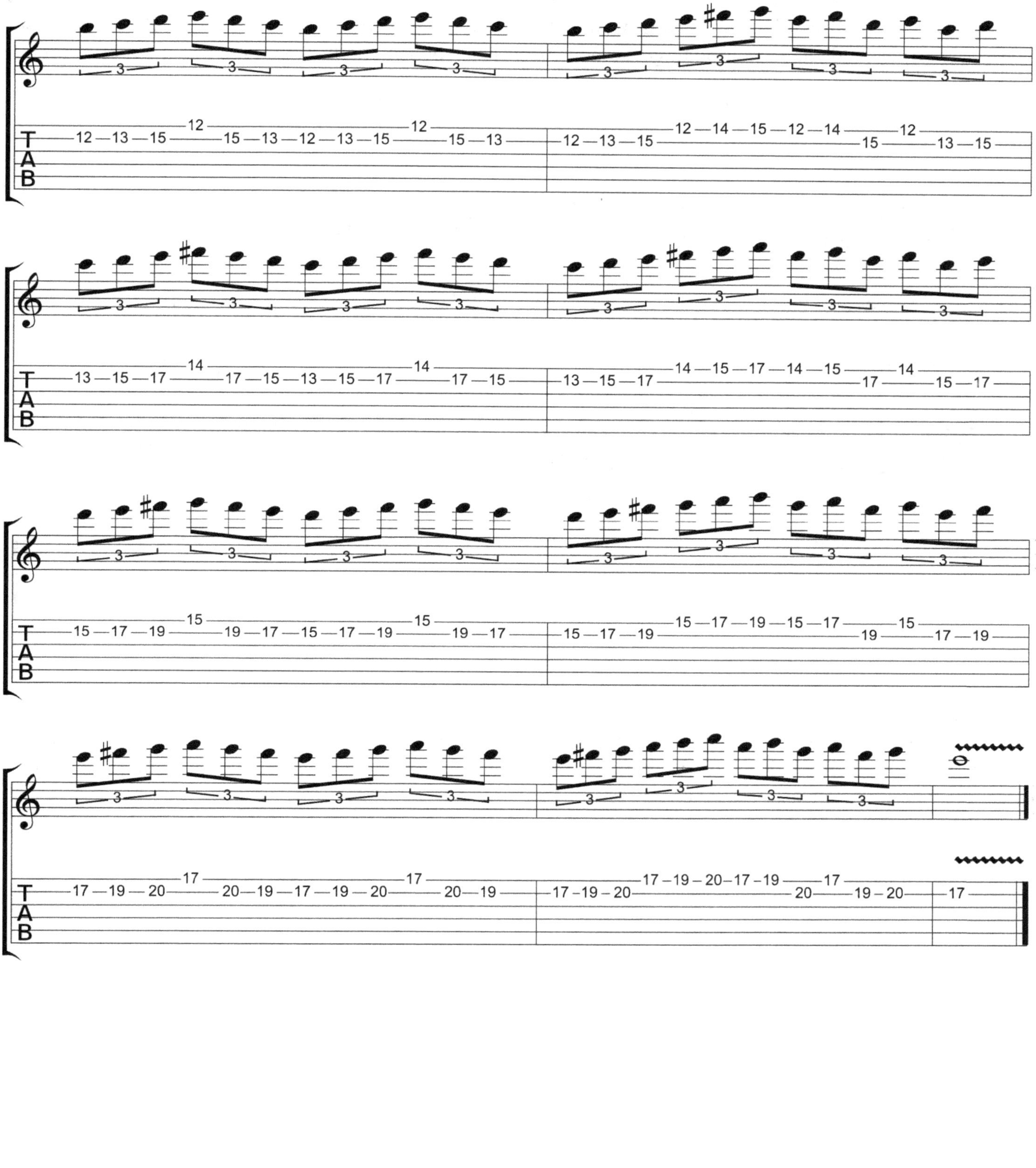

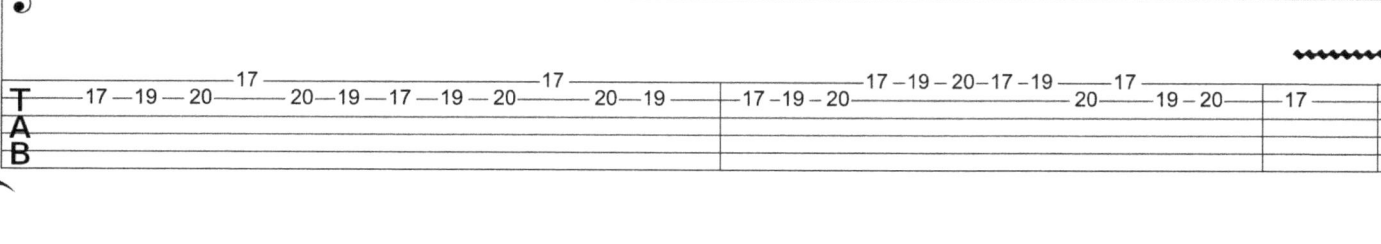

25

The next exercise is made up of several eight-note groups, using a two-string descending pattern that shifts up multiple positions of the minor scale. It has a slight Vivaldi's *Four Seasons* feel about it, so it's an excellent exercise for any shredheads wanting to get some neoclassical sounds into their playing and practice regime.

Example 1t: Two-string descending-ascending shred in E Minor with 1/16th note pulse @ 100bpm

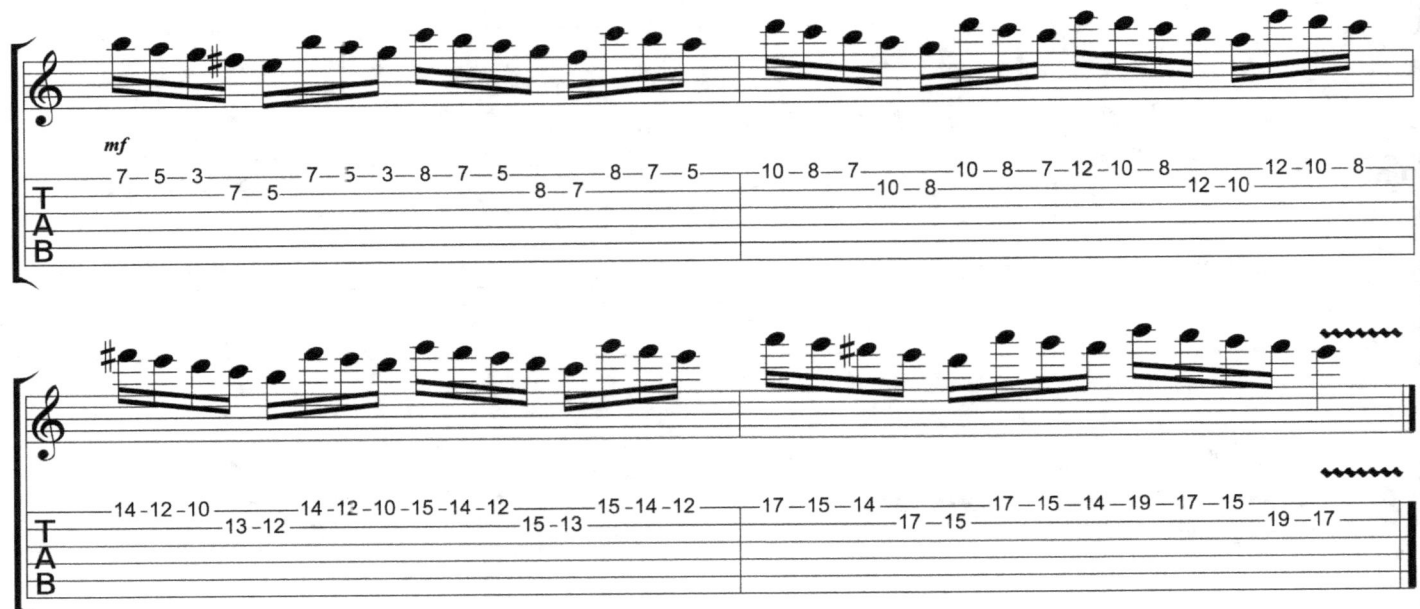

The next exercise uses shredded triplets in the key of F# Minor. It is played across multiple octaves and covers a large expanse of the fretboard. This kind of shredding is stylistically similar to the kind of shred sequences played by Paul Gilbert and Michael Angelo Batio. Once again, pay attention to the picking pattern in the first measure and carry it through the whole exercise.

Example 1u: Paul Gilbert-style F# Aeolian diatonic shred exercise with triplet 1/8th note pulse @ 120bpm

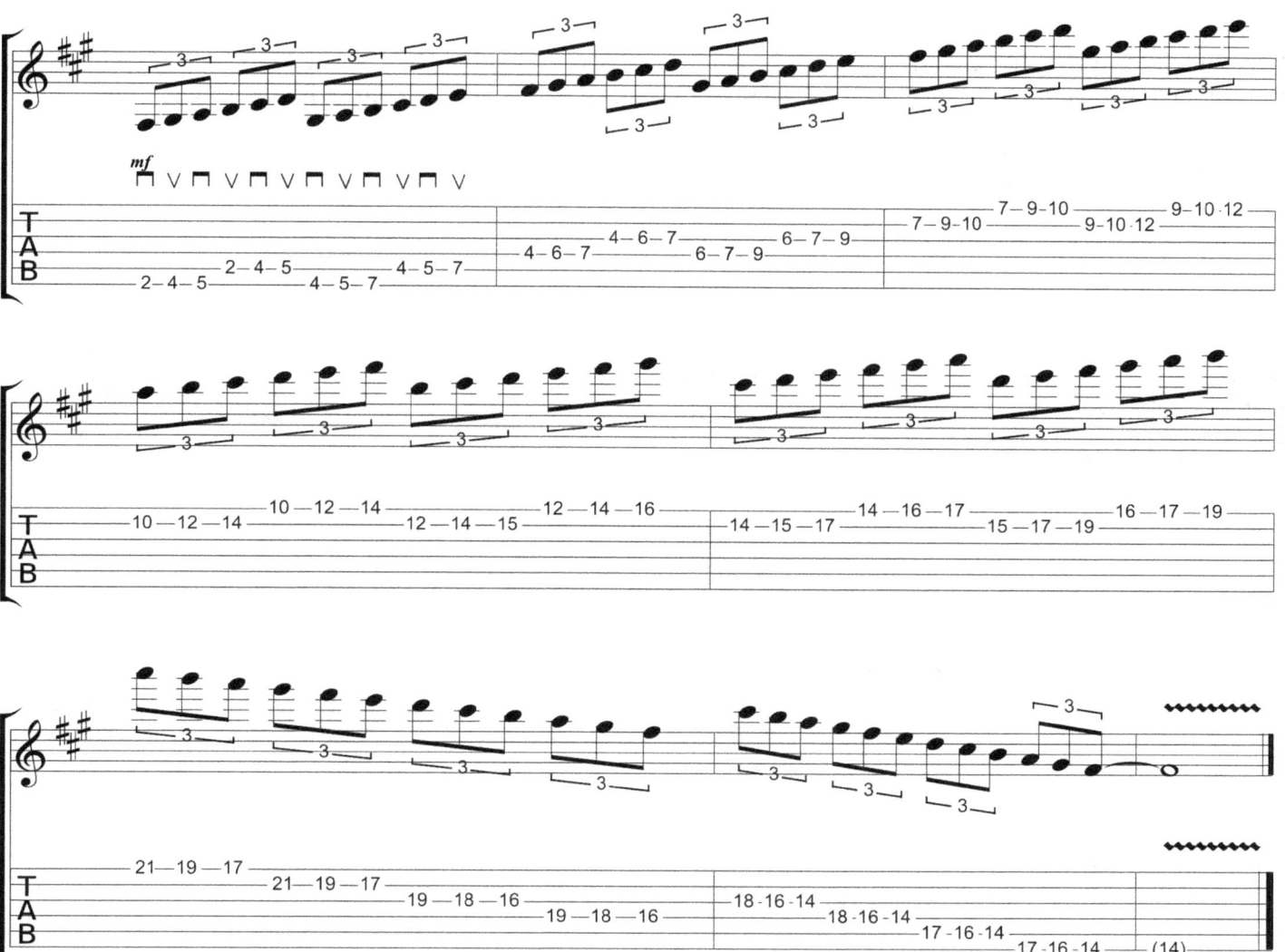

This kind of exercise is quite linear, but will help you execute lengthy shred passages across the fretboard. It will also stop you from being stuck with either CAGED or three-note-per-string shapes as your only methods of shredding a scale. You could always try this kind of scale over multiple octaves with different modes or with some of the more exotic scales.

The next exercise is a little more exotic, sassy and sensual. Think of it as the love child of Antonio Banderas and Salma Hayek, conceived to the music of Al Di Meola – but in scale form!

You may have heard this kind of scale run from players like Alex Skolnick, Yngwie Malmsteen and Dimebag Darrel. One part of this exercise is reminiscent of the opening shred of the solo in Pantera's *Domination*.

We're going to start with an ascending, diagonal E Phrygian Dominant run (the 5th mode of A Harmonic Minor) and work it into a descending wave pattern in a three-note-per-string scale shape.

Example 1v: E Phrygian Dominant crawling shred lick with 1/16th note pulse @ 100bpm

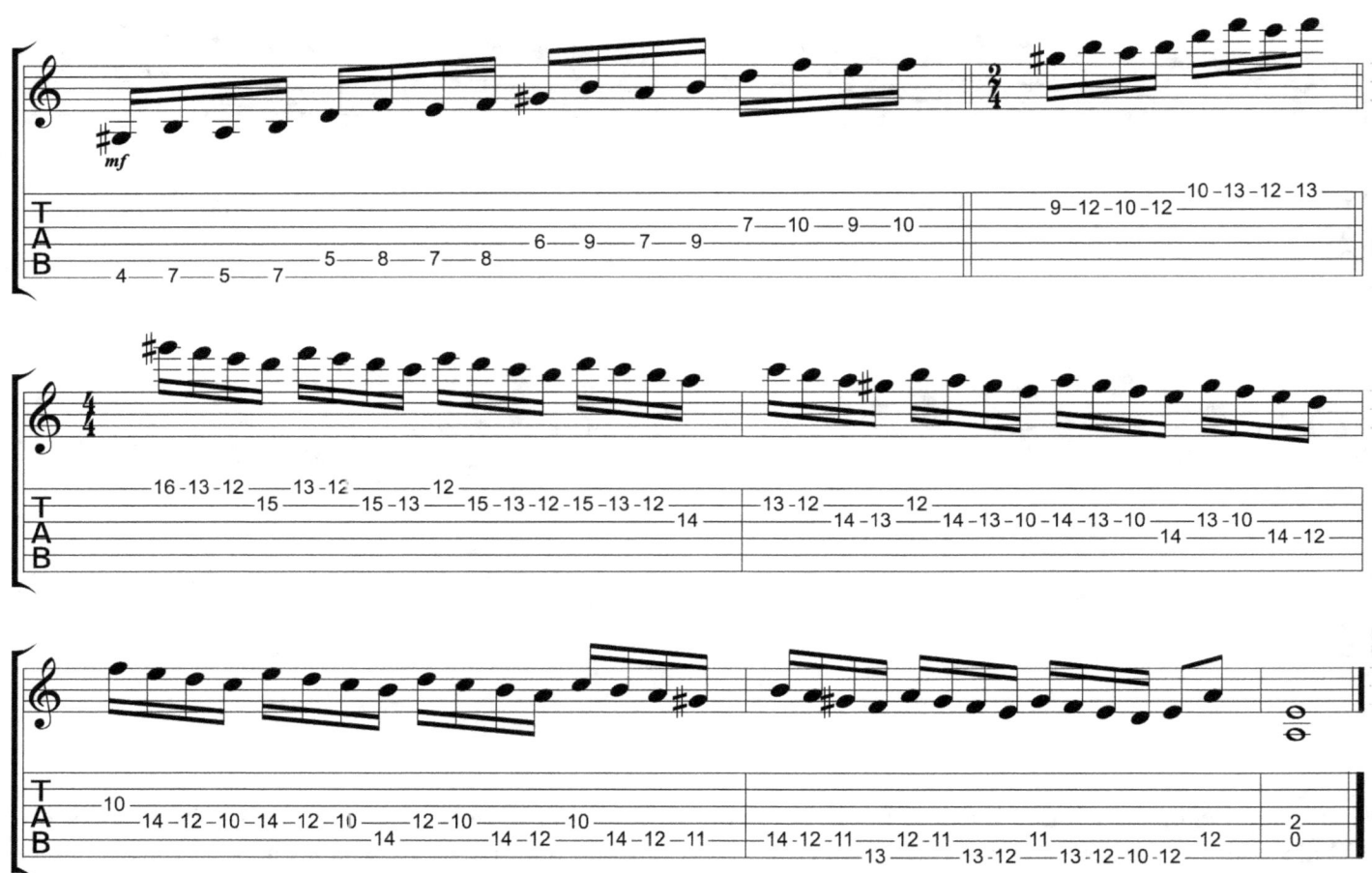

If you ever decide to use a lick like this in your compositions, be sparing with the length of the run. It can sound great and be very effective for a short period, but it soon becomes "scaley" and predictable.

The next exercise is a little crazy, as it blows up some preconceived notions about our old mate, the pentatonic scale! What makes this exercise so unorthodox is that it uses a three-note-per-string pentatonic scale in A Minor that also includes a "blue note" (AKA the diminished or flat 5th, also known as the devil's tritone). This exercise ascends in a diagonal manner across three octaves.

Example 1w: Three-note-per-string A Minor Pentatonic scale shape plus blue note, with triplet 1/8th note pulse @ 110bpm

You'll notice in the latter part of bar two to the end of the exercise we almost have a three-note-per-string box shape, but a lot of notes are doubling up on string changes. This is a cool way to move through a scale more slowly with a lengthy shred run and make it sound more extreme. I've heard players like Dimebag, Dave Mustaine and Jason Hook (*Five Finger Death Punch*) use this "doubling up" concept in solos to create massive shred runs that sound like they could go on forever.

The final three-note-per-string exercise we'll look at on our alternate picking shred journey is probably the most complicated. We'll be dealing with an A Harmonic Minor scale with a 1/16th note emphasis that uses a slightly strange pattern over a 5/4 bar. This exercise spans three octaves and is pretty terrifying!

Example 1x: 5/4 Alexi Laiho-style neoclassical shred in A Harmonic Minor with 1/16th note pulse @ 100bpm

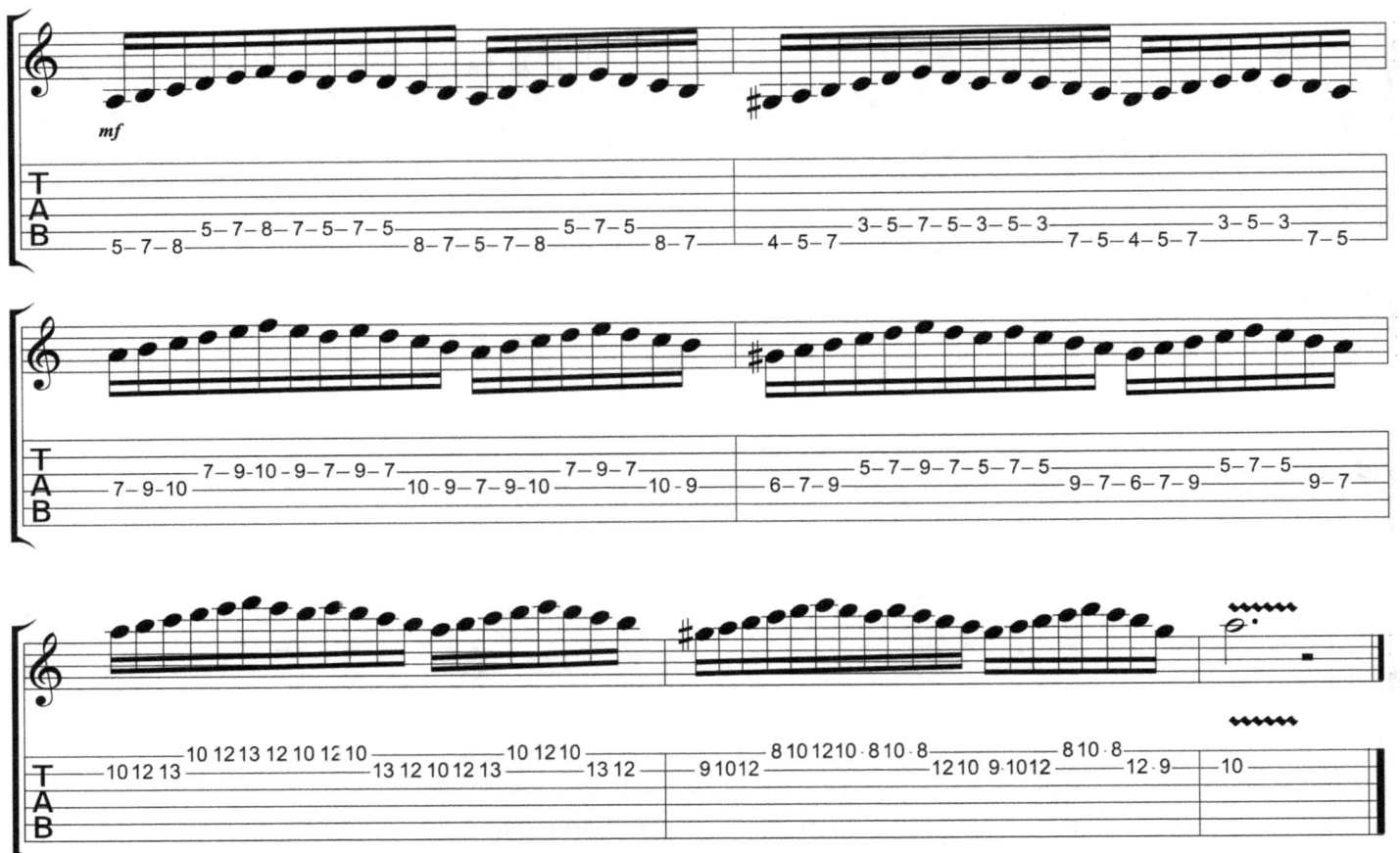

The way this shred pattern ascends and descends is reminiscent of the type of licks played by Alexi Laiho in a handful of great *Children of Bodom* solos.

SIDE NOTE/FUN FACT: I love Alexi's playing so much I named my son after him!

I came up with this next shred a couple of years ago when some of my students got "the need for speed". I did my best to create some interesting sounding exercises that weren't too linear to keep them entertained. I heard a Rusty Cooley song called *Under the Influence* which had a chord progression I liked, so I created an 8-note shred pattern to follow those chord changes: Am C G Am F F#dim7 G G#dim7

Example 1y: *Under the Influence*-style shred in A Minor with 1/16th note pulse @ 100bpm

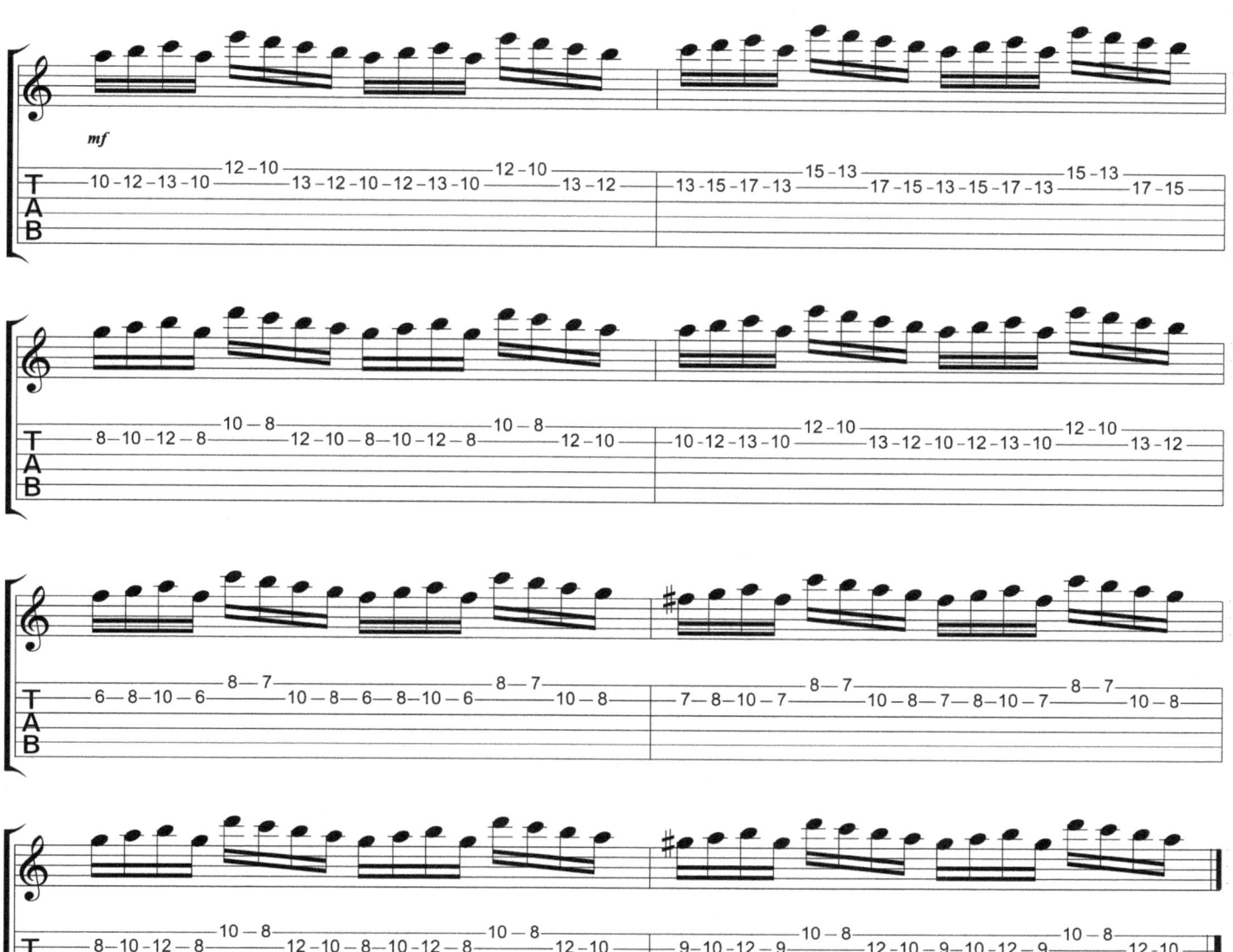

The next exercise is a little different to anything we have seen in this chapter. It uses a pentatonic shape that has four notes on one string, then two on the next. I've seen Emil Werstler from *Daath* use this kind of pentatonic shape and I believe Paul Gilbert might have used it in a few *Mr. Big* solos.

Example 1z: 4 and 2 pentatonic b5 shred in A Minor with triplet 1/16th note pulse @ 85bpm

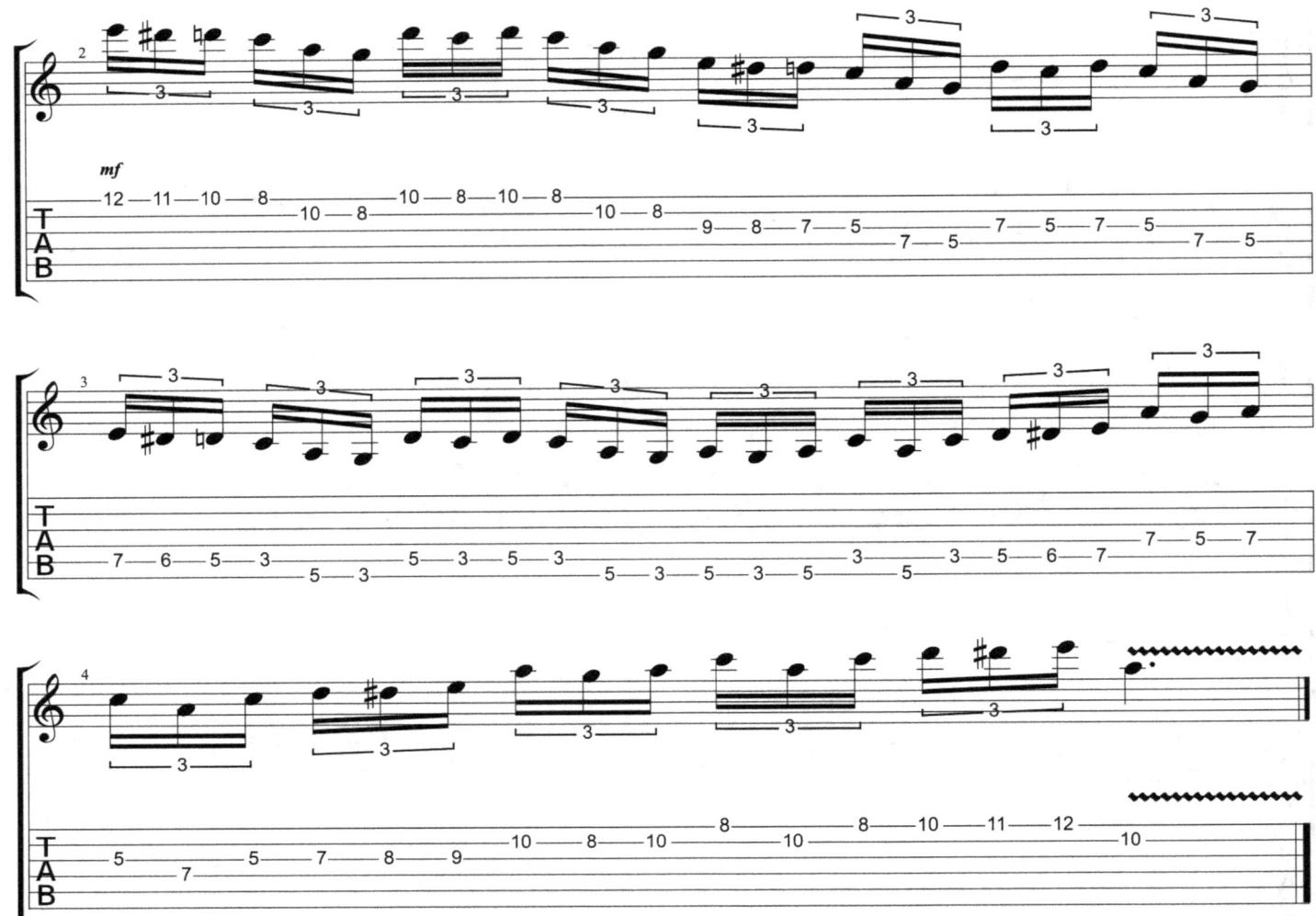

OK, if you have played through all the exercises so far, I applaud your efforts. It delights me to say that I have saved the worst, MOST EVIL and challenging of exercises till last… MWAHAHAHAHA!

This is a lengthy chromatic shred based on Nikolai Rimsky-Korsakov's *Flight of the Bumblebee*. Pay close attention to the 1/16th note triplet pulse running through the exercise. Also, dial down the bpm to a sensible level if you find this too tricky, but don't forget to push yourself either!

Example 1z1: Epic chromatic bumblebee shred sequence with 1/16th note pulse @ 80bpm

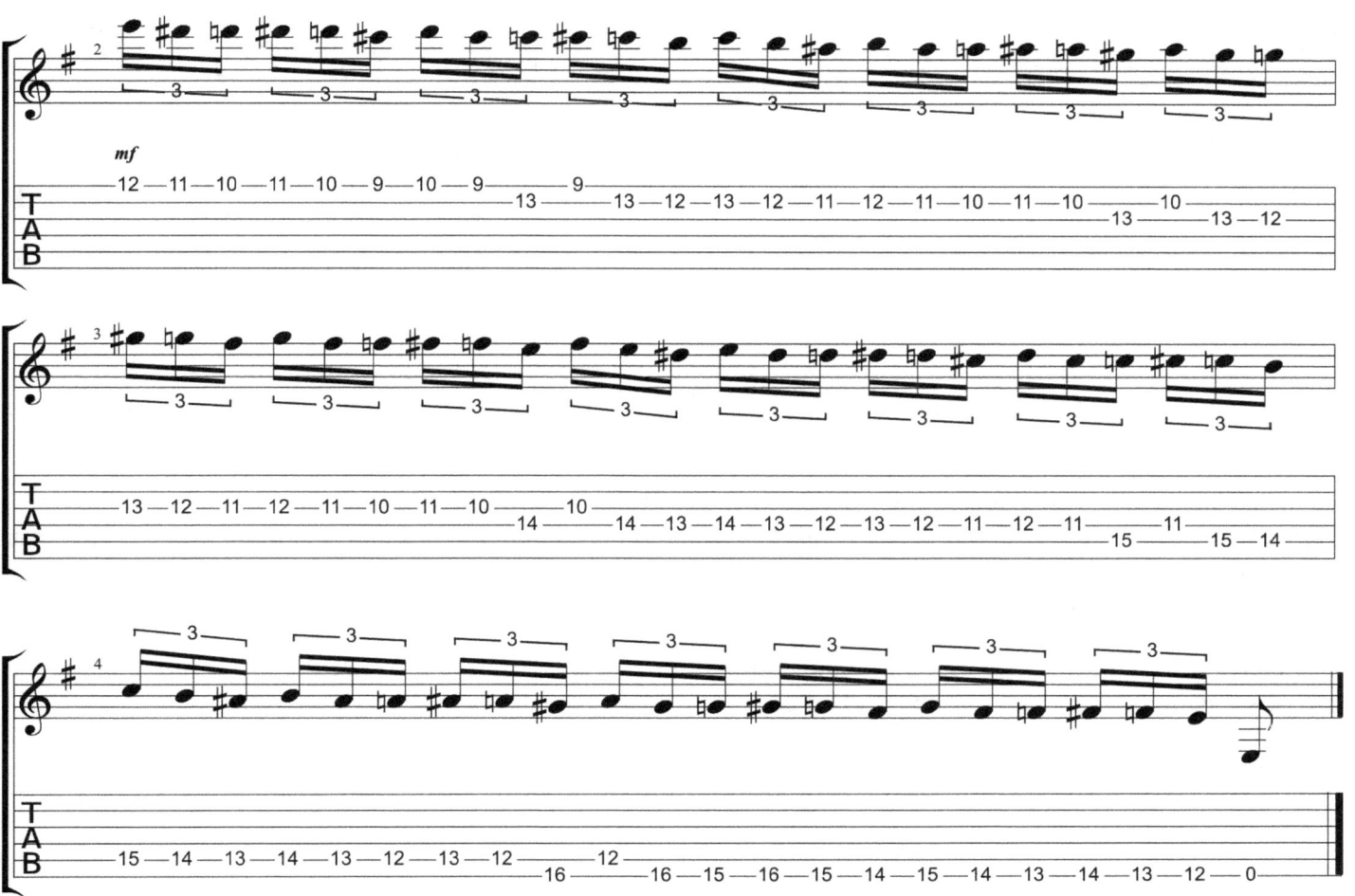

There are infinite combinations you could use to slightly alter any of these exercises, whether that's using a different mode, an exotic scale, or an alternative to a regular minor pentatonic such as the Hirajoshi scale or even a dominant pentatonic scale. The most important thing is your commitment to alternate picking, pulse and metronome usage!

When and How to Use Economy Picking

I promised I'd come back to this. You may ask, "What is economy picking?" Simply put, it is a mini-sweep of the pick to help transition between strings. It is often used as an alternative to straight *alternate picking* if the playing situation calls for it.

For example, if we end a phrase on a down stroke, the next string will also start on a down stroke. Here is a three-note-per-string ascending G Major scale using economy picking:

Example 1z2: Three-note-per-string G Ionian scale with 1/8th note pulse and economy picking @ 85bpm

Notice that every string is picked *down–up–down*. When we leave a string, we end on a down stroke, and the next string is picked with a down stroke.

Economy picking is a great technique when used correctly. It can, however, confuse young or novice shredders in their early stages and stifle progress. If this technique feels unnatural to you, or just plain messes with your head, concentrate on basic alternate pick shreds until you're emotionally ready to tackle this unconventional technique! If you're still keen… READ ON!

The next lick is a crawling A Aeolian scale. It uses the 1st, 2nd, 3rd and 5th notes of the Aeolian scale and ascends diagonally across the fretboard and covers three octaves. Pay close attention to the picking direction and the specific moments where economy picking occurs.

Example 1z3: Three-note-per-string A Aeolian 1 2 3 5 crawl with 1/8th note pulse and economy picking @ 80bpm

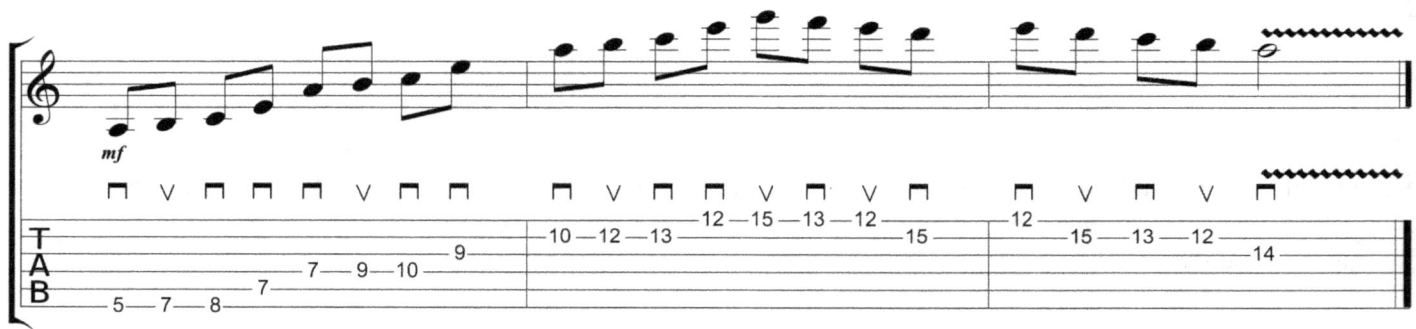

The next lick uses a similar concept, but in a major context. We can take the 1st, 2nd, 3rd and 5th notes of the C Ionian scale (more commonly known as C Major) and use that to crawl diagonally across the fretboard, whilst spanning three octaves.

Example 1z4: Three-note-per-string C Ionian 1 2 3 5 crawl with 1/8th note pulse and economy picking @ 80bpm

The final lick on our brief economy picking journey is based on an E Minor Pentatonic with an added blue note. I often find economy picking works great if there are uneven or inconsistent amounts of notes from string to string. This exercise goes from two notes on one string to three notes on the next and repeats that across all six strings. Pay close attention to the picking direction and try thinking of this exercise in groups of five notes.

Example 1z5: E Minor Pentatonic plus blue note with 1/8th note pulse and economy picking @ 80bpm

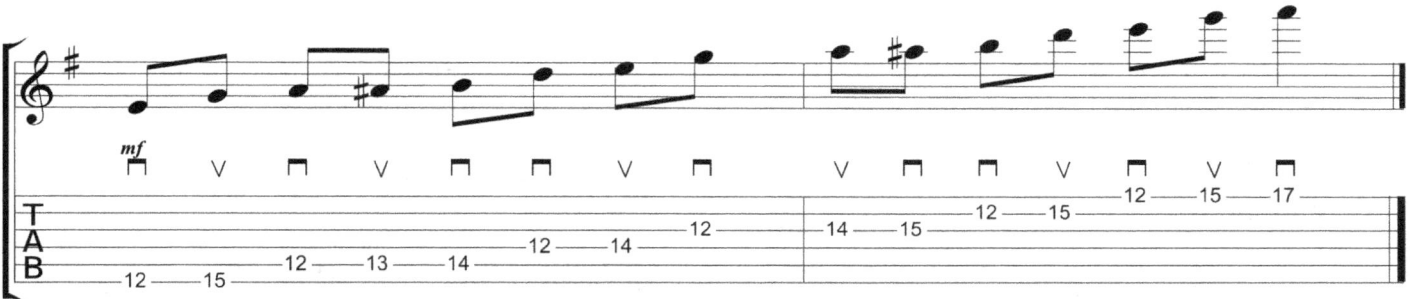

At the end of the day, you may want to avoid economy picking altogether. Doing so will force you to get used to employing a new picking direction on all string changes. In most cases, avoiding economy picking and using only alternate picking will work fine. But perhaps 5% of the time you'll come across a meddlesome lick on which it would make more sense to use economy picking. My advice is, you can never be "too prepared". All techniques (some more superfluous than others) will be useful at some stage in your shredding journey.

String Skip Shredding and Dexterity Builders

I think string-skipping is the most under-practised and most overlooked of all guitar techniques. "Why is it under-practised and overlooked?" you may well ask. Because it's far too easy to play linear scale shapes and sweep through arpeggios. That mind-set and skill-set is enough to get you through a substantial amount of songs, or to compose the things you hear in your head when writing. But it will limit your creativity and the melodic possibilities at your fingertips when it comes to creating lines with bigger intervallic jumps.

In last part of this chapter we will focus solely on SHREDDED string skips. In later chapters we'll also look at legato and tapped string skips.

This first exercise is a simple descending chromatic warm-up, based on what we played way back in Example 1d. This time, however, we'll include string skips.

Example 1z6: Descending chromatic string skip warm-up with 1/16th note pulse @ 100bpm

We'll now take a similar ascending chromatic idea to the one in Example 1m but incorporate the string-skipping technique. Pay close attention to the 1 4 2 3 fingering pattern on the fretting hand.

Example 1z7: Four-note-per-string, string skipping chromatic ascending and descending 1 4 2 3 exercise with 1/16th note pulse @ 80bpm

This kind of finger twisting exercise can be very challenging and, of course, becomes even more challenging with the addition of string skips. If it becomes too frustrating to practise, you can always return to Example

1m and practise that exercise until you have mastered it. You can return to this string-skipping, finger twisting monster when you have built up your confidence again.

We're now going to return to the descending spider crawl idea we saw in Example 1n but add in string skips.

DISCLAIMER: This exercise sounds terrible… Like, Yoko Ono levels of terrible. Please keep an open mind, as it's designed for dexterity and coordination, not to be sonically pleasing.

Example 1z8: String-skipped four-finger spider crawl descending into ascending with 1/8th note pulse @ 100bpm

We can also to return to the ascending spider crawl idea we saw in Example 1o, but now add string skips. I would like to reinforce how terrible these chromatics and crawls sound. Please don't rage quit!

Example 1z9: String-skipped four-finger spider crawl ascending into descending with 1/8th note pulse @ 100bpm

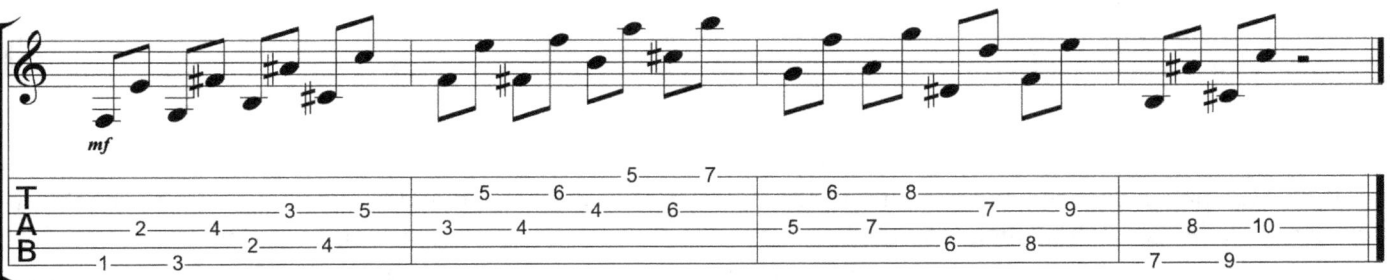

The next exercise is made up entirely of string-skipped arpeggios. Its ascends through the diatonic chord structure in G Major, using basic triads.

Example 1z10: String-skipped diatonic arpeggio ascending with 1/8th note pulse @ 100bpm

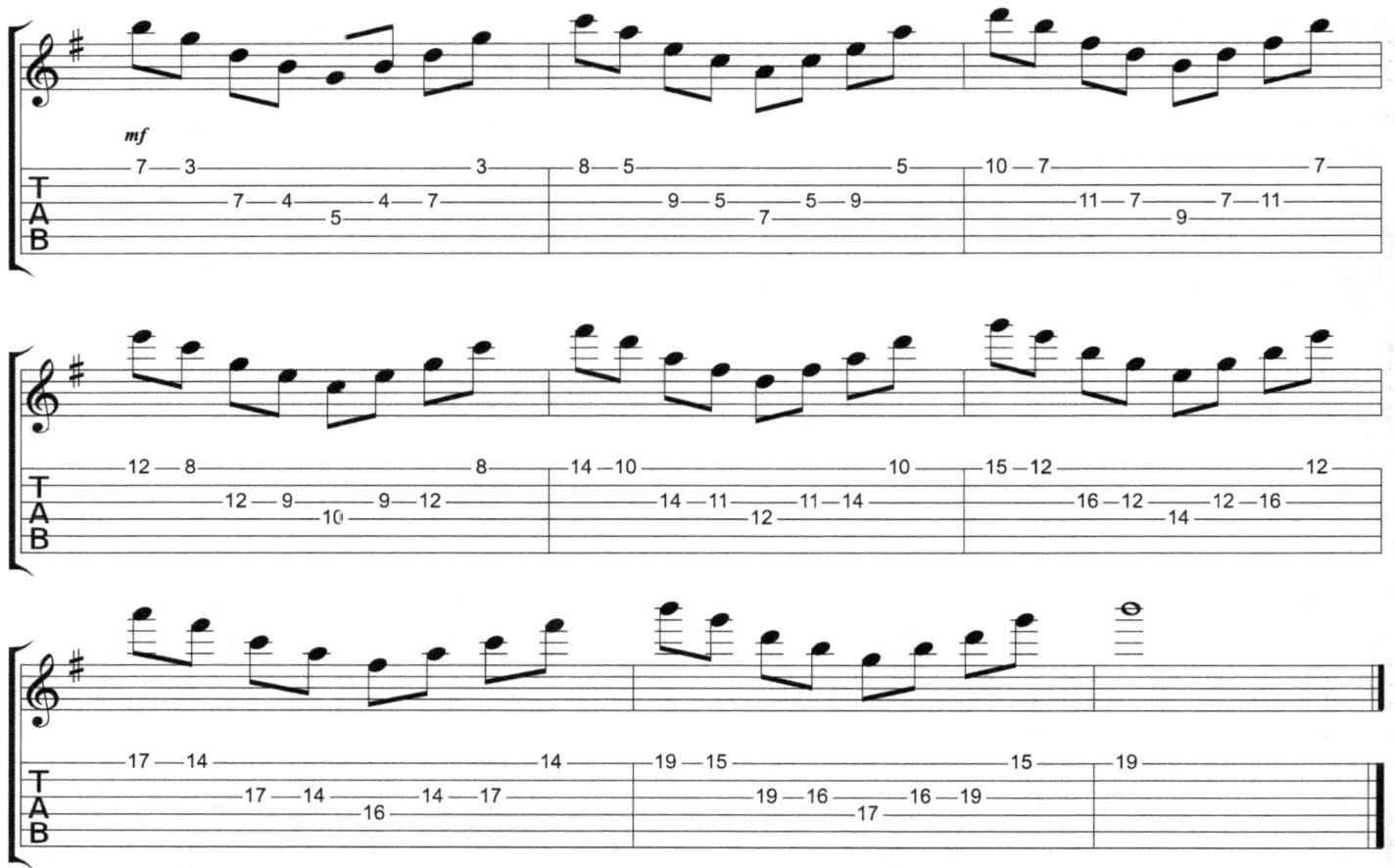

The arpeggio shapes seen in this particular exercise are used often by players like Paul Gilbert and Marty Friedman. I've heard both of them say that the "sweep approach" to arpeggios can be boring and unmusical. Marty even likens sweeping to "a trick any monkey can do" (slightly paraphrased). And who could forget the lovable Alexi Laiho? He has a couple of cool string-skipped arpeggios in the second solo of the song *Sixpounder*.

The next exercise uses a three-note-per-string B Phrygian Dominant scale shape, descending across six strings. It has a strange 7-note pulse and has many string skips throughout its duration.

Example 1z11: B Phrygian Dominant string-skipped descending shred with 1/16th note pulse @ 100bpm

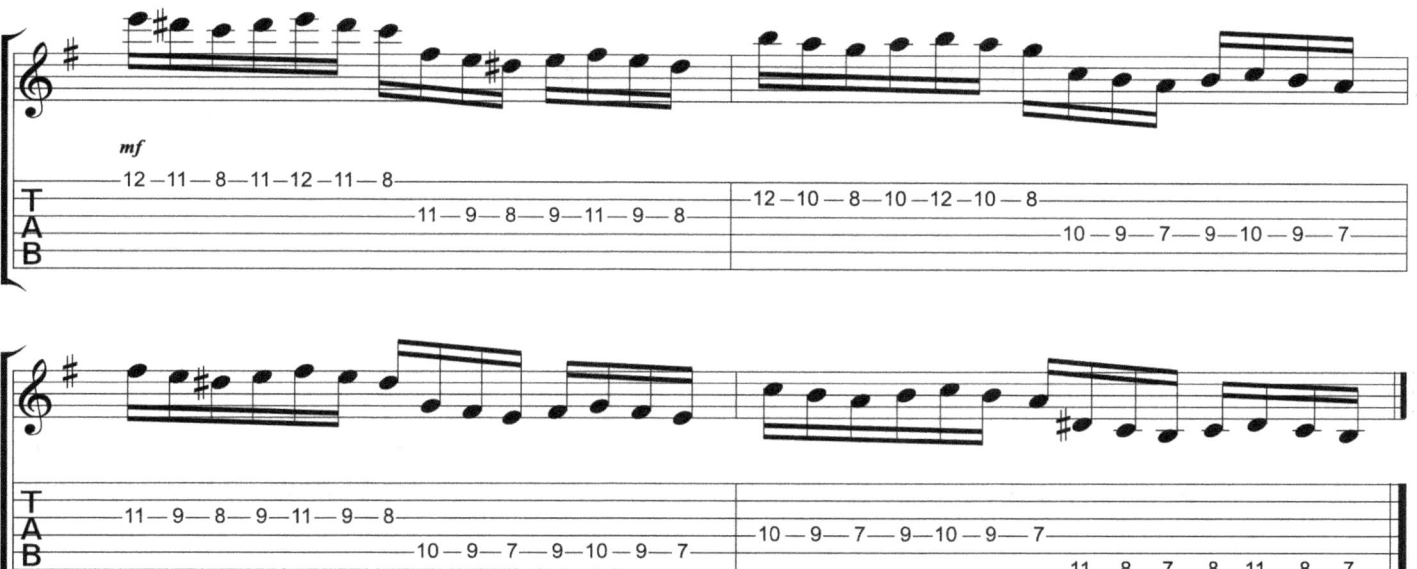

A Gentleman's Conclusion to Shredding

Time to summate! Everything you've seen in this chapter, if practised on a regular basis, with thorough metronome monitoring and gradual increments of speed will, in time, make you a better shredder.

One thing I must stress is that it is paramount you don't dive into the crazy stuff too early. By this I mean things like string-skipping or attempting to break the speed of sound with your picking hand. Rusty Cooley wasn't made overnight in a factory by cyborg overlords. That dude did his homework and put in the hours until he was literally (potentially anyway) the fastest shredder on the planet.

Also, you're going to get some haters – those irritatingly opinionated people who insist on giving you their two cents on why shredding is "unmusical" and "lacks feel". It's crazy the amount of times some un-credible jerk will bring up John Fruciante's "slow note choice" or David Gilmour's "feel" in YouTube comments or in that festering, pus-ridden scourge of the music community, The Ultimate Guitar forum. These are the go-to opening lines of the anti-shred community. It would be on the first page of their promotional pamphlet if they had one.

That doesn't mean I have an issue with the aforementioned players. I'm a huge fan of RHCP and Pink Floyd. There is much to be learned from both players' feel and note choices, but that doesn't mean their approach is the gospel of how guitar should be played. I encourage you to tell those closed-mind disciples of "put-downery" to shut their pretentious, boring faces! If there's a 10-year old guitar prodigy on the internet, shredding his/her heart out, playing Jason Becker, Racer X, or other complex music – that's awesome! The work and dedication it takes to move from being a bedroom novice to a virtuoso shredder is admirable and should be praised.

"Where is Chris going with this rant?" I hear you ask. Just this: don't let the sour, belittling rhetoric of tiny-penised keyboard warriors discourage you from your shred dreams! Strive to do what you love; what excites you. Playing fast staccato, shredded notes can be fun and sound cool. Are people still using the word "cool"? I think "lit" is a thing now. What would I know, I'm frickin' 31! Keep shredding. Get out that metronome and put in the work!

Chapter Two: Legato and the Secrets of Smooth Erotic Playing

It's easy to be seduced by the temptation to constantly shred every note at lightning speed. It's important, however, not to discount the subtle eroticism that comes from a smooth legato sequence! If you're able to drift between smooth legato technique and lightning shred, you'll be a more versatile and a more listenable player. It's also incredibly important to be able to express passages of notes in different ways, other than "Picking the living bajebus" out of everything!

Some of the sexiest phrases I've heard have been based heavily on legato technique. You can hear this utilised very tastefully in the playing of Joe Satriani (the whole *Surfing With the Alien* album is full of sweet legato runs), Alex Skolnick, Guthrie Govan and Chris Poland, to name a few.

"What exactly is legato?" I hear you ask.

Legato is an Italian word meaning "to tie together" or "to bind". In musical terms it describes "notes flowing together smoothly" or "notes tied together" and is the opposite of *Staccato* ("to detach") which describes "notes played sharply and separate from one another".

In simple layman's guitar terms:

Legato = lots of hammer-ons and pull-offs.

Staccato = lots of shreddy short notes

In this chapter we will look at a bunch of shapes, exercises and drills to get you legatoing (not a real word) smoother than the top of Kerry King's head, a fine Kentucky bourbon, or a crème brulee cooked to perfection.

Legato Fundamentals, Common Issues and Building Finger Strength and Dexterity

The first major issue that arises from using legato technique is the lack of picking involved. This may seem like an obvious, "Well, duh!" moment. But when you remove picking from the equation, the majority of the burden falls on your fretting hand. This can result in sloppiness, finger or forearm fatigue and, most offensive of all, *uneven volume of attack* from note to note.

The first legato exercise we'll look at is a fairly straightforward chromatic exercise. It will primarily focus on building finger independence and dexterity and will use the hammer-on technique across all four fingers on the fretting hand.

Example 2a: Chromatic finger independence hammer-on exercise with 1/8th note pulse @ 100bpm

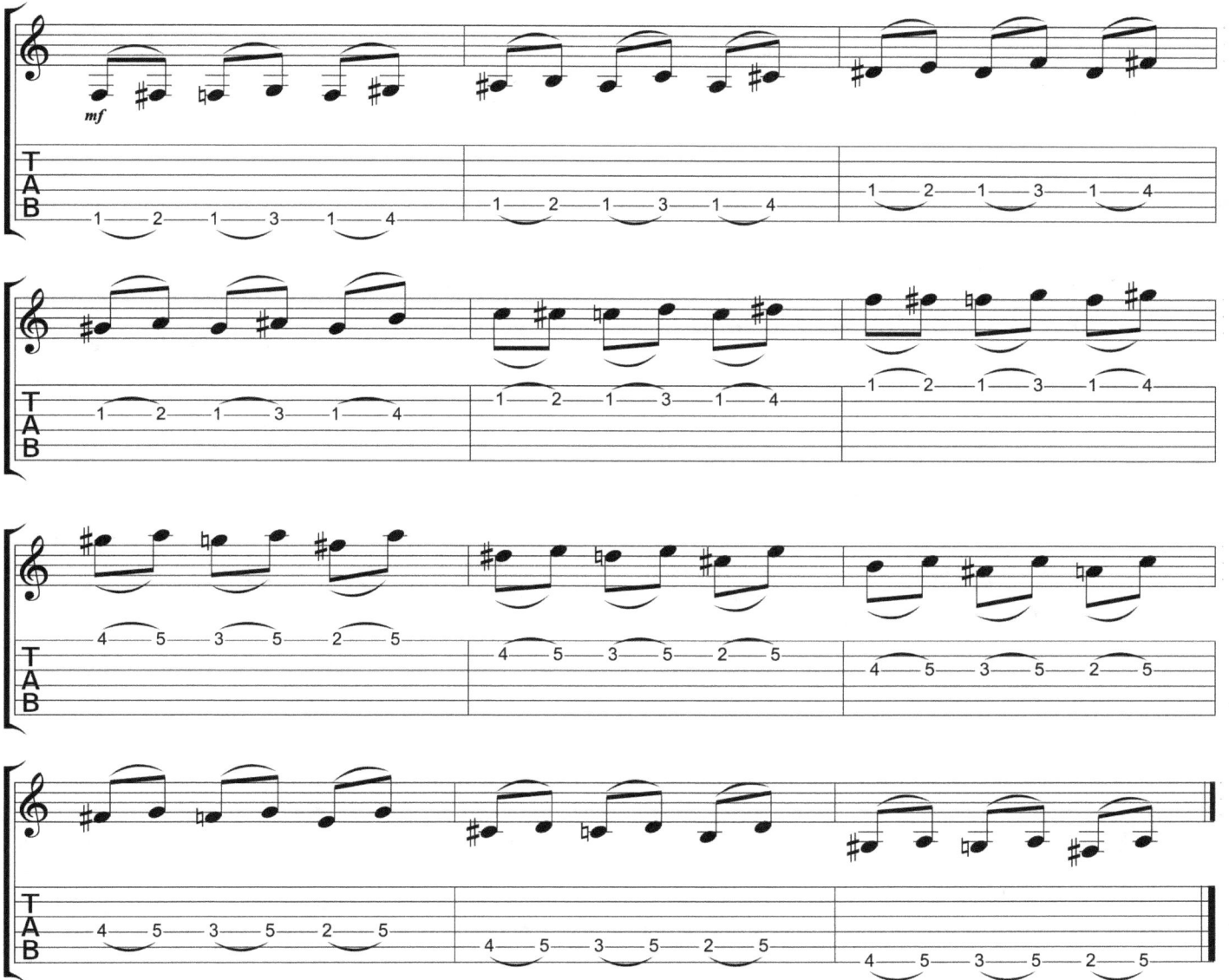

Drilling this exercise repeatedly will cause your forearm to feel like you're receiving a Chinese burn from your older sibling, or that kid in the playground who was just misunderstood and struggled to connect with others. I've often referred to working on legato stamina as "forearm cardio". Indeed, you will see many fruitful results if you put in the practise time!

In a similar vein, we're now going to look at a chromatic exercise that is heavily focused on building finger independence and dexterity, but in this exercise, we will use the pull-off technique across all four fingers of the fretting hand.

Example 2b: Chromatic finger independence pull-off exercise with 1/8th note pulse @ 100bpm

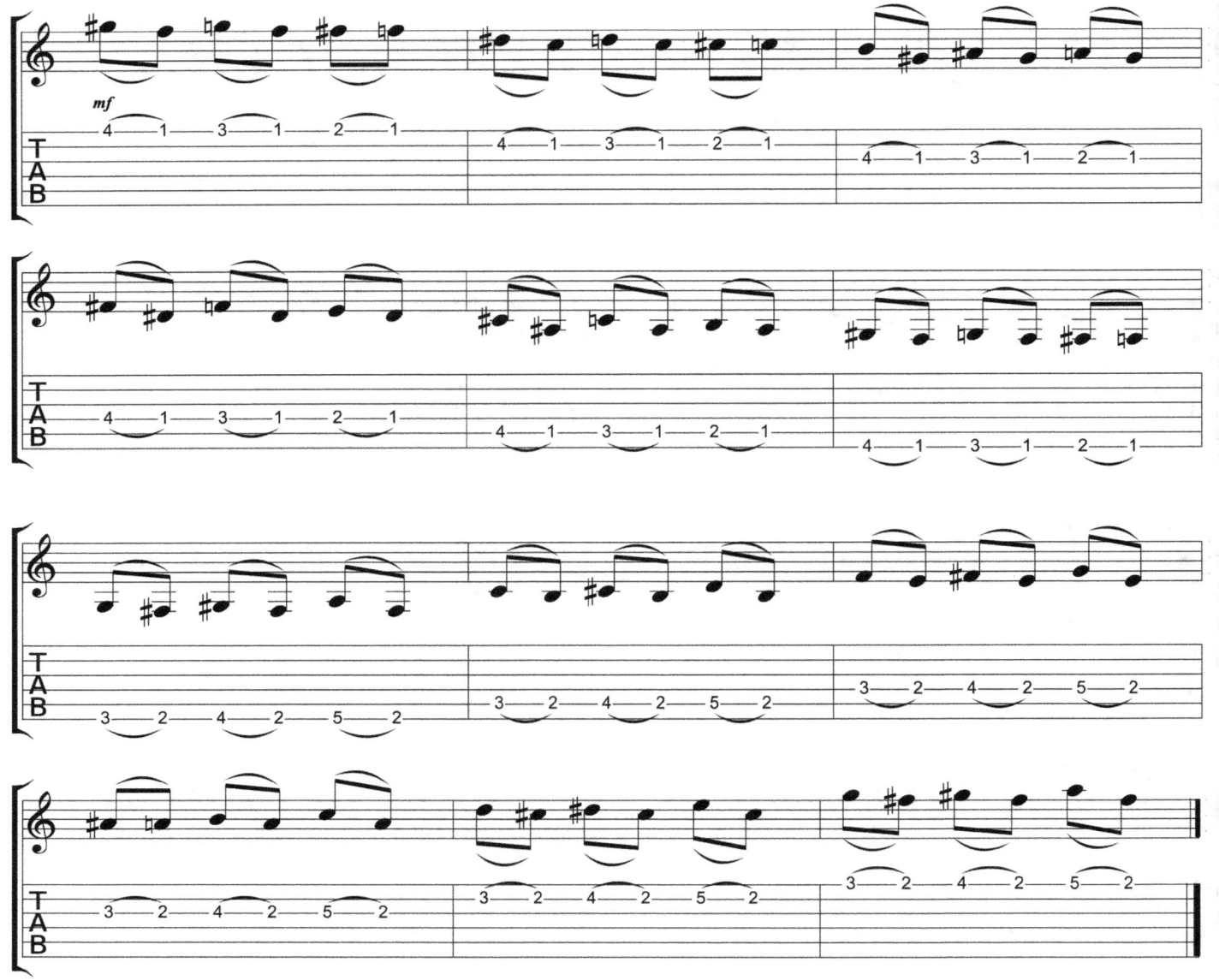

One incredibly important point to make about pull-offs and the descending legato technique is that you can't just be reactive, like when you play hammer-ons. In other words, a pull-off *is not a reverse hammer-on.* You need to prepare by holding down the note you're going to pull-off to, *before* the note that precedes it has been picked. Think of it this way: your fretting hand is plucking the string to *reveal* the note behind it. This might seem like a long-winded explanation, but trust me, it will save your life one day. Well, probably not your life, but it will save you hours of crap legato attempts in which you ask yourself, "Why doesn't this sound right?"

Now that we've looked at monotonous, unmelodic, chromatic legato exercises, let's take a look at some that are more pleasing to the ear. We'll start with a simple pentatonic lick in A Minor, ascending with the hammer-on technique and descending with pull-offs.

Example 2c: A Minor Pentatonic ascending and descending legato exercise with 1/8th note pulse @ 130bpm

The great thing about practising legato using the Minor Pentatonic scale is that we can do relatively simple hammer-on and pull-off drills with easy-to-remember scale shapes. It doesn't take long to get exercises like this one sounding musical and un-robotic (if such a term exists). You could even implement short fragments of this exercise into a lick for use in improvisation or solo composition.

It's also important to keep in mind that you are not just limited to the minor pentatonic for two-notes-per-string scales and exercises. The next few legato exercises will focus on modal scales.

Example 2d uses an A Dominant Pentatonic that is used frequently in mixolydian contexts or played over dominant 7th chords. We'll ascend and descend through this exercise using the same string-crossing pattern we saw in Example 2c.

Example 2d: A Dominant Pentatonic ascending and descending legato exercise with 1/8th note pulse @ 120bpm

As you can hear, this exercise has an interesting sound and will prepare you for less generic and more interesting contexts, other than straight minor blues.

The next two-note-per-string exercise is based on the Hirajoshi scale. This is a Japanese pentatonic scale that uses the 1st, 2nd, 3rd, 5th and 6th notes of the natural minor scale. If we lead from the 6th note and play 6, 1, 2, 3 and 5, we get a very Lydian sounding two-note-per-string pentatonic pattern. Once again, we'll ascend and descend through this exercise using the same string-crossing pattern we saw in examples 2c and 2d.

Example 2e: A Lydian Hirajoshi Pentatonic ascending and descending legato exercise with 1/8th note pulse @ 120bpm

Make That Damn Pinky Cooperate!

As you probably know, the Pinky is the weakest, least cooperative finger, and has the slowest response time of the hand digit family. In short, compared to the rest of the family, the Pinky is prone to letting you down or just being a heartbreaking disappointment.

Long-winded rants aside, I thought it might be fitting to dedicate an entire section of this chapter to taming and strengthening the Pinky, so he (or she) can become a cooperative and useful member of the legato team.

This first Pinky exercise will focus on the relationship between the Pointer and the Pinky, which will create a gap of two whole tones (four frets). We'll use hammer-ons when ascending and pull-offs descending.

Example 2f: Pointer and Pinky legato strengthening exercise with 1/8th note pulse @ 90bpm

Don't be too concerned about the bpm you use for this exercise. The main objective is to develop strength, stretching ability, note clarity and a stronger relationship between Pointer and Pinky.

The next exercise works with all four fingers and emphasises the Pinky's relationship with all of the other fingers. It will vary between hammer-ons and pull-offs and go between Pinky-Pointer, Pinky-Ring and Pinky-Middle.

Example 2g: Four-fingered Pinky legato relationship strengthening exercise with 1/8th note pulse @ 90bpm

The next exercise has a somewhat neoclassical, Malmsteenesque sound to it and uses more diatonic sounding scales. We're going to play through multiple six-note triplet phrases that all begin with the Pinky in the key of E Minor.

Example 2h: Malmsteeny legato exercise in E Minor with triplet 1/8th note pulse @ 110bpm

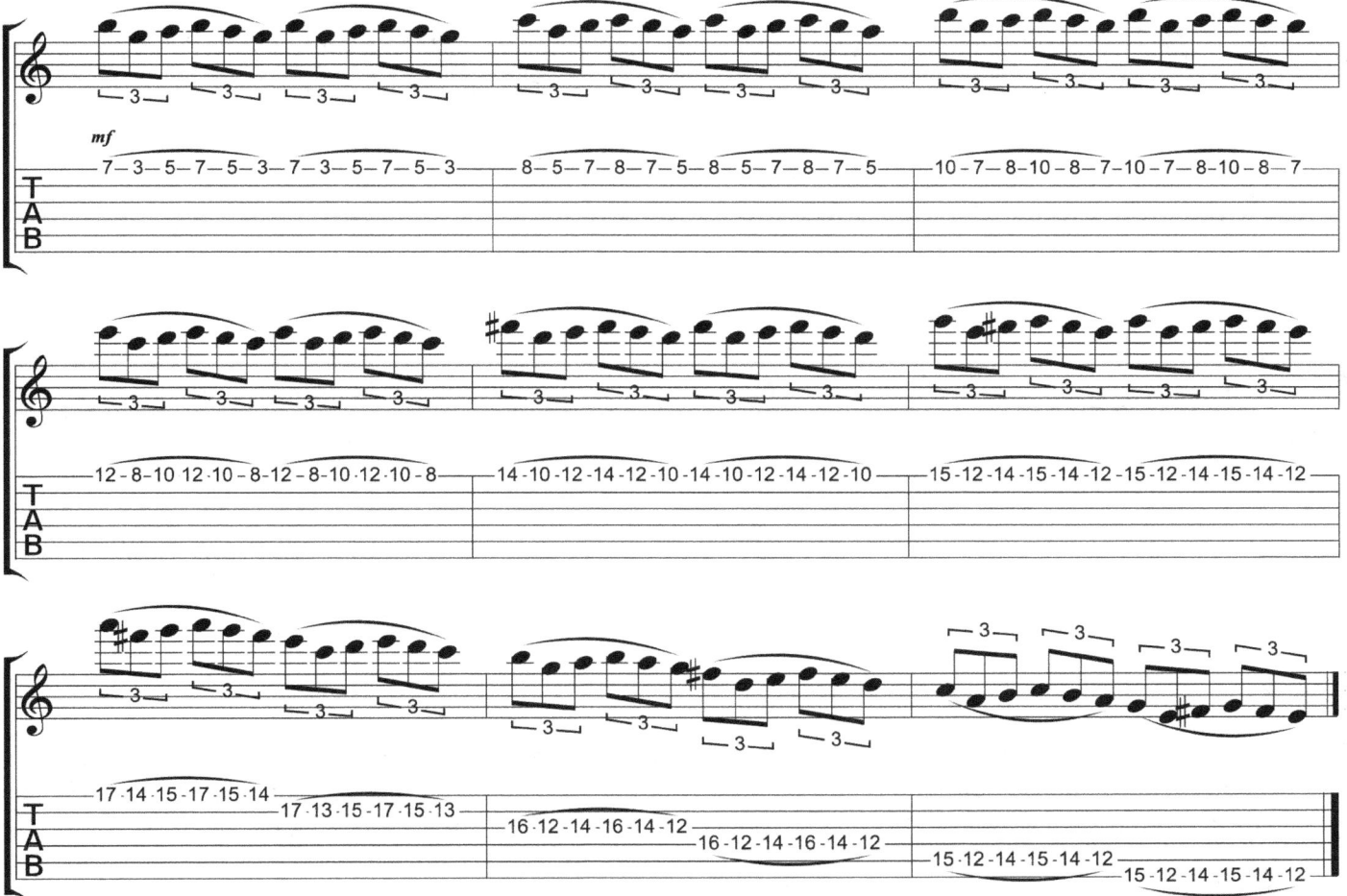

Good Time Rock Legato

The next section of this chapter is based on some pretty cool rock licks and exercises. Some of the shapes and patterns will sound familiar to you. I'm drawing from the influences of Thin Lizzy, KISS, Kirk Hammett, Jimmy Page and, of course, Satch (arguably the king of rockin' legato).

The first exercise is a descending into ascending A Minor Pentatonic scale with a back-tracking triplet feel. It's played over a few bars of 5/4 and uses all six strings. Oh, and don't be scared by the weird time signature – you'll find it feels quite comfortable after a few playthroughs.

Example 2i: 5/4 rockin' pentatonic legato exercise in A Minor with triplet 1/8th note pulse @ 85bpm

You'll hear this style of legato triplet pattern a lot on Kirk Hammett's solos on Metallica's first two albums (*Kill 'Em All* and *Ride the Lightning*) and it's used quite a few times in the Thin Lizzy song *Chinatown*. (If you haven't heard *Chinatown* or much Thin Lizzy you must rectify both of these things immediately!)

The next exercise uses a similar concept to Example 2i, but with D Dominant Pentatonic to get a Mixolydian-type sound. It still has that cool triplet emphasis.

Example 2j: 5/4 D Dominant Pentatonic legato exercise with triplet 1/8th note pulse @ 85bpm

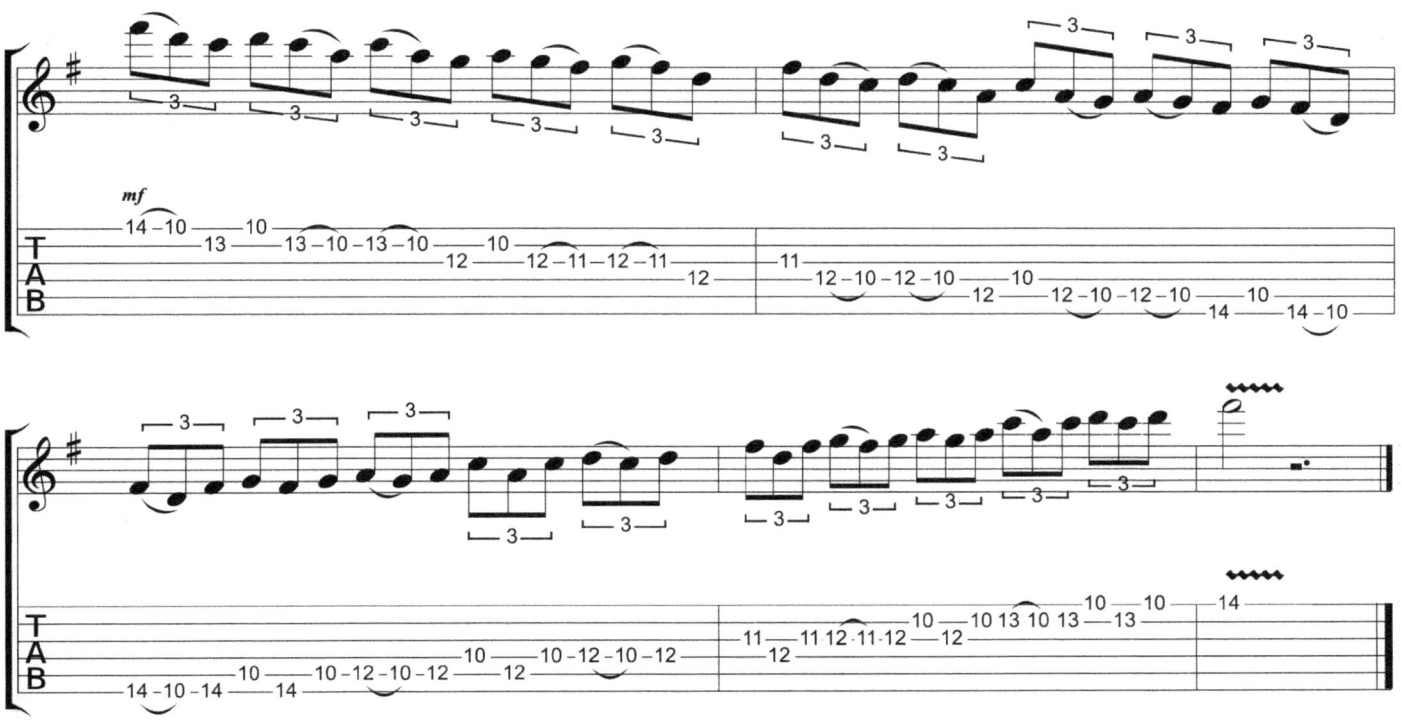

Again, we can recycle the last two examples using the Hirajoshi Japanese Pentatonic in E Minor, emphasising the note C to give it a more Lydian sound, and still retaining the triplet feel.

Example 2k: 5/4 C Lydian Hirajoshi Pentatonic legato exercise with triplet 1/8th note pulse @ 85bpm

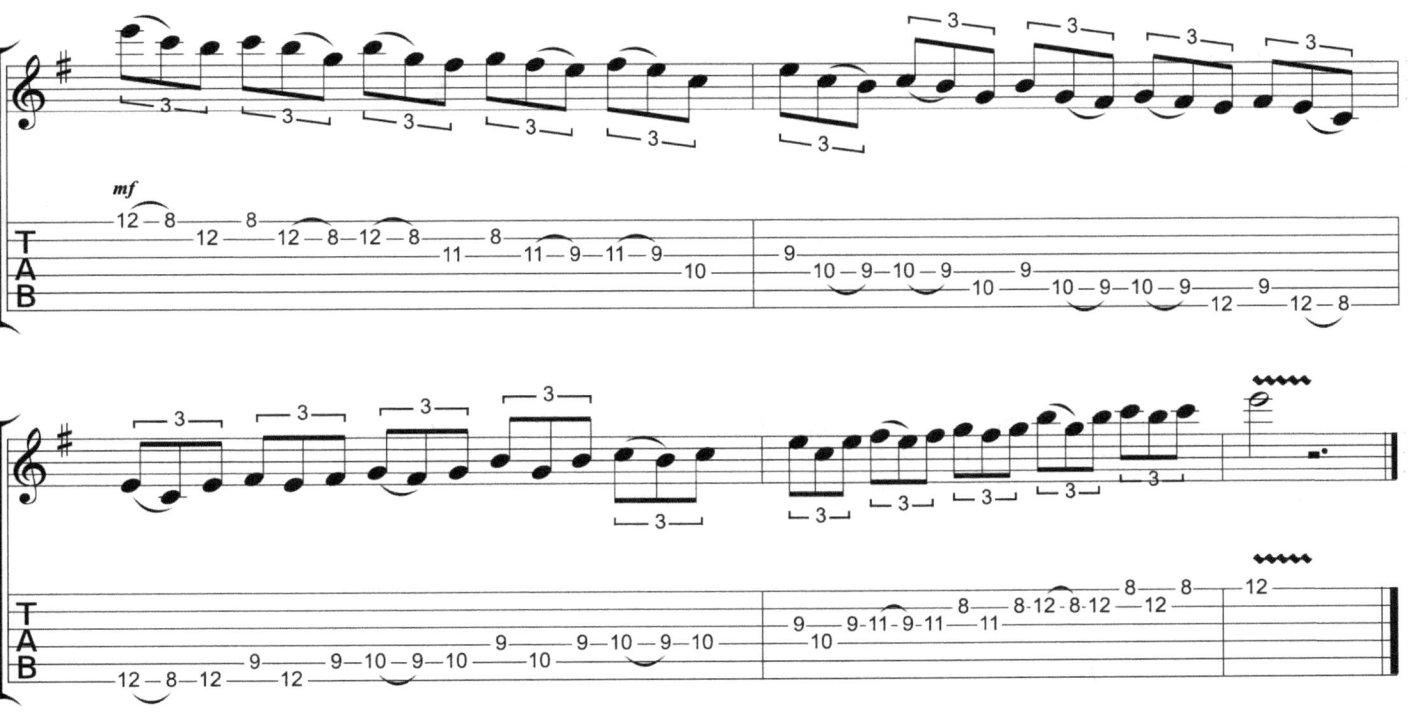

Oddly Timed and Oddly Grouped Legato

One thing that happens a lot in exercises and runs is the use of very predictable note timing or emphasis. If we're dealing with 1/8th or 1/16th notes, you'll often see note groupings and patterns of 2, 4 and sometimes 6 notes. This pattern will then repeat through the exercise or to the end of the run. If we're in either a triplet 1/8th or 1/16th note context, you'll generally see note groupings and patterns of 3, 6 and – on rare occasions – 9 notes. This issue comes up a lot in an alternate picking context too.

For that reason, I want to focus on some five-note groupings that will shake you out of your predictable note grouping comfort zone!

The first exercise uses position 1 of the A Minor Pentatonic scale and ascends in groups of five.

Example 2l: A Minor Pentatonic ascending fives legato exercise with 1/8th note pulse @ 105bpm

In a similar vein, using the same position of the A Minor Pentatonic scale, this time we'll descend in groups of five.

Example 2m: A Minor Pentatonic descending fives legato exercise with 1/8th note pulse @ 105bpm

We can also use different pentatonic scales, such as the Hirajoshi and the Dominant. If you want to get super creative, you can combine ascending and descending ideas. Let's take a look at a B Dominant Pentatonic lick using positions 5 and 1, ascending in groups of five and descending in groups of five.

Example 2n: B Dominant Pentatonic ascending and descending fives legato exercise with 1/8th note pulse @ 92bpm

Again, let's utilise this same concept using E Minor Hirajoshi scale.

Example 2o: C Lydian Hirajoshi Pentatonic ascending and descending fives legato exercise with 1/8th note pulse @ 92bpm

As you can see, five-note groupings are totally bitchin' and they create an interesting flow and emphasis.

The final exercise in this section uses fragments of the 5th, 1st and 2nd position of the A Minor Pentatonic scale. In a similar vein to the fives, this exercise has a less predictable pulse when compared to straight 1/8th or 1/16th note runs. What I like about this pattern is that it drifts between a five-note group and a six-note group.

Example 2p: A Minor Pentatonic ascending fives and sixes legato exercise with 1/8th note pulse @ 120bpm

This idea can work for other pentatonic scales and positions too. Try implementing these strangely grouped legato runs into your playing if you feel like it is becoming stale and predictable.

Rollin' Rollin' Rollin'…Legato

The final section of this chapter will focus on the most terrifying form of legato. "Rollin" legato commonly occurs in a three-note-per-string situation and can create a very cool, flowing sound. In order to achieve these runs, the player will be rolling their fingers back and forth (hence the term "rollin", for which I take full credit for arguably coining, and which works on two clever levels – for which I'm patting myself on the back and smiling!)

Let's begin with an exercise in G Major that focuses on an ascending three-note-per-string legato line.

Example 2q: Three-note-per-string G Major ascending legato exercise with triplet 1/8th note pulse @ 85bpm

Now let's look at an A Dorian three-note-per-string scale, but this time with a descending legato line. As I mentioned near the beginning of this chapter (and feel compelled to reiterate, as it's most important to three-note-per-string descending legato sequences), please don't think of these rolling pull-offs as "reverse hammer-ons"! On the first string you'll need to be holding down frets 10, 8 and 7 before you pick the first note, in order to roll through the notes smoothly. You'll want to carry this thought process, finger preparation and attack all the way through each string of this exercise.

Example 2r: Three-note-per-string A Dorian descending legato exercise with triplet 1/8th note pulse @ 85bpm

Now that we've addressed three-note-per-string ascending and descending lines separately, here is an exercise that brings them together. It ascends through a three-note-per-string A Aeolian shape using septuplets, then drifts into a desending C Ionian shape.

Example 2s: A Minor to C Major ascending and descending three-note-per-string legato exercise with septuplet 1/8th note pulse @ 100bpm

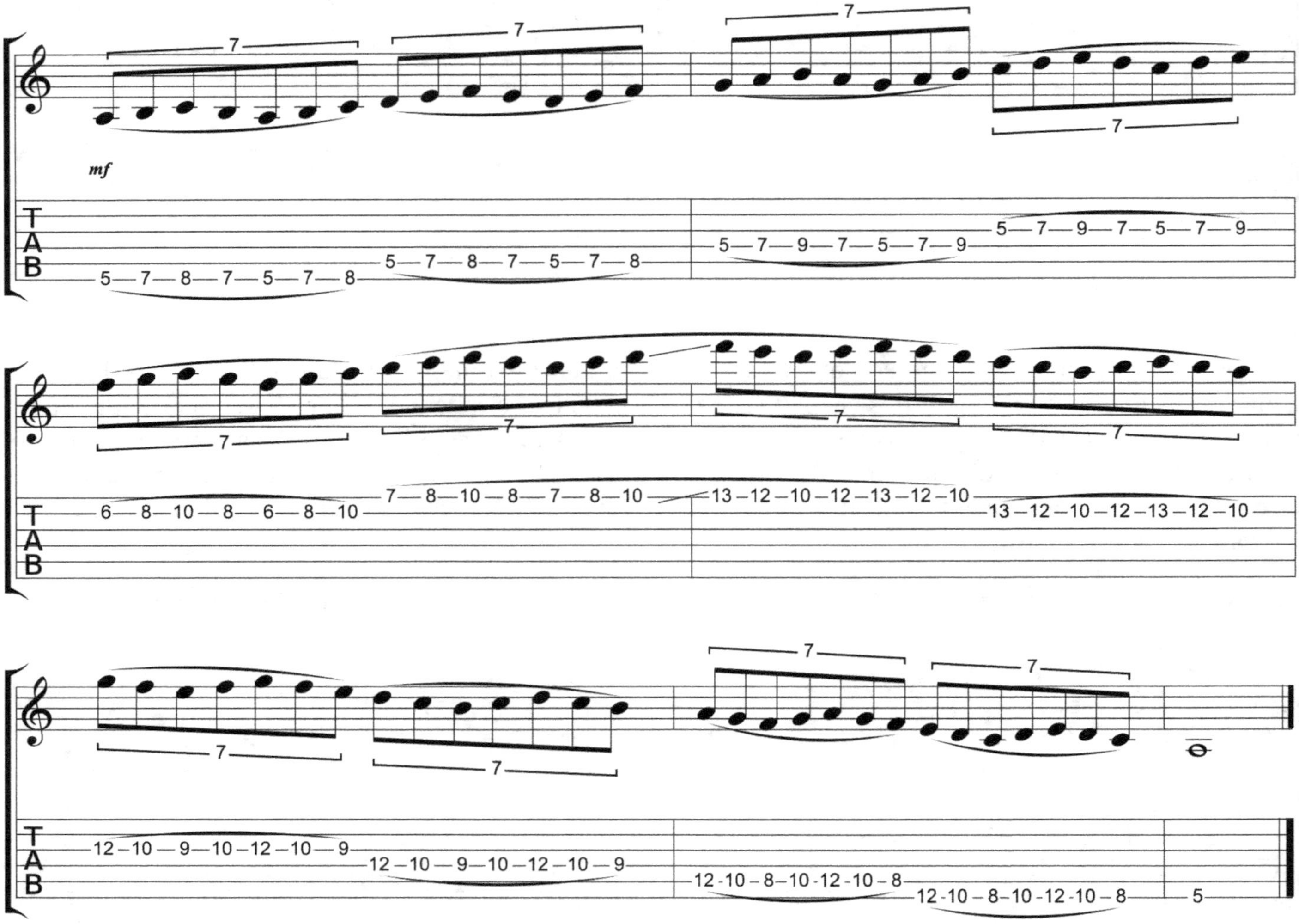

The next exercise is a little unorthodox, which is why I love it! It's an E Minor Pentatonic idea that drifts between 5, 3 and 1 note per string. Keep in mind that since we're not using a traditional scale, this can be a little stretchy on the old fretting hand.

It might be worth mentioning here that large stretches can be painful and strenuous. Poor technique can cause chronic pain or, worse, cacophonic tripe (AKA crappy note execution). It's important that when it comes to dealing with big legato stretches, shredding, or arpeggio stretches, that you keep your thumb on the back of the neck in line with your middle and ring fingers. Hold the neck like you would hold a taco. If you're a little hazy on how to hold a taco, let this jog your memory and inspire you.

Example 2t: E Minor Pentatonic legato exercise with triplet 1/16th note pulse @ 92bpm

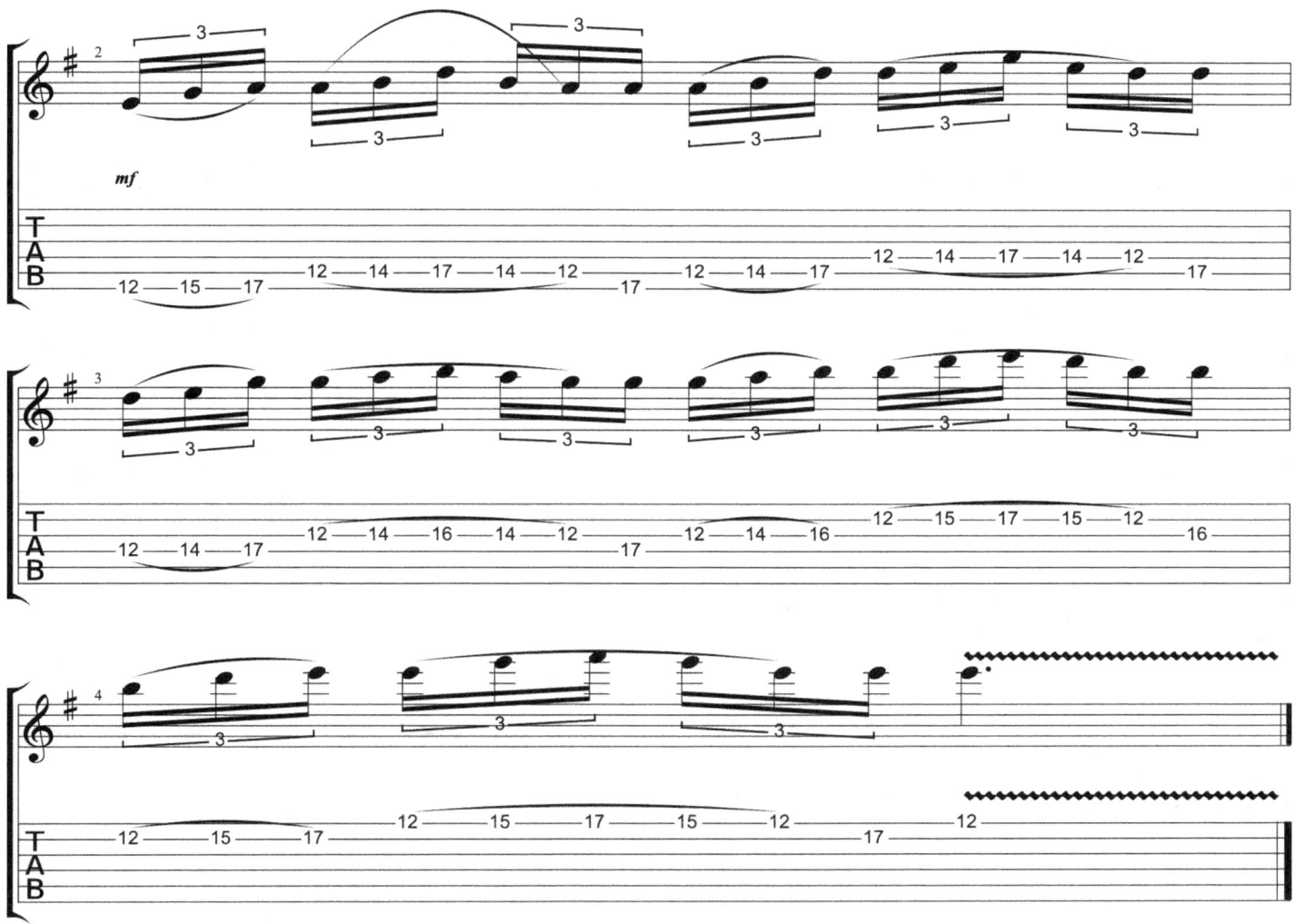

The next exercise in D Phrygian uses rolling legato across two strings. Pay close attention to the quick string changes and multiple position shifts.

Example 2u: D Phrygian position shift legato exercise with triplet 1/8th note pulse @ 115bpm

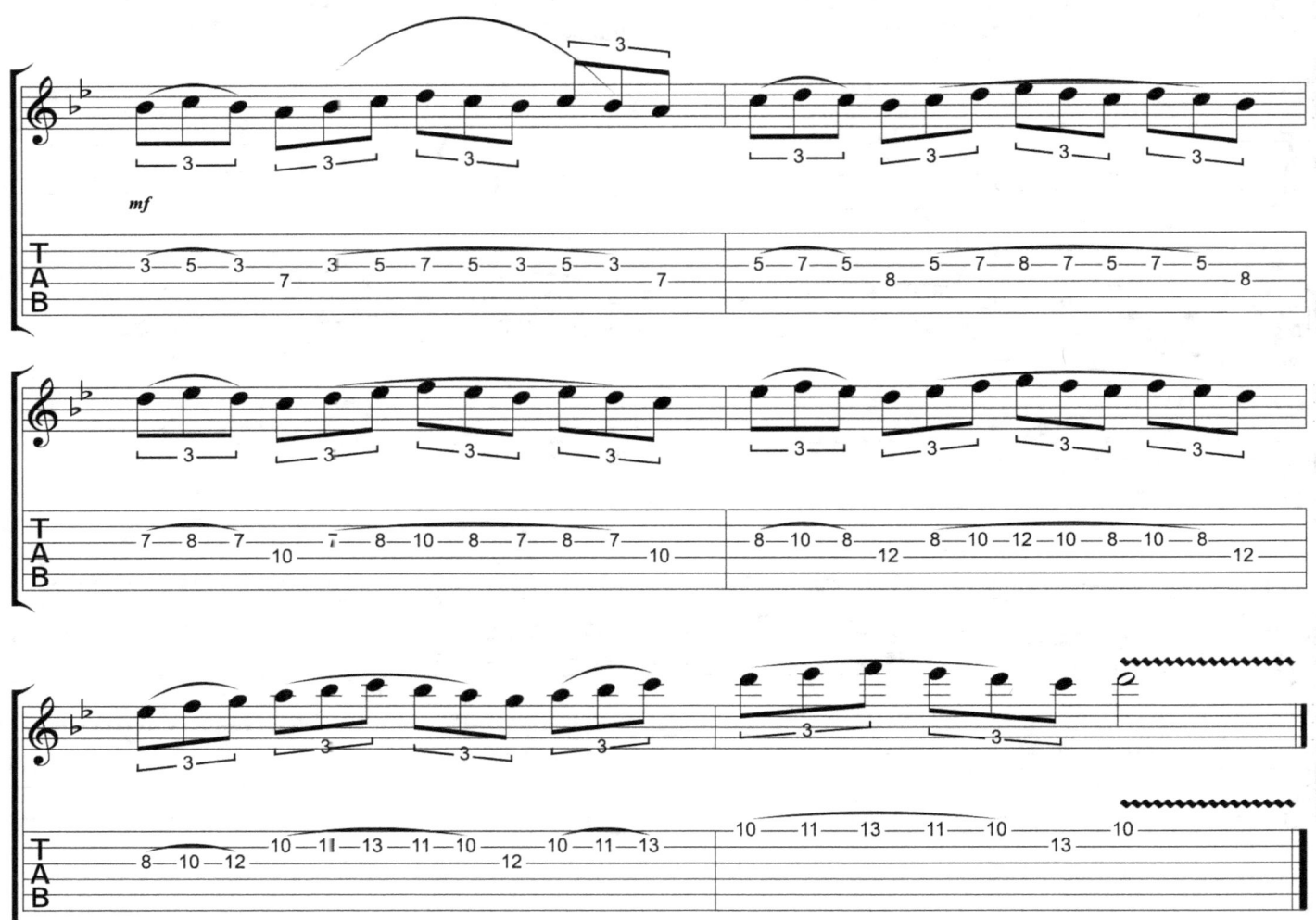

The next exercise uses what I call the "nonsense" Whole Tone scale in the key of F#. It's a good way to drill the most commonly stretched three-note-per-string shape up and down the fretboard. Pay close attention to the triplet emphasis and the rolling groups of either three notes or five notes per string.

Example 2v: F# Whole Tone ascending pattern legato exercise with triplet 1/8th note pulse @ 102bpm

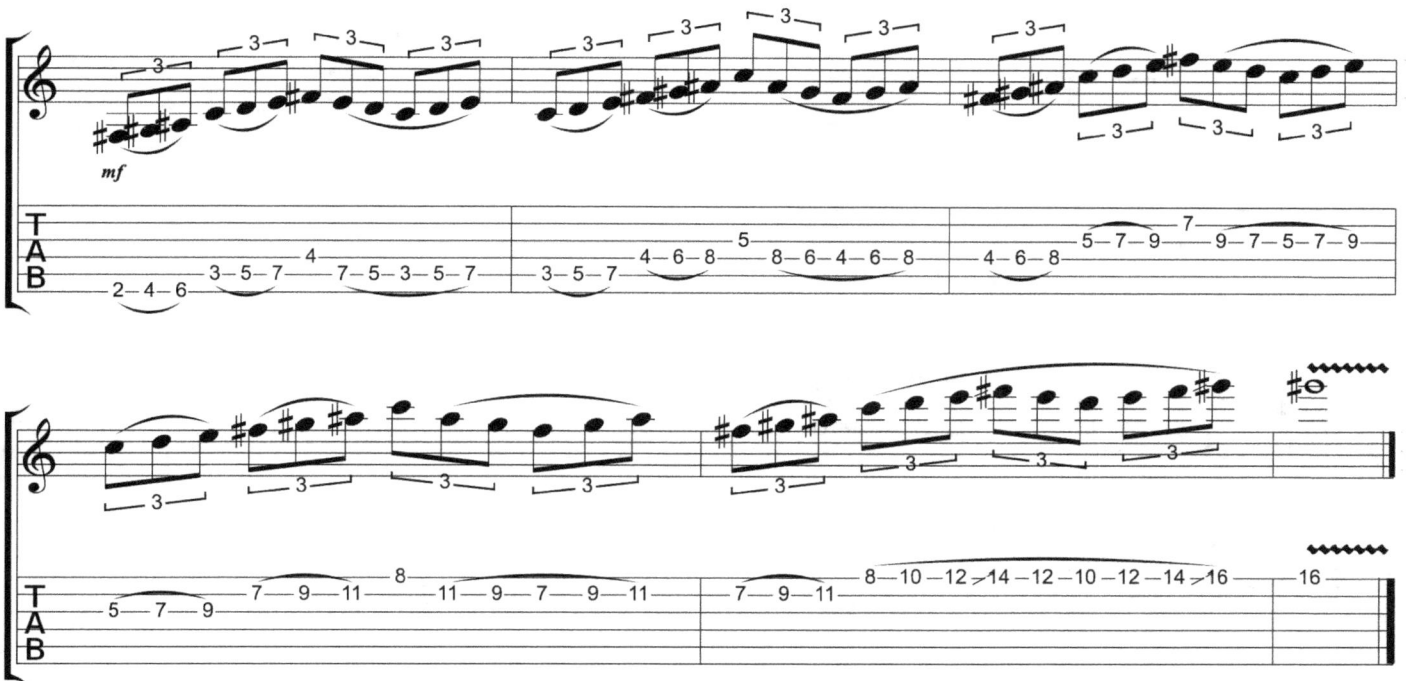

In a similar vein, the exercise in Example 2w shows that we can use the F# Whole Tone scale to drill a rolling septuplet technique. This is an excellent way to keep your legato stamina up. It will also force you to practise ascending and descending legato equally.

Example 2w: F# Whole Tone rolling sevens legato exercise with septuplet 1/8th note pulse @ 102bpm

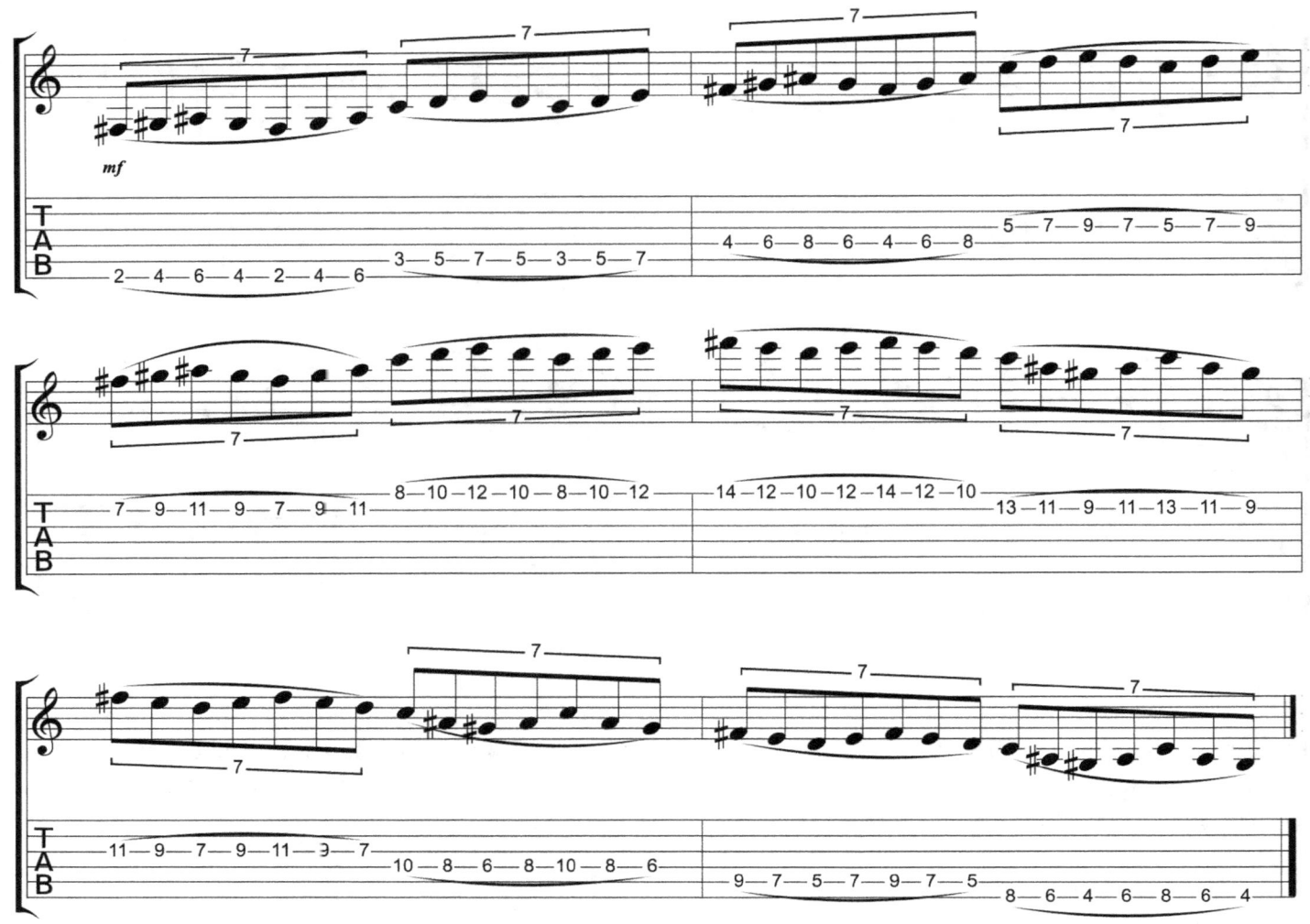

The final exercise in this section is stretchy and incredibly silly. I first saw this shape in the solo to the Pantera song *Domination*. It's a one-string diminished arpeggio that spans a whopping six frets. We'll essentially be playing diminished arpeggios in E, jumping in 4ths, and playing a septuplet on every string.

Example 2x: E diminished sevens legato exercise with septuplet 1/8th note pulse @ 130bpm

String Skip Legato

The final section of this chapter is devoted to string-skipping legato. It's so easy to forget to practise string-skipping in a variety of contexts, so I've decided to put together a few legato exercises in some diatonic and pentatonic situations.

The first exercise is a simple A Minor Pentatonic in the first position, ascending with string skips.

Example 2y: A Minor Pentatonic position one string-skip legato with 1/8th note pulse @ 100bpm

We'll now take the principles used in Example 2y and stretch the A Minor Pentatonic scale across the fretboard using all five positions. It will also include descending patterns from one position to the next.

Exercise 2z: A Minor Pentatonic in all five positions string-skip legato exercise with 1/8th note pulse @ 100bpm

The next exercise is rather controversial and risqué. We'll use a three-note-per-string pentatonic pattern in the key of B Minor, and also include string skips and a position shift. I've seen Rusty Cooley do some crazy stuff with pentatonic string-skipping very similar to this. It's a great way to get a more Satriani sounding legato feel with a pentatonic scale and also creates more interesting intervals than the more common two-note-per-string pentatonic shapes.

Example 2z1: Three-note-per-string B Minor Pentatonic string-skip legato exercise with "tens" pulse @ 92bpm

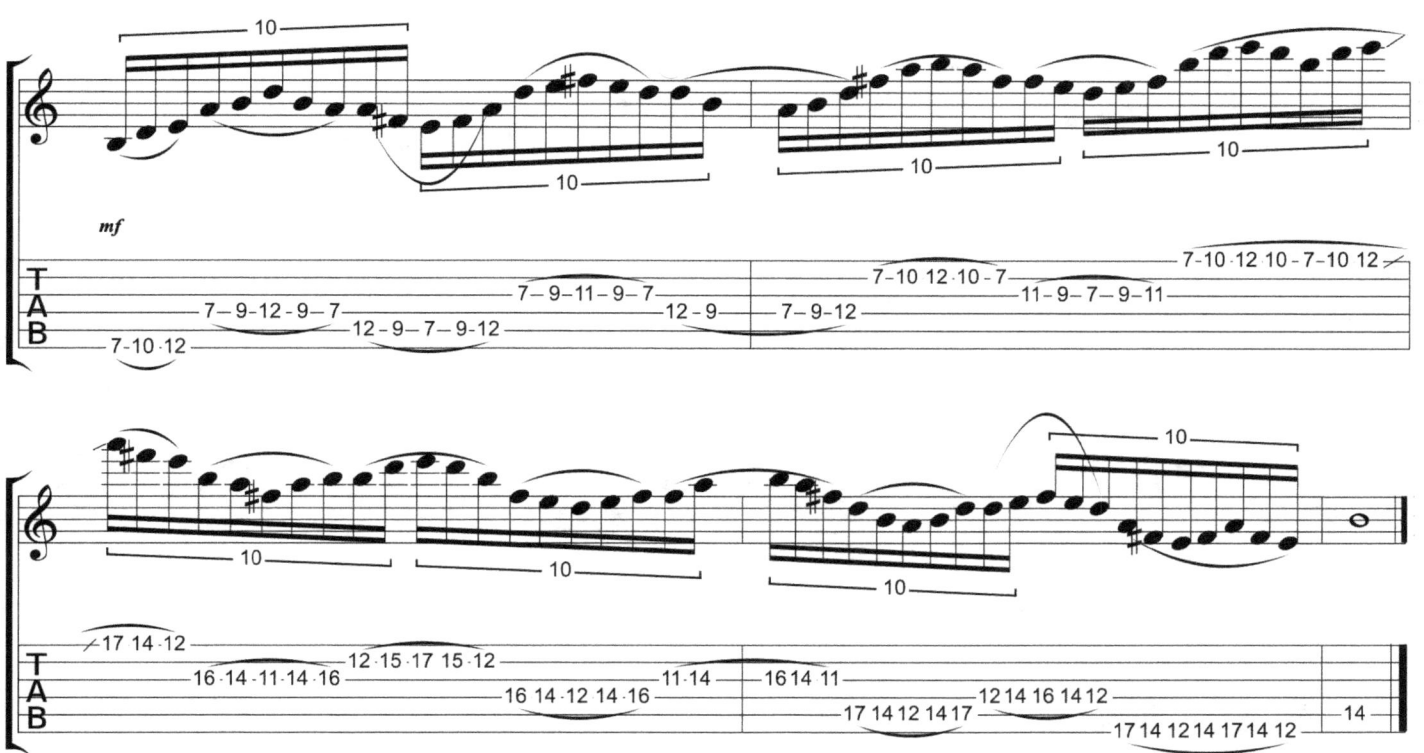

The final legato exercise works through multiple positions and modes of G Major using string skips. This is an interesting way to get some larger intervallic jumps into your legato passages, and also create something of an arpeggio sound as well. I've heard Paul Gilbert and John Petrucci use this concept to create arpeggio substitutes and more interesting legato, and even shred sequences. Apologies in advance for the 13th note pulse!

Example 2z2: Three-note-per-string G Major string-skip legato multiple position shift exercise with "thirteens" pulse @ 130bpm

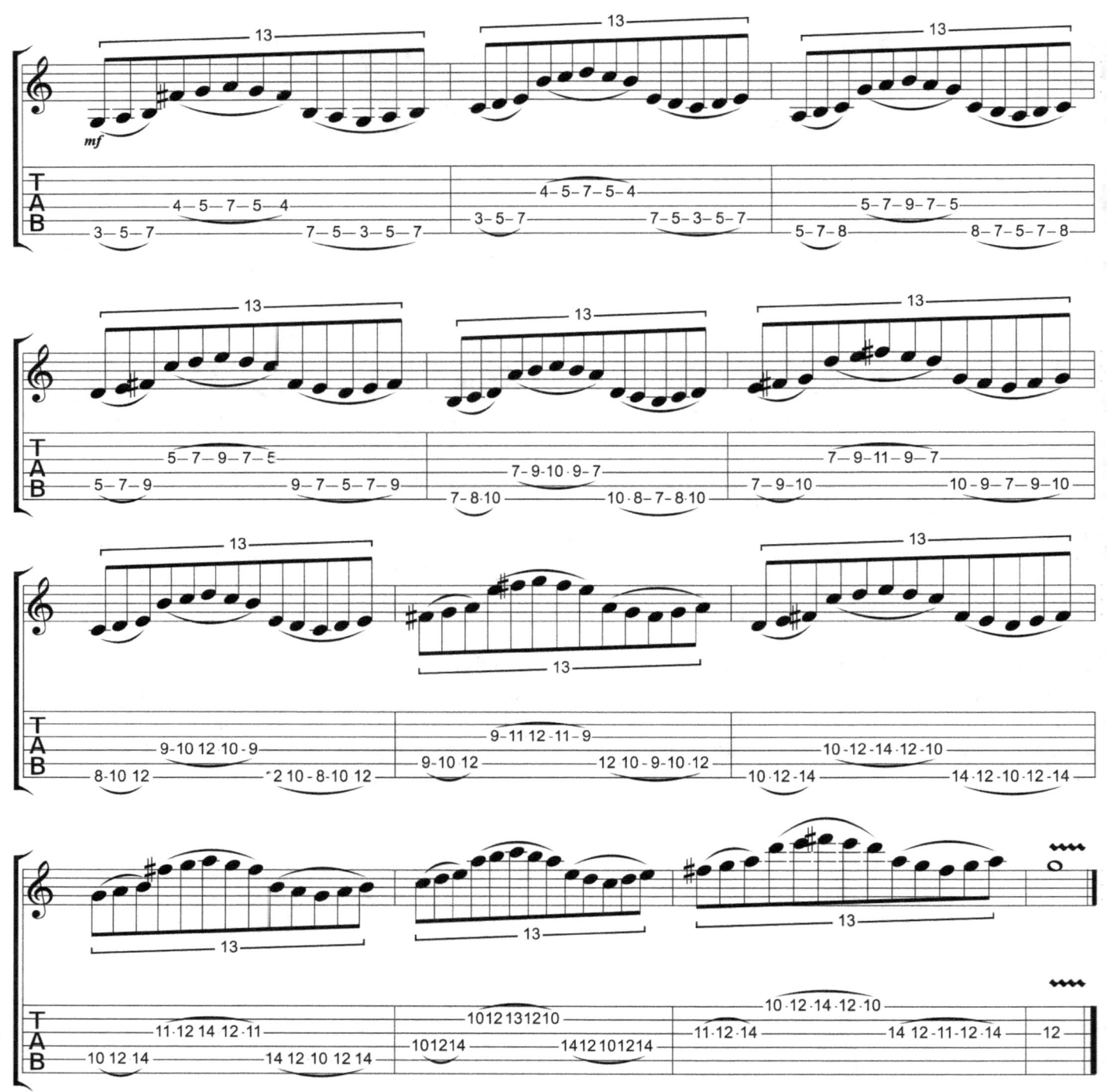

A Smooth Summation

Contrary to popular belief, I think legato is more important than shredding (at least in regard to the way I play, hear melodies and express my ideas in my original compositions). I find that the legato technique can bring speed, emotion and tasteful melody together in a way that common staccato attack, shredding and sweeping cannot. This may differ according to each person's taste, so don't take the way I play as gospel. It's more important for you to find the techniques that enable you to "speak" through your playing and compositions. My goal is that all the techniques discussed in this book will work together to make you a well-rounded player and, of course, the ultimate shred machine!

Chapter Three: Tappin' Like A Boss!

Since its popularisation by Eddie Van Halen in the 1980s, the art of finger tapping (sometimes referred to by dorks and squares as "right-handed hammer-ons") has changed the way we think about the instrument. A once large hand-stretch or impossible position shift can be easily achieved with a cheeky tap. Things like a single-string three-note arpeggio that was once near impossible to execute can now be played effortlessly and at lightning speed.

In this chapter we'll look at many different ways to use the tapping technique. We'll mainly be focusing on diatonic and exotic scales as well as pentatonics and a few cheeky arpeggios.

Simple Tap Licks and Fundamentals

In this first section, we'll concentrate on simple tapping patterns to get you comfortable with the technique and iron out any kinks before we venture into the realm of *ridiculum*.

Guitarists like Steve Vai and Guthrie Govan use their middle finger, whilst still having a firm grip on the pick. The majority of players do this. However, there are anomalies in players like Eddie Van Halen and myself who will use the Pointer (index) finger. It's really down to personal preference.

This first exercise is a one-string E Minor scale working in triplets. It uses a simple tap followed by a pull-off into a hammer-on pattern throughout.

Treat the initial tap like a hammer-on, straight onto the fretboard. Treat the note that follows like a pull-off, otherwise it will have a weak attack. Essentially, you need to "pluck" the string with your tapping finger as it leaves the fretboard. You can pull away slightly in either direction – towards the ceiling or the floor – but just be aware not to hit any other strings in the process. Note that you can also dampen the other strings by resting your forearm across them.

Example 3a: One-string E Minor diatonic tap exercise with triplet 1/8th note pulse @ 100bpm

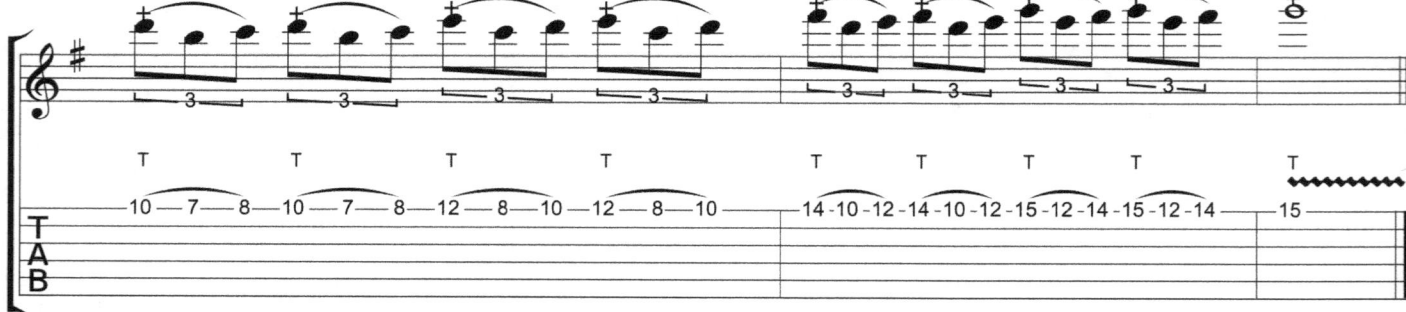

Keep in mind that the premise of tapping is similar to that of hammer-ons and pull-offs: the notes you play won't get a picked attack.

The next exercise is a one-string E Minor diatonic arpeggio sequence. We're creating arpeggios with taps which would otherwise be virtually impossible to play with just our fretting hand. Once again, the pattern throughout the exercise is a simple tap, then a pull-off into a hammer-on.

Example 3b: One-string E Minor tap diatonic arpeggio sequence exercise with triplet 1/8th note pulse @ 100bpm

The next exercise is made up of six-note triplet groupings from the same diatonic notes used above. Each position will begin with a double tap into a pull-off. This tapping style is similar to that used by Randy Rhoads at the beginning of his classic *Crazy Train* solo.

Example 3c: One-string E Minor diatonic double tap exercise with triplet 1/8th note pulse @ 100bpm

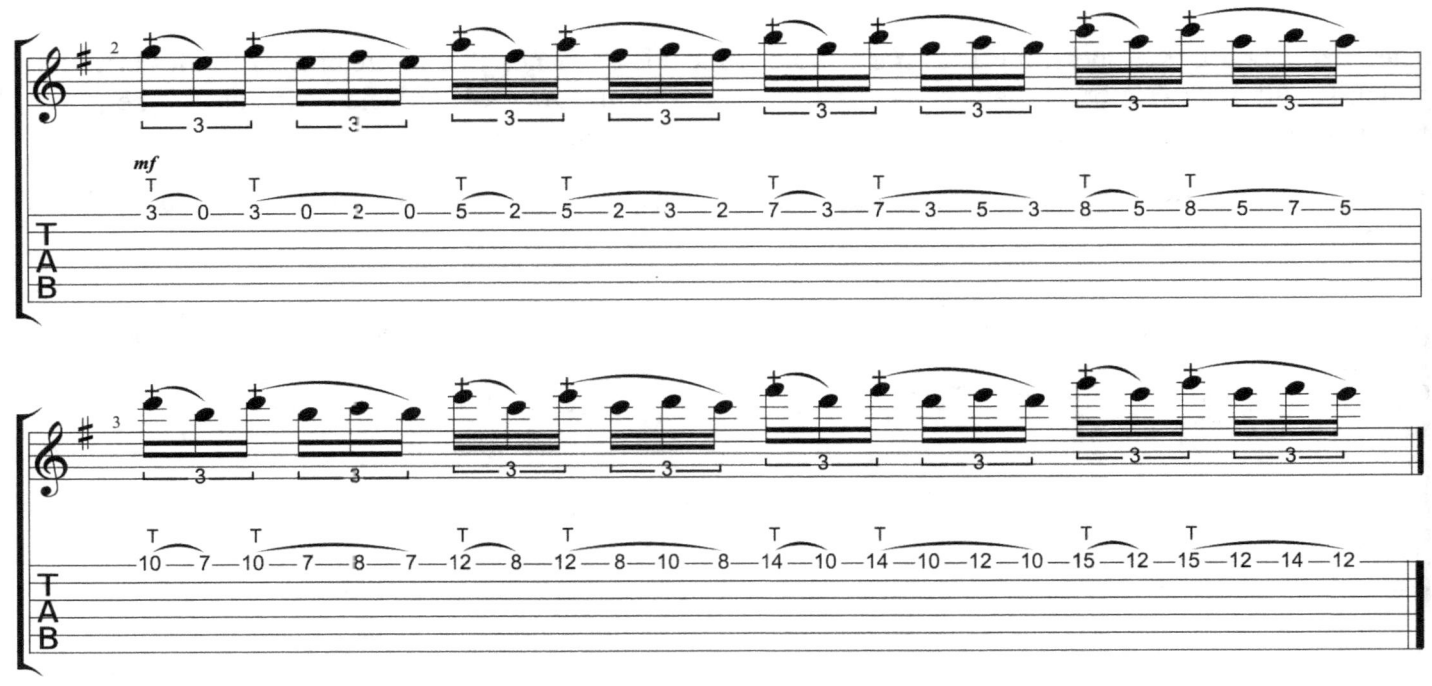

Now let's try a similar diatonic idea to Example 3a, but this time with three ascending notes played by our fretting hand, before our tapping hand gets involved.

Example 3d: One-string E Minor diatonic four-finger tap exercise with triplet 1/8th note pulse @ 100bpm

The final exercise in this section uses similar shapes to those in Example 3d, but we'll begin with a double tap, which will transition into an ascending-descending rolling legato.

Example 3e: One-string E Minor diatonic four-finger double tap exercise with 1/16th note pulse @ 100bpm

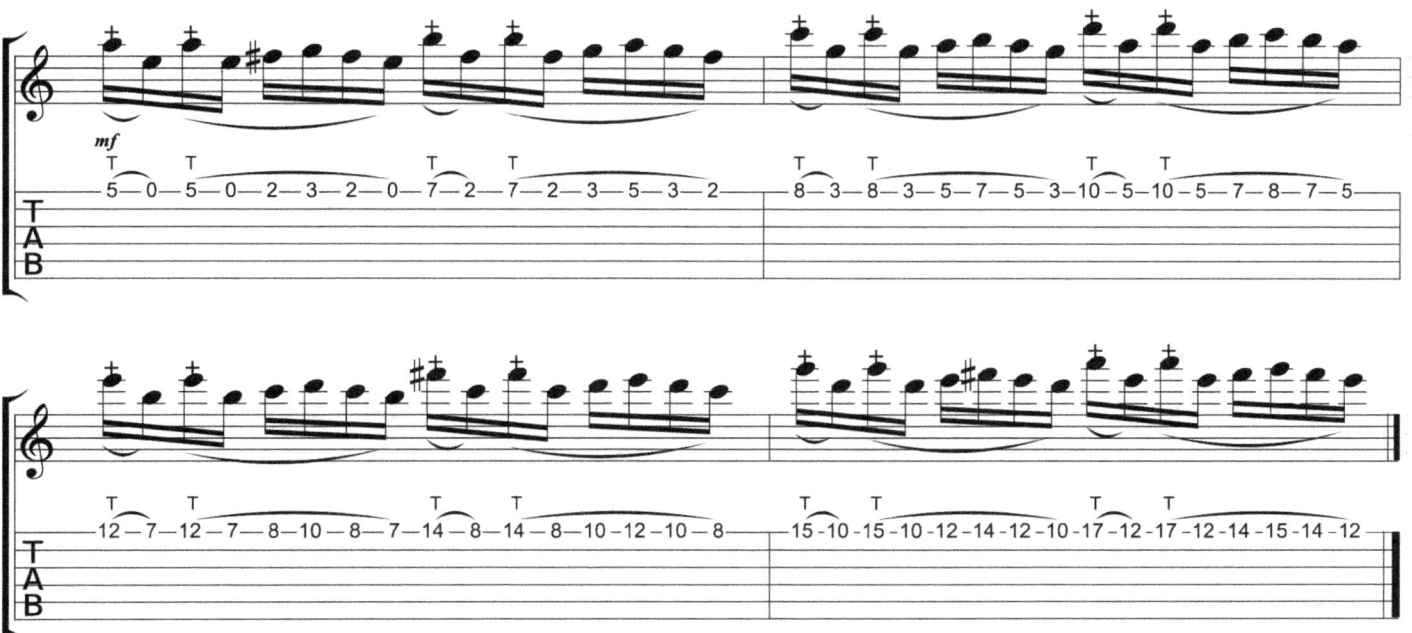

Multiple String Tapping

Now that you have some tapping fundamentals under your belt, it's time to start experimenting with some more extreme tapping concepts. As always, we will ease into it! This section of our tapping journey will focus on multiple-string scales with taps included. We'll look at things like six-string pentatonic and other scales, and even some arpeggios – all with the delightful addition of some cheeky taps.

This multiple-string tapping exercise is a descending into ascending A Minor Pentatonic scale in the 1st position, with notes tapped from the 2nd position.

Example 3f: A Minor 1st position descending-ascending tap exercise with 1/8th note pulse @ 115bpm

Now we'll take the same scale shape/concept as above, but add a *Crazy Train*-style Randy Rhoads double tap. This epic exercise will descend and ascend through multiple positions of the A Minor Pentatonic using a quintuplet pulse over a 3/4 bar.

Example 3g: A Minor multiple-position descending-ascending double tap exercise with quintuplet pulse 3/4 @ 100bpm

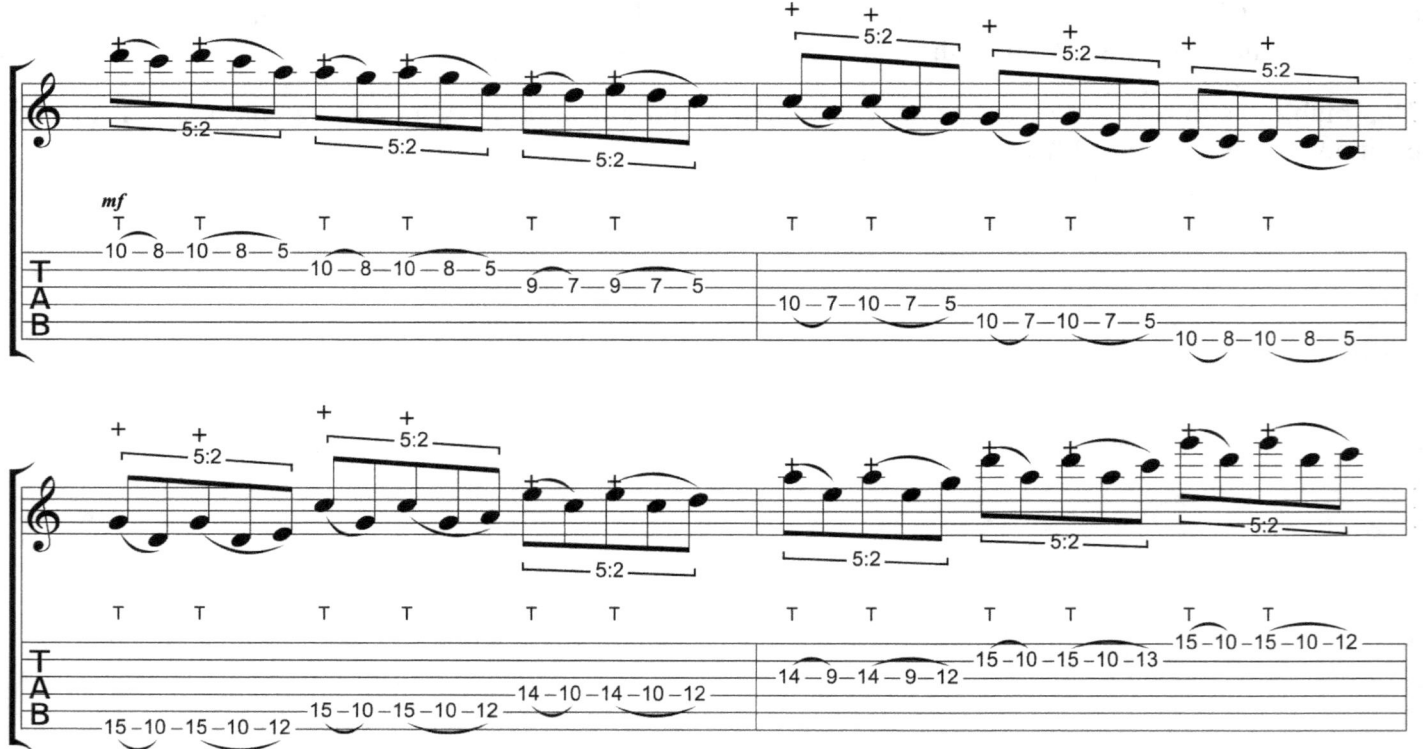

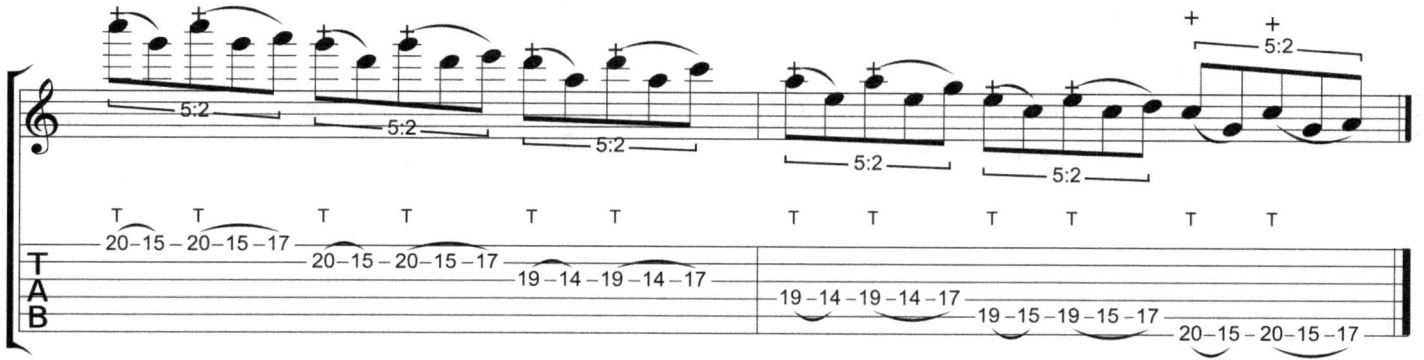

The next exercise uses the 1st position of the C# Minor Pentatonic scale. It has a triplet pulse and descends through the scale shape with taps and three-string groupings. Pay close attention to tapping placement and the backtracking patterns that occur every three strings!

Example 3h: C# Minor 1st position wave tap exercise with triplet 1/8th note pulse @ 120bpm

Let's take a look at some scales with an added tap. Your fretting hand will be working through three-note-per-string shapes. We'll be adding a tap to create one more diatonic note per string. The first exercise uses the A Ionian scale, working across three octaves.

Example 3i: A Ionian fifth tap exercise with 1/16th note pulse @ 110bpm

The tapped note and the first fretted note you pull off to are a fifth interval apart. This creates a melodic "distance" that sounds more interesting than the semitone or whole tone intervals commonly found in diatonic scales.

Now let's look at an exercise similar to the previous one, but this time using the F# Aeolian three-note-per-string shape.

Example 3j: F# Aeolian fifth tap exercise with 1/16th note pulse @ 110bpm

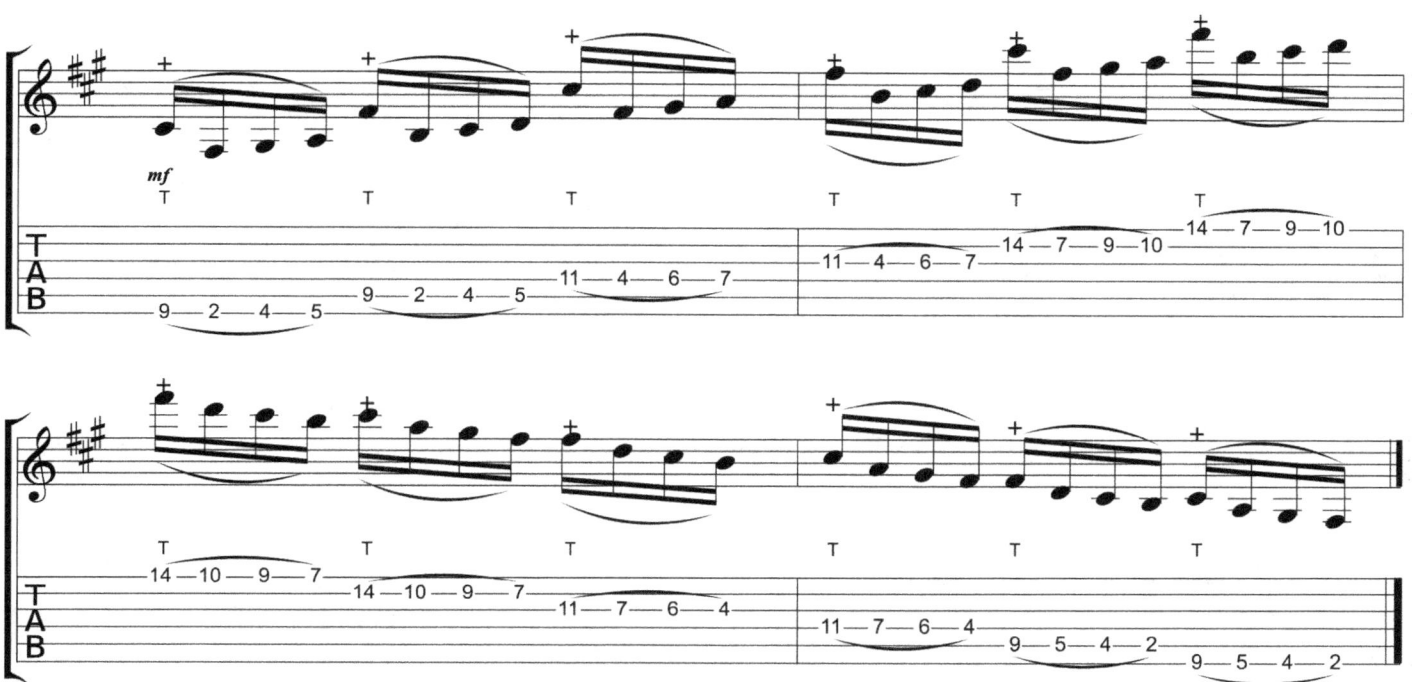

The next diatonic tap exercise uses an ascending E Locrian scale shape and utilises all six strings. It employs rolling legato technique and a tapped note in order to give us nine notes per string.

Example 3k: Three-note-per-string plus tap E Locrian ascending diatonic exercise with triplet 1/16th note pulse 100bpm

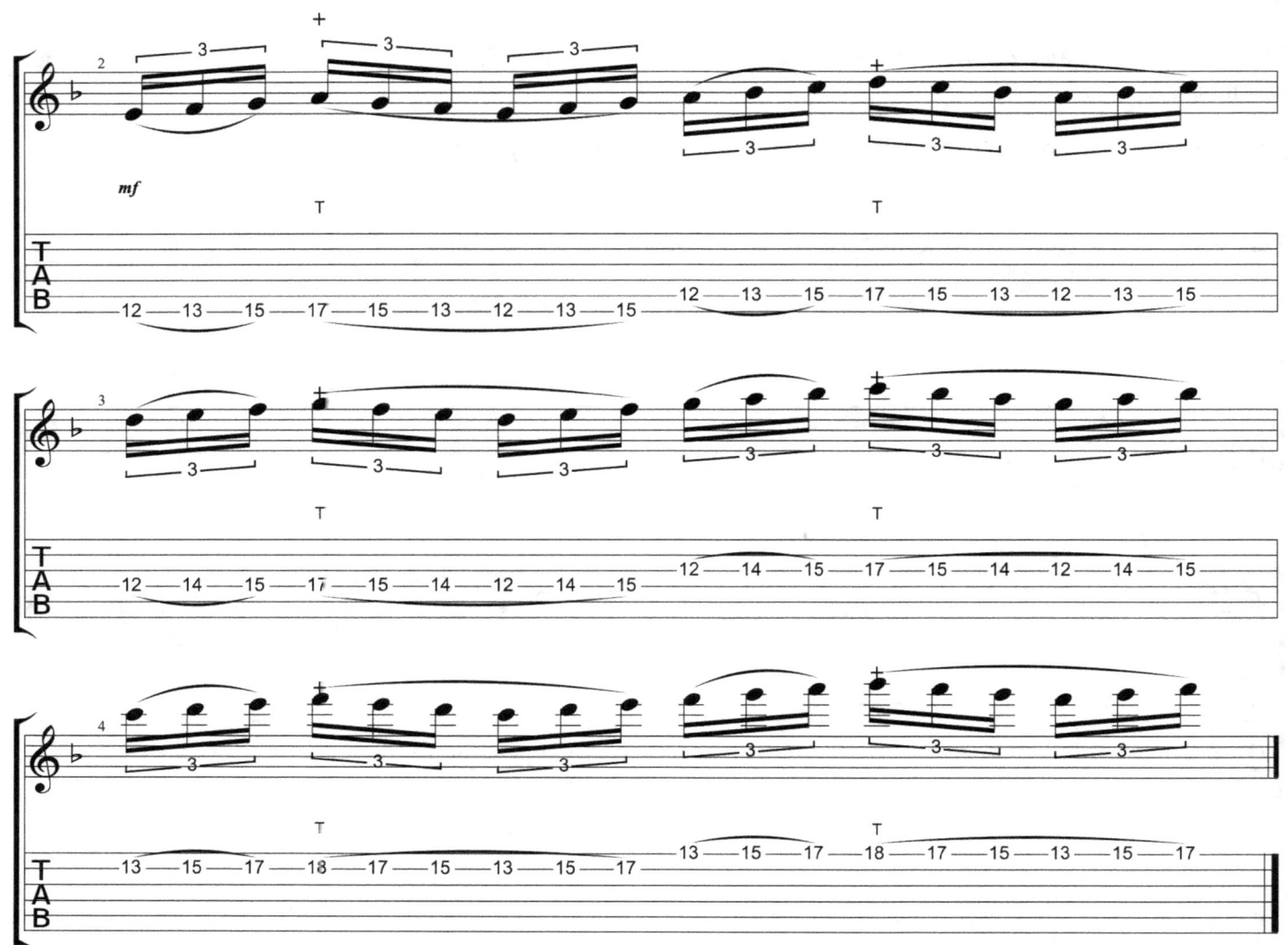

The next example involves rolling legato with slides and, most importantly, an added tap. It descends down the F# Aeolian scale in triplets and has a few position shifts across the neck. Pay close attention to the tap emphasis, as it's not as linear and predictable, as in previous exercises.

Example 3l: Three-note-per-string plus tap F# Aeolian descending diatonic exercise with triplet 1/16th note pulse @ 100bpm

Now here's an idea that uses the Whole Tone scale and ascends and descends in a diagonal manner across the fretboard. The fretting hand will use only two fingers and the tapping hand will do two taps per string. Pay close attention to the tap and the hammered notes that follow on the same fret. It's incredibly easy to get confused, so I would suggest working through this exercise one string at a time in groups of two triplets.

Example 3m: Whole-Tone Racer X-style tap exercise with triplet 1/16th note pulse @ 100bpm

The way this exercises drifts from a tap into a hammer note is characteristic of the tapping I've seen Paul Gilbert do. This kind of exercise will help you get you tapping around the fretboard and build your tapping chops. Stick with it and you'll be able to tackle Racer X songs like *Scarified* or even *Frenzy*.

In a similar vein to Example 3m, the next exercise uses three-note diminished arpeggios, ascending and descending in a diagonal manner across the fretboard.

Example 3n: G Diminished tap exercise with triplet 1/16th note pulse @ 100bpm

This is a cool way to get a lengthy diminished sequence into your playing without having to fall back on sweeps. If you can master this exercise, I would suggest you make it a new feature of your solos when improvising or composing using the Harmonic Minor or Phrygian Dominant scales.

Sliding Taps and Two Finger Tapping

This next section will focus on exercises and licks based on playing more complex sequences and patterns on the tapping hand. We will look at *sliding taps* as well as incorporating a second tap finger.

The first exercise uses the 1st and 3rd positions of the A Minor Pentatonic scale. The fretting hand will play position 1 and the tapping hand will do an ascending into descending slide to play the 3rd position simultaneously.

Example 3o: A Minor Pentatonic position 1 and 3 sliding tap exercise with septuplet 1/8th note pulse @ 100bpm

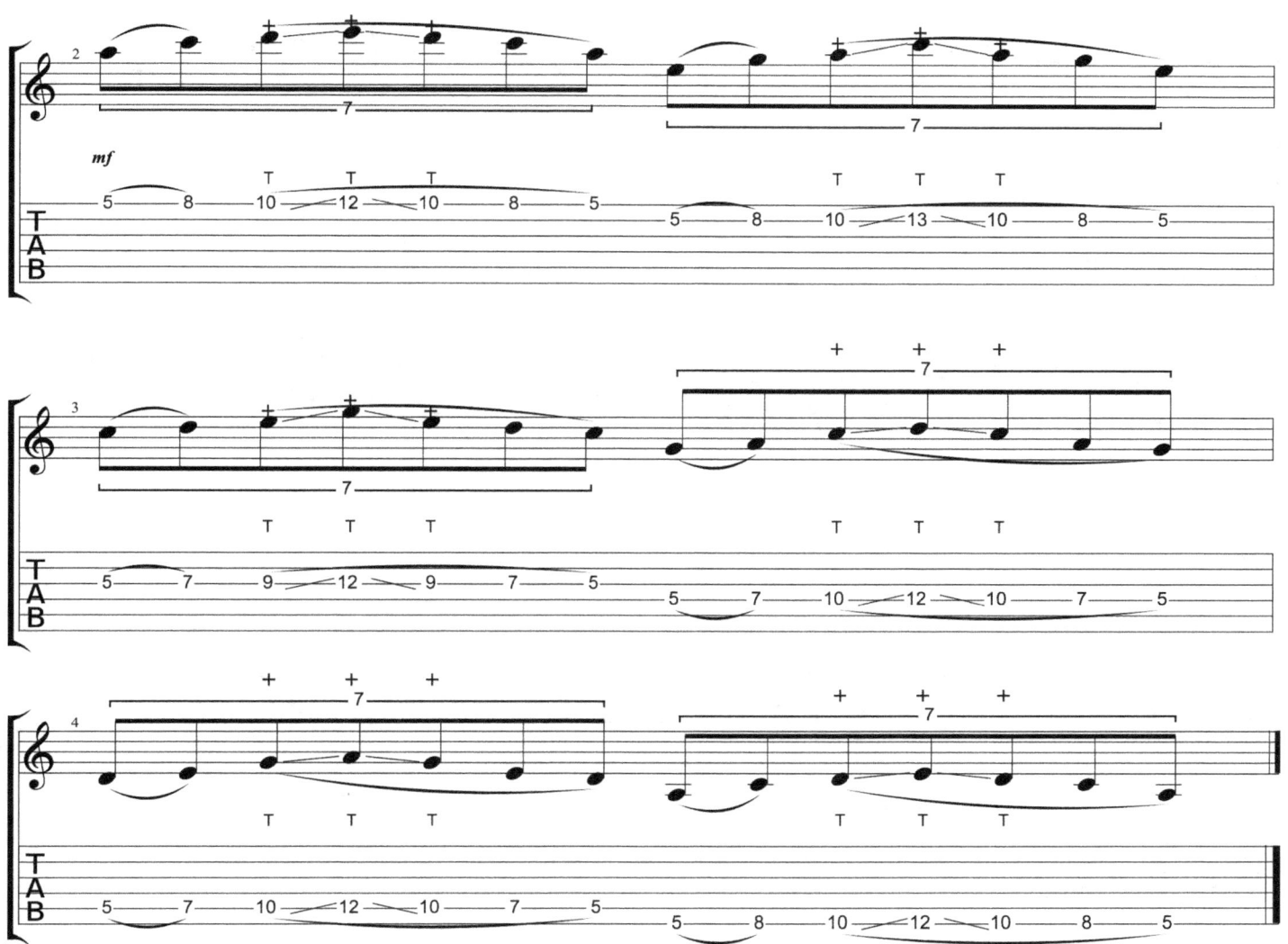

The next exercise uses a three-note-per-string C Ionian scale shape, but also incorporates two tapping fingers. This creates a five-finger legato effect on each string. As it ascends, descends, then ascends again, we'll end up with 12-notes-per-string. Pay close attention to how far the tapping notes are from one another and try alternating tap fingers depending on the intervals.

Example 3p: C Ionian two-finger tap exercise with triplet 1/8th note pulse @ 100bpm

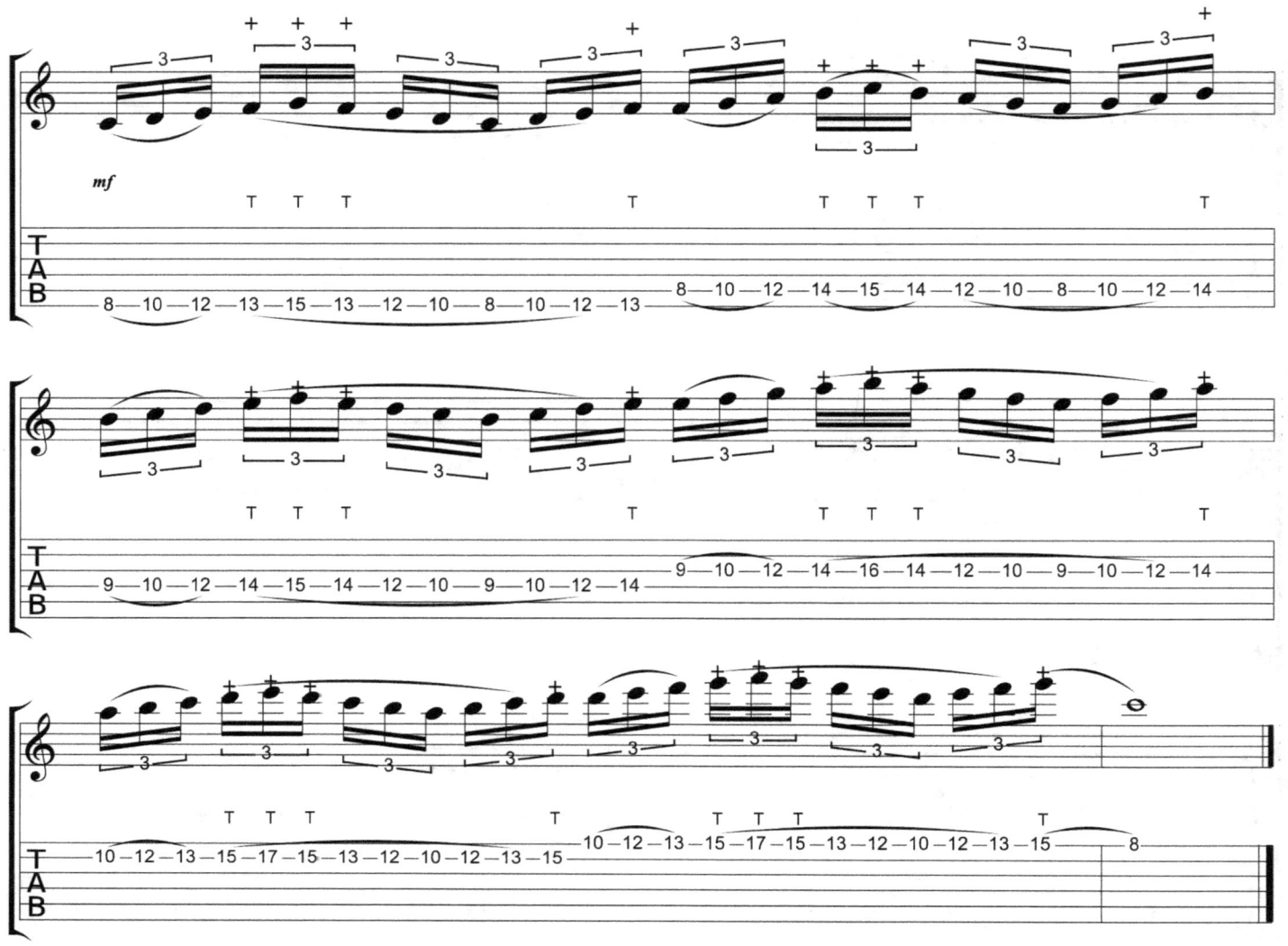

Sweep Arpeggio Taps for the Discerning Gentleman (and Gentlewoman)

Men, women and children of all races, nationalities and religious groups think sweep taps are awesome. This is a *scientific fact* – which, of course, I have no studies or papers to back up. But in saying this, I have set the scene (one riddled with hyperbole, flash and pizazz), and the tone for this section.

I'm going to devote an entire section of this book to a few exercises to help you get on the *Dragonforce* and Skwisgaar path your dreams are made of.

We're going to begin with an exercise that uses a few three-string triad arpeggios in the key of A Minor, but we'll include a 7th as a tapped note, to make the arpeggio more interesting and fancy.

Example 3q: Three-string A Minor arpeggios with 7th tap exercise with 1/16th note pulse @ 100bpm

If three-string arpeggios aren't fancy enough for you, we can use this tapping concept with five-string arpeggios. The next exercise will use arpeggios from the key of D Major. The arpeggios are swept through and there is an octave tap at the end of each one. This kind of shape is used by players such as Alexi Laiho of Children of Bodom and Muhammed Suiçmez of Necrophagist.

The chord progression is: D F#m Em G F#m Bm A D

Example 3r: Five-string D Major arpeggios with octave tap exercise with triplet 1/16th note pulse @ 100bpm

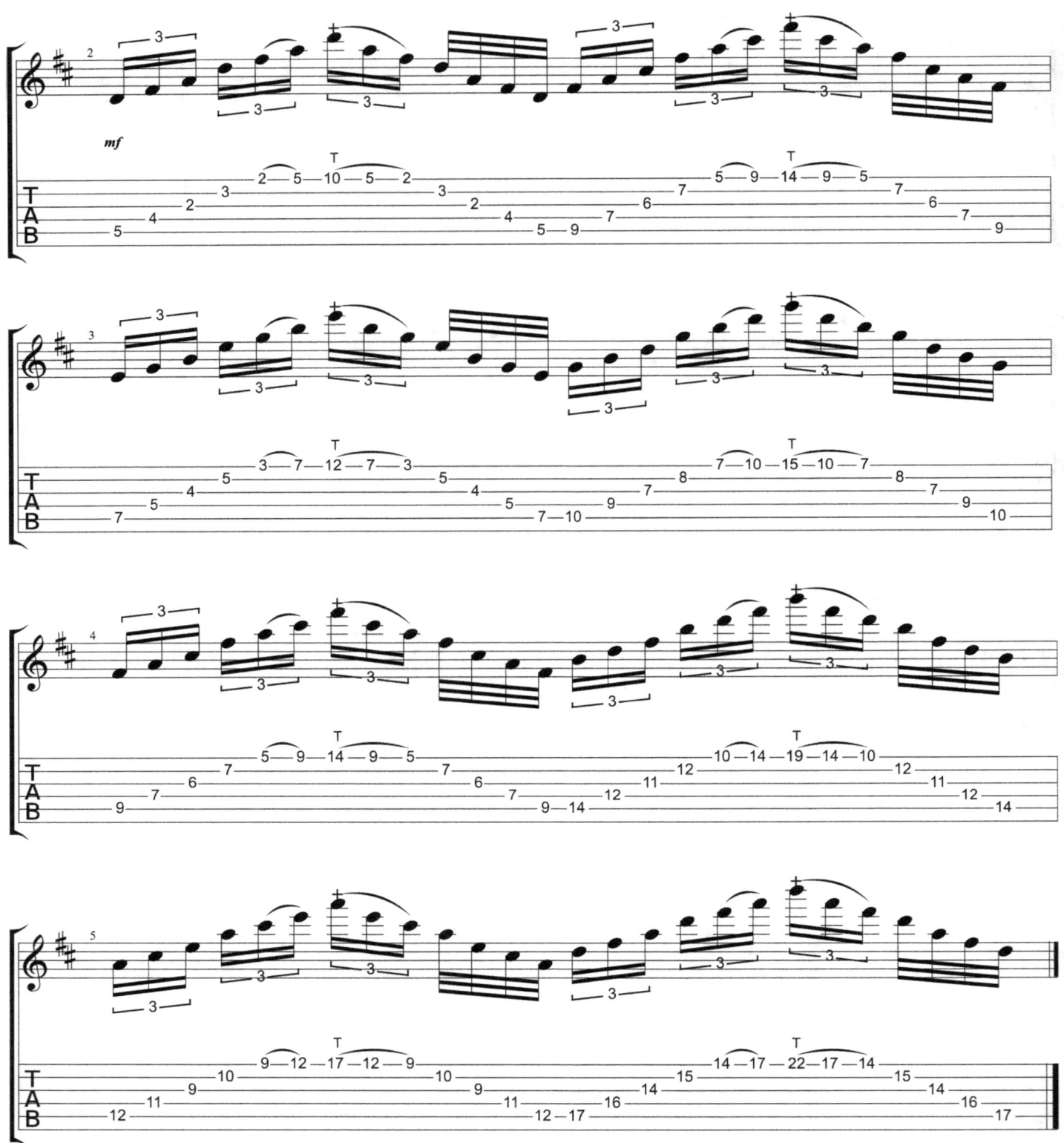

The next few arpeggios exercises use a cool concept where we essentially play two shapes of one arpeggio at the same time. We create this impossible and crazy idea by using the fretting hand and the tapping hand to play different shapes and positions simultaneously.

Let's start by looking at two simple five-string A Minor arpeggio triads. Play both of them separately as normal arpeggios, then practise playing the second arpeggio one note at a time entirely with taps.

Example 3s: Two five-string A Minor arpeggio shapes

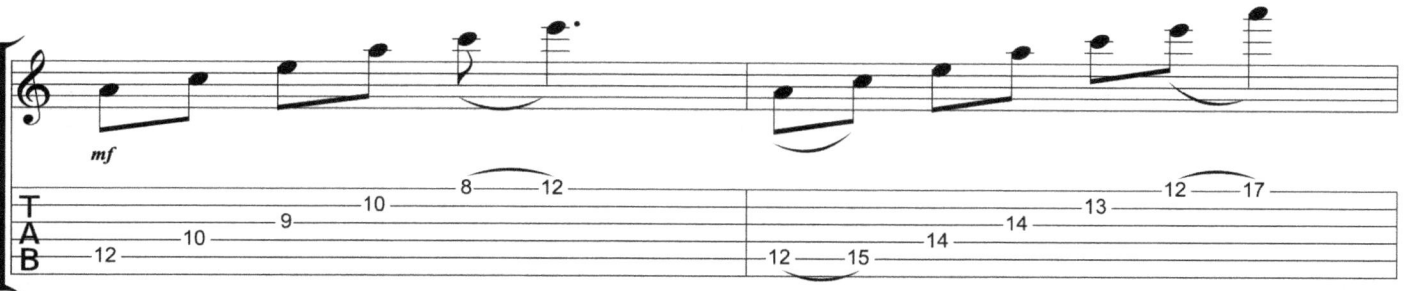

Now we can join both arpeggios together. We can begin with a simple ascent on the first arpeggio shape, but when we descend, we'll have a back-tracking triplet sound when we add in the tapped arpeggio using the second shape. You may also want to use a technique called "hammer-ons from nowhere" on your fretting hand on the descent, when jumping from one string to another. (If you haven't heard that term before, look it up, Greg Howe regularly uses and talks about it).

Example 3t: Two five-string A Minor arpeggios with tap exercise with triplet 1/16th note pulse @ 100bpm

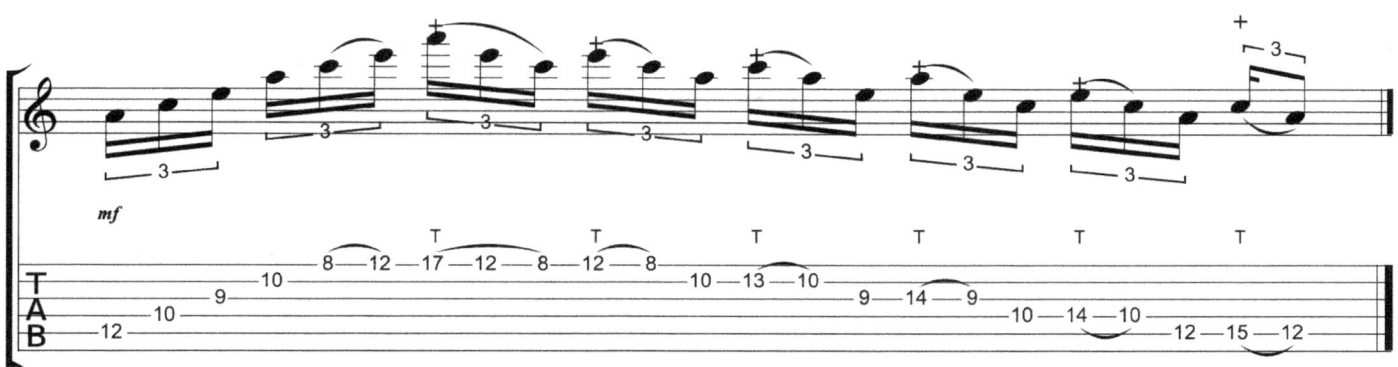

Let's try a similar concept, but using G Major arpeggio triads. Similar to Example 3s, we'll use two simple five-string arpeggios and play both of them separately to learn the shapes. Run through them as normal arpeggios first, then practise playing the second arpeggio one note at a time, entirely with taps.

Example 3u: Two five-string G Major arpeggio shapes

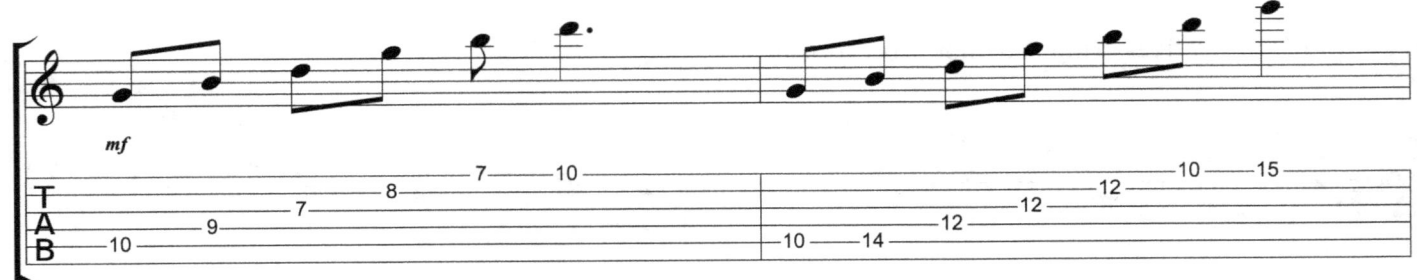

As in the previous exercise, we will ascend through the first shape in a normal swept fashion, then add triplet taps and "hammers-ons from nowhere" on the descent.

Example 3v: Two five-string G Major arpeggios with tap exercise with triplet 1/16th note pulse @ 100bpm

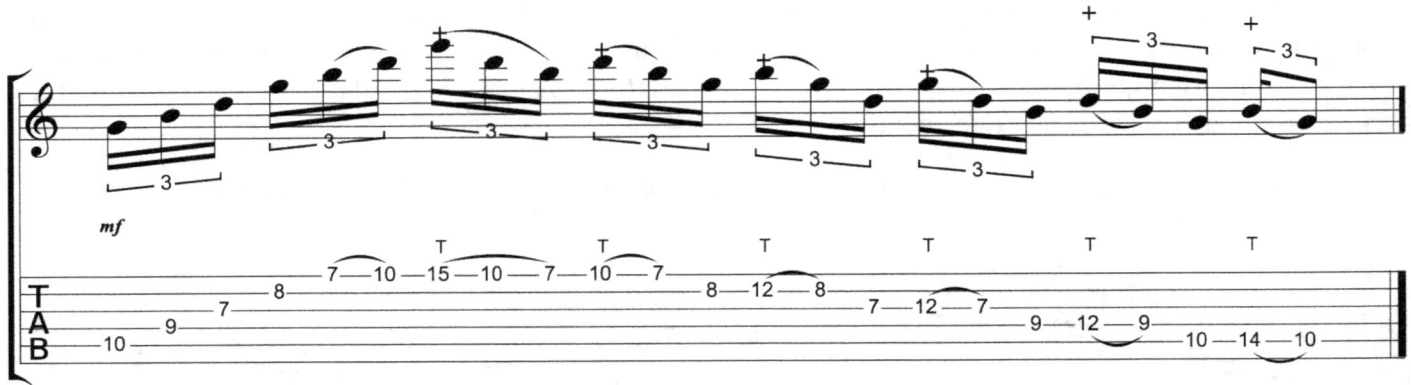

To finish in the most *redonkulous* manner possible, I've decided to take the concepts from Examples 3t and 3v and use them over a six-string F Diminished 7th arpeggio.

Example 3w: F Diminished 7th six-string arpeggio with mirrored tap exercise with triplet 1/16th note pulse @ 100bpm

One thing that is interesting about the descending phase of this arpeggio is that the tapping hand directly mirrors the fretting hand. If you like the sound of diminished arpeggios, this can be a cheeky way to get some interesting sounding diminished licks into your playing without falling into the trap of dragging the same shape up and down the fretboard three frets at a time (I'm looking at you *Trivium* and *Falling in Reverse*!).

String-skipped Taps and Other Advanced Malarkey

The final section of this chapter is going to concentrate on string-skipped tapping licks using scales, pentatonics and arpeggios. As we've seen in previous chapters, string-skipping is a cool way to get some larger intervals between notes and is an excellent way to break up the monotony of a predictable ascending or descending scale or arpeggio.

Let's start by looking at a simple A Minor Pentatonic idea in position 1. We'll be adding string-skipped taps that create a 5th interval between the first two notes on every string to spice things up.

Example 3x: A Minor Pentatonic string skip with fifth interval tap exercise with triplet 1/8th note pulse @ 135bpm

Now we will use the 1st and 3rd strings to create diminished arpeggios, incorporating position shifts in minor 3rd intervals, jumping up the neck. I've heard James Malone of *Arsis* use this tapping concept in a few solos. You can also get a Jeff Loomis-ey sound out of this exercise as well, if you don't want to do hilarious stretches or hand contortions.

Example 3y: Diminished string-skip arpeggio tap exercise with triplet 1/8th note pulse @ 100bpm

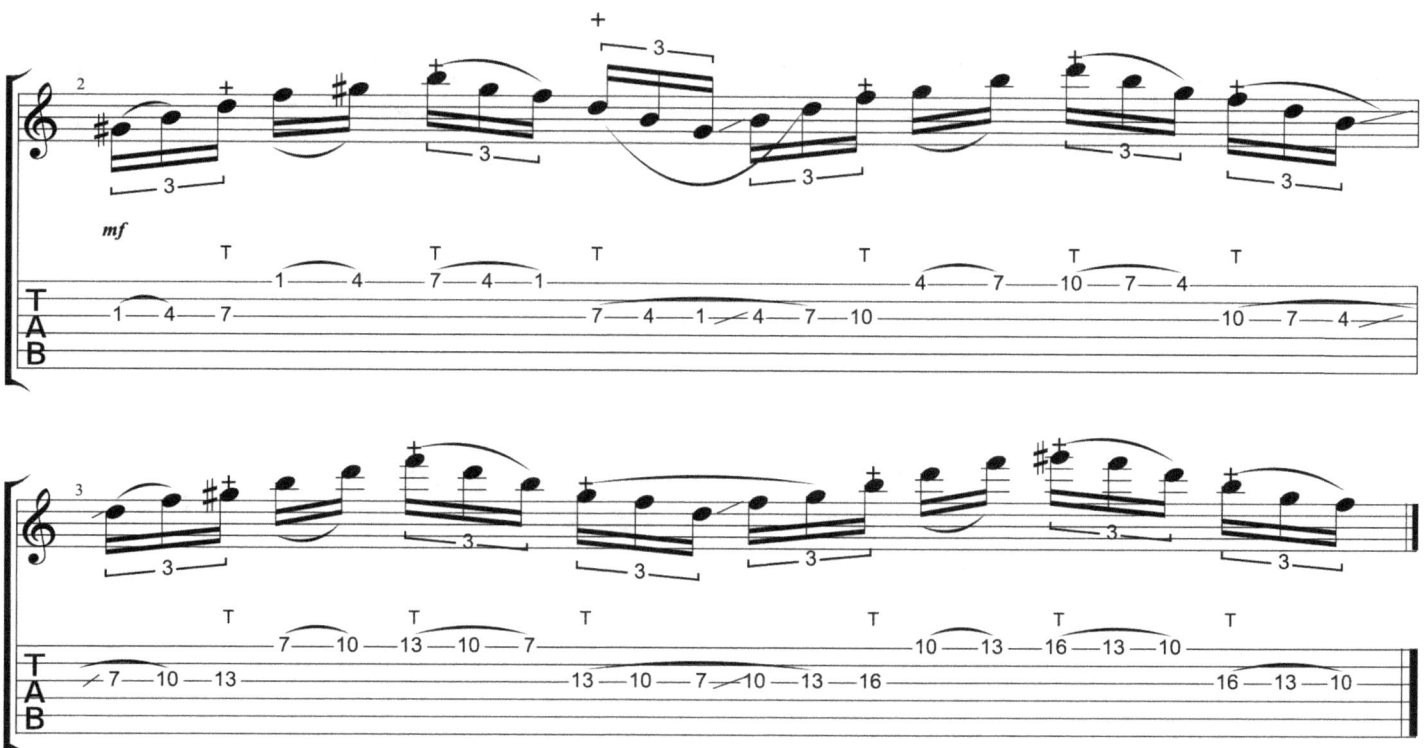

Next we have an ascending diatonic sequence in C Major that uses tapped, string-skipping, 7th arpeggios. The whole exercise takes place on the 1st, 3rd and 5th strings and will use Major 7th, Minor 7th, Dominant 7th and m7b5 arpeggios.

Example 3z: C Major diatonic string-skip arpeggio tap exercise with triplet 1/8th note pulse @ 100bpm

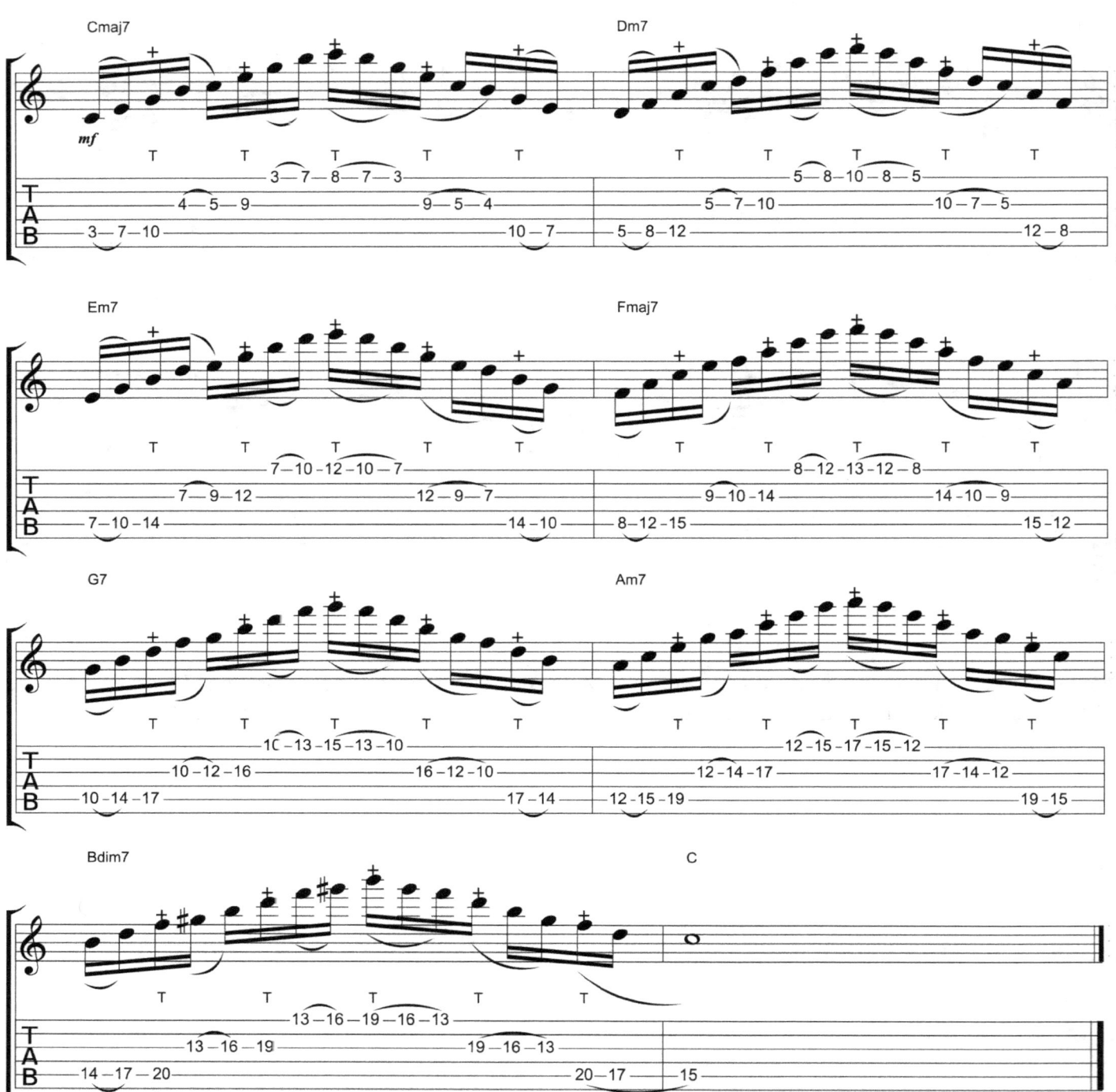

The next exercise uses a basic G Major three-note-per-string diatonic shape, but includes string skips and taps. This kind of exercise could be used in licks and solos as a way of adding a bit of extra speed and variation to an otherwise meat and veg legato string-skip lick.

Example 3z1: G Major diatonic string-skip legato tap exercise with triplet 1/8th note pulse @ 100bpm

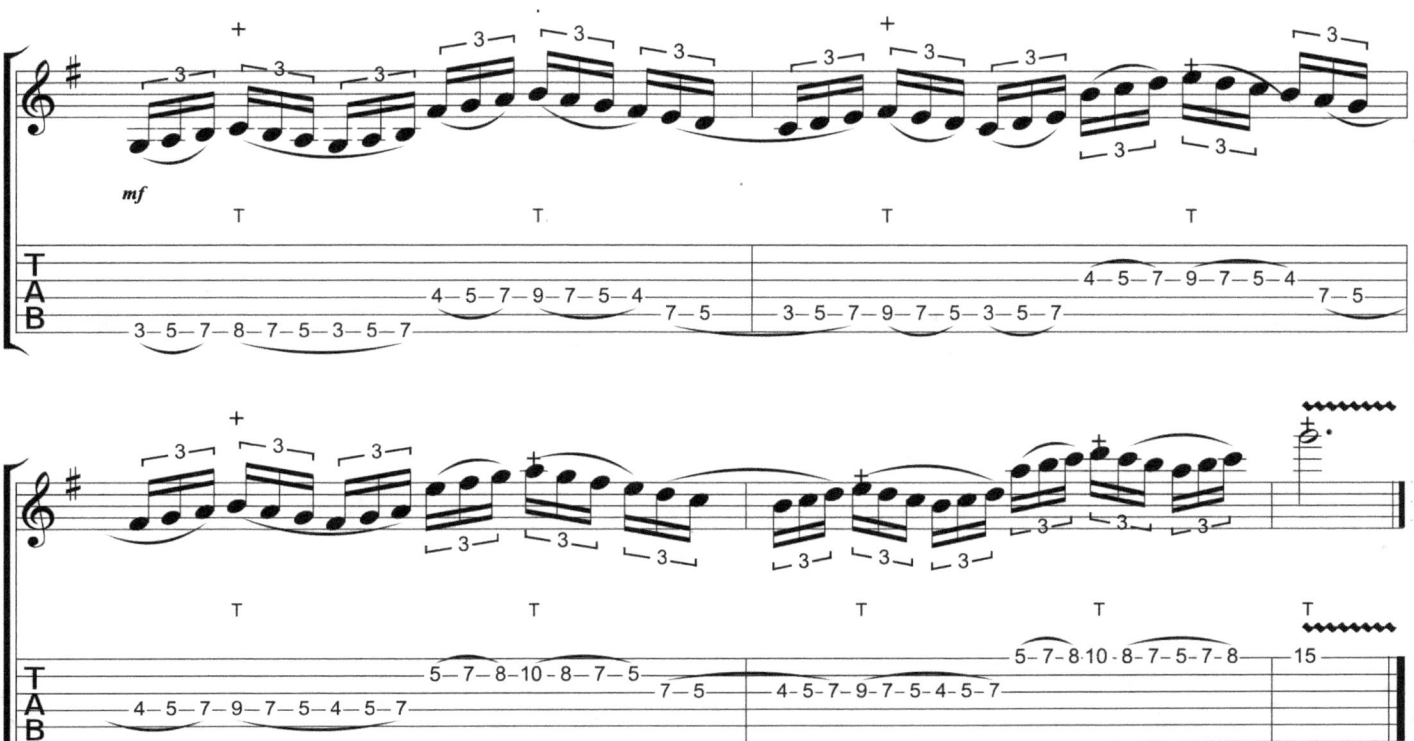

The final exercise in this chapter uses a three-note-per-string pentatonic scale shape in the key of E Minor, and also has a cheeky tap on each string. It is mostly played with legato technique and is a little stretchy on the ol' mittens. This is a great way to play the pentatonic scale if you want to get some cool intervals into your playing, but also want to avoid sounding too stereotypically bluesy.

Example 3z2: E Minor Pentatonic string-skip arpeggio tap exercise with triplet 1/8th note pulse @ 100bpm

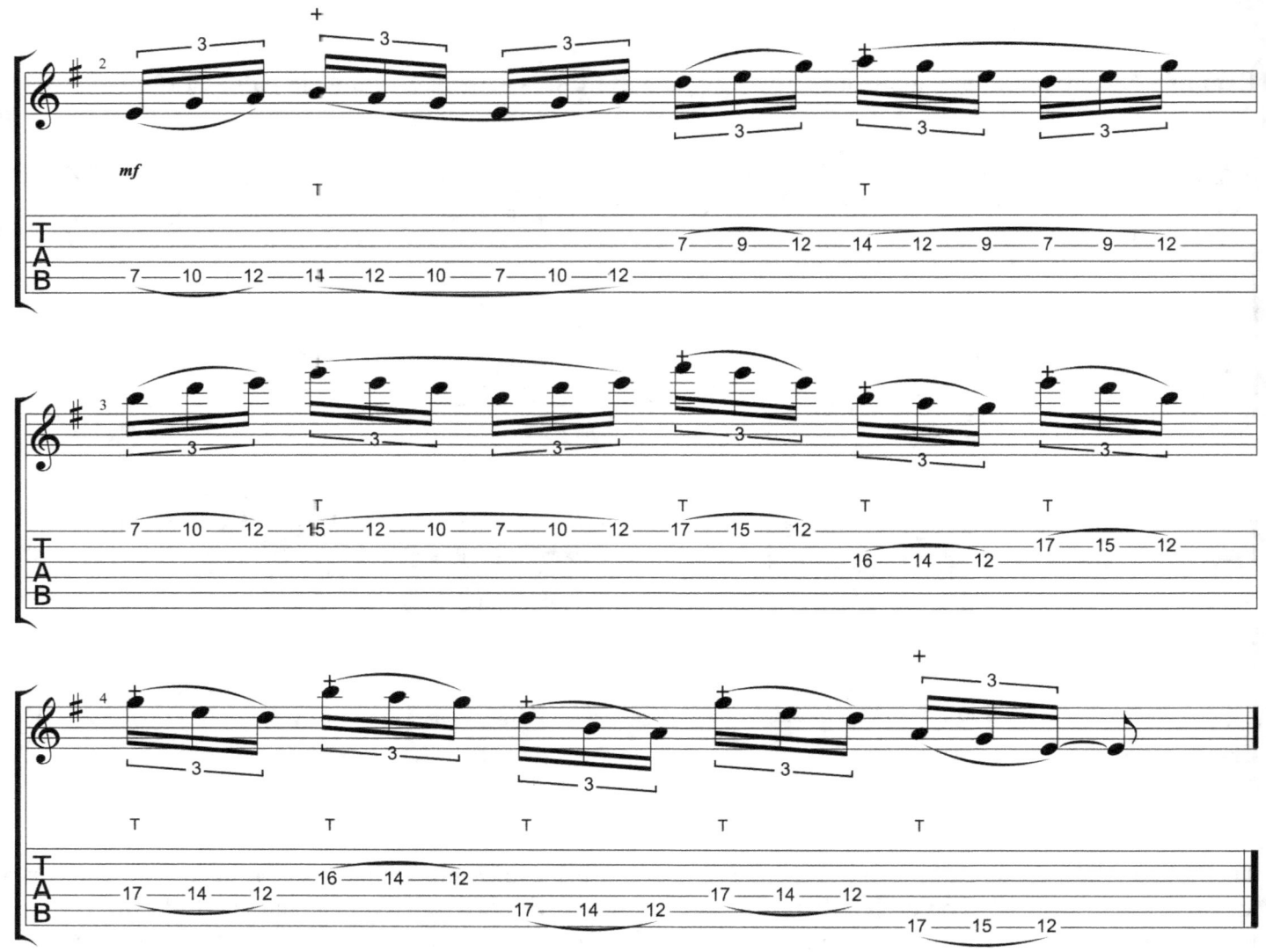

To Tap or Not to Tap? A Summation to the Ultimate Question

Tapping can be used as a cool effect that can *pop* when used correctly. It's also an excellent way to make up for having disappointing Pinky length or a lame hand size. You can use it to impress other non-guitarist folk, or even noobs, with your pseudo awesomeness. Saying that, nobody likes that person who taps too much (except Eddie Van Halen, Yvette Young, Sarah Longfield and Josh Martin of *Little Tybee*), so please, use this newfound superpower responsibly.

Speaking for myself, I love a cheeky, well-placed tap. But I like to use tapping like paprika on cottage fries… sparingly and tastefully. If I sound like a broken record I apologise, but the key to incorporating this into your playing is experimentation and finding the sounds you like. Ask yourself, "How can I use tapping to bring out a new side to MY shred and lead guitar playing?"

Remember, there is no one magical technique that makes you a better or more enigmatic guitar player. The magic has been in you all along (I'm pretty sure I heard something similar in one of the *Air Bud* movies).

Chapter Four: Sweeping Arpeggio Tips and Exercises (Unleash Your Inner Janitor!)

Sweeping is often viewed as the paramount technique needed to be a flashy and respected guitarist. I've even heard people use the phrase, "Sweeping gets the girls!" Well, I am here to tell you that it doesn't. Whoever told you such nonsense cries themselves to sleep at night with a bag of Doritos watching reruns of *Arrow* and spends their spare time blogging about their *My Little Pony* collection in "safe space" chat rooms for *bronies* (men who collect My Little Ponies… Seriously, Google it).

More important than crushing your deluded dreams of *sweeping seduction*, however, is the topic of this chapter: the fundamentals of a good sweep arpeggio technique.

QUICK DISCLAIMER: Before we dive in, I should mention that it's incredibly important (especially in the early stages of sweeping) that you learn your arpeggios inside-out with basic, regular picking. Why? Because your arpeggio shapes need to be extremely fluent in your fretting hand before you add a new technique with your picking hand.

Without further ado, here are some tips that might not get you the babes, but will help you conquer even the most offensive of swept arpeggios!

The Gliding Motion

Over the past few years, I've found the most common problem people have with the sweeping technique is their picking hand. Guitarists wrestling with this concept tend to rush the "gliding" motion, almost treating it like a chord strum. Alternatively, they try to do a lot of consecutive down picks in a row, which is not only impractical, but sounds awful. I recommend starting with all dead notes on the fretting hand (you can even tie a sock around your guitar neck) and practise pushing through one string to rest on the next without lifting in between. This may sound clunky to begin with, but will eventually become a fluent sweeping motion.

On the ascending part of the sweep, I want you to picture a "sawing" motion, or imagine gently punching yourself in the knee. When you descend, picture starting up a lawnmower with a pull-cord, and pull up through the strings. The main thing I reinforce whenever I teach this technique is to make sure your sweep motion is *coming from your elbow* and NOT your wrist!

Let's begin by practicing ONLY the downward gliding motion. The first exercise in an ascending two-string diatonic arpeggio sequence in the key of E Major. Pay close attention to the picking direction and hammer-on emphasis.

Example 4a: E Major diatonic two-string arpeggio with triplet 1/8th note pulse @ 100bpm

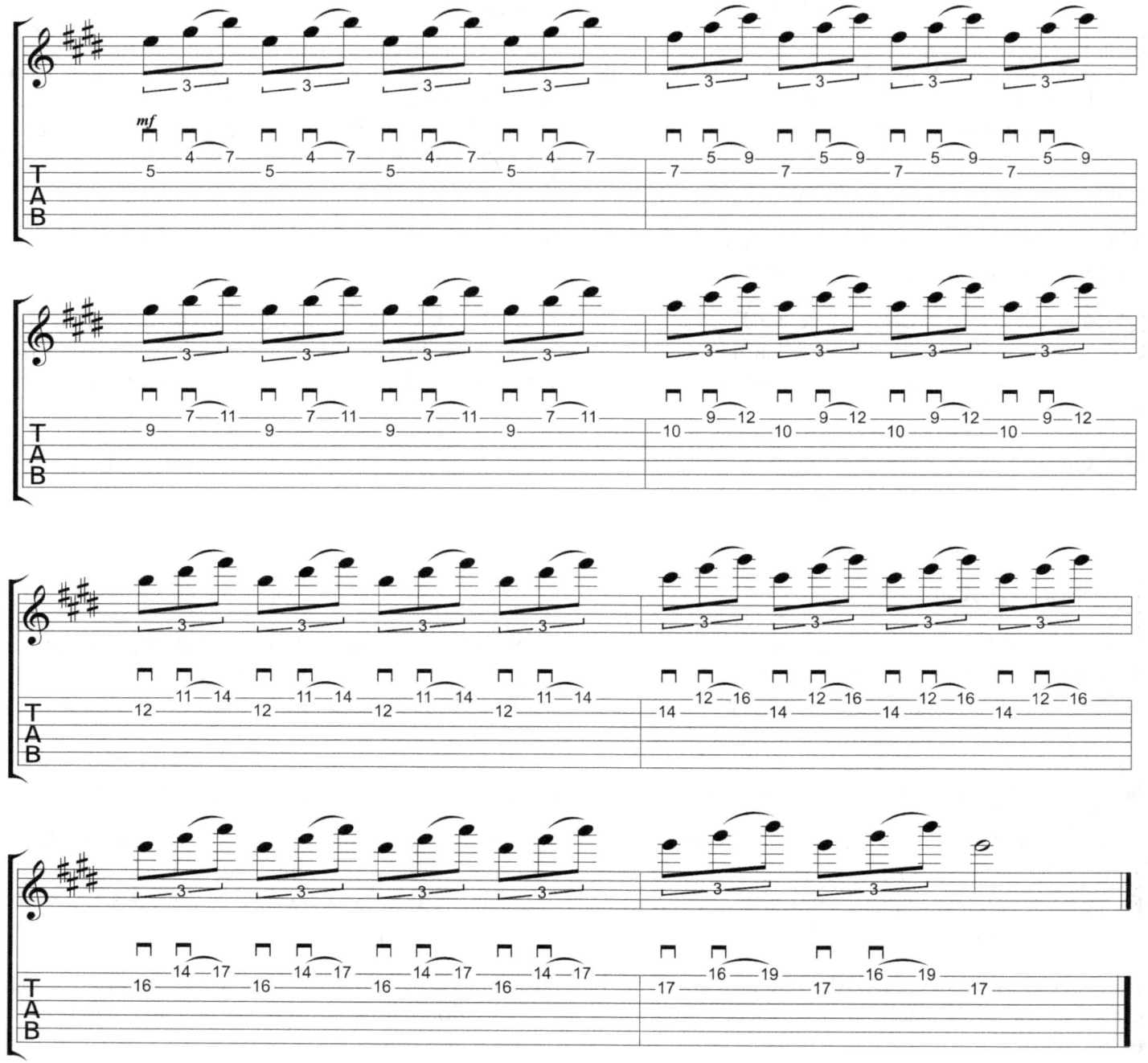

The first stage of this sweep is the ascent and we'll need to get from the 2nd string to the 1st string. Start by pushing your pick through the 2nd string till you're resting on the 1st. If we had a five-string arpeggio, you'd start from the 5th string then keep pushing through, string by string until you were at the 1st string. In the early stages, keep your gliding motion relatively slow, so that each string gets individual and equal attention. Once the 1st string's hammer-ons and pull-offs have finished, we can start gliding in the opposite direction for the descending part of the sweep, but we'll save that for later.

Although it may seem simple, getting the sweeping motion fluent and consistent takes time. These exercises are a great place to start honing that skill.

In a similar vein, we'll now take the E Major two-string diatonic arpeggio sequence and use three-string arpeggios. These are far more commonly used for sweeping than two-string sweeps. Once again, pay close attention to picking direction and hammer-on emphasis.

Example 4b: Three-string E Major diatonic arpeggio with 1/16th note pulse @ 90bpm

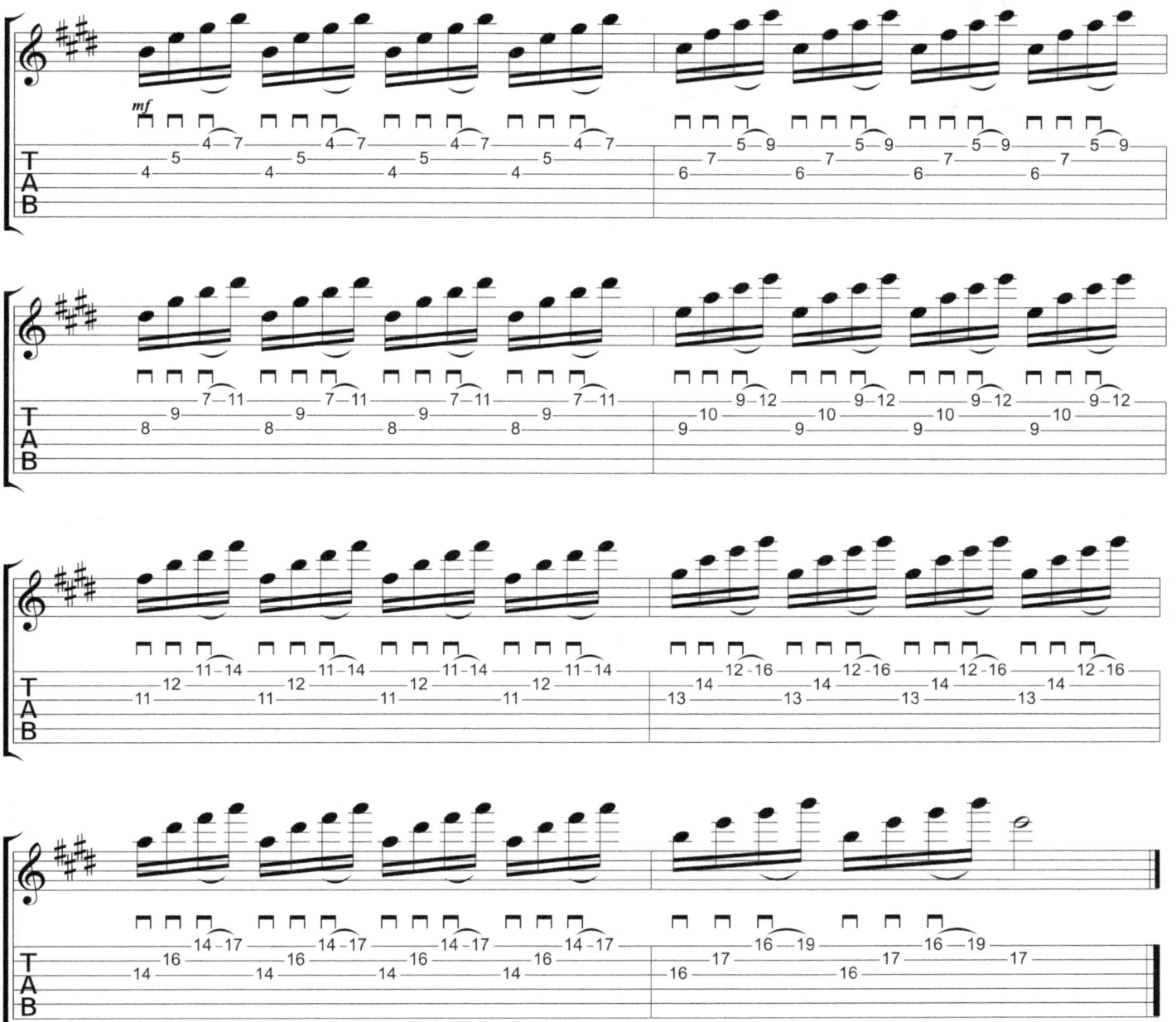

You need to keep in mind the same gliding principles I mentioned in Example 4a, adjusting them to the three-string arpeggio.

Now that we have spent some time talking about the ascending part of a sweep arpeggio, I'd like to focus on the descent. The next exercise uses descending arpeggios in the key of D Harmonic Minor. You'll notice that each arpeggio starts with a down pick and a pull-off, then the next two notes of the arpeggio are played with up-picks. After the down pick, you'll need to slightly adjust the angle of your pick to suit an upwards gliding sweep motion (illustrated below).

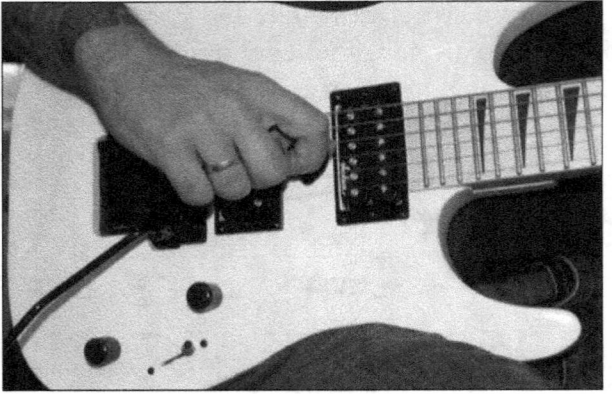

Downward pick slant and Upward pick slant

Pay close attention to the picking directions and try to keep your gliding motion slow and accurate. Resist the urge to Jason Richardson it!

Example 4c: D Harmonic Minor three-string arpeggio sequence with 1/16th note pulse @ 90bpm

The British Cup of Tea Flick

Joining the ascending and descending sweep techniques together can be tricky. The most important part of an ascending into descending sweep is the preparation required for the change in direction, while the hammer-on-pull-offs occur on the highest string of the sweep – which is often on the 1st string.

I've coined the term "The British Cup of Tea" to explain this movement. When a hammer-on into a pull-off happens, you flick your wrist to change the picking direction while waiting for the appropriate time to execute the descending sweep, and for your fretting and picking hands to sync up. Handily, it's the same movement you do if you're having tea with the Queen and she lifts her cup and you lift yours and say, "Charmed" and take a regal gulp. This motion has also been referred to on the odd occasion as "The Gentlemanly Conductor".

Let's try applying both directions of this ascending and descending gliding motion to a simple five-string C Major arpeggio. Pay close attention to the picking direction and the hammer-on, pull-off emphasis.

Example 4d: Five-string C Major arpeggio with triplet 1/8th note pulse @ 90bpm

One of the key benefits of working the sweep technique into longer arpeggios is that we can look more closely at the mechanics involved in both sweeping directions. More often than not, the common problems occur on the back sweep.

With the five-string C Major arpeggio, the ascent is pretty easy. After we've reached the hammer-on and pull-off stage on the first string, you need to make sure your pick is slightly tilted (British Cup of Tea), so that you can do the "pulling the lawnmower starter cord" motion. This will start from the 2nd string, moving to the 5th, with the same speed and gliding principles applied as the ascending motion.

To make things more interesting, we're going to join a few five-string arpeggios together to create a diatonic chord sequence in the key of D Major. We'll be ascending through one arpeggio then using a slide to transition into the descent of another.

Example 4e: Five-string D Major slide arpeggios, diatonic chord sequence, triplet 1/8th note pulse @ 100bpm

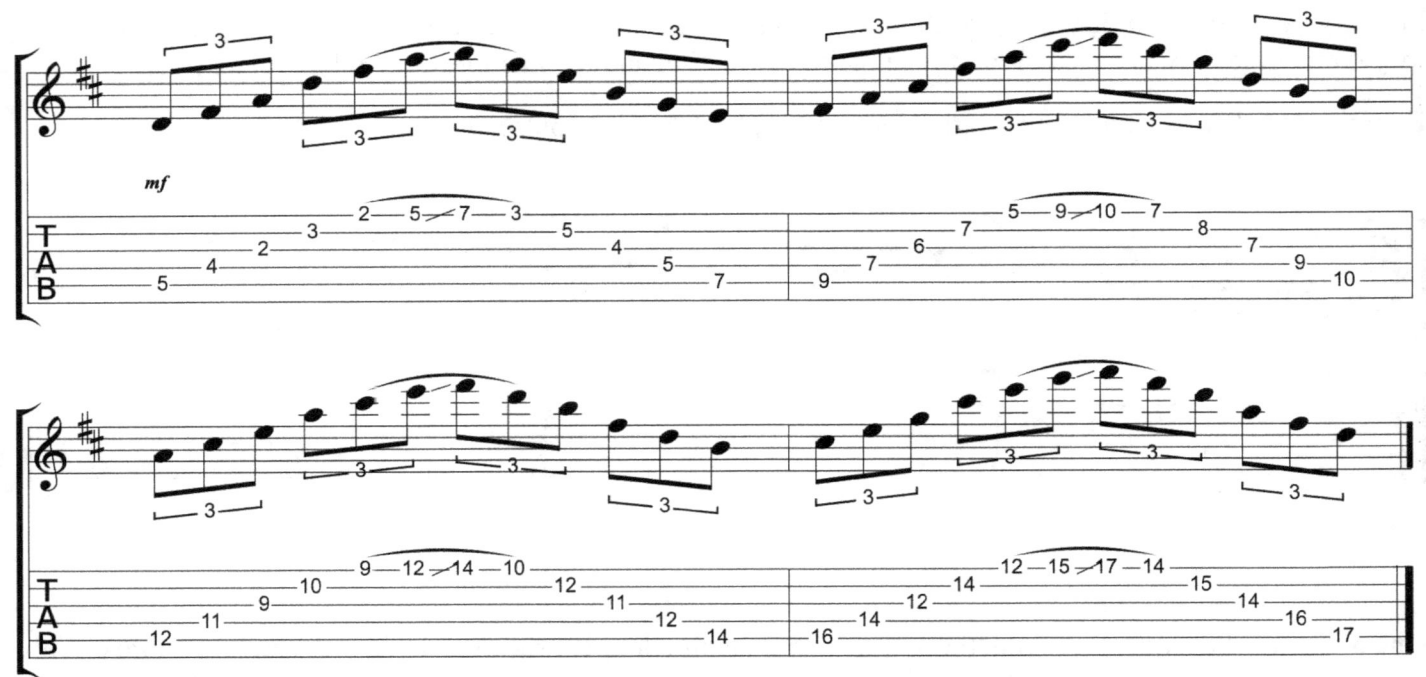

Stringing arpeggios together in this manner is a simple and effective way to use the sweep technique and highlight chord changes in a very poignant manner. I've seen Alexi Laiho from Children of Bodom join arpeggios together like this in quite a few songs (*Bed of Razors* is a personal favourite of mine), as well as other proficient sweep arpeggio professors like Jason Becker and Brendon Small from Dethklok.

To finish on a more ridiculous note, I want us to look at a sus2 arpeggio shape drifting up and down the fretboard.

The chord progression is: Gsus2 A#sus2 G#sus2 Bsus2 Asus2 Csus2 A#sus2 D#sus2

Example 4f: Four-string Sus2 slide arpeggios chord sequence with triplet 1/16th note pulse @ 90bpm

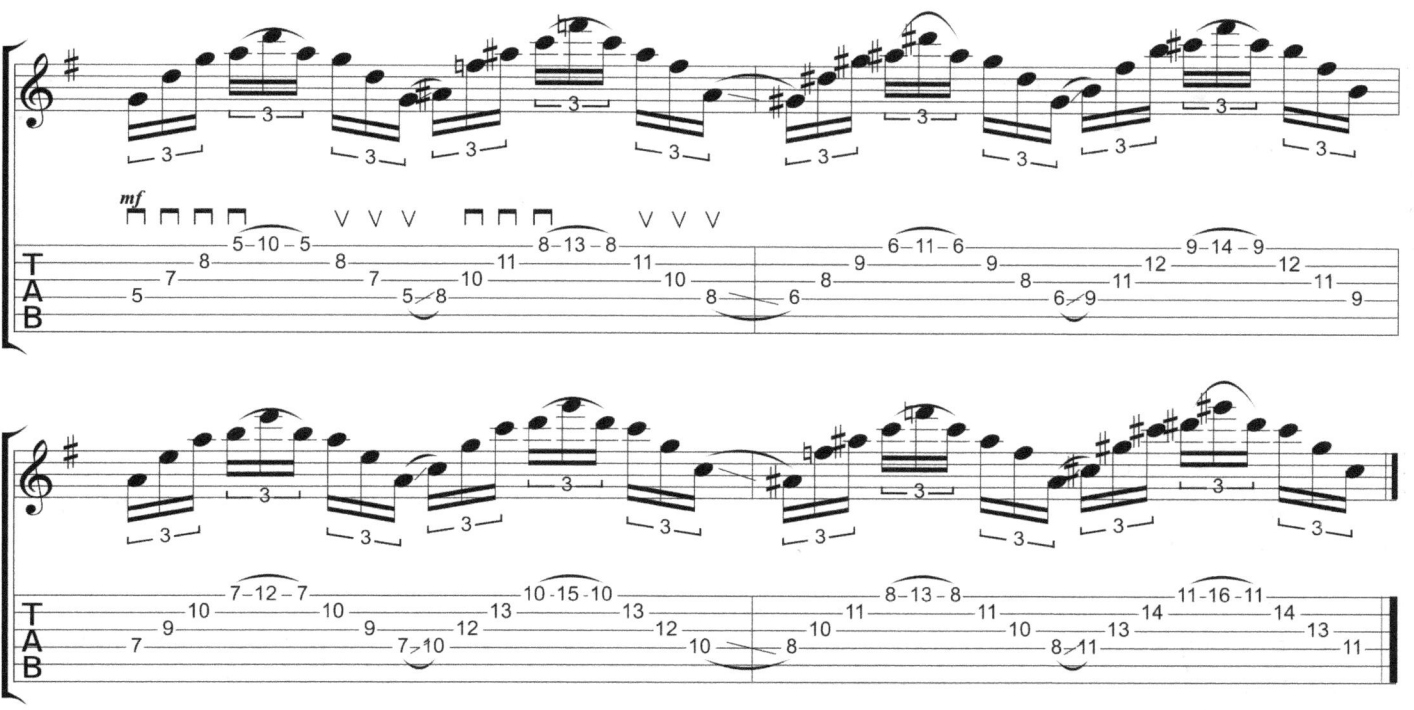

Keep in mind that the sweep arpeggio technique is not just limited to triad arpeggios. In the previous example we dealt with sus2 arpeggios. Later on in this chapter we will look at some more complicated 7th arpeggios like Major 7th, Minor 7th, Dominant 7th, Diminished 7th and who could forget m7b5 – the loveable rascal?!

Hammer-ons, Pull-offs and Hand Synchronicity in Sweeps

I can't stress enough the importance of hand synchronicity; syncing up the hammer-ons and pull-offs of your fretting hand with a controlled, gliding motion with your picking hand. If your confidence is building and you've done your homework, you should be quite proficient with the gliding motion and "British Cup of Tea" sweep techniques. Now, however, it's time to talk about some of the more terrifying arpeggios.

These arpeggios will have more than one string with hammer-ons and pull-offs and will pose a few more challenges than the previous arpeggio shapes in this chapter. As a general rule, the more complex an arpeggio is, the more difficult it is to achieve fluent fretting and picking hand synchronicity.

Let's start with a five-string A Minor arpeggio that has two-strings each with two notes. Pay close attention to hammer-on emphasis and picking direction.

Example 4g: Five-string A Minor arpeggio Pointer-Pinky hammer x2 with 1/8th note pulse @ 100bpm

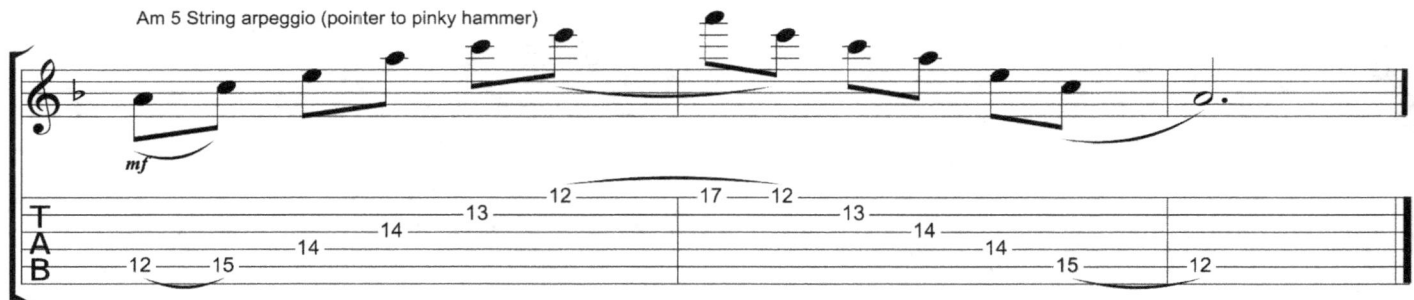

This particular A Minor arpeggio ascends and descends. A hammer-on occurs on the ascent at the beginning of the arpeggio, then there is a hammer-on into a pull-off on the highest string, after which it descends into a pull-off at the end of the arpeggio to arrive back where we started.

The next exercise drifts between D Natural and Harmonic Minor keys and uses similar shapes and hammer-on-pull-off principles as the A Minor arpeggio in Example 4g. It will also use major, minor and diminished arpeggio shapes that will join together to create a melodic progression. Pay close attention to the hammer-ons, pull-offs and the slides used to transition from one arpeggio to another.

Example 4h: Five-string D Harmonic Minor Pointer-Pinky arpeggio progression with 1/16th note pulse @ 100bpm

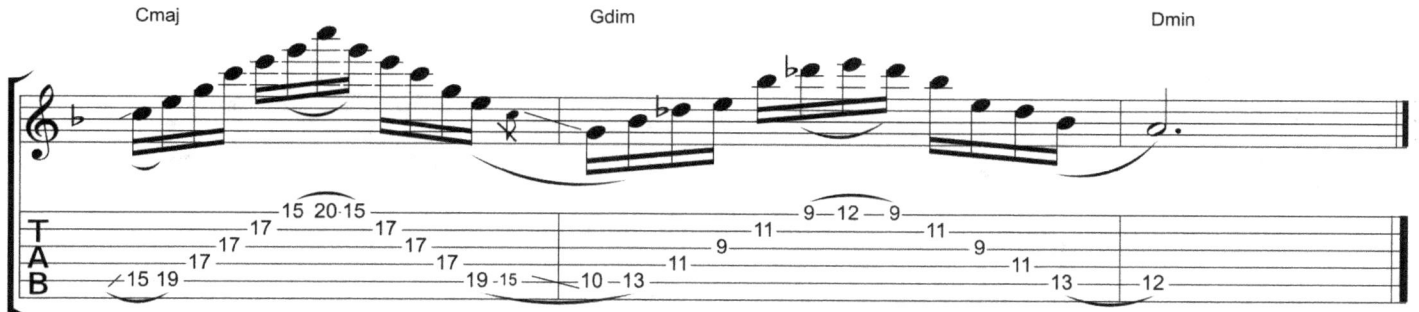

To make matters worse, we're now going to look at 7th arpeggios. These bad boys have three strings with two notes on each, which means even further terror when it comes to hand synchronicity. Let's start with a five-string Cmaj7 arpeggio. Pay close attention to picking direction and the placement of hammer-ons and pull-offs.

Example 4i: Five-string C Major 7th arpeggio with 1/8th note pulse @ 120bpm

You'll notice we have to add an extra pause on the 3rd string in the arpeggio, to allow the picking and fretting hands to sync up again. You can do this with a simple lift or an extra "British Cup of Tea" flick.

When the C Major 7th arpeggio above starts to feel natural, try joining several 7th arpeggios together. The next exercise involves every chord in the C Major diatonic chord progression, but every chord has a 7th. It includes Major 7th, Minor 7th, Dominant 7th and m7b5 arpeggios.

Example 4j: Five-string C Major diatonic 7th arpeggio progression with 1/16th note pulse @ 105bpm

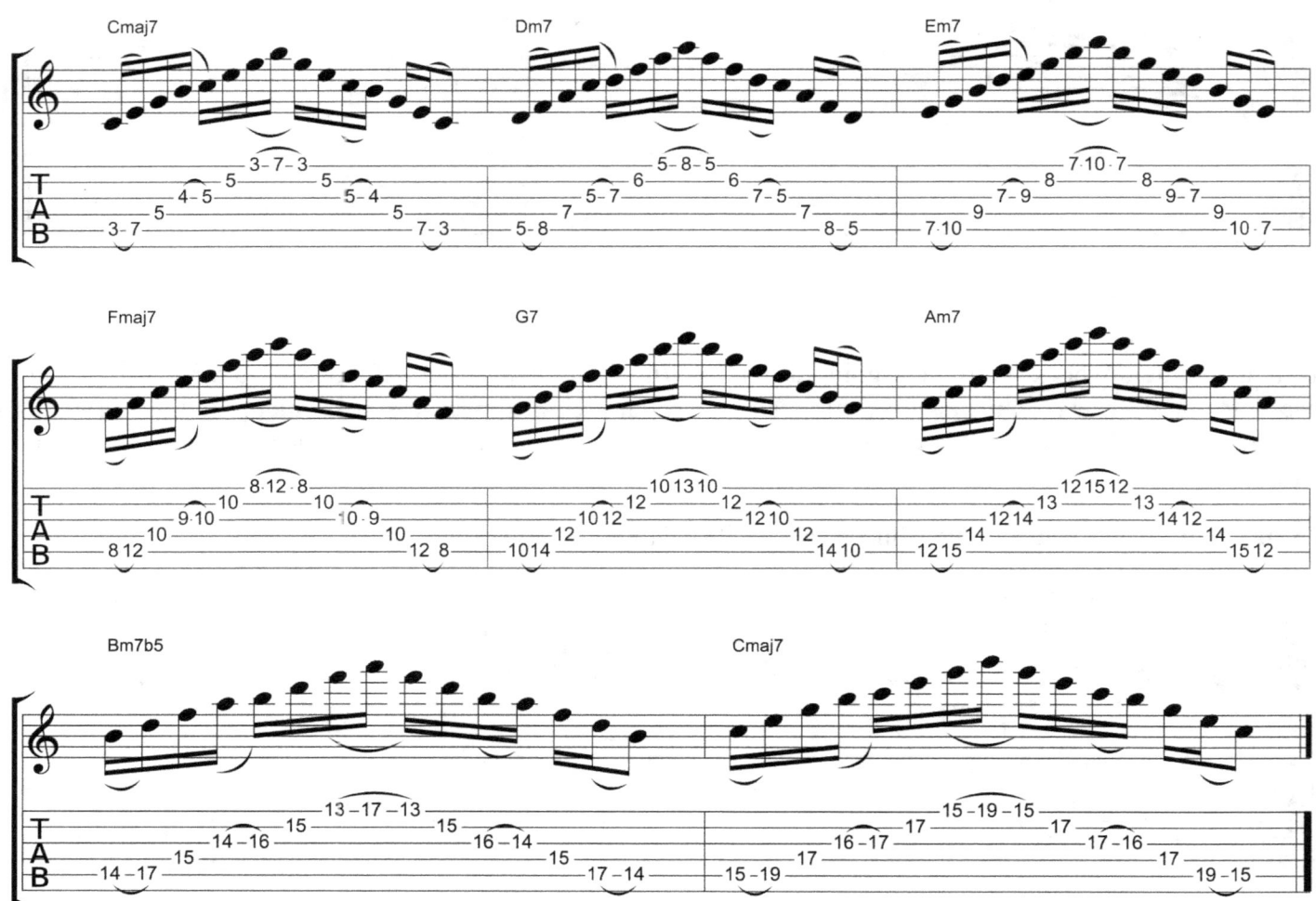

Multiple hammer-ons and pull-offs mid-arpeggio is quite advanced and stringing together a crapload of them is no walk in the park! But repetition of this exercise will eventually increase your fretting and picking hand synchronicity. It all comes down to preparing for when your hammer-ons and pull-offs occur and slowing down or speeding up your glide when you need to.

The next exercise is made up of six-string 7th arpeggios using diatonic chords in the key of G Major. Pay close attention to the multiple hammers and slides and be sure to add sweep glides when you need to.

Example 4k: Six-string G Major diatonic 7th arpeggio progression with 1/16th note pulse @ 95bpm

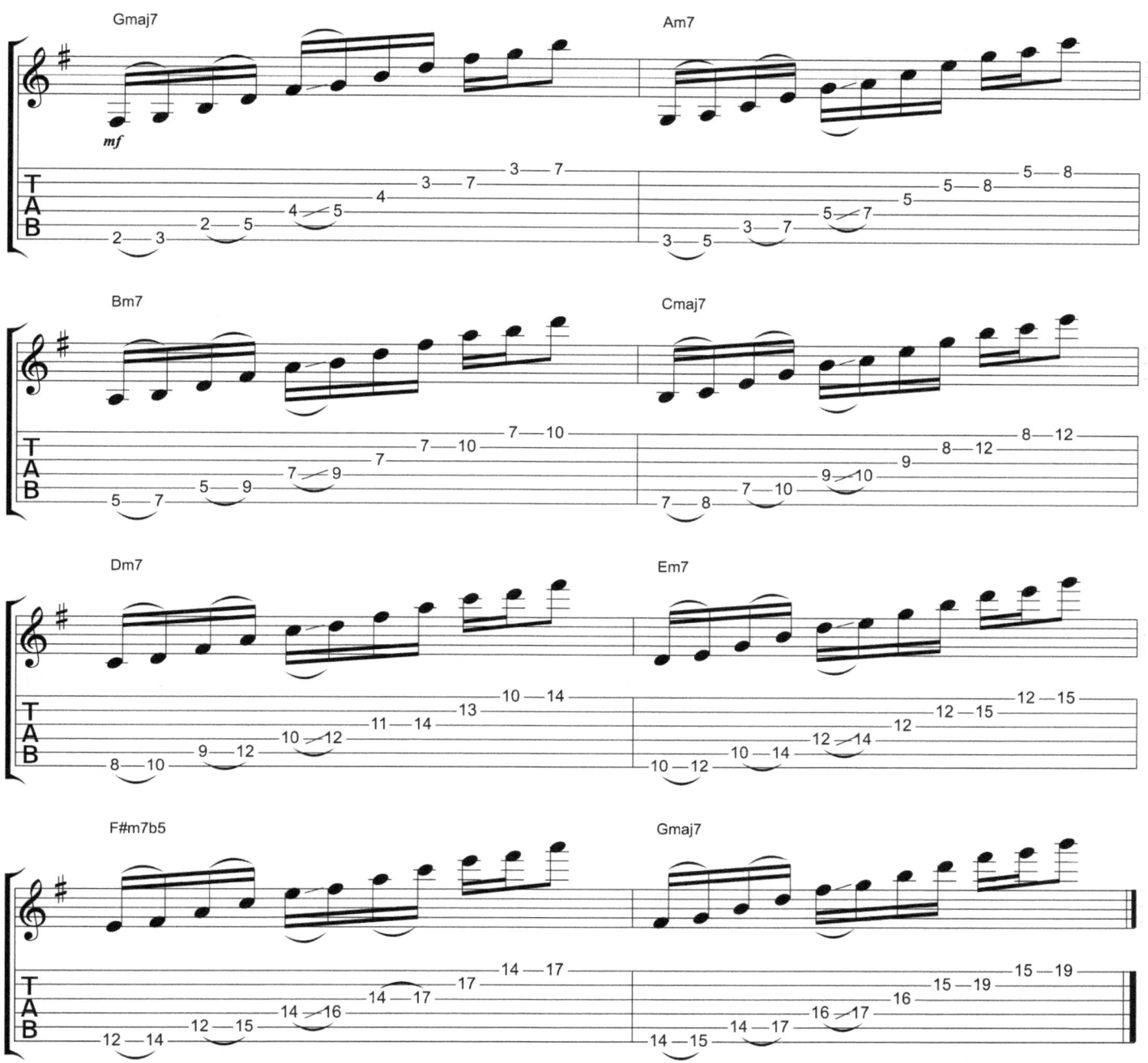

This next idea takes one arpeggio and builds it gradually in mini three-string sweeps. It uses a multiple position G# Diminished arpeggio with an ascending and descending build.

Example 4l: Four-string G# diminished multiple position arpeggio build with 1/16th note pulse @ 110bpm

Now we're going to take the principles from this example and apply them over a chord progression in C Major using building 7th arpeggios. The chord progression is: Cmaj7 Em7 G7 Am7

Example 4m: Four-string C Major multiple position arpeggio building progression with 1/16th note pulse @ 110bpm

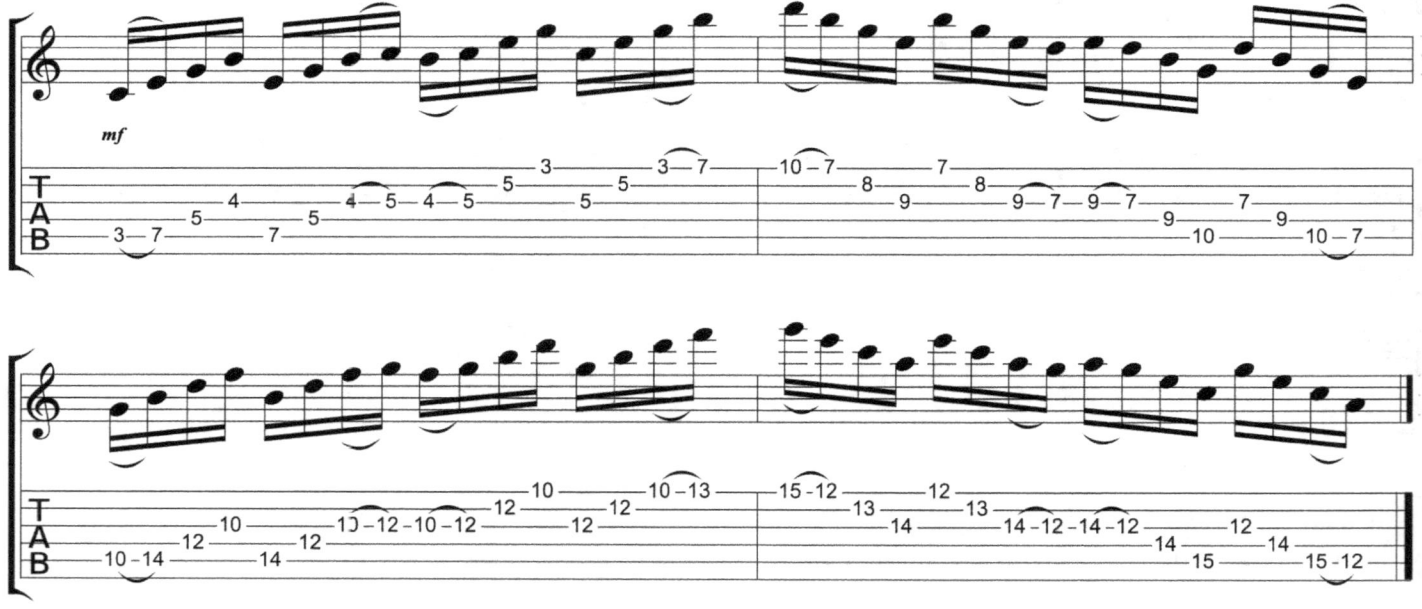

The final exercise in this section uses multiple three-string arpeggios from the 6th string to the 3rd string, to get you more used to the kinds of shapes you'll see in the bass and lower-mid register. The sequence uses chords from the B Major diatonic chord structure and moves predominantly in 4th intervals.

Example 4n: Four-string B Major multiple position bassy-arpeggio diatonic progression with 1/16th note pulse @ 100bpm

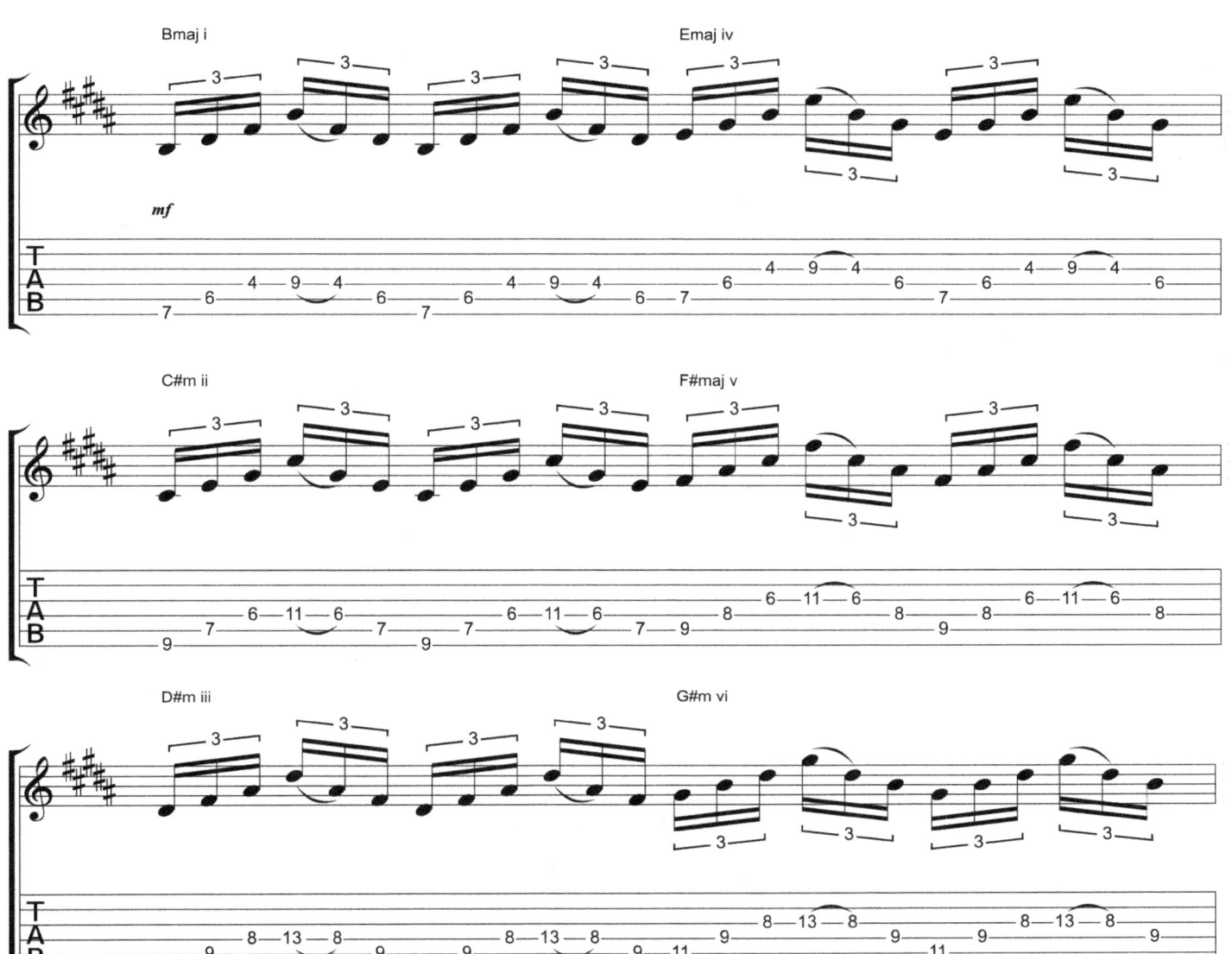

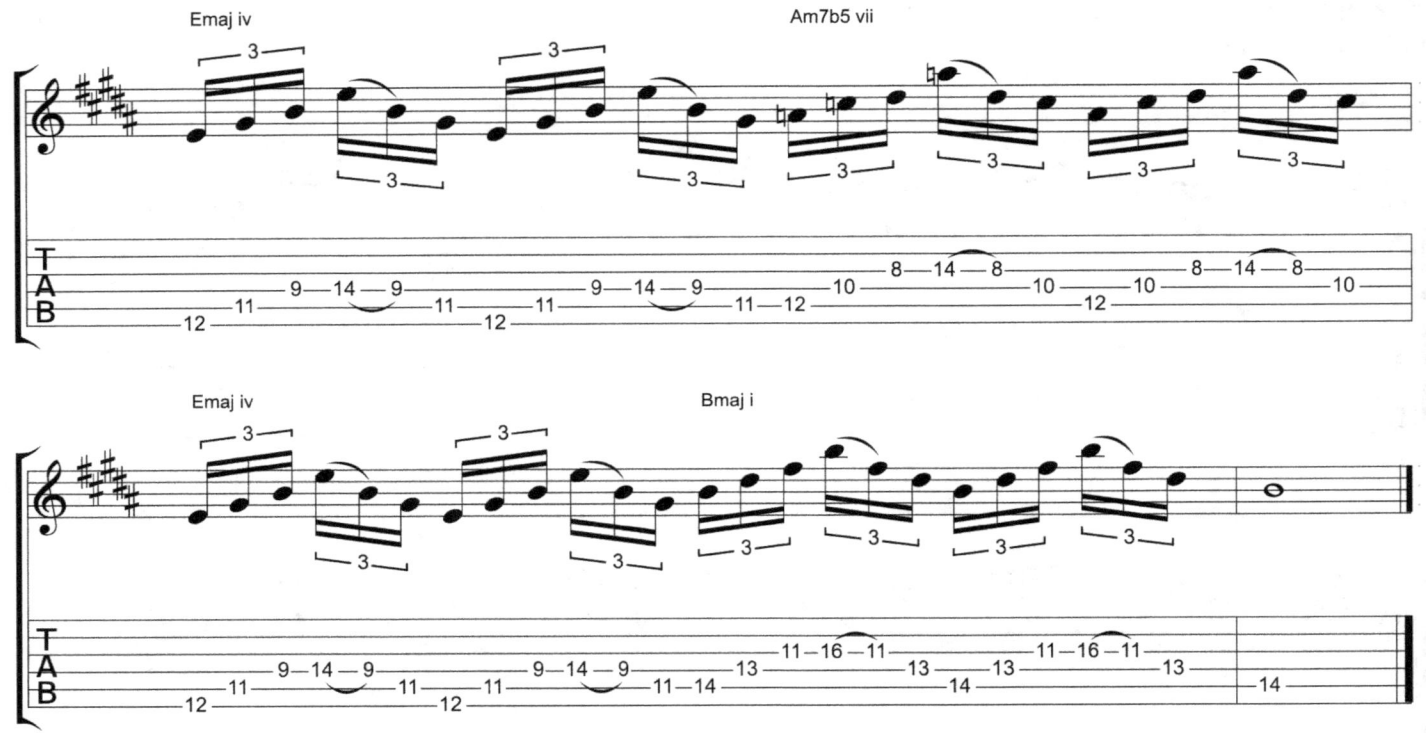

I've seen arpeggios like this countless times in Cacophony and Jason Becker compositions. Although they are much less common than the previous arpeggio shapes we've discussed, you might find you will need them at some point in your own compositions or improvisation, so better safe than sorry!

The Dreaded Flat Finger, Elbows and Uppercuts and the Palm Mute of Destiny

Many a man has had his life torn apart and his dignity and self-worth destroyed when addressing advanced arpeggios with the *rolling flat finger* technique. This is where multiple strings on an arpeggio are fretted with the same finger. In order to stop the notes blending (or bleeding) into one another, the flat fingers need to be rolled from one note to the next.

Let's take a look at an ascending and descending six-string E Minor arpeggio. There are two flat fingers within the arpeggio and both will require a roll.

Example 4o: Six-string E Minor arpeggio with 1/8th note pulse @ 110bpm

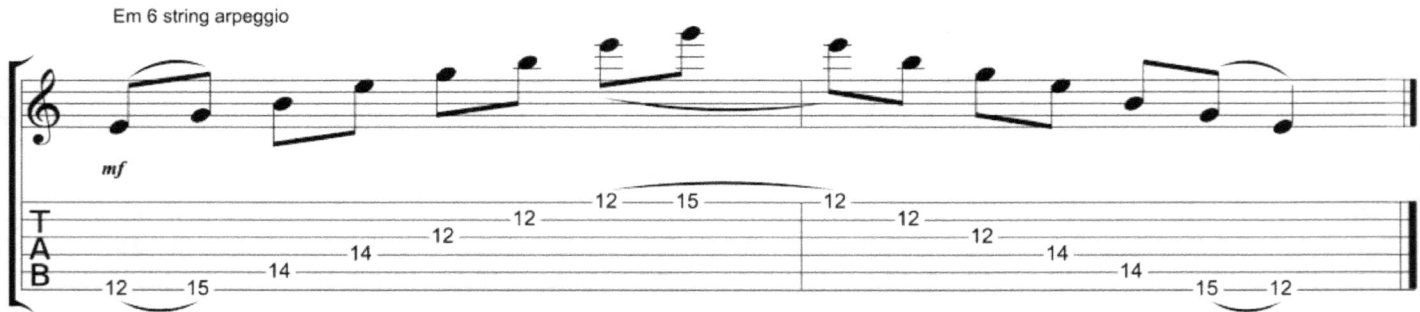

On the ascending part of this arpeggio we'll play the 5th and 4th string on the 14th fret with the flat ring finger, then use a flat pointer rolling on the 3rd, 2nd and 1st strings. On the descent, we'll reverse those concepts. One common misconception is that this rolling motion can be executed entirely from the wrist, but the best results I've seen come from knowing how to position and swing the elbow.

When I'm ascending an arpeggio with a rolling finger, I gradually move my elbow to the back wall as I work through the arpeggio. However, when I'm descending an arpeggio, I do the exact opposite. This means when I roll the middle finger I'm also doing an uppercut motion *Ryu*-style (this is a *Street Fighter 2* reference). It's optional to yell "Shoryuken" if it helps!

Let's try stringing together a few major and minor six-string arpeggios using a basic chord progression in G Major.

Example 4p: Six-string G Major *Closing Time*-style flat finger arpeggio sequence with 1/16th note pulse @ 100bpm

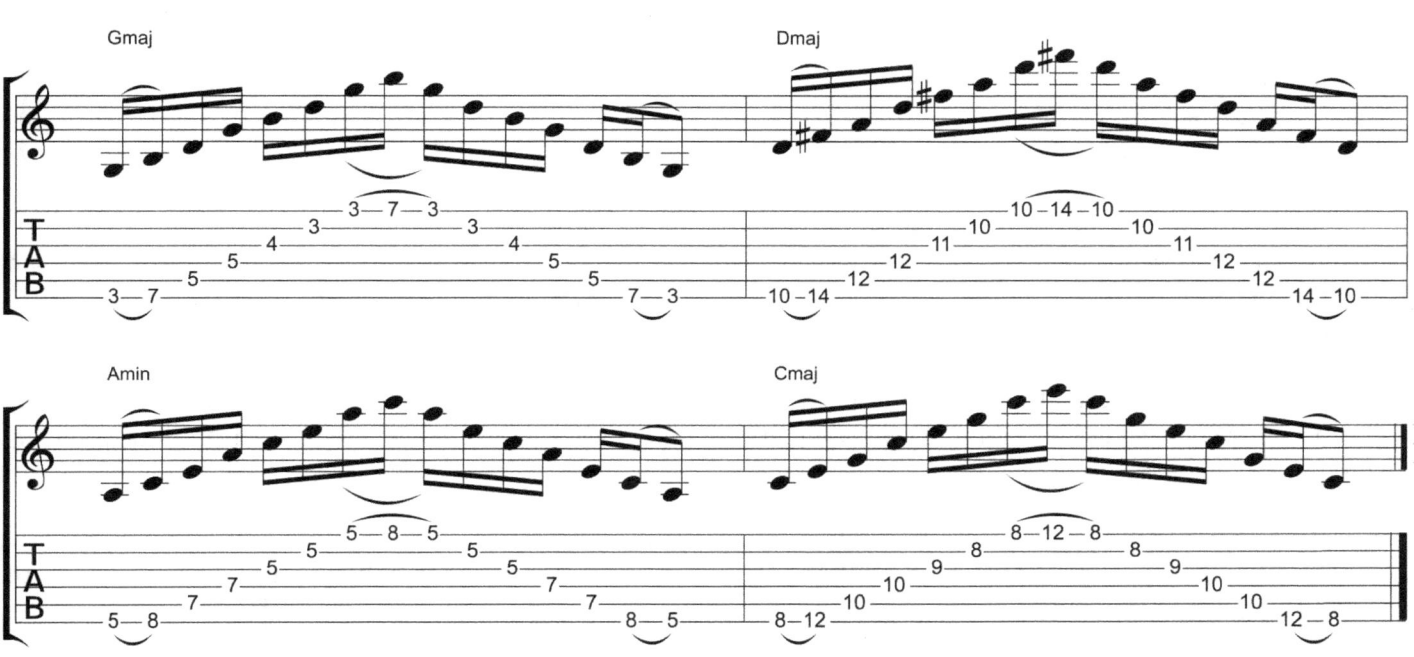

When arpeggios only use the first three strings, the flat finger roll and elbow motion can be quite fiddly and annoying. You may find it hard to get clarity between each individual note. Let's take a look at a three-string arpeggio sequence using flat finger shapes on all of the arpeggios. You might have seen similar arpeggio shapes in Yngwie Malmsteen's *Blitzkrieg* or Dethklok's *Crush My Battle Opponent's Balls*.

Example 4q: Three-string A Major flat finger arpeggio sequence with triplet 1/16th note pulse @ 100bpm

This sequence is based on a chord progression consisting of: A Minor, C Major, D minor, E Diminished 7 and B Diminished 7. The pointer finger is flat on at least two strings through this whole sequence and we'll want to keep up with flat finger rolls and elbow technique.

Keep in mind that it's incredibly easy for notes to bleed and sustain into one another on these shorter arpeggios. By doing a very controlled palm mute, you can increase note clarity and decrease the possibility of notes over-sustaining or bleeding.

The last exercise in this section is the most extreme in the chapter so far. It will require excellent hand synchronicity, as well as moments of the flat finger rolling technique. It drifts between multiple inversions of six- and five-string major and minor arpeggios, using a diatonic chord sequence in G Major.

This trademark style, joining multiple arpeggios of the same chord together, was made famous by Jason Becker in the sweep solo *Serrana* and is also used on multiple tracks on his masterpiece album *Perpetual Burn*. If you don't have that album, go get it... RIGHT NOW!

Example 4r: Five-string and six-string G Major Jason Becker-style arpeggio sequence with 1/16th note pulse @ 100bpm

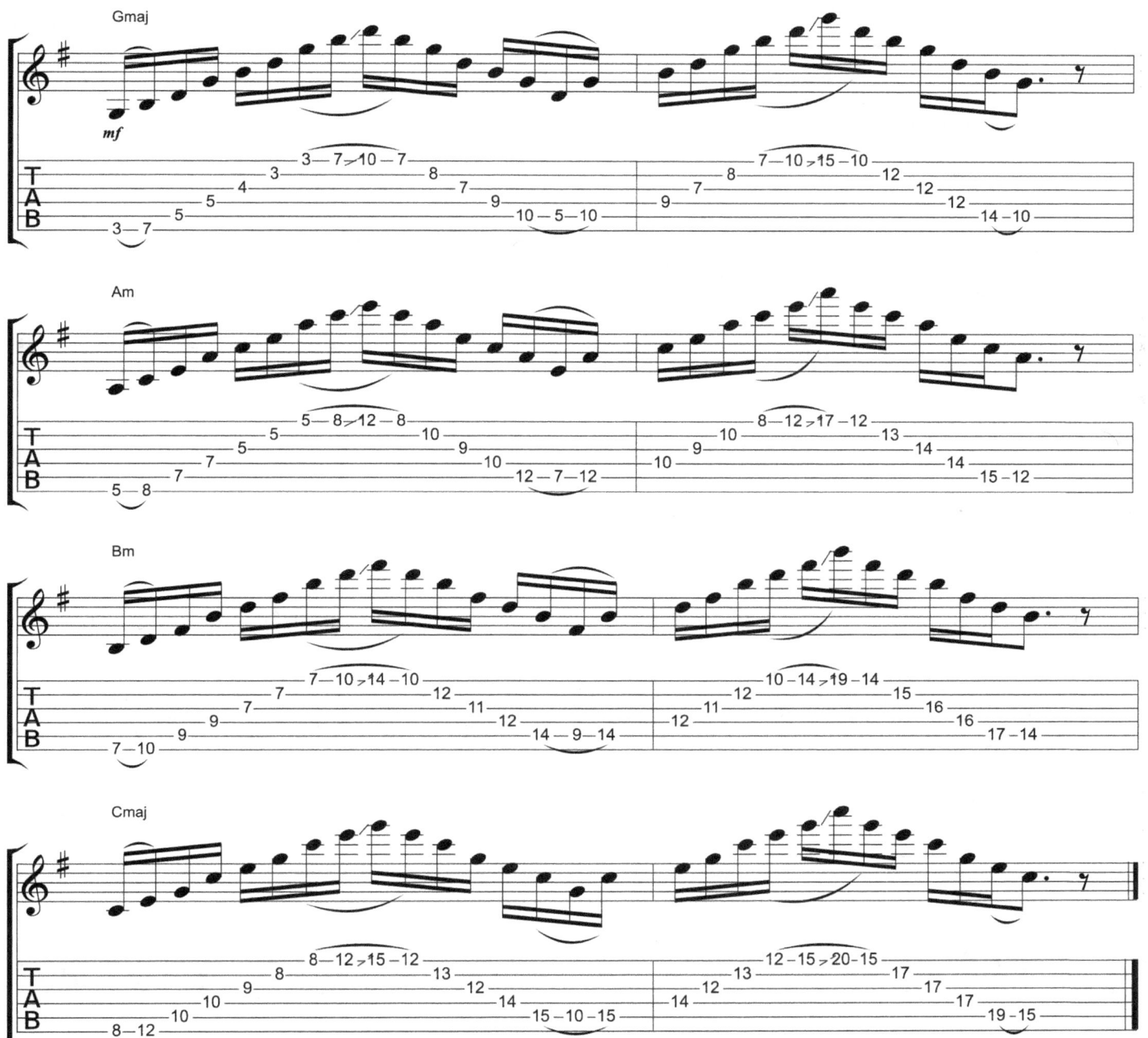

Combining Sweeps and Shred!

Occasionally you're going to come across a shred sequence that begins with a swept entry. The next section of this chapter is devoted to combining a swept arpeggio with diatonic runs. We're going to start with three-string 7th arpeggios in the key of A Minor. This exercise has some similar shapes and position shifts to *The Zephyr Song* by Red Hot Chili Peppers.

Example 4s: Three-string A Minor *Zephyr*-style 7th arpeggio sequence with 1/8th note pulse @ 120bpm

The next exercise uses similar principles to those in Example 4s, but this time we'll use an ascending five-string sweep arpeggio into a lengthier descending diatonic pattern. There are patterns similar to this in the Children of Bodom's *Triple Corpse Hammer Blow.*

Example 4t: Five-string A Minor COB-style arpeggio with shred sequence with 1/8th note pulse @ 120bpm

104

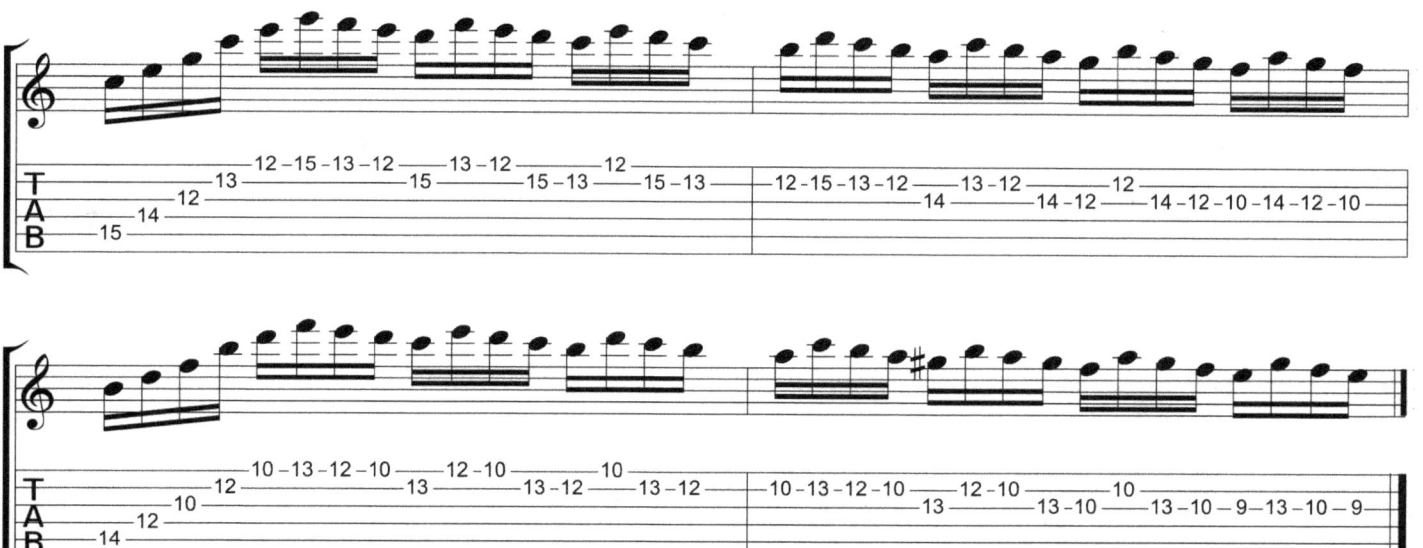

The next exercise uses two-string arpeggios, similar to shapes we saw in Example 4a, but played over three octaves and covering all six strings. It will also descend through scales in the key of E Minor/G Major.

Example 4u: Multiple two-string, three octave E Minor arpeggio with descending shred sequence with 1/16th note pulse @ 135bpm

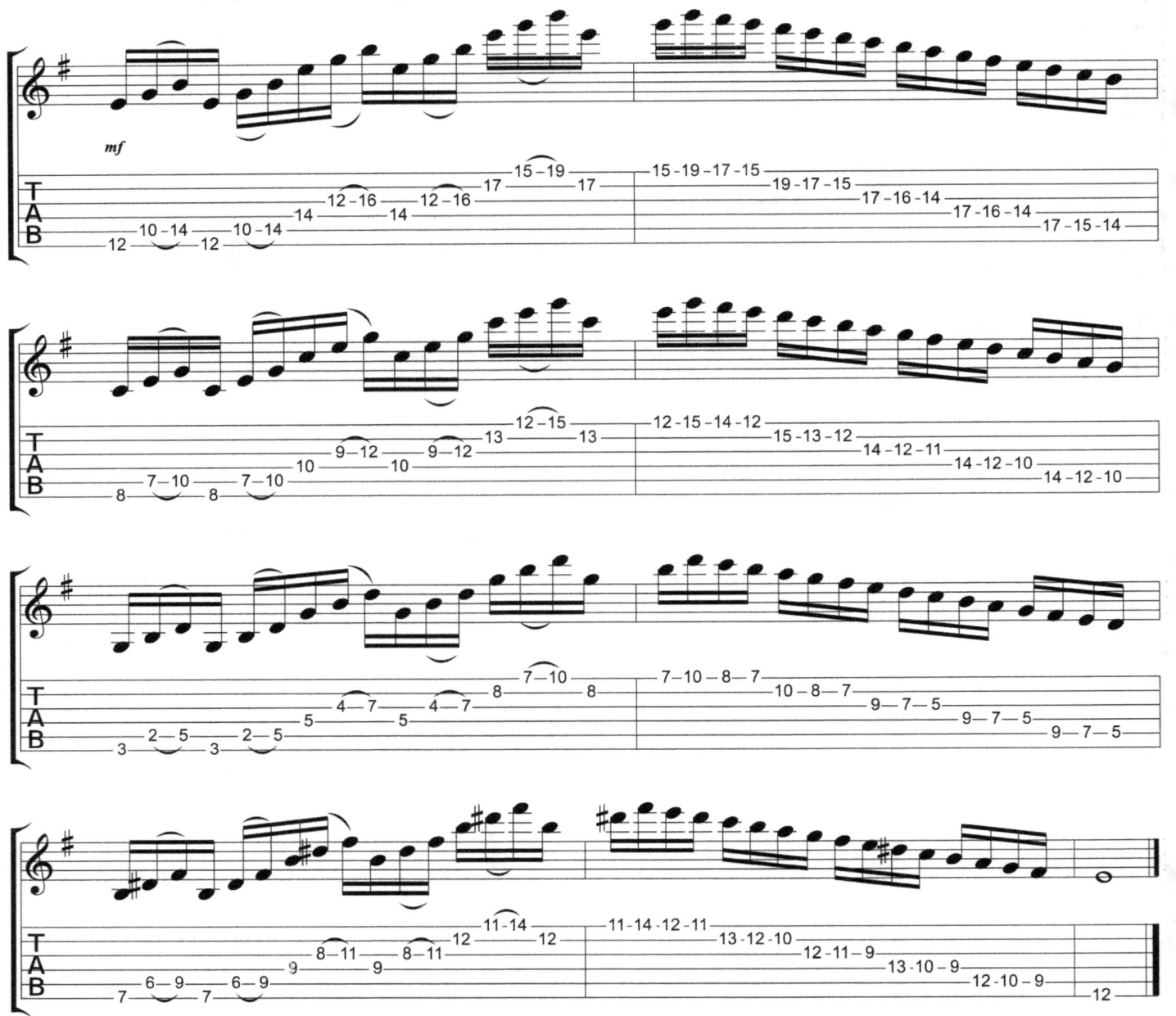

Now we will combine three-string, descending and ascending diminished sweeps with chromatic shredding. I have seen this used in countless Cacophony songs and it's used to great effect in the climax of the solo in Trivium's *Pull Harder on the Strings of Your Martyr*.

Example 4v: Three-string diminished arpeggios with chromatic shred with triplet 1/8th note pulse @ 105bpm

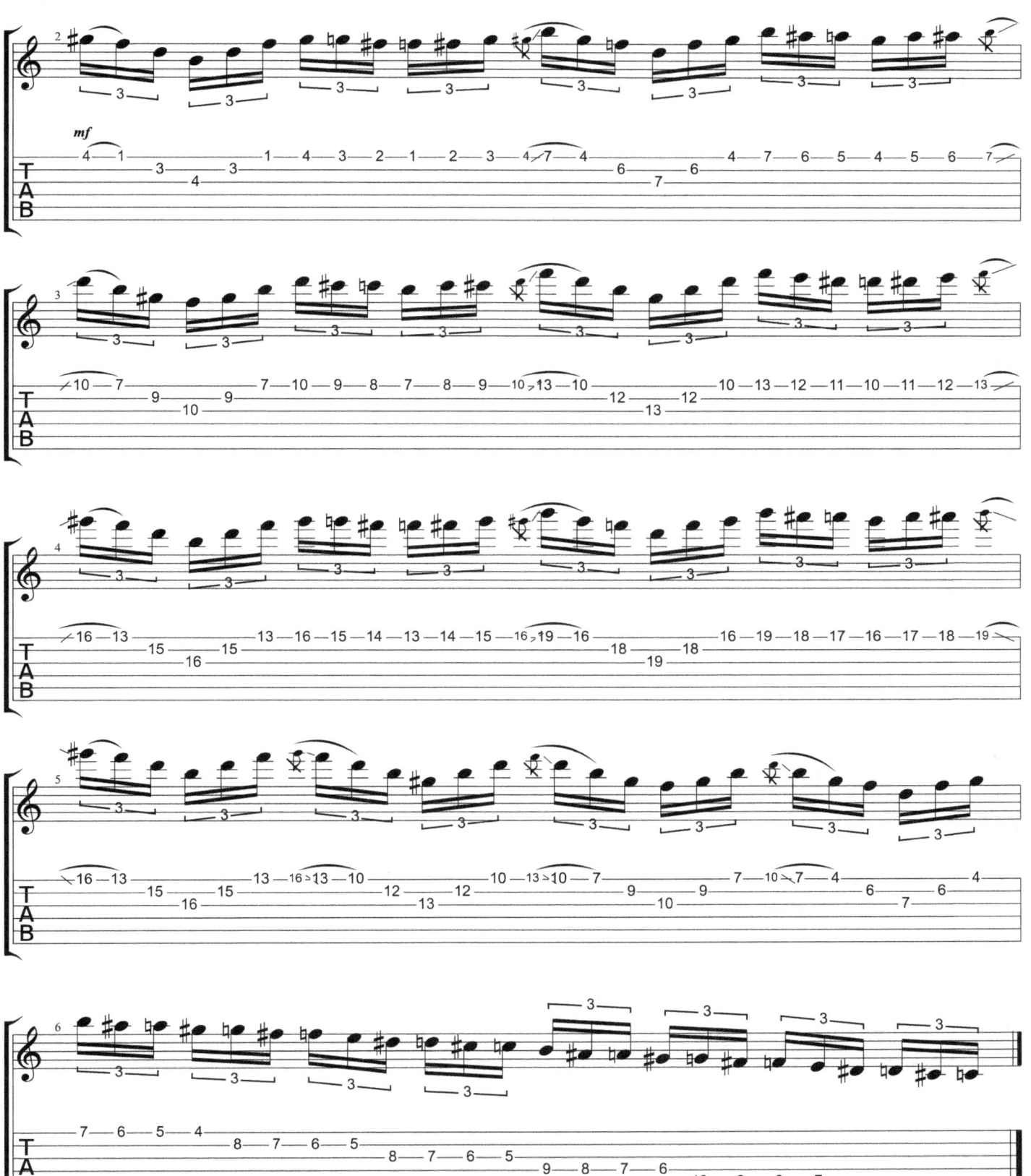

This final exercise uses five-string sweep arpeggio triads, but also includes descending scale runs. I've heard Alex Skolnick from Testament use this concept in a few solos to create a more exciting and melodically colourful entry to a diatonic run or lick.

Example 4w: Five-string sweep arpeggios with descending diatonic shred with triplet 1/8th note pulse @ 105bpm

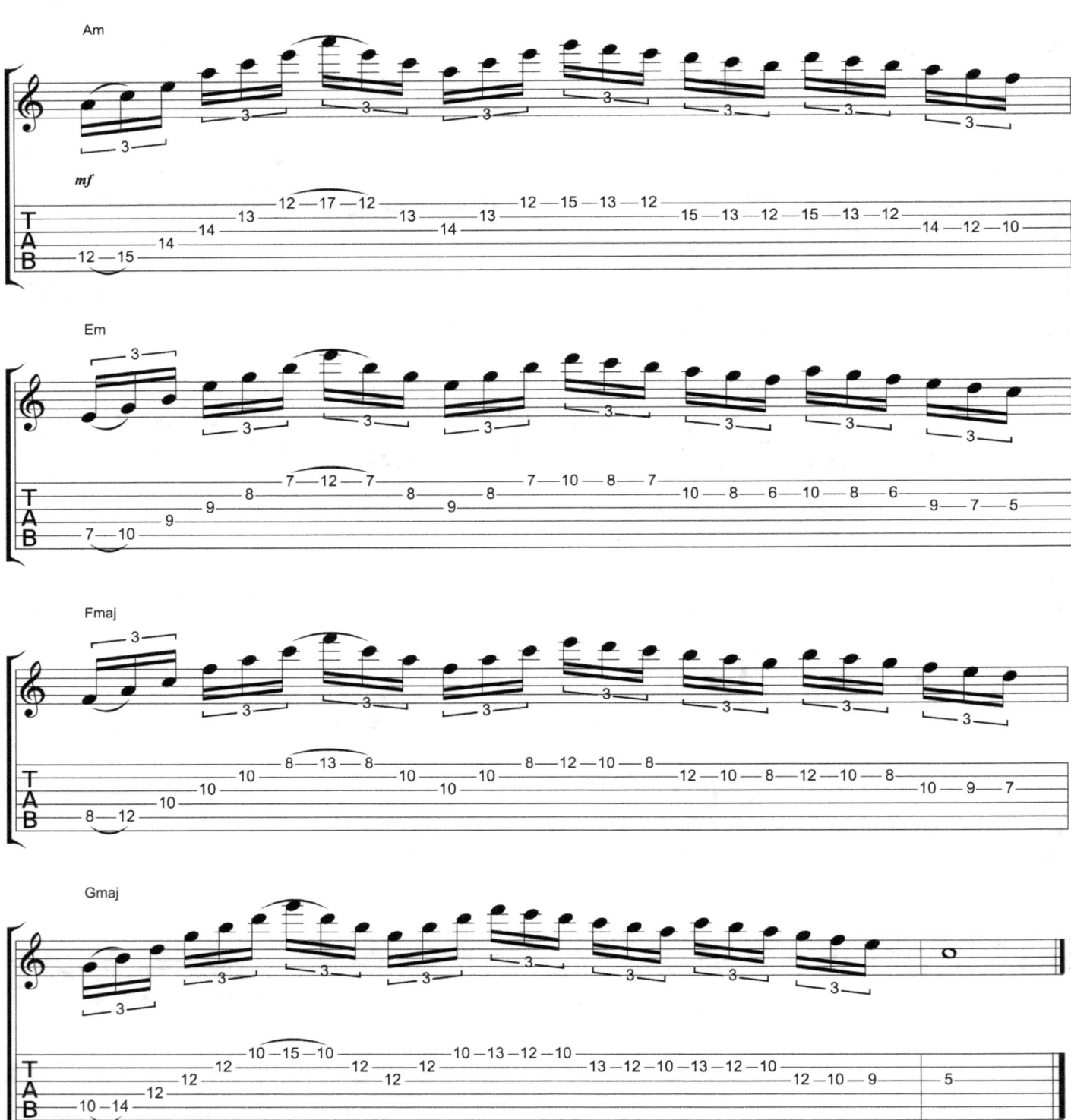

Secrets of a Janitor and Bringing it All Together

Trying to master all the details and idiosyncrasies of sweeping is a little overwhelming at first. However, you will reach your goals when you can bring together a sexy gliding motion, hand synchronicity and well-placed finger rolls, as well as speed and note clarity. When the arpeggios start to sound clear and musical, the most important thing to remember is, USE THEM IN MODERATION!

At some point in your life and musical journey, you'll hear a guitarist improvising, or writing a solo, just going completely overboard with the use of sweep arpeggios. For seasoned musicians and people with a more developed, mature musical palate, the sound of "Wadilop, wadilop, wadilop" is excruciating. It's like when a toddler ruins a dinner party by running around shaking their willy (as they've literally just discovered it) and you're sitting there with your Salmon in butter sauce thinking, "I get it kid… Good on you, but settle down." So, remember, "With great power comes great responsibility." Sweep responsibly!

Epilogue and Acknowledgements

Holy Jenna Elfman! Here we are at the end of my first book… AND I'm glad it's done.

Seriously, has anyone who has read my book ever written one? It's hard, isolating and causes you constantly to question your intelligence – not only in your field of expertise, but as a person too.

This book was a long time coming and I'm glad it's over. If I could liken my joy to its completion to a film, I would describe it like the first (and only) time I saw *Beowulf* at the cinema. I was like, "Yay, it's over. Now I can get on with my life." If I could liken the relief I felt to an illness, it'd be like having food poisoning, when you know you can't possibly poo or vomit any more, then you just drink Gatorade and sleep.

I want to thank all of my students from Melbourne and across the world who push me every week and force me to get super creative dreaming up new ways to push *them*. There are times when I get stuck in a rut as a teacher and as a musician/songwriter, and I owe it to you guys for slapping me in the face and reminding me how lucky I am.

I'd like to thank the friends I have made in the Melbourne music scene and through YouTube. Especially, Jens Larsen, Kevin Goetz, Levi Clay, Stratten Hammond, Dave Dunsire, Noemi Terrasi, Adam Duquemin, Tyler Larson and the gorgeous Ben Eller. You have all been an enormous support and have inspired me to be less crap at my instrument, less crap at life and less crap as a person (#allthecraps).

Lastly, I want to thank my beautiful wife, Lucie, my son, Alexi, and my cat, Senator Andrew P. Rodriguez (AKA Emperor Puddpatine). To quote Brian Adams, "Everything I do, I do it for you." You all manage to make me smile every day and are the greatest family I could hope for. Everything I have achieved is with your, help encouragement and love.

ROCK GUITAR MODE MASTERY

A Guide to Learning and Applying the Modes
to Rock and Shred Metal Guitar with Chris Zoupa

CHRIS ZOUPA

FUNDAMENTAL CHANGES

Foreword

I started teaching guitar when I was 15 years old. I talked to a couple of other kids at school about, "Comin' 'round for a shred." My sales pitch consisted of, "Yeah, I teach" and "Yeah, I can show you some stuff!" I also put an ad in the school newsletter that read:

Rock and Metal Guitar Lessons. 1st LESSON FREE!

Eventually the phone rang, with someone *actually enquiring* about guitar lessons.

Initially, I was freaked out about the idea of people paying ME to teach them guitar. The reality was, I was untrained, I lacked knowledge, and had little understanding of how to pass on information. Basically, I was going to have to wing it. But I got lucky. I found that I had a knack for it and fell in love with teaching straight away. Of course, like most young teachers, the early years consisted of fooling around with Metallica, Megadeth, Slayer and Guns N' Roses riffs – all the fun stuff.

When I was about 19, theory, improvisation and composition started to interest me and I became infatuated with the modes. The more I used them, and the more epiphanies I had, the more I wanted to teach them and share what I believed to be "amazing discoveries". I didn't care who it was, I just needed someone to share my excitement with – even if it was one of the tiny kids who could barely hold a guitar.

Now, as a gentleman of thirty-one and a half years (insert adult level sigh here), I decided to write a book to help those who want a "plain English" guide to the modes. A book that would show guitar players how to use the modes in context, without the fear of playing wrong notes or, worse, having a spontaneous head explosion. I've lost count of the number of times I've begun naming the modes to a student, saying "Mixolydian" or "Locrian", and they've looked at me as if to say, "I'm sorry, sir. I did not realise I was paying for an astrophysics class taught in ancient Aramaic!"

I'm hoping that this book will remove your fear of new, scary words, and give you the confidence and understanding to apply modal music theory. The moment you start understanding the modes and their theoretical application is an exciting and liberating one. It will have a great effect on your composition of chord progressions, riffs, solo writing, and how you approach improvisation.

Did someone say, "That's a good place to throw in a m7b5 arpeggio"?!

Alas, let's get learning.

Chris

Get the Audio

The audio files for this book are available to download for free from **www.fundamental-changes.com.** The link is in the top right-hand corner. Simply select this book title from the drop-down menu and follow the instructions to get the audio.

We recommend that you download the files directly to your computer, not to your tablet, and extract them there before adding them to your media library. You can then put them on your tablet, iPod or burn them to CD. On the download page there is a help PDF, and we also provide technical support via the contact form.

For over 350 Free Guitar Lessons with Videos Check out:

www.fundamental-changes.com

Twitter: **@guitar_joseph**

Over 10,000 fans on Facebook: **FundamentalChangesInGuitar**

Instagram: **FundamentalChanges**

Get your audio now for free:

It makes the book come alive, and you'll learn much more!

www.fundamental-changes.com/download-audio

An Introduction to Modes

Since the dawn of time, modes have freaked people out – especially guitarists. The pretentious and pompous musicians of the world have used their modal knowledge to look down smugly from their pedestals and dismiss the rest of us "theory-less, self-taught peasants" and make us feel all the more basic and pedestrian.

Before we delve too far down the theory rabbit hole, we need to be able to understand and answer a very simple question: *what is a mode?* We need to understand their purpose, and their theoretical and practical application, so we can use them to make awesome music.

Put simply, a mode is a scale derived from the notes of a parent scale. For example, given the parent scale of C Major (C D E F G A B), the second mode will consist of the notes D E F G A B C. The third mode will consist of the notes E F G A B C D, and so on.

A major scale is always built from a set pattern of tones and semitones. Looking at our C Major scale we can see that,

C to D = Tone

D to E = Tone

E to F = Semitone

F to G = Tone

G to A = Tone

A to B = Tone

B to C = Semitone

(notated for convenience as T T St T T T St)

When we start from a different note in the scale to create a mode, we create a different pattern of tones and semitones. For example, it we begin with a D note we get,

D to E = Tone

E to F = Semitone

F to G = Tone

G to A = Tone

A to B = Tone

B to C = Semitone

C to D = Tone

(T **St T** T T St T)

This pattern of tones and semitones sound *very* different from the pattern of tones and semitones in our original C Major scale. So just by playing a major scale beginning on a different note, we can create a whole different mood in music very easily.

This can be tricky to hear when simply playing an isolated sequence of notes (from D to D, or E to E, for example). However, when we *harmonise* (make chords out of) the modes, and play over progressions built from chords in the mode, they quickly take on very distinct personalities. We have the funky chilled out jazz of the Dorian mode (D to D), the country-blues of the Mixolydian (G to G), and the dark, dislocating dissonance of the Locrian (B to B).

Modes are used to convey different moods, feelings and textures. They are often used to create a precise sound or mood that characterises a specific musical genre. Modes can even be used to create a sound evocative of certain time periods, countries, religions or cultures.

In this book we'll cover the seven "church" modes of Ionian, Dorian, Phrygian, Lydian, Mixolydian, Aeolian and Locrian. Every mode we discuss will be compared to its parent major scale, to help you understand why it sounds different.

By now, you're probably asking yourself,

"How does playing a scale using the exact same notes, but in a different, order create a different sound?"

That's a solid question.

One simple way to understand it is that, although we are using the same seven notes, the "home base" is different for each mode. The home base is the note the scale begins and ends on. There is also a home base chord to go with it, that the mode works beautifully over. So, even though the notes are the same, the change of home base means that they function differently. In fact, the notes have varying degrees of importance from one mode to the next.

Let's explore this a bit further:

In the key of C Major, the home base note is C and the home base chord is C Major. The *strong* chord sounds in C Major are C Major, F Major and G Major. Every melodic lick or line you play is heard in relation to these strong chords and your ears interpret them as "happy".

If we begin from the second note in the C Major scale (D), we are now in D Dorian. The home base note is D and the home base chord is D Minor. The *strong* chord sounds in this mode are D Minor, G Major (or G7) and A Minor. Every melody you play is heard in relation to these strong chords (normally the first, fourth and fifth chords in the harmonised scale) and suddenly your melodies sound completely different. Even though you are playing all the same notes as the C Major scale, now your ears interpret them as "sad" or "melancholy" because you hear all the scale notes in relation to different strong chords.

Each mode has its own character and mood and the chords produced by each mode are like the colour of a wall where you hang a painting. The same painting can evoke a different mood, just because it's hanging on a different coloured wall.

Now we're going to explore the modes. We'll start off by learning each one over one octave to establish an immediate understanding of its characteristic sound and intervals. Then we'll dive in deep for a thorough analysis with lots of example licks to learn.

Chapter 1: Owning your Ionian

The beginning of one's modal journey can be a terrifying one. It is a quest riddled with new and scary words, accompanied by the unjust composity of that one jazz nerd who loves to think they have something over you!

Now that we've looked at the basics of modal theory, we're going to explore the *sound* of each mode in turn and learn some licks that highlight its unique flavour. I'll also suggests some songs you can listen to, based around each mode.

Let's start at square one and talk about the Ionian mode. Known for its happy, joyous nature, the Ionian mode is often used to create uplifting moments in classical music and film scores. It has been used in children's nursery rhymes and lullabies for centuries, and has made frequent appearances in pop music for the last 60+ years.

Don't let this mystical new word fool you – you've already heard this mode close to a Bajillion times in your lifetime.

DISCLAIMER: "Bajillion" is not a real number and I have no science to back up my previous statement.

Part 1: Finding the Ionian sound

The Ionian mode is the first of the seven diatonic modes and is often referred to simply as "the major scale". It's predominantly used to convey a sense of triumph and joy and you will have heard it used repeatedly in modern and classic pop music. It's the happiest sounding of the seven modes and is the easiest to identify.

The Major scale is the basis of all the "rules" of music that have been around for hundreds of years. It's the yardstick by which all other scales are described and, as such, it's given a very simple formula.

Starting on any note on the guitar and ascending using the pattern "Tone Tone Semitone Tone Tone Tone Semitone" will form a major scale. This pattern of notes is given the formula 1 2 3 4 5 6 7

Let's look at the sound and characteristics of the Ionian mode. Listen carefully to the relationship between the notes and think about what mood the scale conveys. Here's a reminder of the Ionian mode in one octave in the key of C Major. Try playing it over the C Ionian backing track.

C Ionian: C D E F G A B C

Example 1a:

The intervals (distances between each note) of the Ionian scale are T T St T T T St (T = Tone; St = Semitone).

The scale formula for the Ionian mode is 1 2 3 4 5 6 7

Tip: As we progress, try to memorise the intervals for each mode. This will help you to differentiate each mode's characteristics, emotions and superpowers!

In any mode, the 3rd interval defines whether it is major or minor. A Major 3rd (four semitones) tells us that the scale is major and will have a happy quality to it. A Minor 3rd (also known as a b3 = three semitones) tells us that the scale is minor and will have a sad quality.

Apart from the 3rd, the most important "character" intervals of the Ionian mode are its 4th and 7th. These notes distinguish it from the Lydian and Mixolydian modes (the two other major modes that contain a major 3rd).

It is difficult to hear the unique qualities of a mode when playing it in isolation. We can get a better feel for its character if we hear it played over a simple progression built from the chords of the mode.

Example 1b is an Ionian chord progression. First play through the chords, then play the ascending and descending versions of the scale. Try playing the scale over the C Major backing track provided and create your own melodies. Listen to which notes sound tense and which notes sound resolved.

Example 1b: C Ionian chord progression and scale ascending & descending

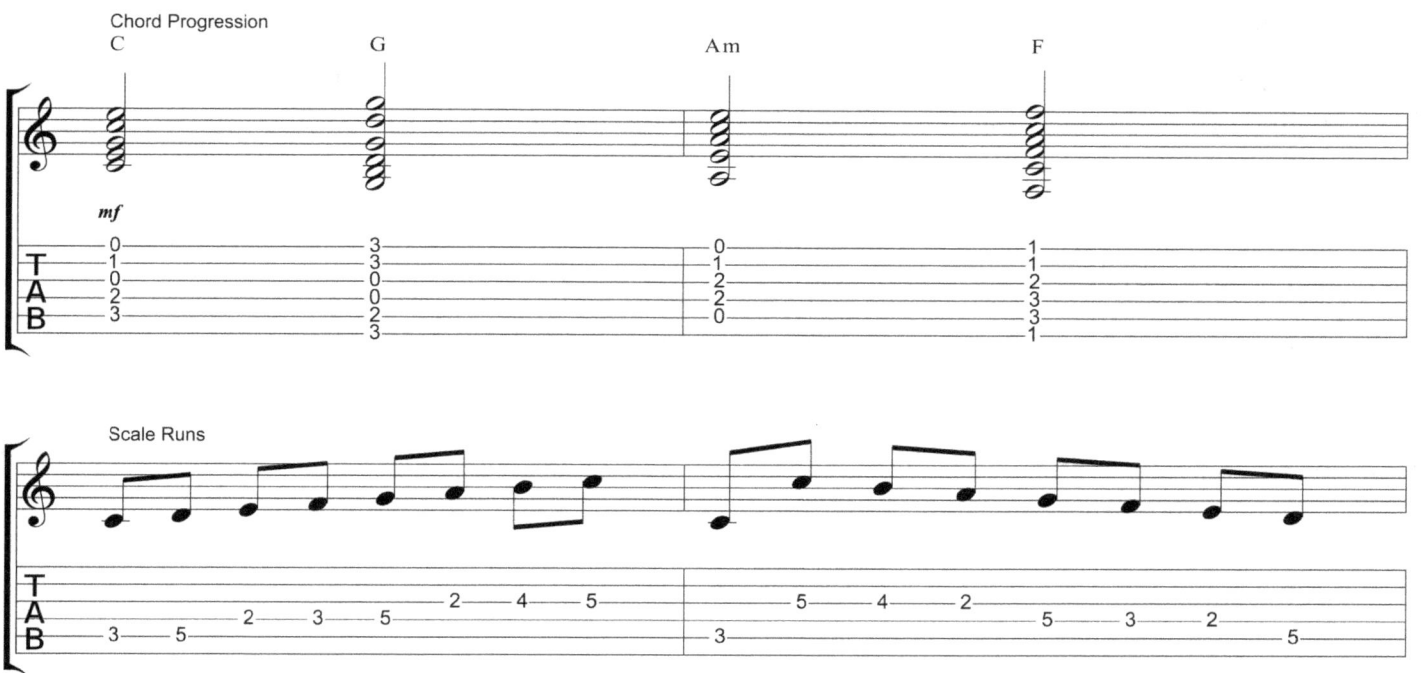

The combination of these chords, even without the scale runs, is enough to create the happy, joyous Ionian signature sound, because they contain important notes of the scale. Painting a modal "picture" isn't just about the notes of the scale – it's about the chords and harmonies that occur within the scale, and the interplay of melody against those chords.

Tip: a dedicated study of music theory, scale shapes, and note/interval knowledge will certainly make you a more *learned* player, but nothing beats understanding the melodic sound and feel that a mode creates. This is something internal to you as a player – you can't write it down on a piece of paper and play it on the fretboard.

Here are some well-known songs built around the Ionian mode for you to go and check out:

- Better Be Home Soon – Crowded House
- Let It Be – The Beatles
- You And Me – Lifehouse
- Stand By Me – Ben E. King
- Runaway – The Corrs

Listen carefully to how these songs sound and see if you can identify and add other songs to the list.

Part 2: Diatonic Chords

I've mentioned that each mode has certain chords that belong to it, and now we'll look at how to construct them. "Diatonic chords" simply refers to chords that are built from each degree of the scale. Understanding which chords belong to which mode will help massively when you come use them in a musical context.

Remember that the notes of C Ionian are C D E F G A B.

To form a chord, we simply stack alternate notes from the scale. For example, we start on C and take the 1st, 3rd and 5th notes (C E G), and play them together to form a C Major chord.

(C) D **(E)** F **(G)** A B C

Next, we move to the note D and treat it as our "1". The 1st, 3rd and 5th notes (D F A), played together form a D Minor chord.

Repeating this process for every note of the C Major results in the following chords:

C major (C E G)

D minor (D F A)

E minor (E G B)

F major (F A C)

G major (G B D)

A minor (A C E)

B minor7b5 (B D F A)

In "proper music theory" (I know, snore-fest), each chord is given a Roman numeral to identify it. The Roman numerals are normally displayed as upper case for major chords and lower case for minor chords.

Taking each note of the Ionian mode in turn, the harmonised scale is as follows:

I	ii	iii	IV	V	vi	vii
maj	min	min	maj	maj	min	min7b5 (or 1/2 diminished)

Here they are played as simple open chords:

Example 1c:

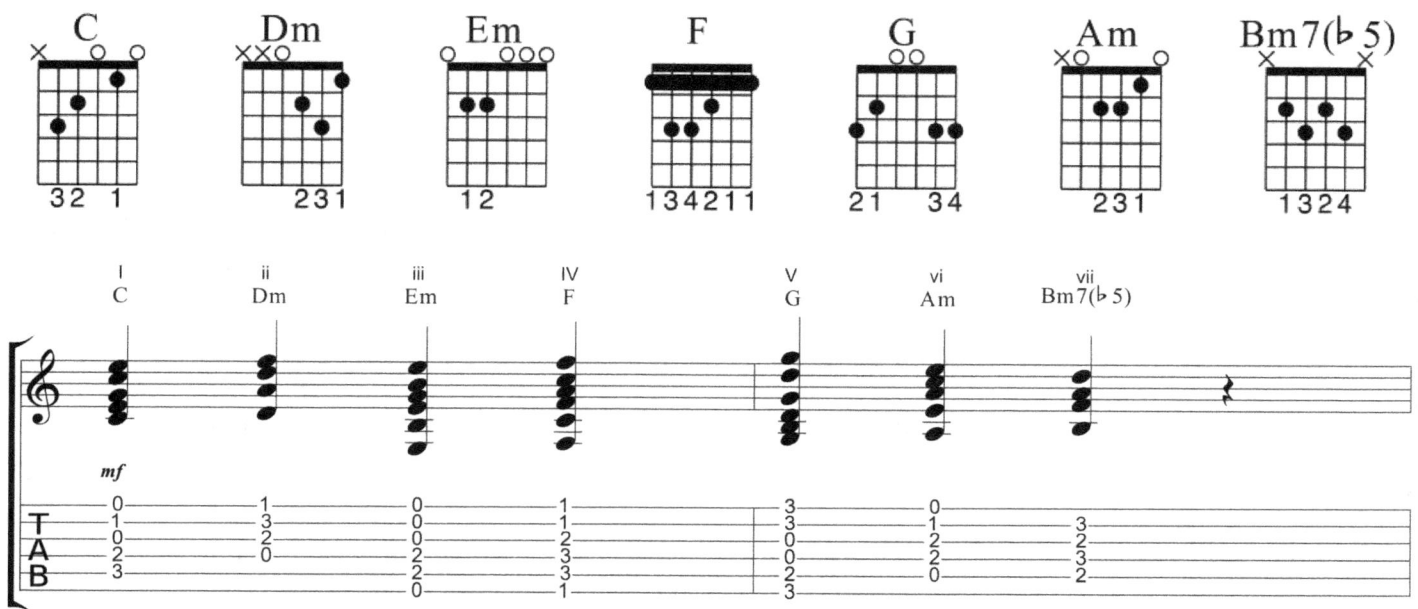

These chords should be familiar to you as they are foundational to guitar playing and make up the majority of "beginner" guitar songs. Try writing a few chord progressions with them, preferably beginning and ending on a C major chord, so that you get a feel for the Ionian sound. Here are a couple of examples:

Example 1d – progression 1:

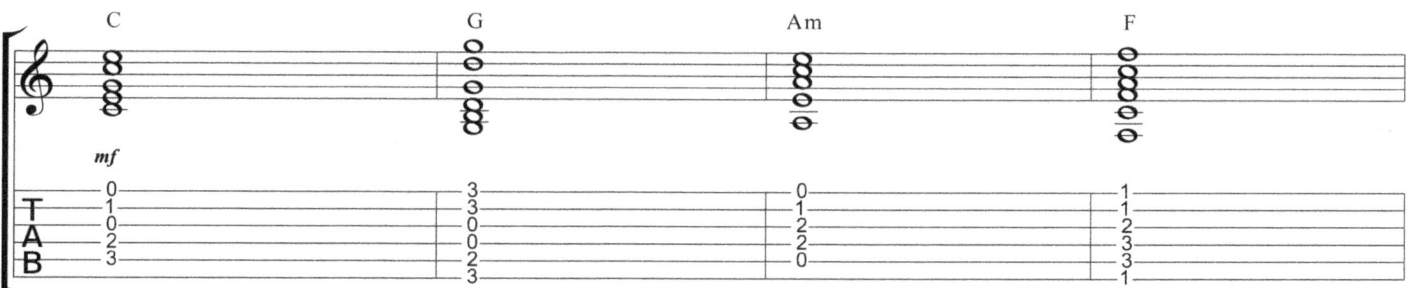

Example 1e – progression 2:

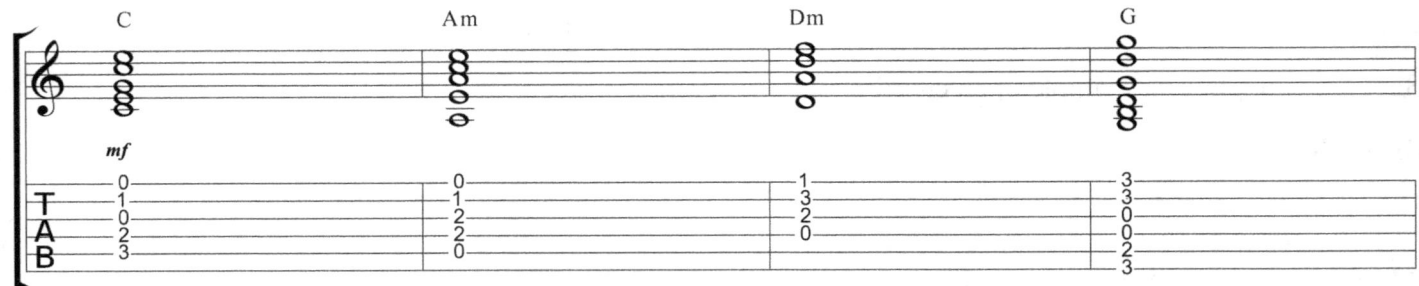

Part 3: Soloing in Ionian using scales and arpeggios

I've probably said this thousands of times over the years to students: "In the beginning, it's often hard to know where to start when soloing modally." So to make things easier, before I start writing or improvising, I ask myself these questions:

1. What is the three-note-per-string pattern for this mode from the root?

2. What kind of pentatonic scales are hiding in the mode. E.g. regular, custom or relative minor?

3. What types of arpeggios will bring out the flavour of the mode?

Let's look at each of these in turn before learning a load of cool licks that use each approach.

First, let's take the simple Ionian scale from the start of the chapter and stretch it across six strings with a three-note-per-string pattern.

Example 1f:

This is the fastest way to play and hear the mode across two and a bit octaves. As a pattern, it's also fairly easy to use in composition and improvisation. Learn it over the C Major backing track.

Pentatonics

Another effective way of playing the Ionian mode is to take just five of its seven notes and turn them into a pentatonic scale. The major pentatonic scale is made up from the 1st (C), 2nd (D), 3rd (E), 5th (G) and 6th (A) notes of the Ionian scale. Having five notes instead of seven means there are fewer notes between the root and the octave, which creates wider intervals and allows us to make bigger harmonic jumps. Let's take a look at that scale in a box-shaped pattern.

Example 1g:

If you feel the box pattern is too restrictive, you can use a crawling pentatonic shape that works diagonally across the neck.

Example 1h:

Side note: C Major Pentatonic and A Minor Pentatonic share identical notes, just played in a different order:

C Major Pentatonic = C D E G A

A Minor Pentatonic = A C D E G

This means you can use them interchangeably. If you are playing in C Ionian or A Aeolian, both shapes can be used over both modes. Here they are side by side:

Example 1i:

If you're more comfortable with the minor pentatonic shape, use that one instead. Remember that you can use your original three-note-per-string shape and the pentatonic scale shape to mix things up and break the monotony of running up and down one pattern.

Arpeggios

Another cool way to emphasise the sound of the Ionian mode is to use major triad arpeggios. (These are the simple chords we made earlier: C major – C E G, D minor – D F A, etc). We can also add a fourth note to these triads to create a major 7th arpeggio (Cmaj7 has the notes C E G B). Example 1j illustrates how the triad arpeggio (made from the 1st, 3rd and 5th notes of C Ionian) sounds compared to the major 7th arpeggio (1st, 3rd, 5th and 7th).

Example 1j:

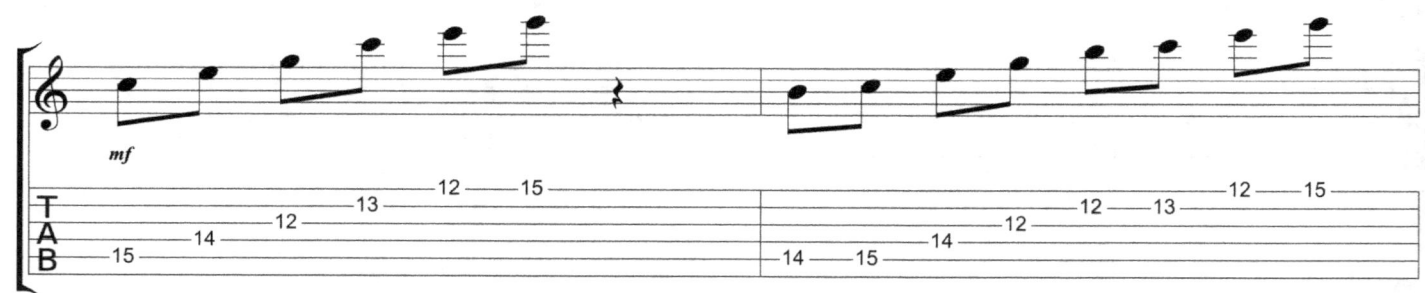

Example 1k:

Experiment with both arpeggios. Straight triads can sound a little predictable. Overuse the major 7th, however, and it can sound too jazzy.

You can play both triad and major 7th arpeggios in a lower register with different shapes:

Learning more arpeggio positions gives you more options and means you can shift between endless ideas that span the fretboard. Listen to the multiple arpeggio inversions of the same chord used on Jason Becker's masterpiece album, *Perpetual Burn*. The title track has an amazing sequence of arpeggios joined together at 1:41.

Lastly, I want to show you my two favourite ways to play a major 7th arpeggio so that it spans all six strings. This first shape leads from the major 7th (B) then plays the 1st, 3rd and 5th scale intervals. There's a slide in the middle of the arpeggio to help position the hand for the major triad. It also helps the arpeggio sound less robotic and more like a phrase.

Example 1l:

The second shape also leads from the major 7th and works across three octaves. This shape is more predictable as each octave is played identically. I've seen guitarists like Marty Friedman (Megadeth, Cacophony) and Corey Beaulieu of Trivium use this shape spectacularly in a few solos!

Example 1m:

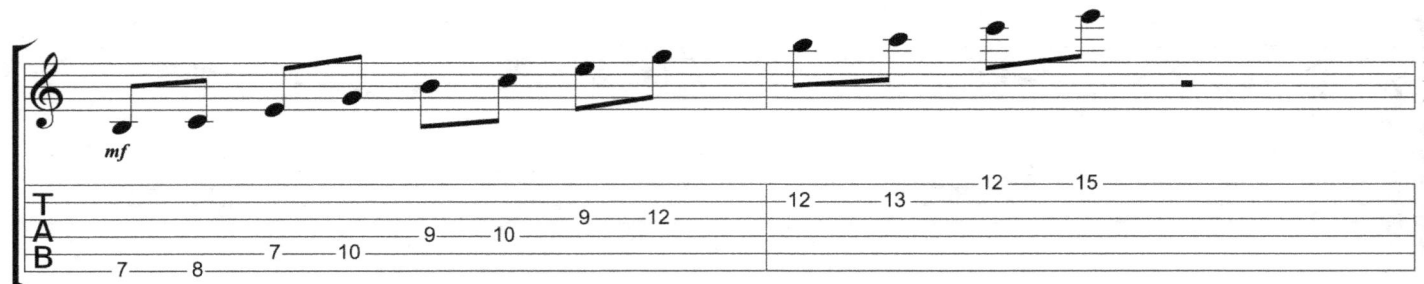

Experiment with different patterns using this arpeggio. You don't always have to lead from the seventh or the root note. Your main consideration should be how what you're playing sounds over the backing chords and key signature.

Tip: These shapes work equally well in a Lydian context. That means you can play them over a I chord (Ionian) or IV chord (Lydian) in any chord progression.

OK, here's the bit you've been waiting for, let's learn some of my favourite Ionian licks.

Part 4: Ionian licks to help you get creative

I've given you some useful scales and arpeggio shapes already, and at this point you might be thinking, "Thanks Chris, that's all I need!" However, you may then sit down to improvise and everything you'd play would sound linear and robotic – boring runs or, worse, up-and-down arpeggios! At which point you'd say to yourself, "That evil jerk face! Chris lied to us. He lied to all of us – even the sooty orphans at CHRISTMAS no less!"

Firstly, calm down! Secondly, I haven't properly shown you how to get the most out of those ideas yet. For the final part of this chapter, I've prepared several Ionian licks to show you how to bring these melodic ideas together in an expressive way in a musical context.

The first lick I want to show you is a major pentatonic pattern, crawling across the neck, using slides and hammer-ons to add flavour. Play all the ideas in this section over the C Ionian backing track.

Example 1n: Sliding C Major pentatonic lick

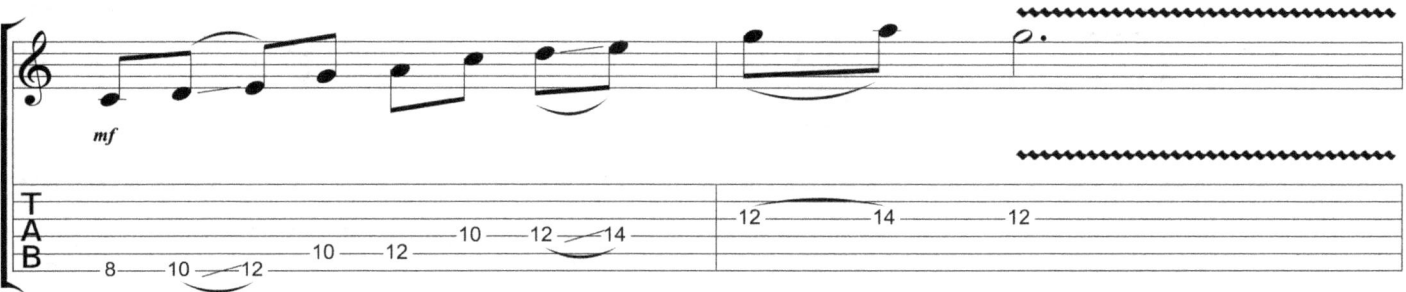

I'm a massive fan of licks like this that encourage you to use the whole neck of the guitar and force you to execute positions shifts. They can help you break out of rigid box patterns and can be used to transition from one position to the next.

In the next example, we'll use position 1 of the A Minor pentatonic, then shift up the neck.

Example 1o: A Minor pentatonic drifting positions lick

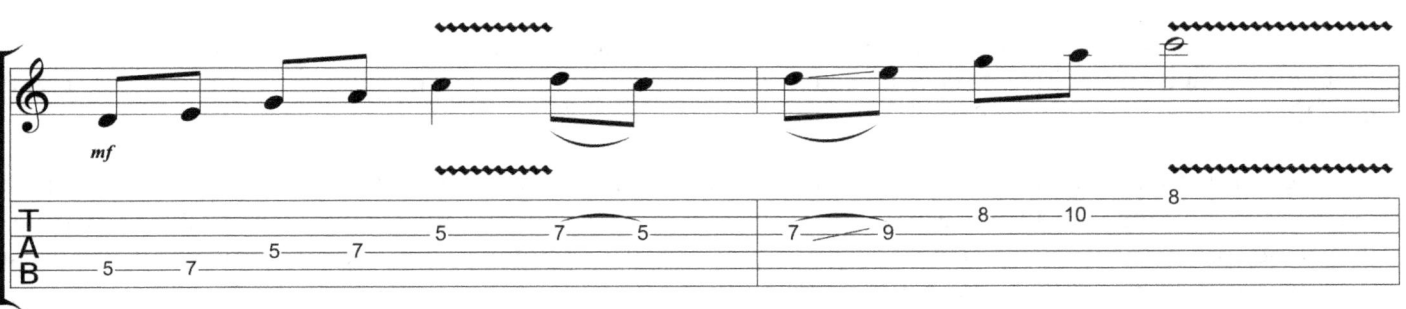

This is a relatively simple idea. I decided to target and rest briefly on the C note – the root note of a C Major chord. However, you could also target the major 3rd (E) or 5th (G) to support the chord. Your target notes will change if you play this lick over a different chord in the progression, so tinker with it accordingly. Try using this lick to drift from one minor pentatonic position to the next.

Example 1p uses the C Ionian three-note-per-string scale shape. It ascends in triplets, but varies between 1/8th and 1/16th notes to add an occasional burst of speed. I use this approach a lot in improvisation and composition. I've seen Mark Tremonti play similar licks in a few Alter Bridge solos.

Example 1p: Tremonti-style diatonic building lick

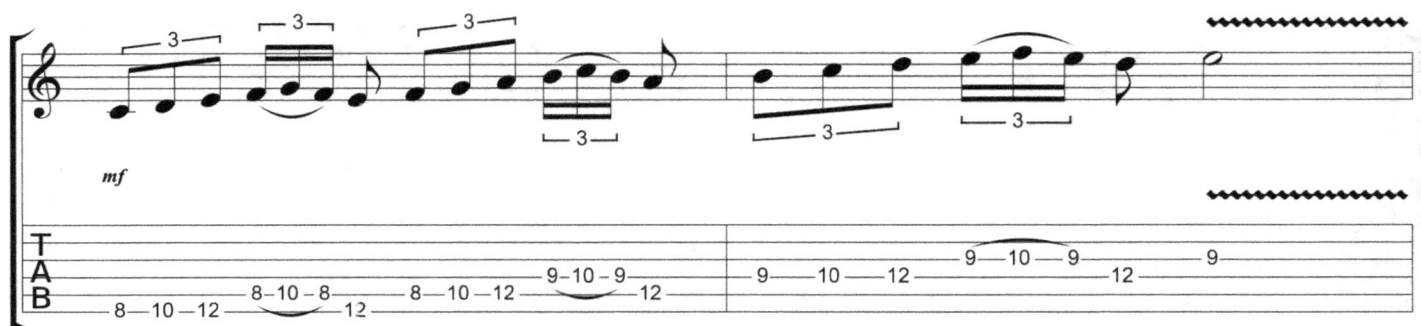

After playing through this lick a few times, you'll notice that the addition of speed variance and legato are a great way to break up the monotony of a linear ascending scale run. It's also really interesting to switch between legato technique and shredding in the same lick. This lick can also be applied to any three-note-per-string modal shape.

Side note: I may go into detail about more exotic, adventurous modes in a future book. It'll need to have a sassy yet bold name. Until then, let's keep it simple. There's also a very good chance Jens Larsen will write that book before me and do a very good job. SIGH! (Seriously though, check out Jens Larsen on YouTube).

Example 1q combines old school, Chuck Berry-influenced blues rock pentatonics with a few additional scale notes to give a nice mix of both scales. This lick starts with a D note bent a full tone to E. It also ends on an E note to highlight the major 3rd of the C Major chord.

Guitar legends Carlos Santana and Slash use this concept to create moments of triumphant rocking out, mixed with powerful emotion. It's a great way to blend the rocky-blues sound of the pentatonic with the heartstring-pulling emotion of the diatonic scale. The pentatonic scale is completely devoid of semitones – the most emotional sounding of intervals – which is why borrowing diatonic scale notes can be so effective. Think of it as having your rock cake and emotionally eating it!

Example 1q: Chuck Berry A pentatonic lick with diatonic descending notes

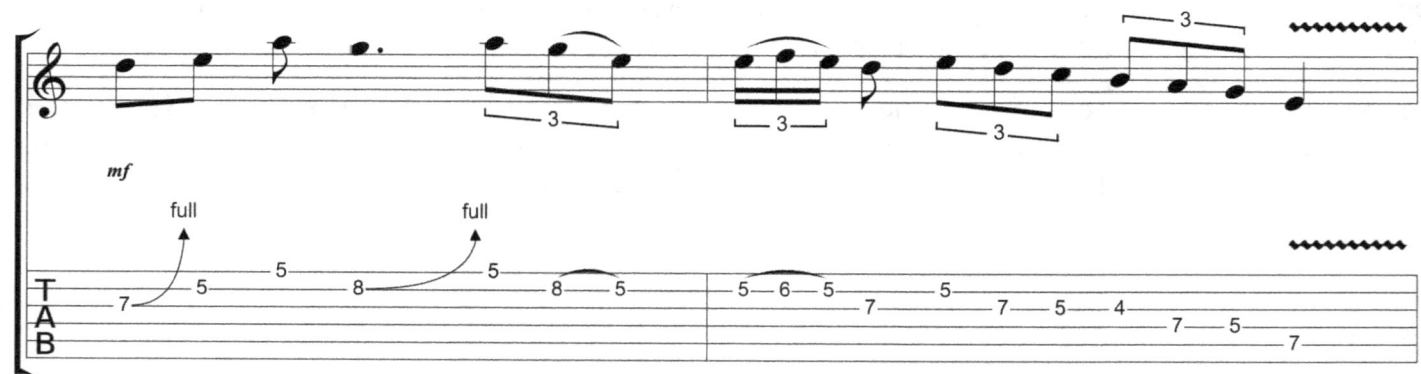

The next example lick uses a G pedal note, while the other notes work diatonically through C Ionian. This kind of lick is cool because it creates tension and has movement, yet the pedal makes it seem as though it's not moving much at all. Players such as John Mayer, Mikael Akerfeldt and Alex Skolnick have used this concept very subtly in some of their solos.

Example 1r: C Ionian pedal note lick

This next idea combines an arpeggio with some passing notes. It's a simple C Major triad (C E G), but I've added a F on the turnaround for extra flavour. Notice that I've also added a slide from D# to E before descending the arpeggio. This "outside" note adds further tension as it doesn't belong to the C Ionian mode. You can use this idea in scales too, not just in arpeggios. Just make sure you move from the outside note (sometimes referred to as a WRONG note) to a scale note – preferably one that supports the chords you are playing over.

Example 1s: Five string C Major arpeggio lick with outside note slide

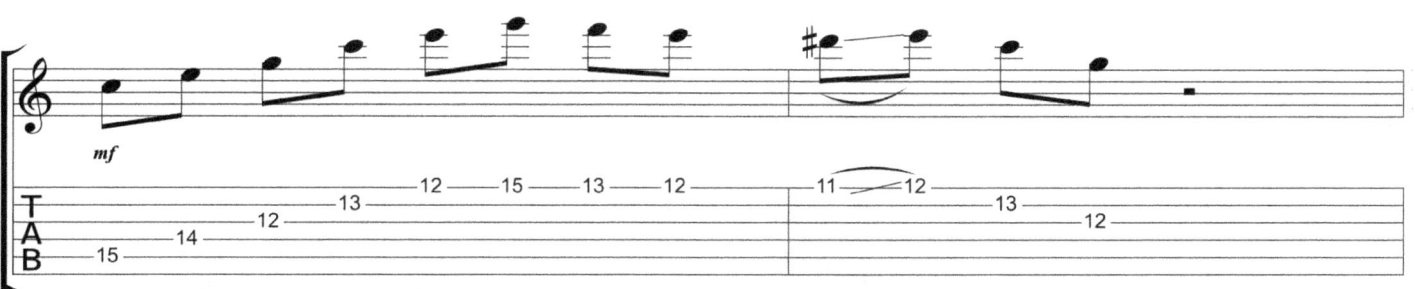

Example 1t has an ascending Cmaj7 arpeggio over three octaves, spanning all six strings, and uses a hammer-on on every string. Descending, we have diatonic notes from C Ionian.

Example 1t: Six-string Cmaj7 arpeggio with descending diatonic legato lick

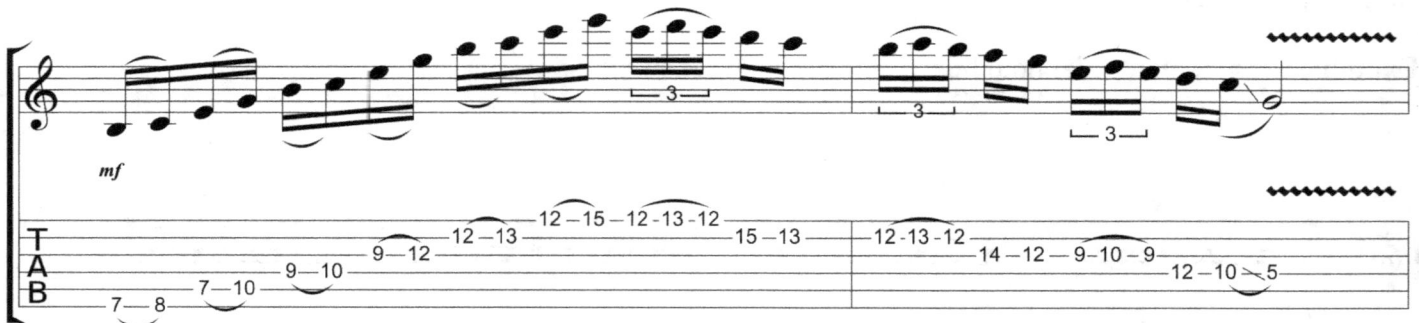

You may have noticed there are several position shifts in this lick. The shifts help avoid this becoming a linear, predictable sounding run.

The next lick uses position three of the A Minor pentatonic scale and ascends in groups of five, using legato technique. There's a sliding position shift into a descending Cmaj7 arpeggio.

Example 1u: A Minor pentatonic with five-note groupings and string skip descending Cmaj7 arpeggio

Did you notice the multiple slides in that lick? I'd like to point out that SLIDES ARE YOUR FRIEND. Not only is sliding a useful, expressive technique, it can also make position shifts seamless and less clunky.

Example 1v uses the first position of the A Minor pentatonic scale, but is played with many string skips. Pay attention to the legato emphasis and be wary of the complications that can occur during string skips!

Example 1v: String skipped legato A Minor pentatonic lick with minor 6th and b5 notes

One cool thing you may have noticed is that string skips create less predictable intervals. It's a very basic trick to make the delivery of a scale or arpeggio more interesting. This intervallic approach need not be limited to the pentatonic, however – it's useable in all scales and modes.

The final example of this chapter uses the three-note-per-string C Ionian scale shape again. It uses a rolling legato technique descending, while adding a few tapped notes which are diatonic to the scale. This adds flavour and a degree of surprise.

Example 1w: C Ionian descending legato lick with taps

It's important to remember that all the C Ionian ideas you've learnt can be modulated to other Ionian keys. Find some jam tracks in different keys to practise over and try your best to nail that happy, cheery major Ionian sound with the notes you play. If your audience is smiling, you're doing it right!

Chapter 2: Deciphering Dorian

Our modal journey continues and we venture into the void of Dorian. This mode is an absolute delight to listen to and play, as it highlights some sexy aspects of minor modality. Yet, it has some of the uplifting qualities of the major too. An extremely versatile mode, it is found in multiple music genres including country, jazz, blues, fusion and lots of RnB.

Dorian is classed as a minor mode due to its b3 interval. Remember that in a scale or chord, 3 = major, b3 = minor.

Dorian is the second of the seven diatonic modes. I often refer to it as "a minor scale with a sense of hope" or "the Pink Floyd mode". Pink Floyd used the Dorian mode poignantly and tastefully to stir great emotion in songs like *The Great Big Gig in the Sky* and *Shine on You Crazy Diamond*.

This mode is also used to great effect in the soundtrack to *The Hobbit* and all of the *Lord of the Rings* films – often to underline the trouble and adversity the hobbits will face, along with their ability to overcome it with the power of friendship and determination.

Dorian is commonly used in jazz, fusion and sometimes rock music. The only thing that differentiates it from the more common and traditional Aeolian mode is that the Dorian scale has a *natural* 6th note (often referred to as the major 6th) and Aeolian has a b6. This single note is the only difference between Dorian and Aeolian, but it makes a huge difference in sound. Really! The difference a single note can make is unbelievable! We haven't even got to Lydian yet… that'll blow you away!

Part 1: Finding the Dorian sound

Let's begin by listening to the sound of this mode in a simple, one octave format. Again, listen out for the relationship between the intervals which yield its distinctive sound. Pay attention as well to the mood it creates and think about how you can convey this in your music.

In this chapter we will switch to the key of F Major and use G Dorian for all the examples.

Let's take a look at the G Dorian scale played to one octave.

Example 2a:

While it's important to learn Dorian as a sound in its own right, in the back of your mind it's important to know that the Dorian mode is just like the Aeolian mode but with a natural 6th. In the diagram below we have G Aeolian and G Dorian side by side.

Example 2b:

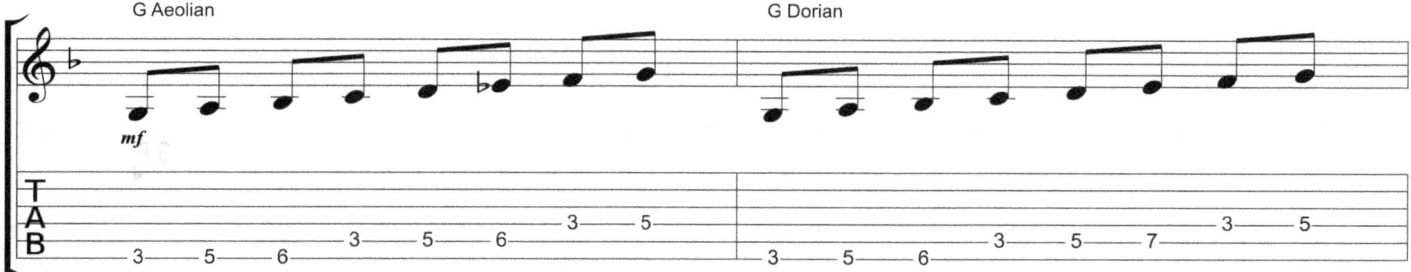

Aeolian scale formula = 1 2 b3 4 5 b6 b7

Dorian scale formula = 1 2 b3 4 5 6 b7

As the Aeolian is the most common minor mode, it's a useful yardstick to help describe the other minor modes (Dorian, Phrygian, and Locrian), just as the Ionian is a great yardstick for the major modes.

The b3 gives the Dorian its minor sound, making it sound sad, but its natural 6th injects an uplifting, hopeful undertone, so it's definitely not as sombre as the Aeolian. The Aeolian has a semitone interval between the fifth and sixth notes, whereas the Dorian has a full tone. It's this full tone "character" note that produces its signature sound – a small injection of hope. Though it's a subtle difference, the natural 6th is more positive sounding than the melancholy minor 6th of the Aeolian.

Though comparing the two scales is a great way to see how they differ, it doesn't give us enough of an understanding of how Dorian will work in context over music. Play through this simple two-chord progression and then play through the ascending and descending versions of the scale. Then try it over the G Dorian backing track.

Example 2c: G Dorian chord progression with scale ascend & descend

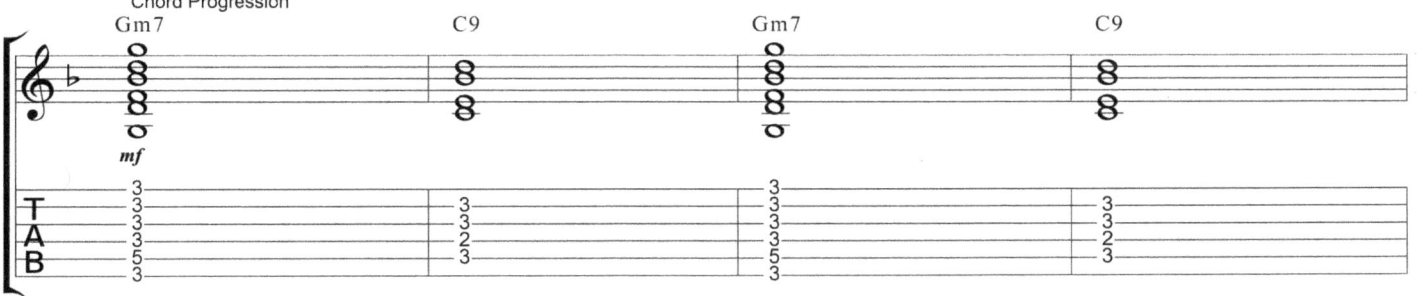

131

Scale Runs

You will notice that the characteristic 6th note (E) reacts with the Gm7 chord to create a Gm6 sound. Gm6 is made up of G, Bb, D and E, and has that characteristically Dorian sound.

The E note is also present as the major 3rd in the C9 chord, which is made up of C, E, Bb and D. We can hear the interplay between the chords and the scale creating a sombre minor feel that's followed immediately by a hopeful major lift. This is a very simple way to create an understanding of the Dorian sound and how you feel when you hear it.

Here are some reference songs that contain the characteristic Dorian sound:

- The Unforgiven – Metallica
- Mad World – Tears For Fears
- Wicked Game – Chris Isaak
- The Extremist – Joe Satriani
- Whatta Man – Salt N' Pepa

Part 2: The Dorian diatonic chords

As discussed, it's important to understand the diatonic chords belonging to each mode because it helps us to determine how to highlight the mode's colour and emotion. Let's look at the diatonic chords of the Dorian mode compared to the Ionian mode.

Diatonic chords built from Ionian:

maj	min	min	maj	maj	min	min7b5
I	ii	iii	IV	V	vi	vii

Diatonic chords built from Dorian:

min	min	maj	maj	min	min7b5	maj
i	ii	bIII	IV	v	vi	bVII

The previous diagram shows that the first chord of the harmonised Dorian scale is minor, whereas in Ionian it's major. The first (tonic) chord is always the most important in defining the mood of the scale, so you can already see that Dorian and Ionian will sound very different. What other differences can you spot in the harmonised scale?

In the same way that we built chords by harmonising the Ionian mode, we can do the same with the Dorian mode to give us the G Dorian chord structure:

Example 2d:

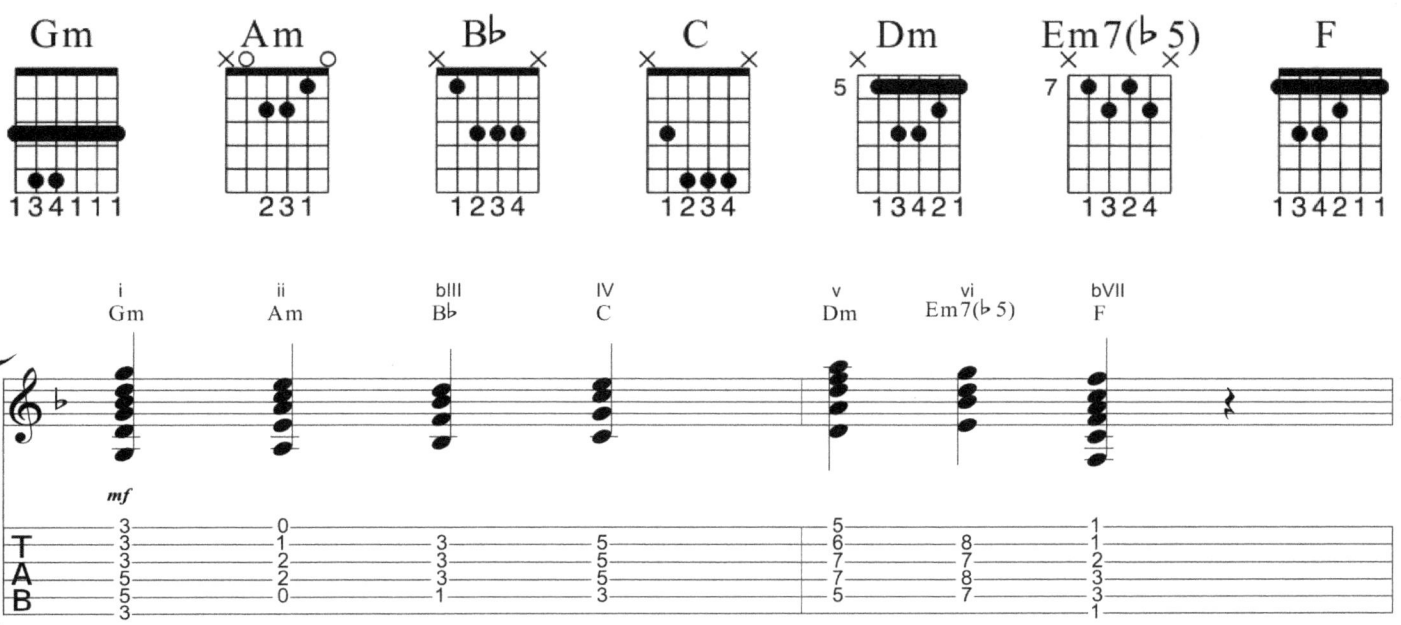

When composing using a mode, we want to choose chords that reflect its characteristic sound. In the case of the Dorian, we can highlight that natural 6th. The natural 6th (an E note in the key of G Dorian) occurs in the chords C Major, Am and Em7b5.

C Major (IV chord) = C E G

Am (ii chord) = A C E

Em7b5 (vi chord) = E G Bb D

Of course, we normally want to include the tonic chord (Gm) too!

Try composing some Dorian chord progressions of your own, keeping in mind to highlight the characteristic sound of the mode. Try to begin and end with a Gm chord. Here are a couple of suggestions to start you off:

Example 2e – Progression 1:

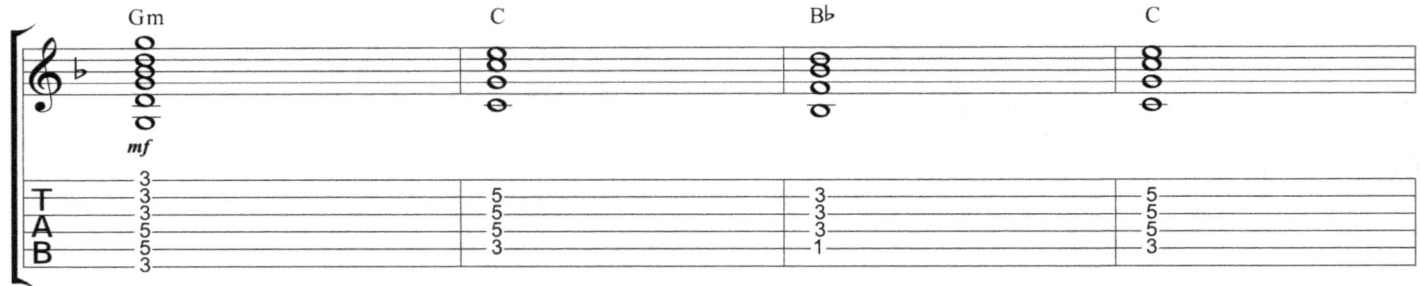

Example 2f – Progression 2:

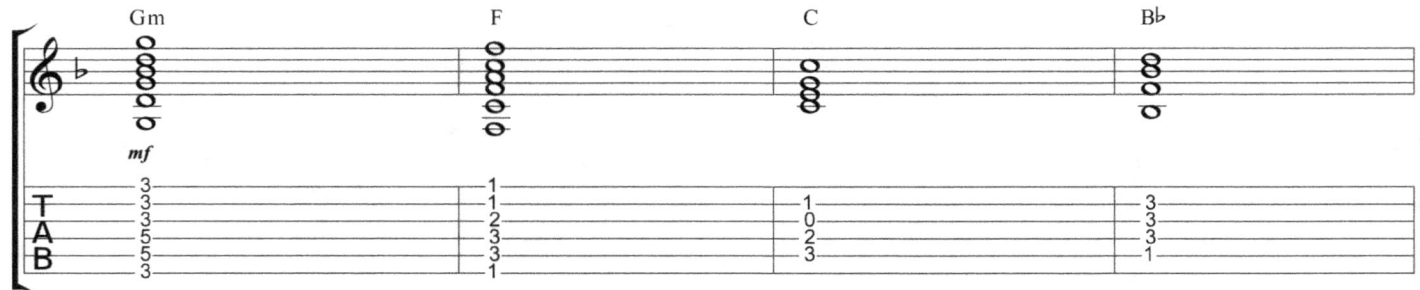

Part 3: Soloing in Dorian with scales and arpeggios

The early stages of modal improvisation and composition can be daunting and it's often hard to know where to begin. My approach to solo writing and improvisation using the Dorian mode uses the same checklist as the previous chapter:

1. What is the three-note-per-string pattern for this mode from the root?

2. What kind of pentatonics can I use e.g. regular, custom or relative minor?

3. What kinds of arpeggios will bring out the flavour of the mode?

First, let's take our G Dorian scale from the start of this chapter and stretch it across six strings with a three-note-per-string pattern. Try it over the Dorian backing track.

Example 2g:

This is the quickest way to hear the Dorian mode working across two and a bit octaves. It's also a good shape to use for solos if you're new to the Dorian. When improvising, I like to highlight:

- The b3rd (Bb in the case of G Dorian) – it's what gives it its sadder, melancholy sound

- The major 6th (E in G Dorian) – it's the most flavoursome note; the natural 6th note gives this scale its bittersweet quality – an unexpected lift you don't find in typical minor scales.

Pentatonics

Let's talk pentatonics – *ye olde faithful* of scales for improvisation. Dorian is a minor mode, so we can play it using regular minor pentatonic patterns made up from the 1st, 3rd, 4th, 5th and 7th degrees of the scale.

Omitting the 2nd and 6th degrees is a smart thing to do, because it leaves us with "neutral" notes that can work in other modal contexts (Aeolian and Phrygian) as well as Dorian. Here is G Dorian starting from the root, expressed as the familiar pentatonic shape we all know and love.

Example 2h:

This simple shape won't sound out of place over any Dorian chord progression, but let's hear it again, adding in that characteristic major 6th note (E). This is so easy to do, but adds so much expression.

Example 2i:

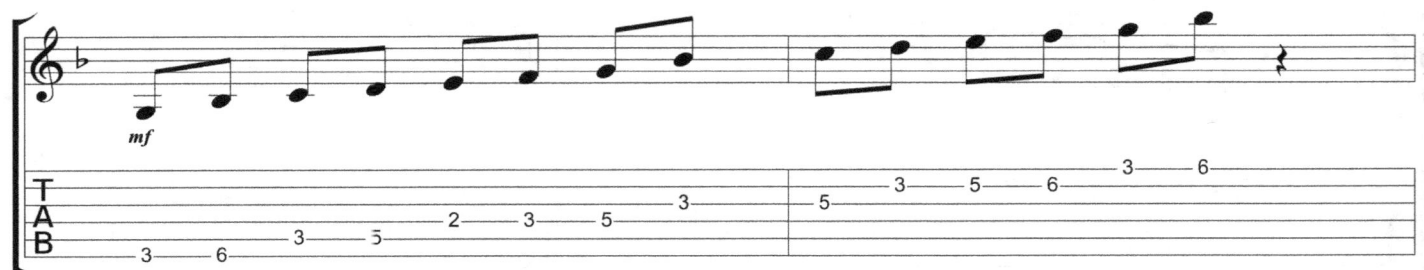

I use this latter shape all the time. You can hear the full effect of adding in the major 6th note when jamming over a Dorian chord progression. Below I've illustrated the other four positions of our pentatonic scale. For each position there is a version without, then with the major 6th, so you can really hear the difference.

Example 2j:

Position 2 Gm Pentatonic — Position 2 Gm Pentatonic + major 6th

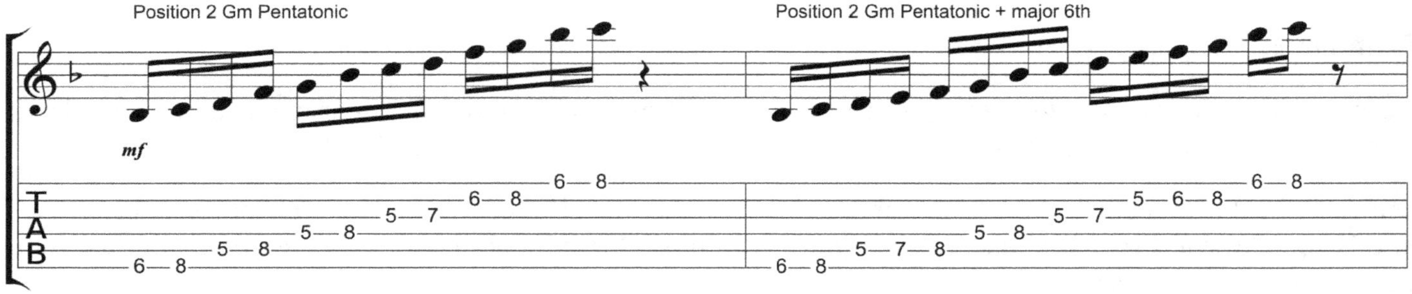

Position 3 Gm Pentatonic — Position 3 Gm Pentatonic + major 6th

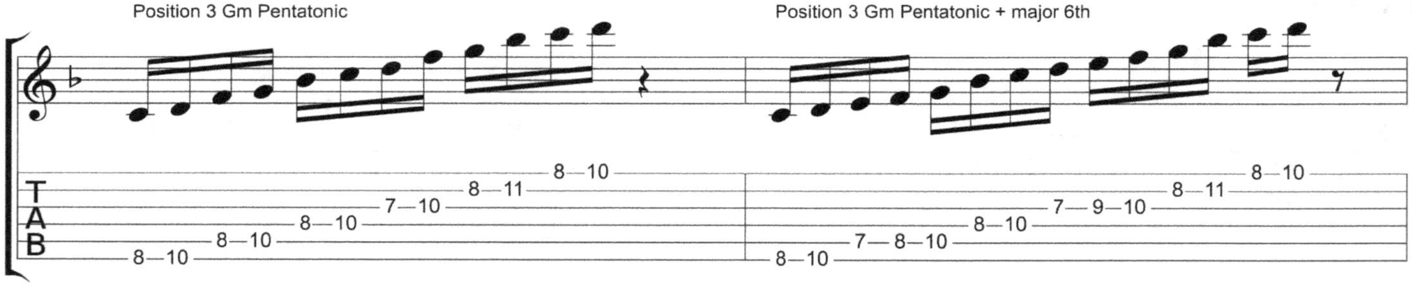

Position 4 Gm Pentatonic — Position 4 Gm Pentatonic + major 6th

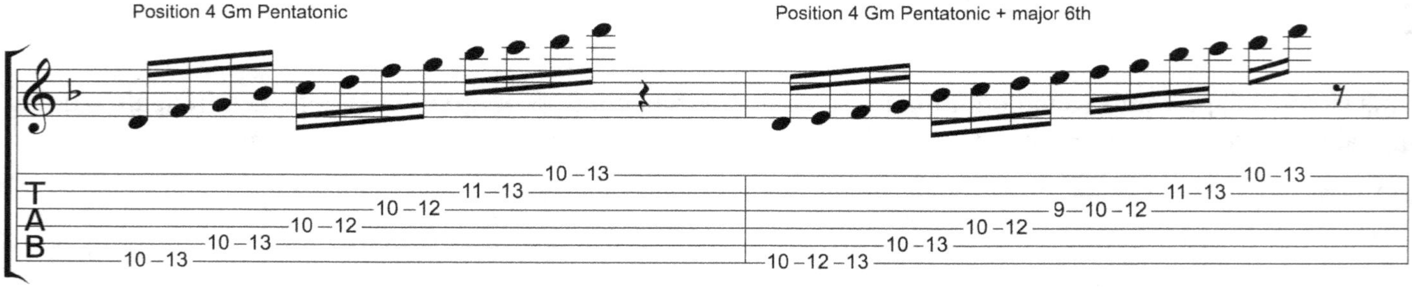

Arpeggios

Now let's accentuate the Dorian flavour using arpeggios. Example 2k illustrates a basic G Minor arpeggio with added major 6th.

Side note/stunning fact: The basic G Minor triad consists of the notes G, Bb and D. The addition of the major 6th (E) turns it into a Gm6. Coincidentally, Gm6 shares all the same notes as Em7b5 (E half-diminished). If you're struggling to play something over a pesky Em7b5 chord, G Dorian works amazingly well.

Example 2k:

This works to perfectly highlight the i or vi chords in a Dorian progression, but also works well used casually over a droning Dorian riff. We could also use a Gm7 arpeggio (G Bb D F) and add in the E again:

Example 2l:

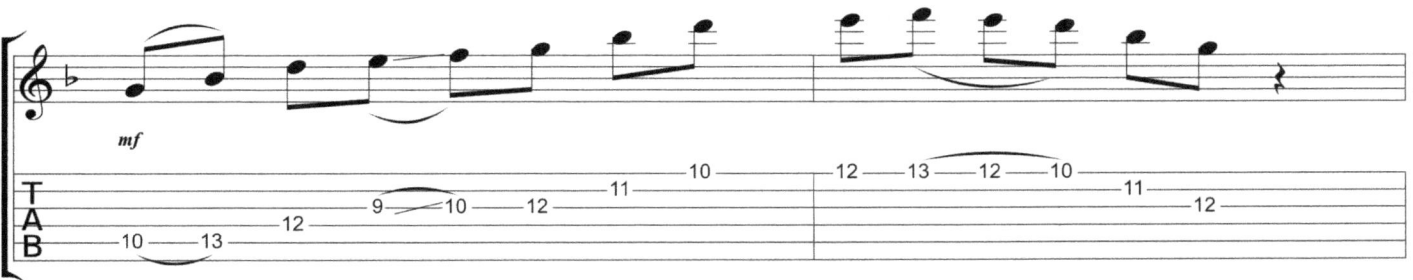

These arpeggios with the special major 6th will sound good over a ii minor chord in any key. And don't forget your Dorian secret weapon when confronted with a m7b5 chord. Dorian is a very versatile mode and can be used in many musical situations.

Part 4: Dorian licks to help you get creative

I've prepared a few licks in G Dorian based on the diatonic and pentatonic scale shapes we've discussed, as well as some arpeggios. These will help you to see how the Dorian can be applied melodically in an expressive, musical context.

The first example uses a simple G Minor pentatonic lick with a cheeky bend from the E note. This is a great way to highlight the natural 6th while keeping things bluesy. Players like Stevie Ray Vaughn, David Gilmour and Joe Bonamassa use this approach frequently when a Dorian situation presents itself.

Example 2m: Bluesy lick with Dorian 6th

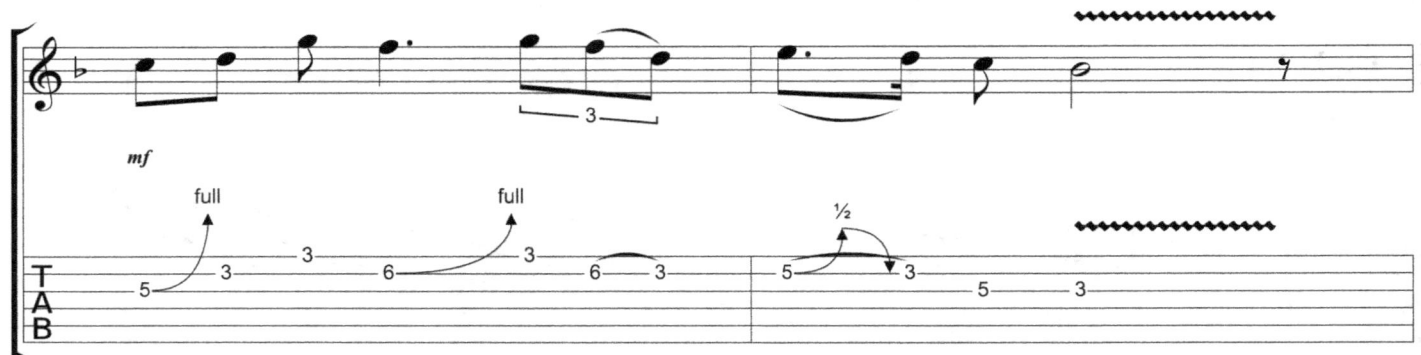

This kind of lick works well over the i chord (Gm) in a Dorian progression, but is also compatible with the IV chord (C7) as it highlights the major 3rd and resolves to the b7 (Bb) note.

Example 2n is a simple three-note-per-string ascending run. To make it less monotonous I've included a few hammer-ons and pull-offs to vary the timing. I've also included a bend from an "outside" note (because that's what cool people do).

Stylistically, it's reminiscent of Mark Tremonti and Slash. I've seen both players use this little trick over diatonic runs to make them more interesting and less linear. You can, of course, apply this approach to any mode using its three-note-per-string scale shape.

Example 2n: Tremonti-style G Dorian three-note-per-string ascending lick

This next idea uses G Minor pentatonic with an added "blue" grace note and a run that descends diatonically through G Dorian.

Example 2o: G Minor pentatonic with blue grace note and major 6th

Joining pentatonic and diatonic scales together is always refreshing to hear. It has melodic impact because the pentatonic scale has no semitone intervals, yet the diatonic scale does. This means you can quickly jump from a rocky-blues sound to something more heart-warming, emotional and bittersweet. Be wary when playing passages like this that you resolve to a note that complements the backing chords. Choose a specific note e.g. ending the run on a Bb over a Gm7 chord to highlight the minor 3rd.

Example 2p combines a basic G Minor triad arpeggio with descending diatonic notes from the Dorian scale.

Example 2p: Five-string G Minor arpeggio with G Dorian diatonic descent

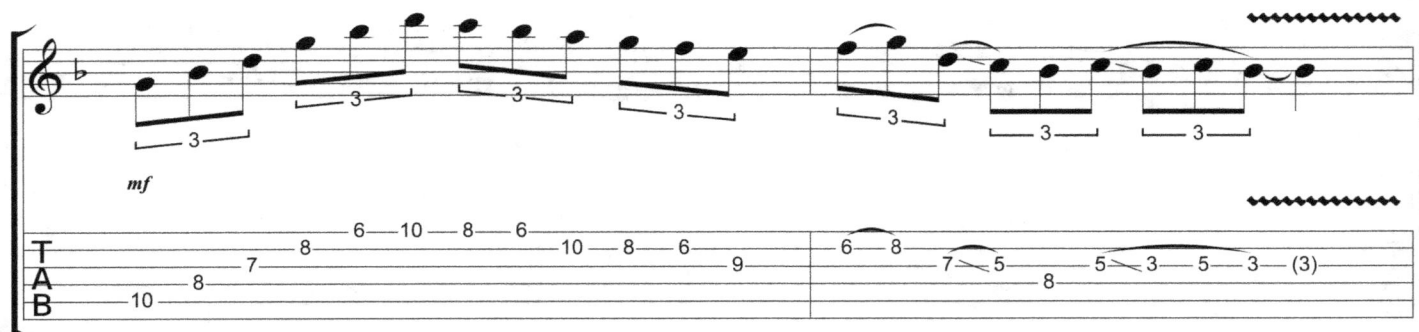

Licks like this can be executed as a slow arpeggio or a quick sweep – it's completely up to you and will depend on your taste and what you think fits the song, composition or solo. I've heard Alexi Laiho from Children of Bodom use licks like this to make his entry into a fast, long descending run more triumphant. You will also notice that I've added slides to make the phrase more interesting and give it some flair. This also forces you to shift to a different section of the neck.

This next lick is based around a Gm7 arpeggio with an added E note to get more of the Dorian major 6th flavour.

Example 2q: Gm7 arpeggio with added major 6th

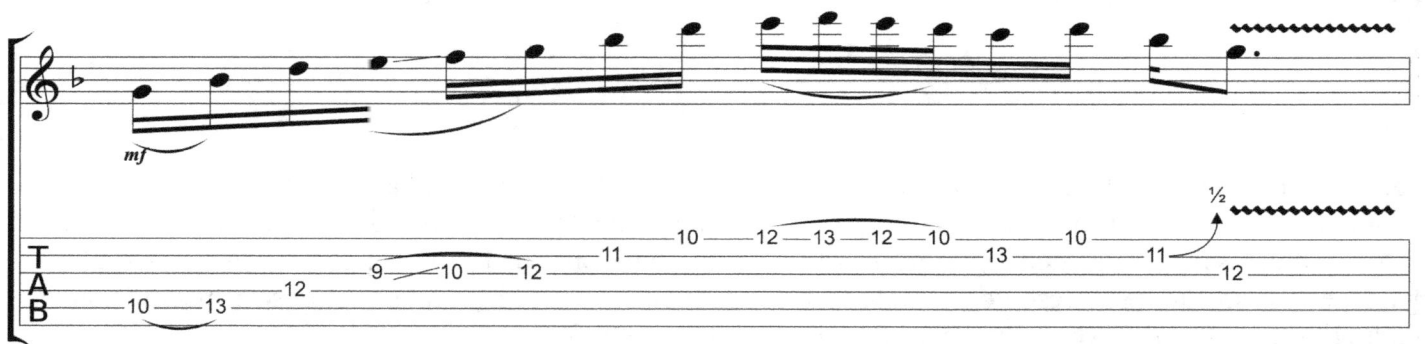

You can mess around with various expressive techniques to make arpeggios (and scales) sound less mechanical. In this instance I used slides, legato and a cheeky bend to give the phrase more feeling and add a fleeting moment of sexy blues.

The next lick features a concept I touched on earlier that I use all the time in Dorian soloing. When playing in G Dorian, the i chord (Gm) can be used as a substitute for the vi chord (Em7b5). Therefore, the reverse is true: the vi chord can substitute for the i chord. Example 2r uses the notes of Em7b5 (E G Bb D) over a G Minor chord. The note order has been rearranged to make the lick less boring and linear sounding.

Example 2r: Em7b5 arpeggio 1 3 2 4 3 5 lick

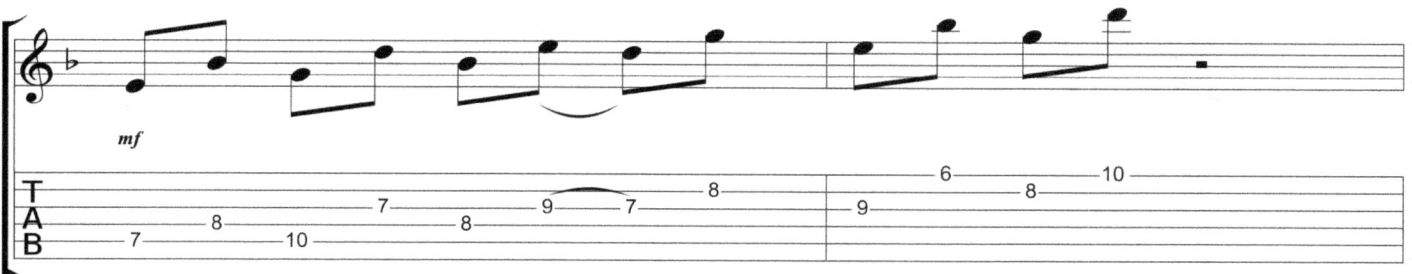

Notice that the notes used in the previous example are essentially a Gm triad (G Bb D) with an E note at the front. Once again we're highlighting that delicious Dorian note. For a great example of this, listen to Marty Friedman's solo on *Symphony of Destruction* by Megadeth. He plays an F#m7b5 arpeggio (ii chord in the key of E Minor) over the A Minor backing chord (chord iv in E Minor). It's well supported by the music and sounds more interesting than straight ascending and descending arpeggio triads.

The next example uses another Em7b5 arpeggio, but rearranges the order of the notes to make a simple, cool movable shape you can use across three octaves. It also uses a few mini-arpeggio triads in the descending part of the lick.

Example 2s: Crawling three octave Em7b5 arpeggio lick with descending mini arpeggios

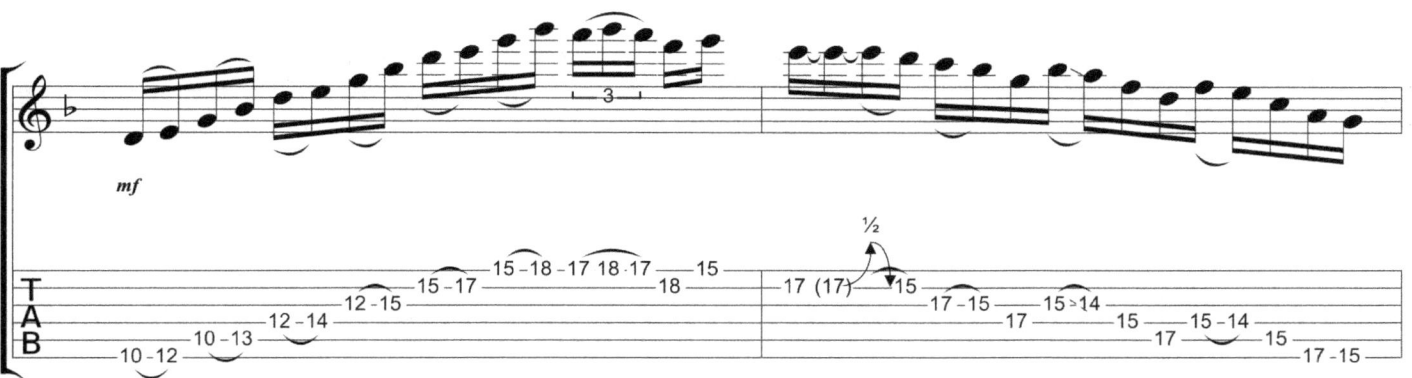

In the next lick we'll be using position four of the G Minor pentatonic scale in an ascending manner with legato five-note groupings. The lick resolves with a descending Gm7 arpeggio with an added major 6th, once again hammering home that Dorian sound.

Example 2t: G Minor pentatonic position four with five-note legato groupings and Gm7 descending arpeggio

As you can see, the lick ends with a bend from a Db note. This is not from the G Dorian scale but is, however, the b5 of G. If we bend it up a semitone, the effect is to change a tense, outside note into a pleasant "in key" note. In this instance I've bent the Db to a D note, the fifth of G.

Example 2u takes a simple G Minor pentatonic shape in the first position with the addition of the major 6th and some tapped notes. The tapped notes suggest G Minor pentatonic in the second position. The fretting hand will occasionally highlight the E note for a more characteristically Dorian sound.

Example 2u: G Minor pentatonic with major 6th and tapped notes

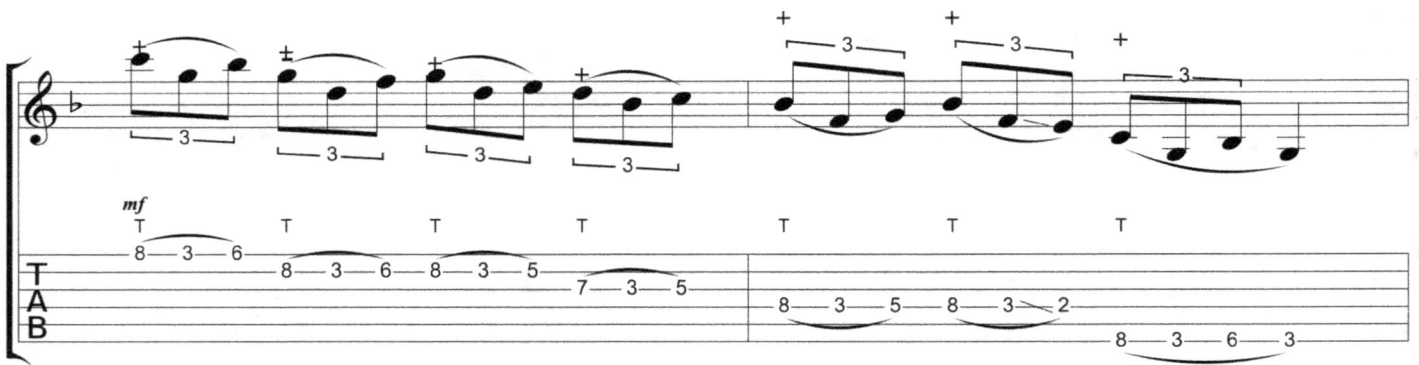

This last lick is easily the silliest and most terrifying. We're going to combine an ascending Per Nilsson style Gm11 arpeggio with a descending Em7b5 arpeggio. This lick also includes a few outside notes, borrowed from the three-note-per-string Lydian diatonic scale shape, but we won't worry about that now!

Example 2v: Gm11 into Em7b5 arpeggio lick with ascending Dorian diatonic notes

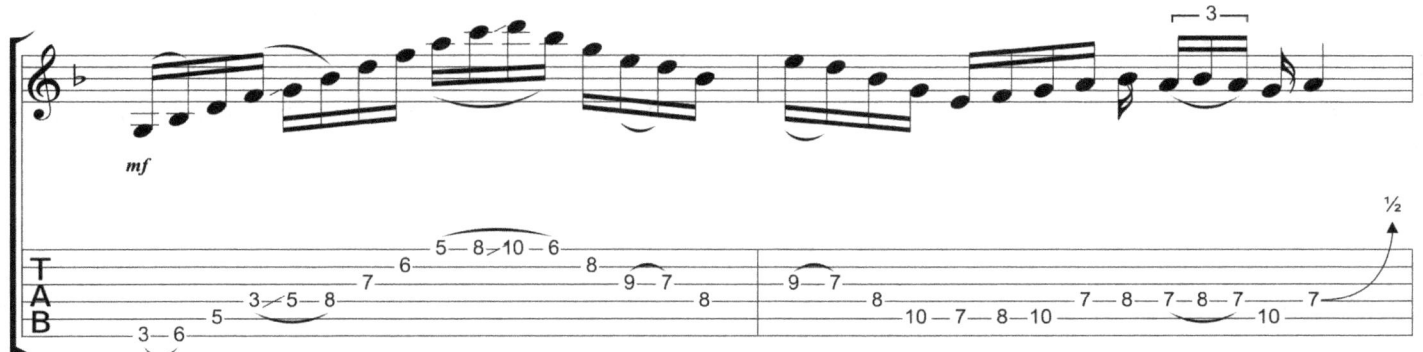

Again, a lick like this forces you to make a position shift. It's a cool way of covering a large distance on the neck and is especially helpful if you have a tendency to get trapped in box positions. You may just like the feeling of longer, more horizontal passages. #whateverfloatsyourboat

Every lick we've learnt in this chapter can be transferred to other keys. Find some jam tracks or Dorian songs to play along to and try out these ideas. The more you play and listen, the more you'll uncover that bittersweet Dorian emotion that has been dying to come out of you.

Chapter 3: Phabulous Phrygian

Since the dark ages, a melodic evil, a mode of great power, has lived at the centre of the earth. It has been foretold in stories of folklore, superstition and urban legend that this mode is the last thing you hear before … being chased and eaten by a shark. Of course, I'm referring to the Phrygian mode.

Phrygian is the third of the seven diatonic modes. It's signature tense, foreboding sound has been used in everything from flamenco to thrash metal and, indeed, any other sub-genres seeking to attain a satanic sounding edge.

Part 1: Finding the Phrygian sound

In this chapter, the B Phrygian mode will be used for all our examples. Let's start by looking at a B Phrygian scale in one octave.

Example 3a:

As always, we should learn every mode as an individual scale in its own right, but it doesn't hurt to bear a few things in mind. B Phrygian can be viewed in a couple of ways:

1. As the third mode of G Major.

2. As a B Aeolian (Natural Minor) scale with a b2.

It's easy to see this if we compare B Aeolian and B Phrygian side by side.

B Aeolian = B **C#** D E F# G A

B Phrygian = B **C** D E F# G A B

Example 3b:

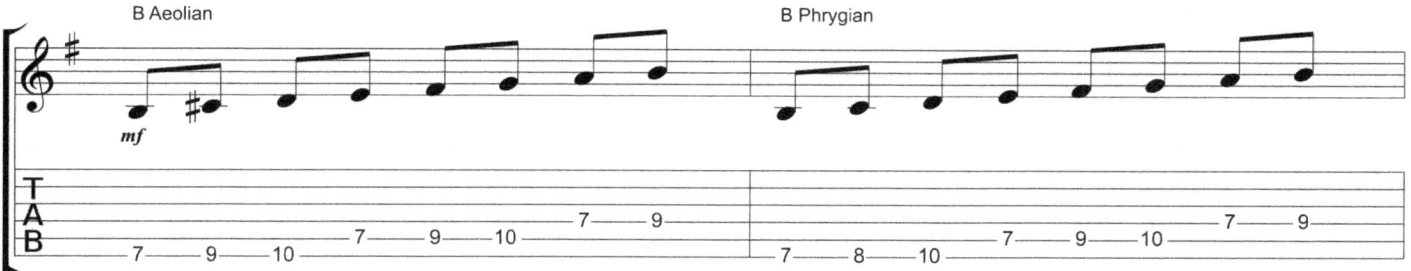

Aeolian scale formula = 1 2 b3 4 5 b6 b7

Phrygian scale formula = 1 b2 b3 4 5 b6 b7

The only difference between the two modes is the second note. The Aeolian mode has a full tone between root and second (B to C#). The Phrygian has just a semitone (B to C), which creates a very tense sound. Just as the major 6th was the "character" note of the Dorian mode, the b2 provides the Phrygian's signature evil sound.

Thinking of the Phrygian mode as "a minor scale with a b2" might seem like enough to get a theoretical understanding of the mode's sound, but the best way to hear a mode's characteristic sound is in context, with a chord progression.

We can hear the Phrygian's characteristic b2 interval by playing it over the simple chord progression shown below. Play through the power-chord progression, then play through the descending and ascending version of the scale.

Try this over the Phrygian backing track too!

Example 3c: B Phrygian chord progression with scale descend & ascend

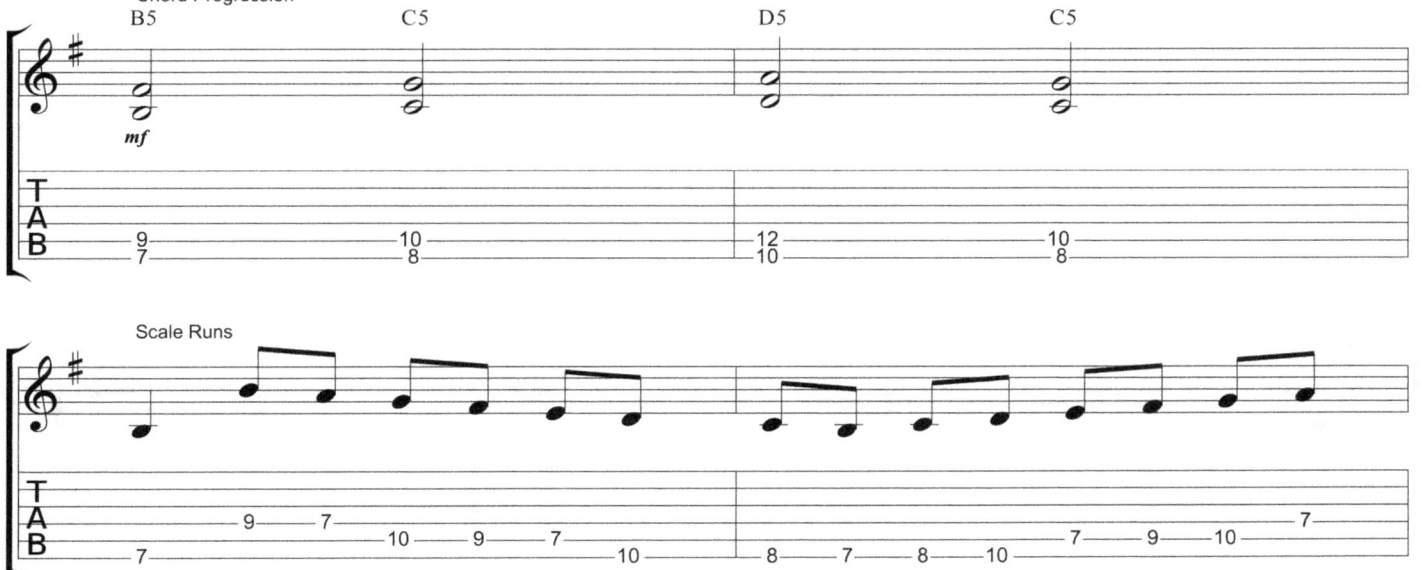

145

The b2 is an outright tense interval, as it forms a semitone clash with the tonic home note (B). We can hear this in the interplay between the B5 and C5 chord. The C note from the B Phrygian scale is obviously present in the C5 chord, and you can the Phrygian mode's characteristic b2 in both the power-chords and the descending and ascending scale runs immediately after.

It's no wonder that the Phrygian is the go-to mode for thrash metal, nu-metal and for conjuring up tension in film scores. Who could forget the shark attack scenes in the *Jaws* films? Possibly the best and most effective use of the Phrygian mode EVER! It's abrasive, dark quality also makes it the perfect mode for adding drama and intensity to flamenco music.

To further familiarise yourself with the Phrygian mode's characteristic sound, have a listen to these Phrygian-based songs:

- Symphony of Destruction – Megadeth
- Wherever I May Roam – Metallica
- Over the Wall – Testament
- She Wants To Move – N.E.R.D.
- White Rabbit – Jefferson Airplane

Part 2: The Phrygian diatonic chords

In the case of the Phrygian, the semitone relationship between the i and the bII chords creates the most poignant tension and produces its signature sound. Let's take a look at the diatonic chords of the Phrygian mode compared to the Ionian.

Diatonic chords built from Ionian

maj	min	min	maj	maj	min	min7b5 (or 1/2 diminished)
I	ii	iii	IV	V	vi	vii

Diatonic chords built from Phrygian

min	maj	maj	min	min7b5	maj	min
i	bII	bIII	iv	v	bVI	bvii

Example 3d:

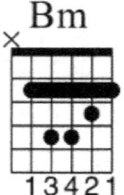 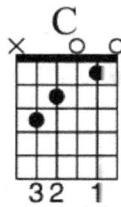 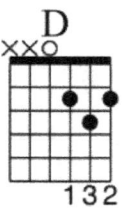 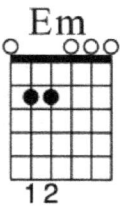 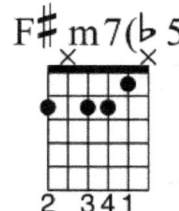 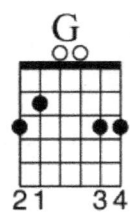 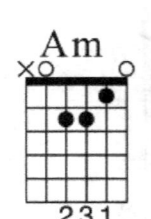

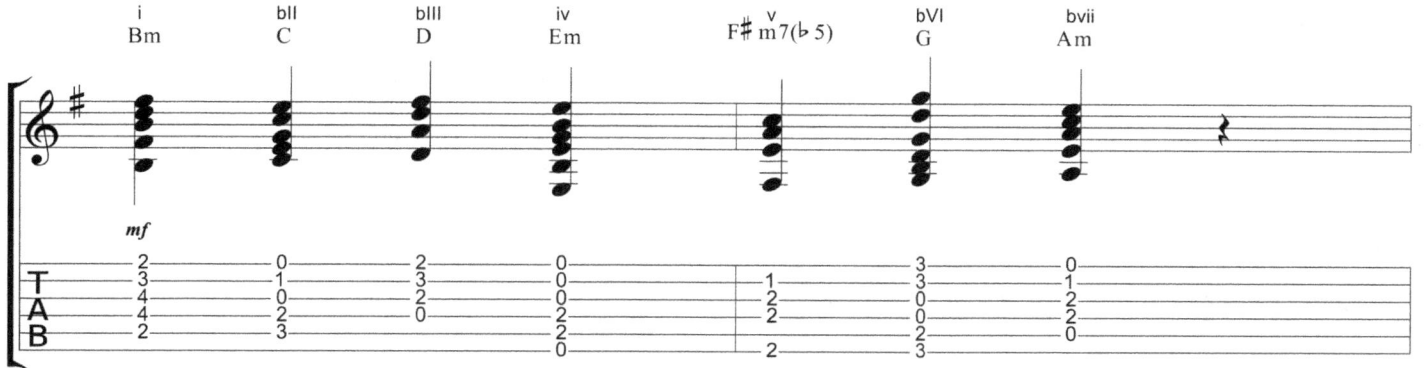

When composing using a mode, we want to pick chords that reflect its distinct character and feeling. In the case of the Phrygian, we'll want to highlight the minor 2nd (b2). The easiest way to do this is to play any chord that contains the b2 flavour note. In B Phrygian, the b2 flavour note is C.

C Major (bII chord) = C E G

A Minor (bvii chord) = A C E

F#m7b5 (v chord) = F# A C E

Try writing a few progressions using these chords, preferably beginning and ending on B Minor. Here are two ideas to get you started:

Example 3e – Progression 1:

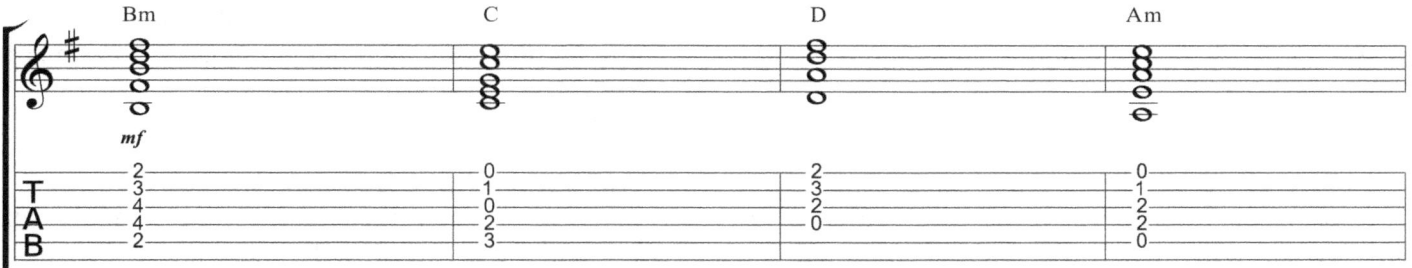

Example 3f – Progression 2:

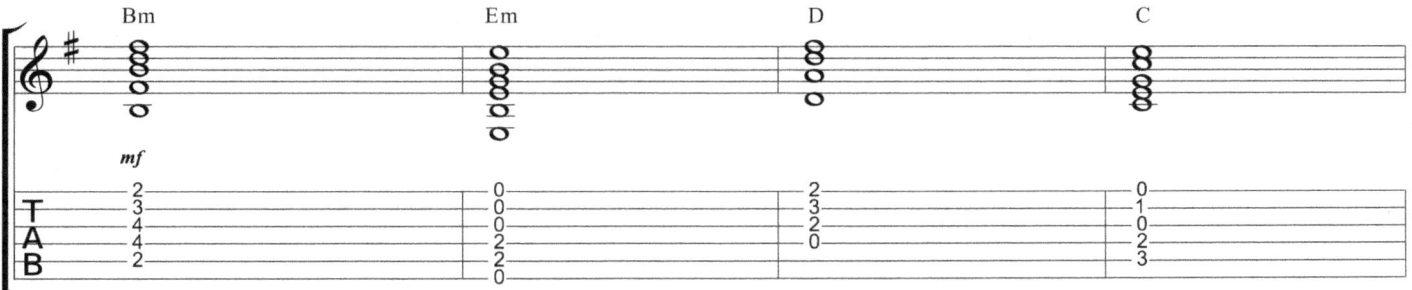

Part 3: Soloing in Phrygian using scales and arpeggios

I've said this 1,000 times, but it's often hard to know where to start when soloing modally! As usual, I ask myself these questions:

1. What is a three-note-per-string version of the scale from the root?

2. What kind of pentatonics can I use e.g. regular, custom or relative minor?

3. What kinds of arpeggios will bring out the flavour of the mode?

Let's take the diatonic B Phrygian scale and stretch it across six strings with a three-note-per-string pattern.

Example 3g:

This is a good scale shape to begin with if you're new to the Phrygian sound. Highlighting the minor 3rd (D) evokes the melancholy sound of the minor scale, but the b2 (C) is the most flavoursome note and the one I always try to emphasise.

Pentatonics

We know that the versatile minor pentatonic scale can work for all of the minor modes – Aeolian, Dorian and Phrygian. It uses the 1st, 3rd, 4th, 5th and 7th intervals only – thus omitting the b2. Here is a regular descending B Minor pentatonic pattern, and the same pattern with added b2.

Example 3h:

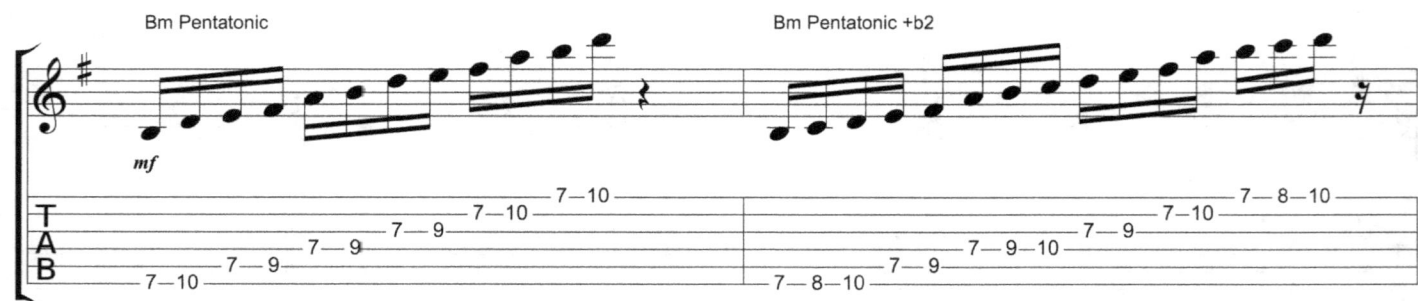

Let's look at the remaining four positions of B Minor pentatonic, comparing the regular scale and the scale with added b2, side by side.

Example 3i:

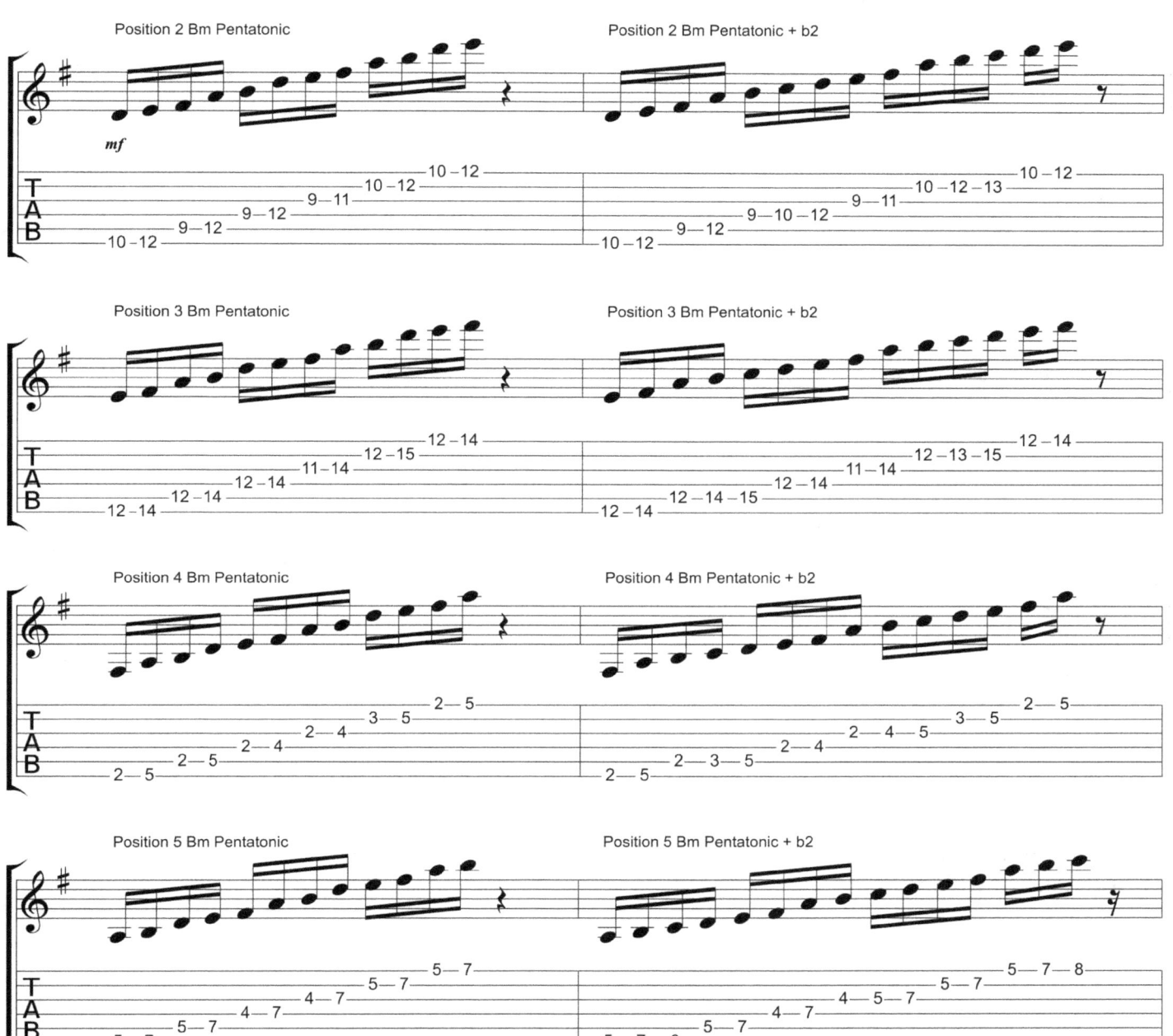

Remember that you can choose to add in the b2, or not, and switch between the two highlighting the Phrygian sound as appropriate.

Arpeggios

Lastly, let's look at how to *Phrygianize* (a term I just coined) our arpeggios. By this I mean to take a simple B Minor arpeggio and add in the b2 (C) to add modal flavour. Compare the two arpeggios below.

Example 3j:

Here is another common five-string minor arpeggio shape, and the same arpeggio with an added b2.

Example 3k:

Finally, this Bm7 arpeggio covers all six strings in a diagonal, crawling manner spanning three octaves. Here it is without, and with, the b2.

Example 3l:

All of these arpeggios are useful for Phrygian soloing and it's good to have options, but they can also be used over a iii chord in any progression or key. You can be subtle and stay with the straight minor, or highlight the more evil Phrygian sound in your playing. All these ideas will work extremely well in death metal, thrash metal and sassy flamenco.

Part 4: Phrygian licks to help you get creative

To avoid giving you a bunch of scales and arpeggio shapes and not showing you how to use them properly, I've prepared some licks to bring all these melodic ideas together in an expressive, musical context.

The first lick we'll look at uses a classic a Chuck Berry pentatonic lick in B Minor, but I've added a C note to introduce the Phrygian b2 sound.

The classic bluesy pentatonic approach with bends is a familiar sound, but the hammer-ons and pull-offs between the B and C notes on the first string create the semitone tension crucial to the Phrygian sound.

Example 3m: B Minor pentatonic Chuck Berry lick with b2 legato notes.

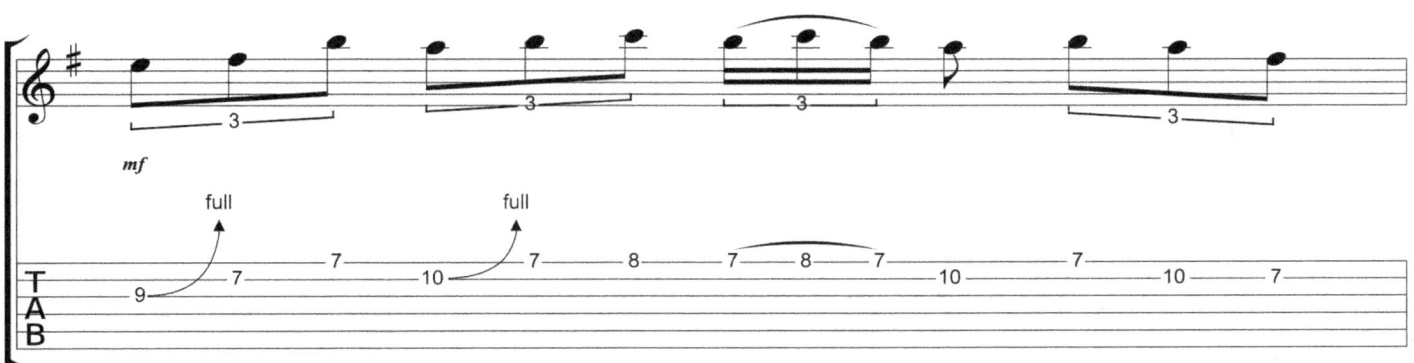

Example 3n uses another custom Phrygian pentatonic that spans multiple octaves. The notes used can also be viewed as the exotic E Hirajoshi scale (E F# G B C). To make the lick more interesting, it crawls in an ascending, diagonal manner that forces multiple position shifts over three octaves. This is much more interesting than a standard two-note-per-string vertical pentatonic box. I've also added a few hammer-ons for smoothness and pace.

Example 3n: Crawling E Hirajoshi with five-note groupings

I wasn't too creative with the order of the notes in this lick, but you can use it to create a shreddy build up to another lick. The main thing is that I've planted the seed of an idea for you to go away and be creative with!

This next idea uses a three-note-per-string B Phrygian scale shape across six strings. I'm using triplet shreds with the occasional cheeky moment of legato to keep things interesting. It's reminiscent of Trivium and Racer X. It's easy to fall into a monotonous pattern with three-note-per-string shapes, so mess around with different legato note placement and timing.

Example 3o: Racer X style B Phrygian building shred lick

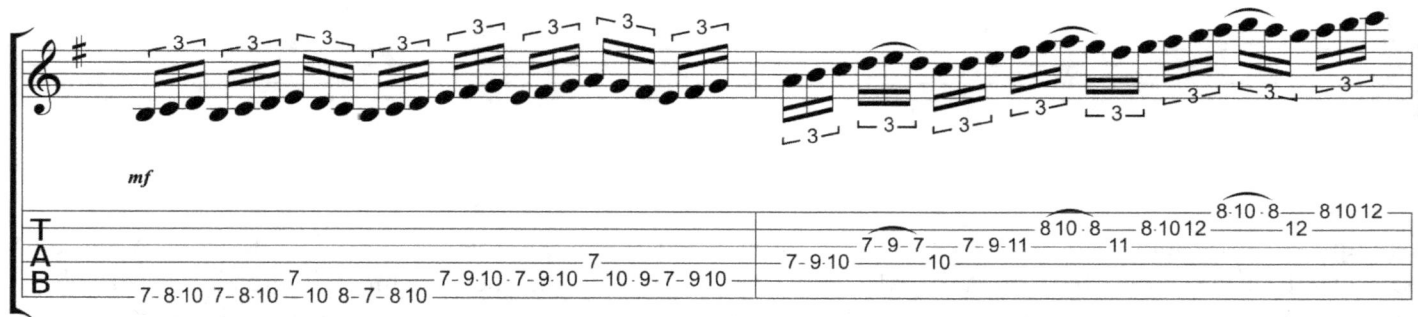

The next lick combines a simple five-string B Minor triad arpeggio with descending notes from the B Phrygian mode. The descending pattern suggests F# Locrian and I have used quavered triplets to add a bit of a swinging bounce to the lick.

Example 3p: Five-string B Minor arpeggio with F# Locrian three-note-per-string descent

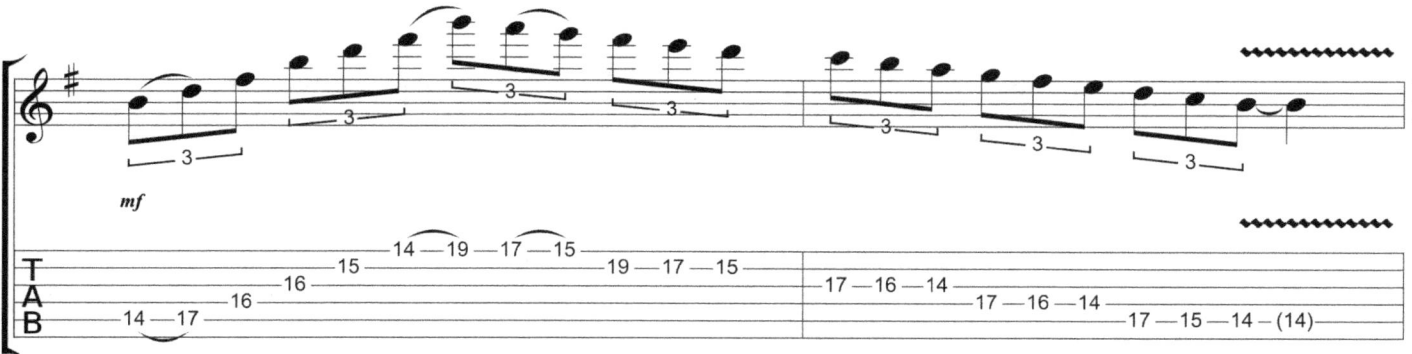

Combining arpeggios and diatonic runs adds interest to an otherwise straightforward descending lick. It means we can jump from the wider intervals of an arpeggio to the closer intervals of a scale. You can apply this idea to any mode and explore it using three-, four- and six-string arpeggios.

Example 3q uses a B pedal note. I tried to keep this lick mainly to one string as I've seen Kirk Hammett and Michael Paget (Bullet For My Valentine) do a similar thing in solos and it's always sounded cool to me. Pedal notes really help to build tension. As the Phrygian is already a tense sounding mode, adding in the pedalling technique makes it an unstoppable force… for evil! Experiment with adding a pedal note on a few different strings and see what you can come up with.

Example 3q: Pedal B Phrygian lick

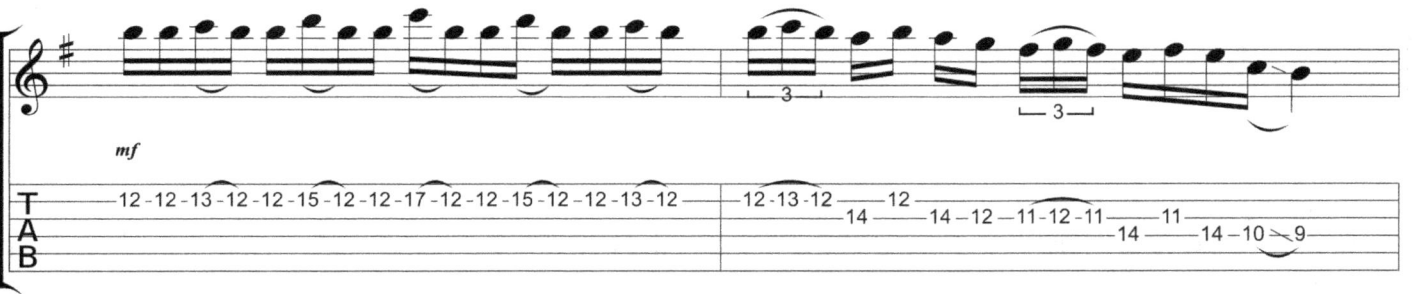

In the next example I thought it would be fun to give you a crazy arpeggio across all six strings using the 1st, 3rd, 5th, 7th, b9th (the b2 up an octave) and 11th intervals of the B Phrygian mode.

This would be a great way to start a solo or a cheeky lick for improvisation. It ticks all those nasty, tense Phrygian boxes. Be careful not to overuse an idea like this. Instead, think of it as a secret weapon for special occasions – like a bazooka loaded with Honey Badgers, or sword made entirely from liquorice (yes, I have just revealed my Kryptonite!)

Example 3r: Bm11(b9) sliding arpeggio lick

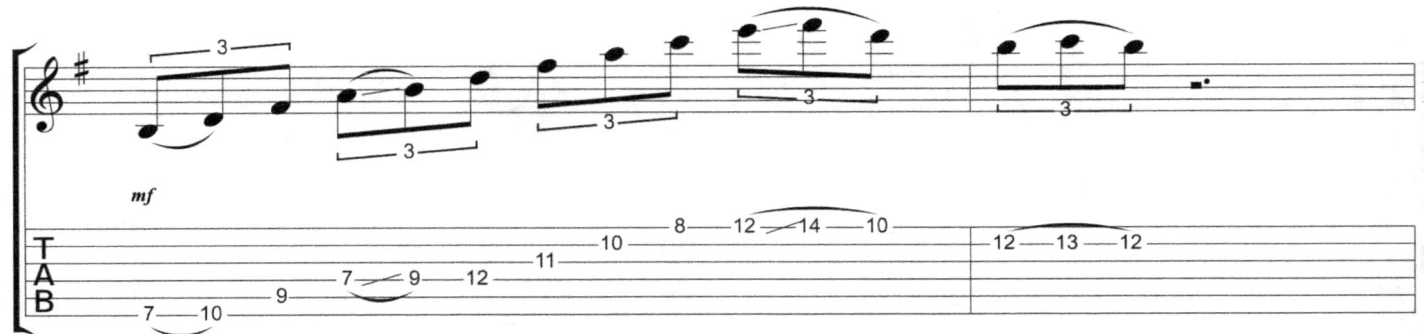

Here is an idea based on the B Phrygian three-note-per-string shape, which combines a few different techniques. It has fast triplet 1/16th notes played using rolling legato, with the addition of taps and strings skips.

Example 3s: B Phrygian three-note-per-string skipped legato lick with taps

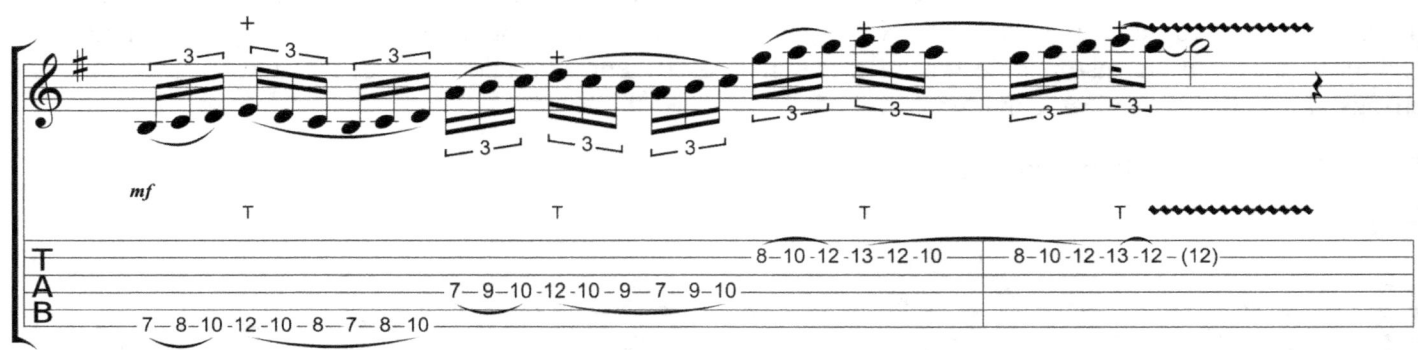

Using rolling legato and taps is a great way to create speed without shredding or sweeping. The string skips create interesting intervallic jumps mid-lick, to provide the listener with some melodic curve balls to keep them intrigued.

Example 3t uses a B Minor pentatonic shape with an added b2. One thing that's interesting about this lick is the inconsistency of the number of notes on each string. Three-note-per-string patterns can cause us to fall into the trap of predictable triplet runs or robotic shred. Using a pattern like this encourages us to think in a less formulaic, mathematical manner and forces much less predictable lines.

Example 3t: B Minor pentatonic with b2 legato lick

The next lick uses a classic rock descending B Minor triplet pattern, then shifts into an ascending scale run using a segment of the A Dorian three-note-per-string shape. We can use A Dorian in a B Phrygian context as both modes come from the same key of G Major, thus they share the same notes.

Example 3u: B Minor pentatonic descending triplet lick with A Dorian three-note-per-string ascent

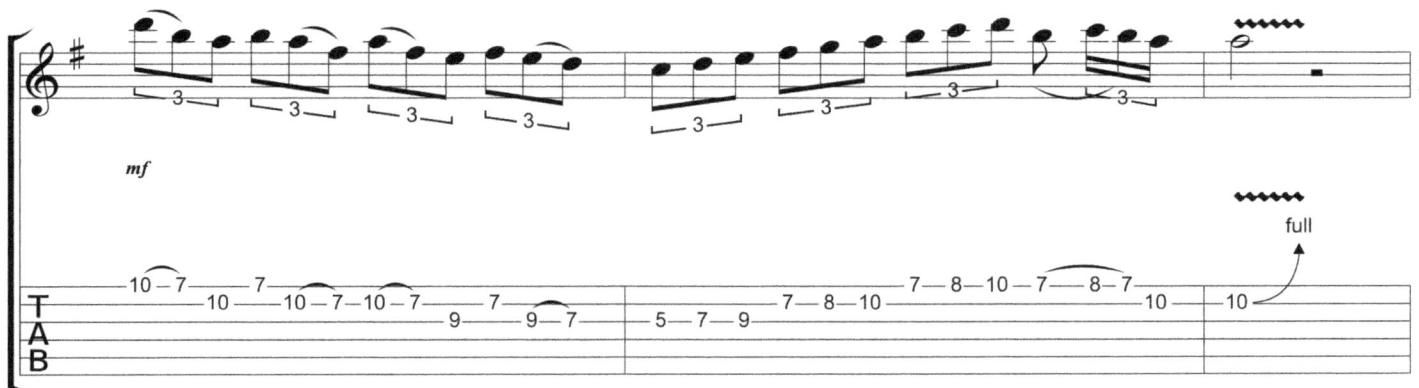

Our final lick uses another pedal idea with the open B string. It has a somewhat ACDC *Thunderstruck* vibe to it. John Petrucci and Alexi Laiho have used this kind of lick in many of their solos. You won't always have the option to use open strings in your licks, so if the opportunity presents itself, *go for it!*

Example 3v: Pedal on open B string lick

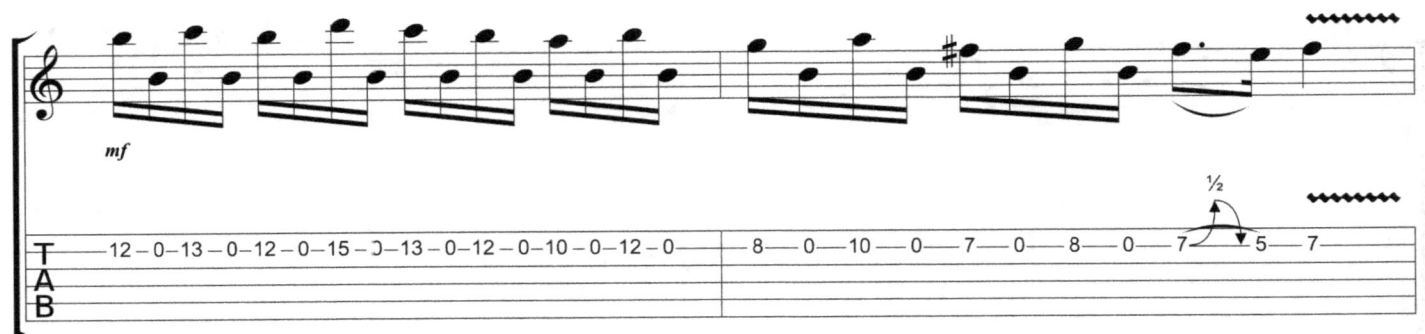

The main consideration with open string licks is just to make sure the fretted notes are derived from the scale. Example 3v is ideally to be used over a B Phrygian chord progression. The fretted note choices would be any combination of C, D, E, F#, G and A to remain in key.

As with all the modes, finding an appropriate jam track to practise to is essential. With any luck you'll summon the thrashy, flamenco beast-yeti-monster that has always lived within your soul and has been itching to come out!

Chapter 4: Luscious Lydian

The next stop on our modal journey plunges us into a misty void; a mysterious, galactic space kingdom known as *Lydian*. Allow me to set the scene that the Lydian mode is so well known for.

Imagine yourself travelling at the speed of light through multiple galaxies, or flying majestically through the air like that kid and the weird dragon dog from *The Never Ending Story* (his name is Falkor, I just Googled it). Imagine yourself casually opening a mysterious treasure chest. Mist flows out and reveals a golden sword, covered in flames. It can achieve many mighty purposes including making the perfect soufflé and has the ability to cure the common head cold.

Now imagine that you have to sit down and compose a soundtrack for all these zany adventures. It must capture feelings of excitement, mystery, uncertainty and surrealism. You feelin' me? Because if you are, we are ready for our Lydian musical adventure to begin.

The Lydian is the fourth of our seven modes and is a major mode, which means it has a generally happy sound. However, it has a raised (or *sharp*) fourth degree. Its #4 is its character note – the note that has been used in countless Sci-Fi and Fantasy film scores. In fact, it is identical to the Ionian mode except for that one note. It has also been used to great effect in many compositions by guitar virtuosos such as Steve Vai, Joe Satriani and John Petrucci. The Lydian mode has even been known to make the occasional appearance in progressive rock/metal.

Part 1: Finding the Lydian sound

In this chapter we will be using C Lydian for all our examples. Let's start by playing the C Lydian scale in one octave.

Example 4a:

We can think of C Lydian in two ways. Again (and I know you're getting bored of this now) it's important to learn the Lydian mode as an individual scale, but it doesn't hurt to know a few of its pseudonyms. Lydian is…

1. The fourth mode of the major scale

2. Identical to the major scale except for its #4 note

Let's compare C Ionian and C Lydian side by side:

C Ionian (C D E **F** G A B C)

C Lydian (C D E **F#** G A B C)

Example 4b:

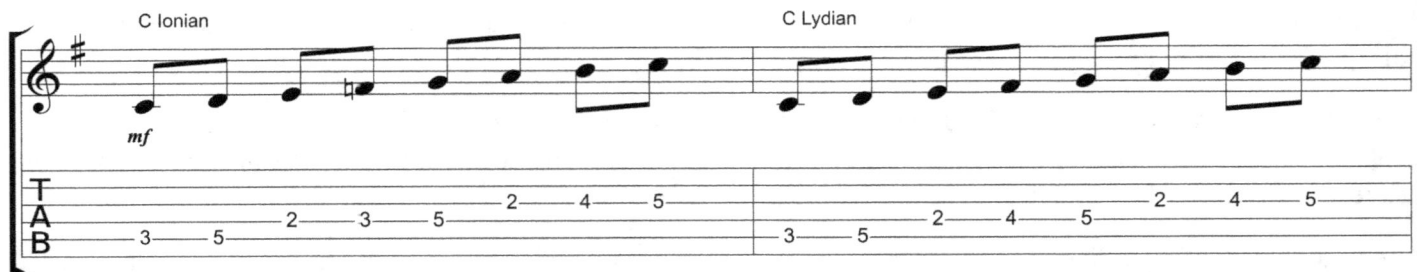

Ionian scale formula = 1 2 3 4 5 6 7

Lydian scale formula = 1 2 3 #4 5 6 7

As you can see, the only difference between the two scales is the fourth note. The Ionian mode has a semitone interval between the third and fourth notes, while the Lydian has a full tone, creating the raised 4th (#4).

The #4 is the most important note in the scale and what gives the Lydian its spacey, dreamlike and somewhat uplifting, characteristic sound.

Comparing the two scales mentioned above gives you a quick overview of the Lydian mode's intervals and differentiating characteristic note. However, having the knowledge that Lydian is essentially a "major scale with a #4" means very little if we have no understanding of how the scale works in context over chord progressions.

Let's look at a simple chord progression using characteristically Lydian sounding chords. We'll play two bars of chords and two bars of simple scale runs that ascend and descend. This will help you get used to not only the sound of the scale, but the chords that create the overall mood as well.

Play the following example and try the scale ideas over the Lydian backing track.

Example 4c: C Lydian chord progression with scale ascend & descend

The #4 (F#) note is the characteristic note of C Lydian and is included in the Cmaj7(#11) and D7 chords. When we combine the scale with these chords, we have a fuller understanding of the Lydian sound.

With these elements in mind, we can use the Lydian mode to create moments of drama, tension and galactic adventure in songs. It is often used as a compositional tool to create a tense dramatic bridge or outro to a song.

Lydian is used repeatedly in film scores. Picture a spaceship landing. The mystery and tension build as the doors slowly open, then … BAM! Out pops an alien. Or, if you're watching Jodie Foster in the 1997 Sci-Fi blockbuster *Contact,* a blurry, possibly alien or monster-like figure in the distance… and it turns out it's her dad. (Cough, cough... insert rolling tumbleweed here).

Here are some examples of Lydian songs to get you used to its characteristic sound. See if you can add some Lydian songs to the list:

- Curve – John Petrucci
- Flying in a Blue Dream – Joe Satriani
- The Simpsons Theme – Danny Elfman
- Dreams – Fleetwood Mac
- E.T. The Extra-Terrestrial OST Far From Home – John Williams

Part 2: The Lydian diatonic chords

In the Lydian mode, there is a strong relationship between chord I and chord II. Having two major chords adjacent to one another contributes to this mode's happy sound, but also creates an unusual tension. Let's look at the diatonic chords of the Lydian, compared to the Ionian.

Diatonic chords starting from chord 1 (Ionian)

maj	min	min	maj	maj	min	min7b5 (or 1/2 diminished)
I	ii	iii	IV	V	vi	vii

Diatonic chords starting from chord four (Lydian)

maj	maj	min	min7b5	maj	min	min
I	II	iii	#iv	V	vi	vii

We can now take the notes of C Lydian (C D E F# G A B) and use them to create chords that relate to the mode.

Example 4d:

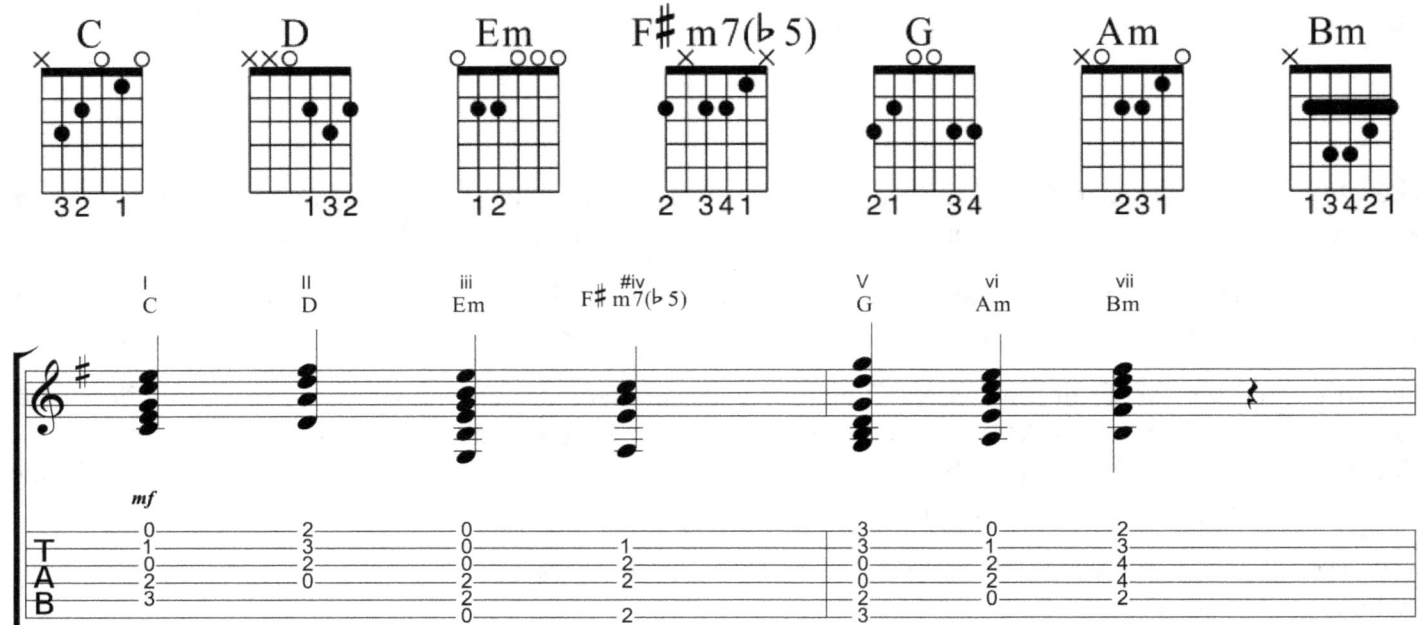

If we are composing with this mode, we'll want to include the chords that particularly highlight its "flavour" note – in the case of C Lydian, the F#. One easy approach is to create a progression that combines the IV and V chords, as there is no other example in a diatonic chord progression where two major chords appear, side by side, a whole tone apart. Other good choices are the vii or #iv chords.

Each of the chords below contain the characteristic F# note:

D Major (II chord) = D F# A

B Minor (vii chord) = B D F#

F#m7b5 (#iv chord) = F# A C E

Try writing a few chord progressions that use these chords, beginning and ending on a C Major chord, and get a feel for the Lydian sound. Here are two examples:

Example 4e – Progression 1:

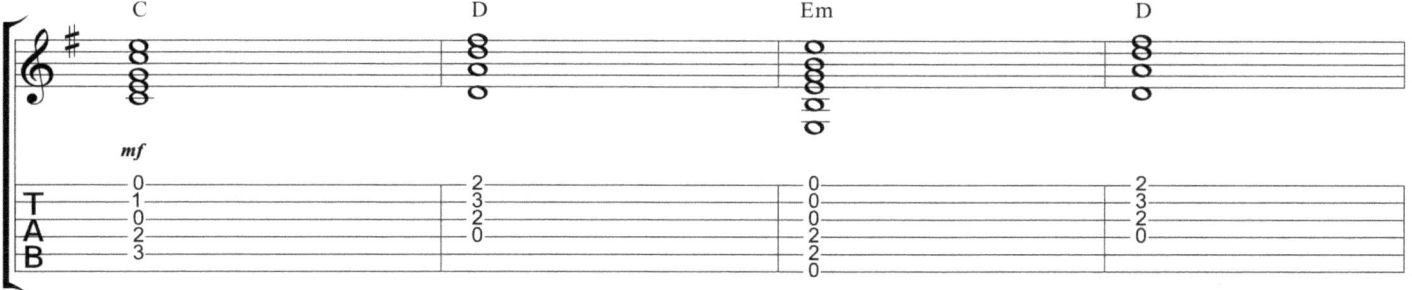

Example 4f – Progression 2:

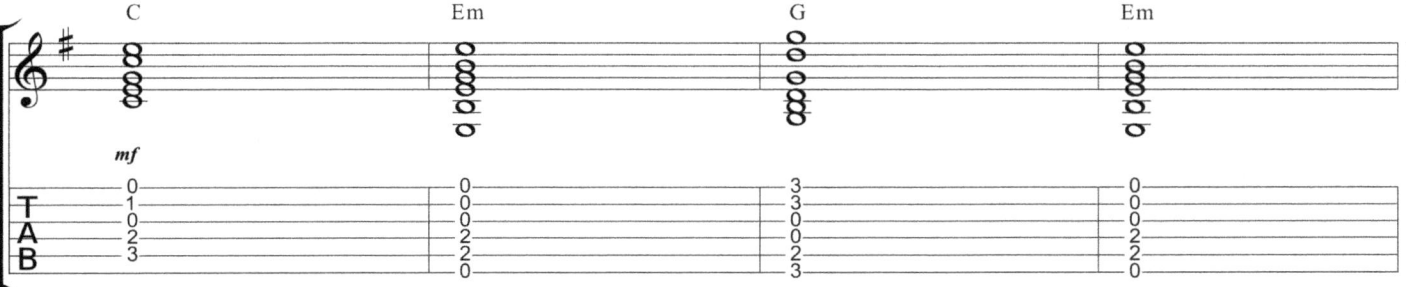

Part 3: Soloing in Lydian using scales and arpeggios

You've heard it thrice! … Now you're going to hear it a fourth time!

1. What is a three-note-per-string version of the scale from the root?

2. What kind of pentatonics can I use e.g. regular, custom or relative minor?

3. What kinds of arpeggios will bring out the flavour of the mode?

Here is the diatonic Lydian scale across all six strings, using a three-note-per-string pattern.

Example 4g:

When playing the Lydian mode, I'll always highlight the major 3rd (E in C Lydian) to conjure up that major sound, but the raised 4th (F#) is the tense flavour note, so I insist on emphasising this too. It's what gives the mode its quirky, spacey sound. If you highlight Lydian's major 7th (B) it can create the sound of a "hanging note" and adds further tension.

Pentatonics

In the case of the Lydian mode, a cool substitution idea is to play a minor pentatonic scale four semitones up from the root. Instead of the C Lydian scale we can therefore play E Minor pentatonic.

Example 4h:

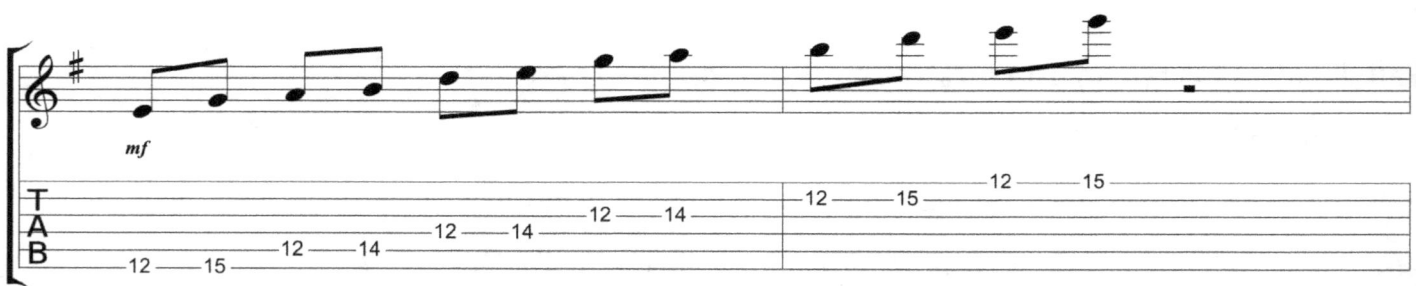

You can also use all the other minor pentatonic box shapes and sneak in a blue note – the b5 of E (Bb).

The E Hirajoshi scale I mentioned in the previous chapter also works really well in place of C Lydian, the notes of which are E, F#, G, B and C (1 2 b3 5 b6).

Example 4i:

Not only does this scale summon ninjas, it has a nice creepy, tense vibe due to its emphasis of the minor 6th. The reason this scale works so well in a C Lydian context is that it also highlights the major 3rd and major 7th notes of C Lydian – both of which are important to its character. If you begin the E Hirajoshi scale on a C note instead of an E, you end up with what I like to call a "Lydian pentatonic box", which is made up of the notes C E F# G and B.

Let's look at C Minor pentatonic and "C Lydian pentatonic" side by side:

Example 4j:

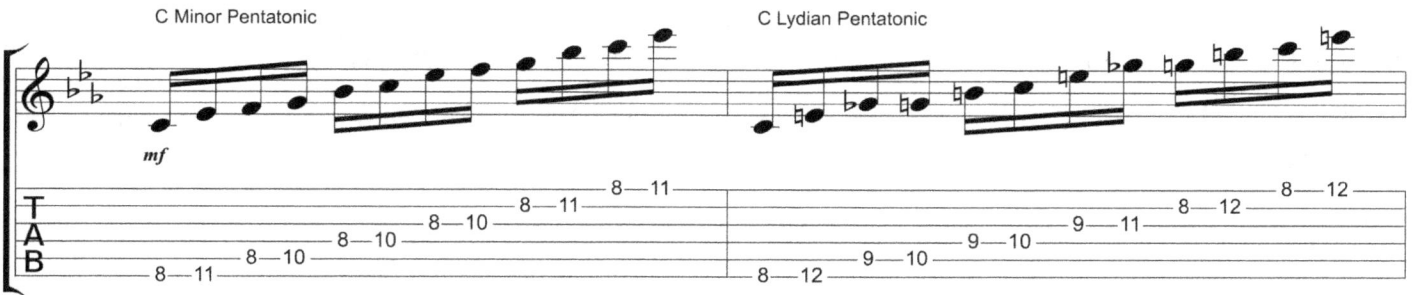

If ninjas played lead guitar, this would surely be the kind of scale they'd play soon after avenging their grandfather's death at the hands of the neighbouring rival ninja clan. In the context of C Lydian there will be five, two-note-per-string E Hirajoshi scales shapes across the fretboard.

Example 4k:

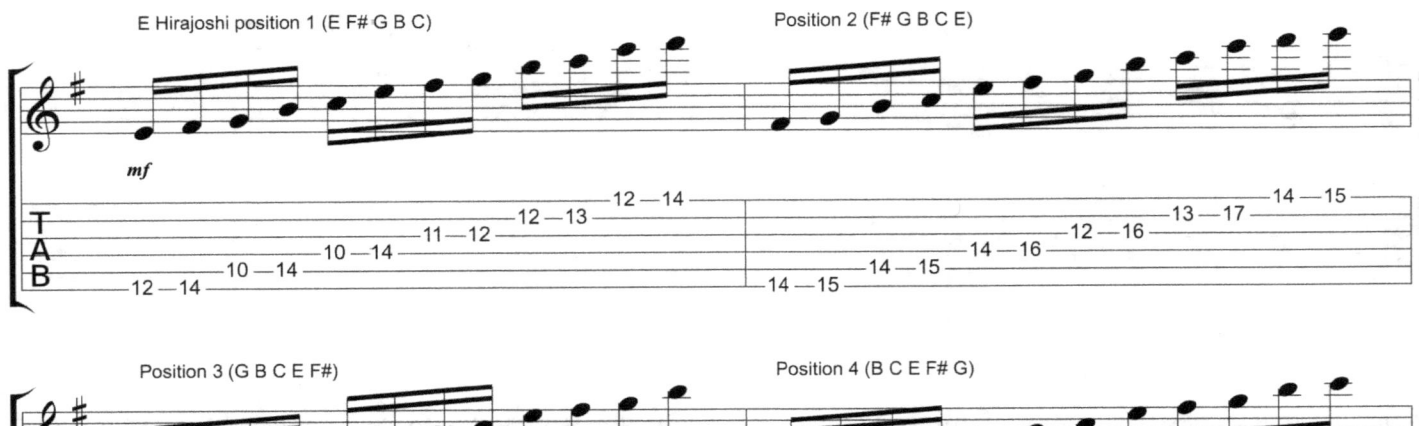

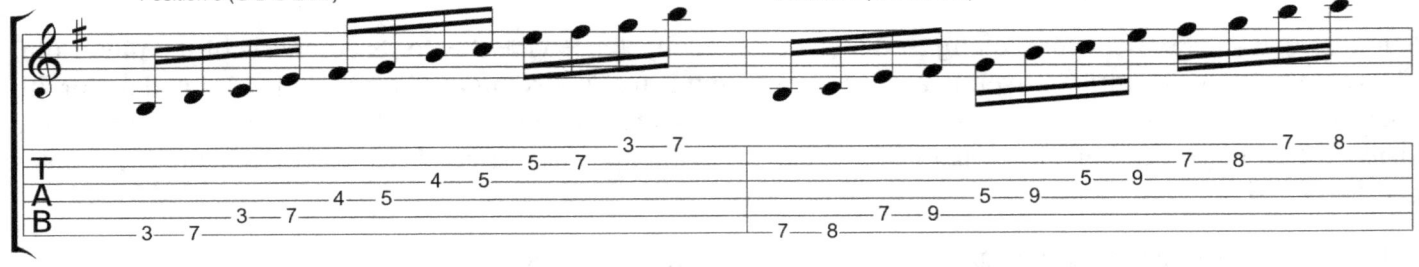

Arpeggios

Let's talk arpeggios. The standard major triad is made up of the 1st, 3rd and 5th notes of a major scale (C, E and G in C Major). To bring out the Lydian flavour we'll add in the raised 4th (F#).

The arpeggio below uses a high register and spans two octaves using the most common five-string shape, with the addition of the #4. Let's compare a standard C Major triad with its *Lydianised* variation.

Example 4l:

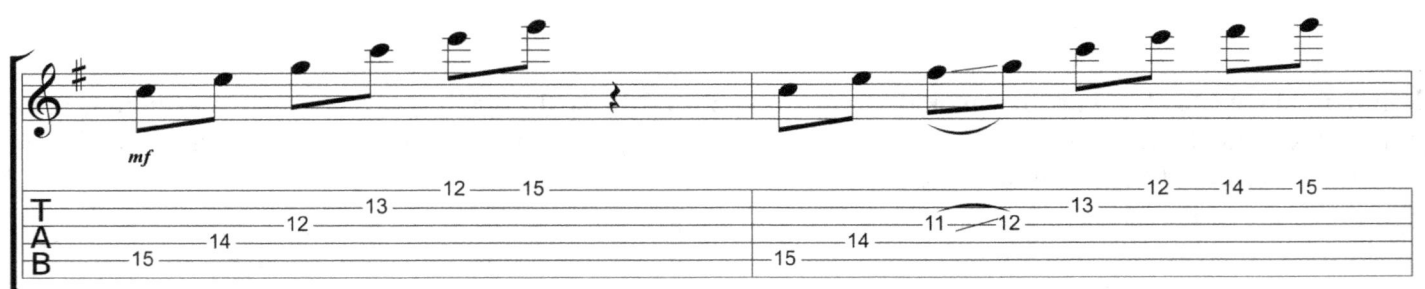

The next arpeggio uses a slightly less common five-string shape, played in a lower register.

Example 4m:

When used over a I chord, or a droning C Lydian riff, these scale shapes and arpeggios are a great way to bring out the poignant characteristics of this mode. You can also use them in any mode or chord progression when the right chord change presents itself! For example, you could use a *Lydianised* arpeggio over a IV chord in an Ionian progression, or a III chord in a Dorian progression, etc.

Part 4: Lydian licks to help you get creative

Now it's time to see how these melodic ideas can be used in a musical context. Example 4n is a three-note-per-string diatonic run I use quite a lot when improvising. This idea can be applied to any mode, but I am particularly fond of using it in a Lydian context.

Notice that I've added in a few hammer-ons and pull-offs to make it less robotic and linear. I've also included two triplets to break up the straight 1/16th note pattern. There are a few moments where the lick descends briefly, to stop it sounding like an ascending scale.

Experiment with changing the placement of legato notes and triplets. Be creative and mess around with this until you find a combination of notes that sound the way you like.

Example 4n: Tremonti-style C Lydian ascending lick

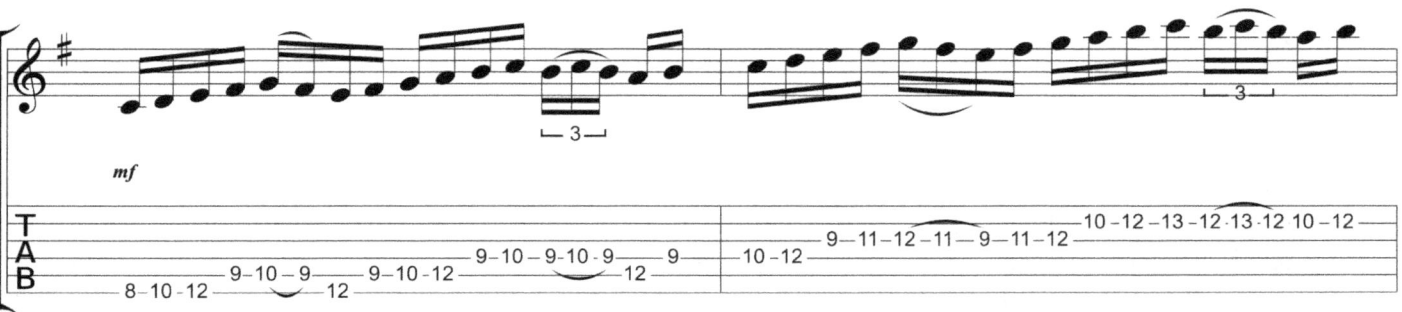

The next example uses the substitute mentioned earlier, E Minor Pentatonic (E, G, A, B and D) which nicely captures the Lydian sound, but in this instance I've added in the missing diatonic notes (C and F#) every so often to add to the flavour.

Example 4o: E Minor Pentatonic with C Lydian diatonic descent

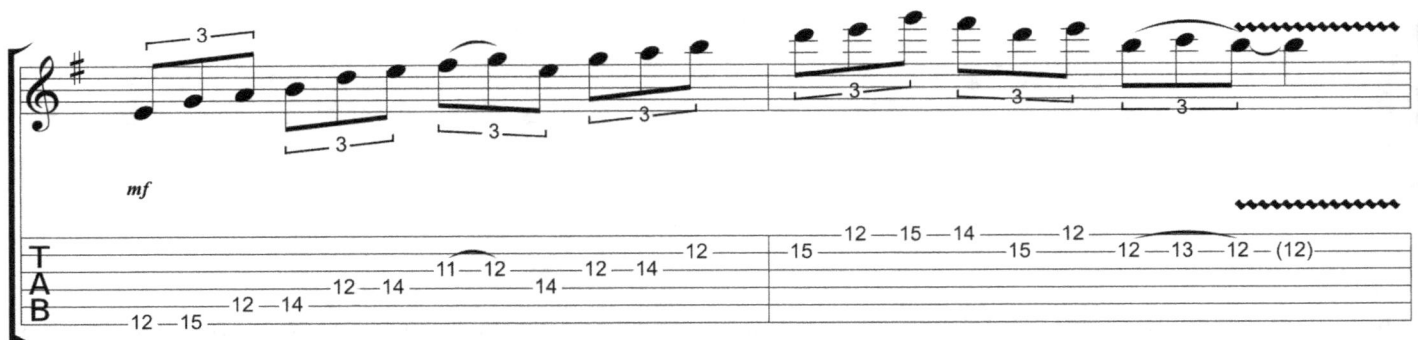

We know from previous examples that the pentatonic has a great bluesy sound that works 99% of the time, but in a Lydian context its lack of semitones is conspicuous. We need that spacey note to create the dreamy Lydian sound, so we'll add in the #4 (F#). The addition of a B note creates an unresolved quality that fits perfectly with the Lydian vibe.

This next lick uses a C Major triad arpeggio with an added #4. This instantly gives us the Lydian sound and I've added some interesting position shifts, as well as a few 5th intervals to add to the futuristic, spacey sound.

Example 4p: Five-string C Major arpeggio plus #4 with descending slide lick

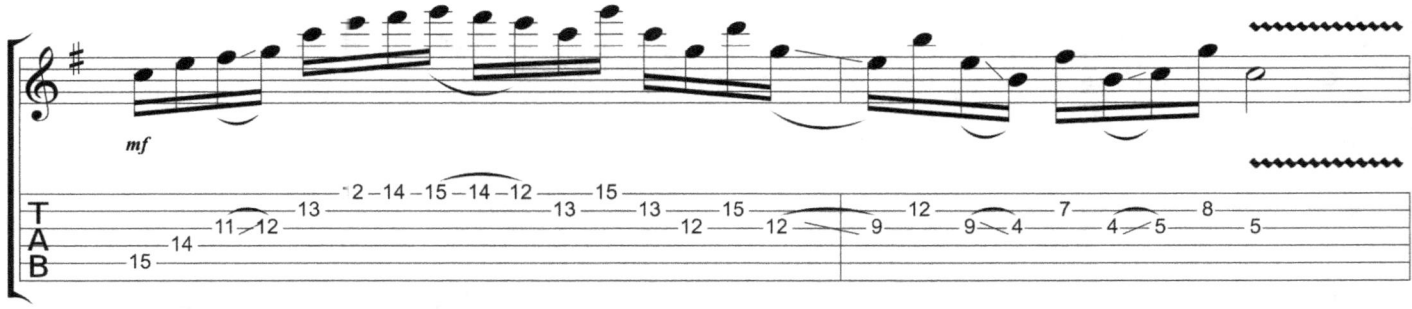

Example 4q uses a pedal C root note and gradually moves through the C Lydian scale. I've heard bands like Testament, Trivium and Judas Priest use licks like this in solos, often as a means of slowing things down and creating tension before a faster, more explosive passage, such as an epic shred or sweep picked arpeggio. Experiment by trying different pedal notes. You could try flipping this idea around and using a high note as the pedal tone while you descend down the scale.

Example 4q: C Lydian pedal lick

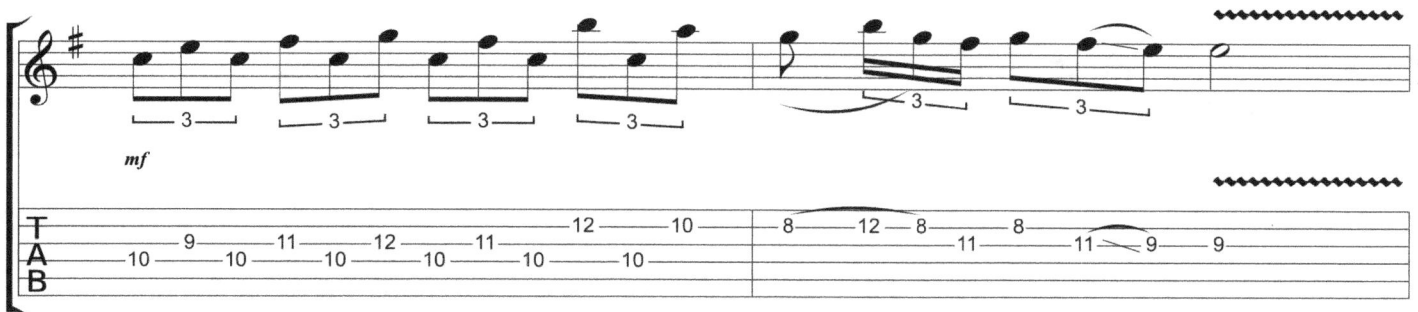

This next idea uses a major 7th arpeggio with a #4 spanning three octaves. I've also included some slides and a string skipped major 7th arpeggio that resolves to a sus2-shaped arpeggio.

Example 4r: Crawling diagonal E Hirajoshi lick with Cmaj7 string skip arpeggio descent

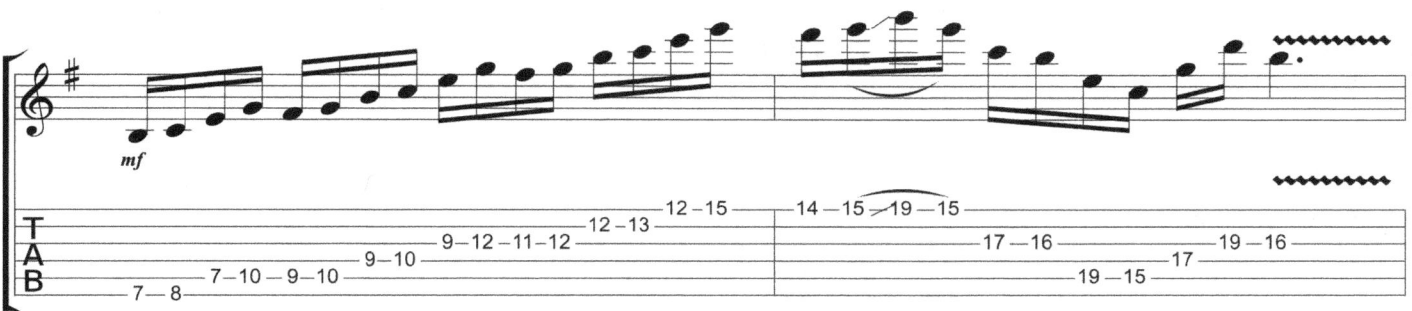

The major 7th interval is a feature of the Ionian mode too, so it's not a "Lydian only" sound, but when paired with the Lydian #4 you get two moments of lovely unresolved tension. This, of course, brings out the weird spacey vibe of Lydian and is a go-to staple for me – especially if I'm running out of material when improvising!

Example 4s uses the Lydian pentatonic (AKA Hirajoshi) idea we looked at earlier and is one of my favourite scale shapes. This example includes hammer-ons, slides, taps, bends and five-note groupings – all designed to make the timing of the phrase less predictable.

Example 4s: C Lydian pentatonic with ascending fives legato lick and taps

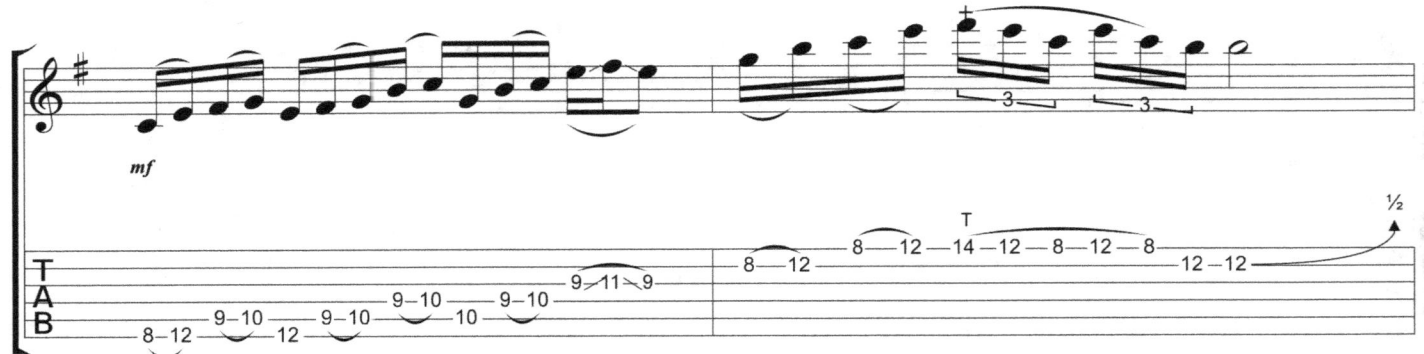

Five- and seven-note groupings are a really simple way to escape predictable four, eight and sixteen note patterns. They bring an element of surprise, as the emphasis falls on unexpected beats in the bar. This kind of lick can be used on any pentatonic or two-note-per-string scale, so mess around with it in a few different keys and modes.

The next lick opens with a combination of a Csus2 shape and an E Minor triad, the effect of which is somewhat like a Cmaj9 arpeggio. The lick drifts into an ascending E Hirajoshi run, then transitions into the E Minor Pentatonic scale.

I love this lick as it's incredibly diverse. Ninth arpeggios are far less used than triads or seventh arpeggios, so it instantly gives a fresher sound. The combination of the Hirajoshi and minor pentatonic scales produces a Japanese sounding hybrid blended with traditional blues.

Combining multiple scale flavours like this makes it hard for your licks to sound like they've been borrowed (stolen) from another player. We've all heard that one guy who *only* listens to SRV and Hendrix, whose licks sound like a stale, grating tribute. So at all costs, don't be that guy. *Never* be that guy!

Example 4t: Csus2/Cmaj9 arpeggio lick with E Hirajoshi run and slide into E Minor pentatonic

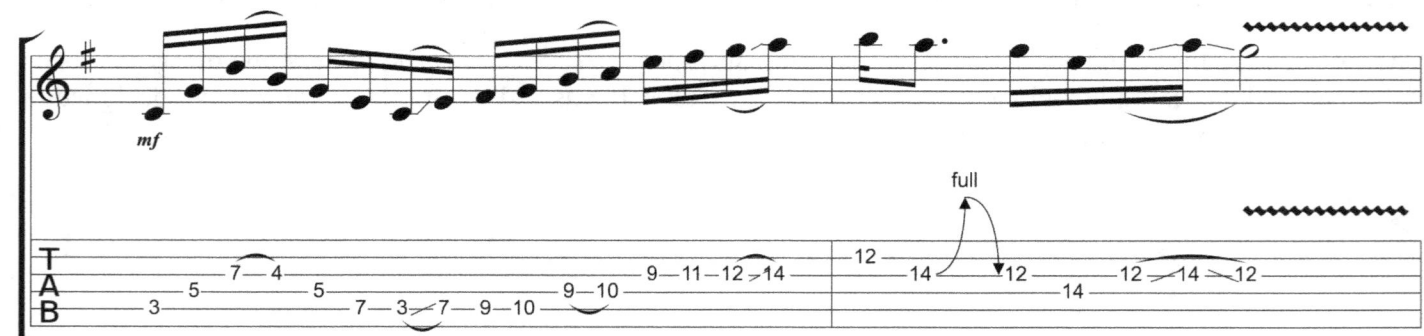

The next example uses the C Lydian three-note-per-string scale shape, but calls for a rolling legato technique as well as tapping. I've also added some string skips to create interesting intervallic jumps!

Remember that you can use this concept with any three-note-per-string mode shape. When adding tapped notes, make sure they are diatonic notes from the parent key. If you're feeling particularly daring, try this concept with the harmonic minor and other exotic scale shapes.

Example 4u: C Lydian three-note-per-string, string skip legato lick with taps

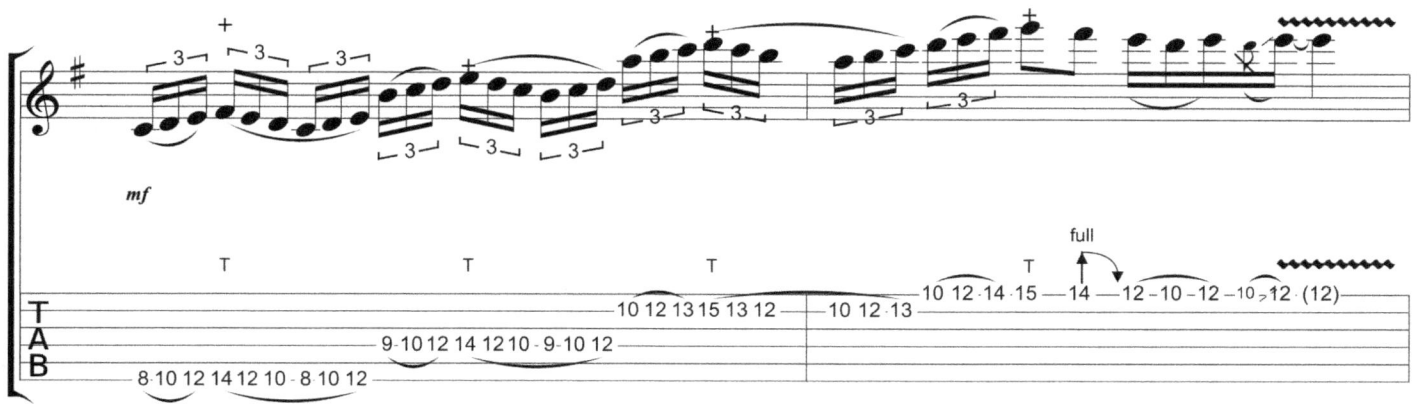

Example 4v utilises the E Hirajoshi scale again. The lick is fairly straightforward as it uses straight 1/16th notes with legato technique here and there to keep the phrasing loose and avoid sounding too robotic.

Example 4v: E Hirajoshi lick with hammer-ons and pull-offs

Don't hesitate to try this idea with other two-note-per-string scale shapes. Be brave, be daring and see what kind of licks you can come up with.

The final lick in this chapter combines a Cmaj7 arpeggio over six strings with the fifth position of the E Hirajoshi scale. This will sound characteristically Lydian. It also has a brief legato descending pattern working in groups of five, which if you haven't noticed, I'm obsessed with!

This lick is very ZOUPAFIED. I love six-string arpeggios with legato and slides; I love five note groupings; and I love resolving phrases that use bends going from outside to inside! That said, it's important when creating your own licks and solos that you gravitate towards what *you* love. This will help you cement your unique playing style and find your voice as a guitar player.

Example 4w: Six-string Cmaj7 arpeggio lick with Hirajoshi descending five and outside bend

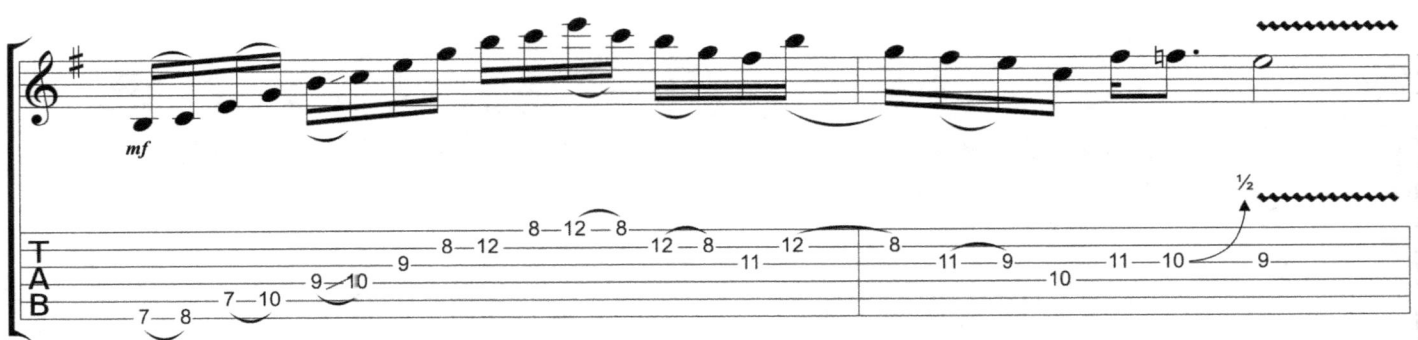

In summary, everything you've learnt here can be moved to other Lydian keys. Find some Lydian jam tracks and play along until you find that spacey, tense, dreamy and sometimes groovy sound.

Chapter 5: The Magic of Mixolydian

In all my years studying music, the Mixolydian has been the standout mode that has fascinated me the most. My fascination stems from its incredible eclecticism and versatility. This can be seen through the mode's broad usage across multiple cultures, periods of time and musical genres.

If there was a planet called Mixolydian it would be inhabited by happy, jigging hobbits and skipping leprechauns. The streets would run rampant with charming parades, filled with painted Indian elephants and everyone would be listening to good time 80s glam metal. Furthermore, if they had floats in such parades, there would be a Steve Vai float, but he would only be allowed to play his guitar using the "mystical sitar" effect. As you can see, Mixolydian would be a mystical and charming world.

Mixolydian is the fifth of our seven diatonic modes. Known for its fist-raising sound and bounding positivity, it's no wonder this mode was used repeatedly throughout the 80s to create rock 'n' roll and glam metal anthems. It is also used frequently in traditional Celtic and Indian music. It was even used in medieval music! (Ask Sven from Skyrim. I apologise if that gag/reference is too obscure!)

Part 1: Finding the Mixolydian sound

In this chapter we will use E Mixolydian for all our examples. Let's start by playing the E Mixolydian scale in one octave.

Example 5a:

As well as being a scale and sound in its own right, we can think of Mixolydian in two other ways:

1. As the fifth mode of the parent major scale (in this case, E Mixolydian is the fifth mode of A Major).

2. As a major scale with a b7.

It's easy to spot what makes the Mixolydian distinct by comparing E Ionian and E Mixolydian side by side.

E Ionian = E F# G# A B C# **D#** E

E Mixolydian = E F# G# A B C# **D** E

Example 5b:

Ionian scale formula = 1 2 3 4 5 6 7

Mixolydian scale formula = 1 2 3 4 5 6 b7

The only difference between the two modes is the seventh note. The Ionian mode has a semitone interval between the 7th and the octave, whereas the Mixolydian has a full tone, which creates a b7 (b7 or dominant 7th) relationship with the root note.

This b7 note gives the Mixolydian mode its signature rock 'n' roll, dark blues and anthemic sounds, whereas the regular major 7th note of the Ionian has an unresolved, peaceful, yet contemplative sound. Even though only one note has been changed from Ionian to create the Mixolydian, the difference in sound and feeling is quite substantial.

As I've stated in previous chapters, comparing one scale to another will give you an understanding of intervals and the different scale formulas, but it will not increase your understanding of how the mode works in a musical context. The best way to achieve this is to hear the mode accompanied by chords.

Have a play through the example below. It's simple chord progression made up of four chords, followed by ascending and descending version of the E Mixolydian scale in one octave.

Example 5c: E Mixolydian chord progression with scale ascend & descend

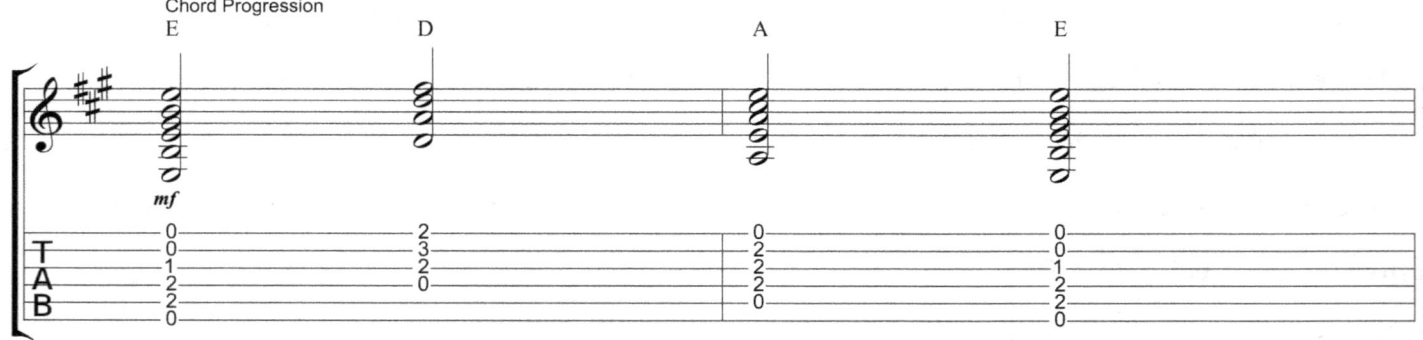

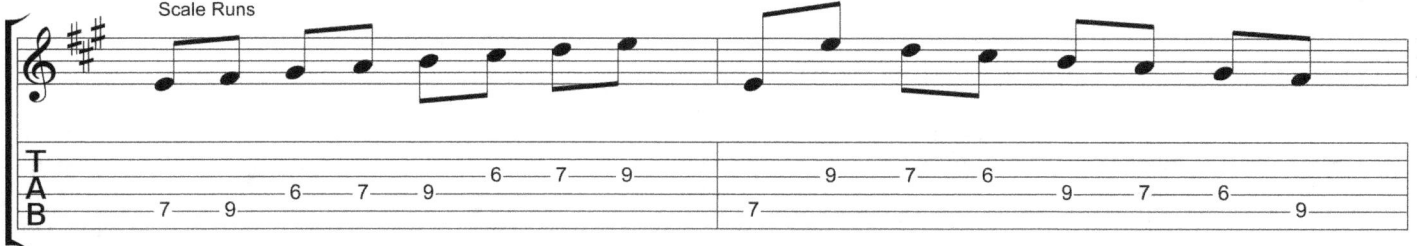

The chord progression consists of E Major, D Major and A Major, which means the progression is made entirely of major chords. Stylistically, this is very common in Mixolydian rock progressions and compositions.

Side note: did you notice the progression above included the chord D Major? It's built on the b7 of the scale (the only difference between major and Mixolydian is that b7 note) so it's a great chord to use when outlining Mixolydian. You'll often see the tonic chord, in this case E Major, followed by a major chord one tone below (in this case D Major) in Mixolydian progressions. An excellent example of this change between the D and C chord occurs in *Sweet Child O' Mine*.

When the chord progression and scale are played after one another, you'll get that sense of a happy, yet kick-ass rock sound. With these factors in mind, it's easy to see why the Mixolydian mode is such an important staple of 80s party rock, glam metal and stadium rock music.

Here are some examples of Mixolydian songs:

- Nothing But A Good Time – Poison
- Glasgow Kiss – John Petrucci
- Royals – Lorde
- Sweet Child O' Mine – Guns N' Roses
- Highway To Hell – ACDC

Part 2: The Mixolydian diatonic chords

The distinct character of the Mixolydian mode comes from the relationship between the I and IV chords, and often the I and bVII chords. The important thing to note is that all three of these chords are major.

Let's compare the diatonic chords of the Ionian and Mixolydian modes:

Diatonic chords of Ionian

maj	min	min	maj	maj	min	min7b5 (or 1/2 diminished)
I	ii	iii	IV	V	vi	vii

Diatonic chords in Mixolydian

maj	min	min7b5	maj	min	min	maj
I	ii	iii	IV	v	vi	bVII

Example 5d:

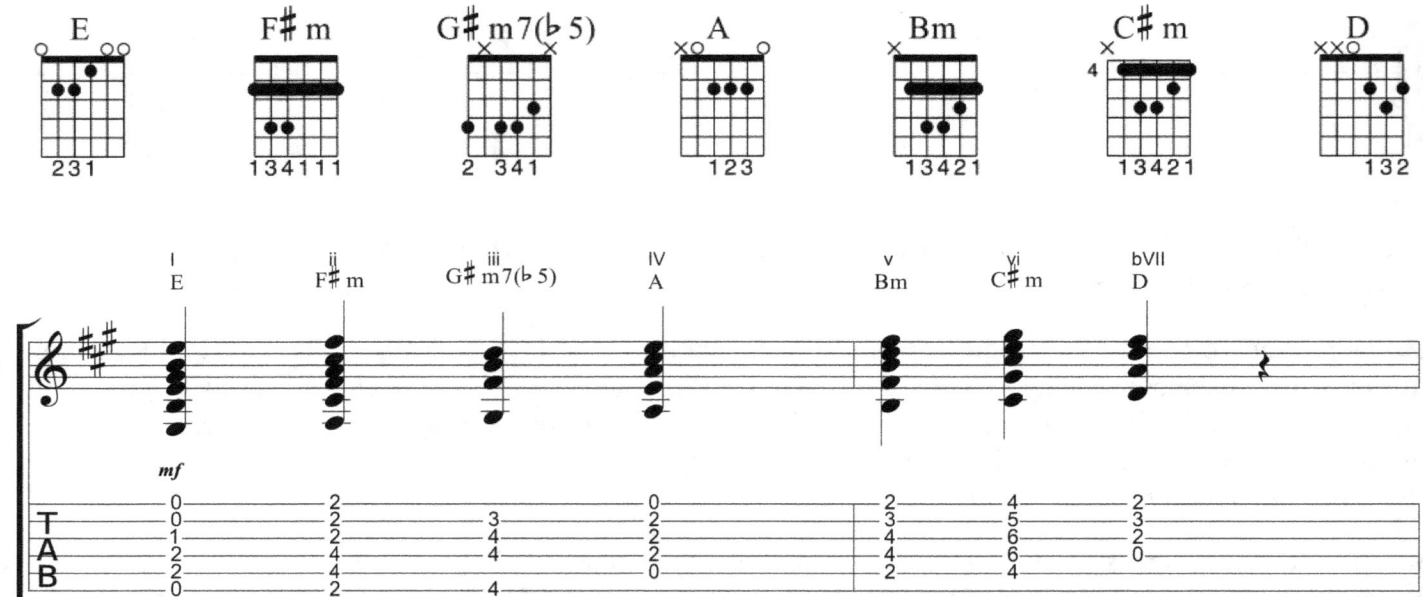

When composing with the Mixolydian mode we normally want to highlight the b7. The easiest way is to pair the I chord in a progression with the bVII chord (the most fist-raising rock chord when it follows the V). Or we can highlight the v or iii chords. All of them contain the characteristic b7 (D).

D Major (chord bVII) = D F# A

B Minor (chord v) = B D F#

G#m7b5 (chord iii) = G# B D F#

Try writing a few chord progressions using these options, preferably starting and ending on E Major to capture the Mixolydian feel. Here are a couple of ideas:

Example 5e – Progression 1:

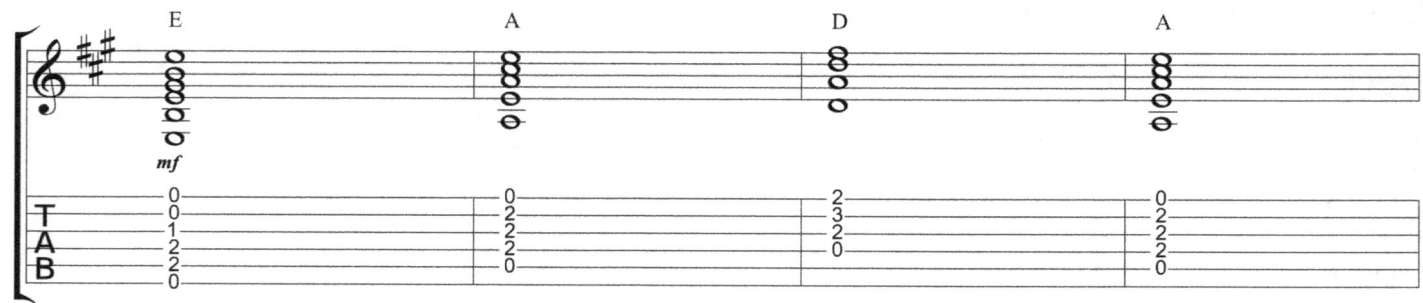

Example 5f – Progression 2:

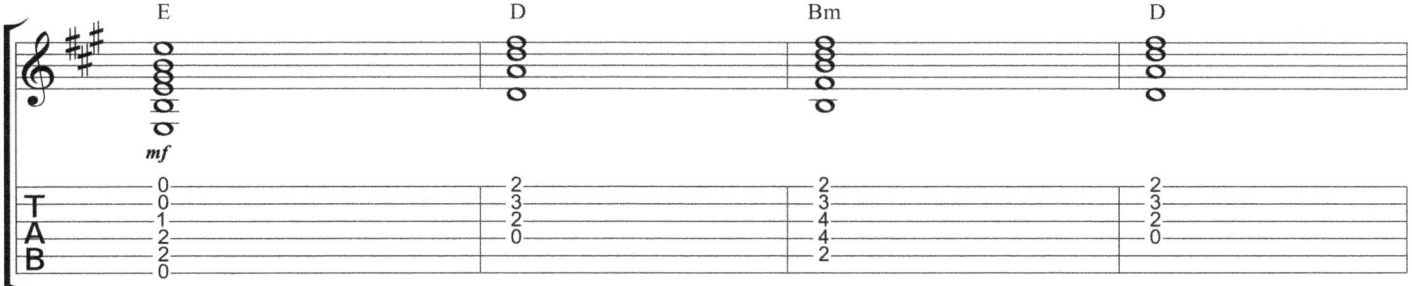

Part 3: Soloing in Mixolydian using scales and arpeggios

Sorry if I sound like a broken record by now, but…

1. What is a three-note-per-string version of the scale from the root?

2. What kind of pentatonics can I use e.g. regular, custom or relative minor?

3. What kinds of arpeggios will bring out the flavour of the mode?

Here the is three-note-per-string pattern for the Mixolydian across all six strings:

Example 5g:

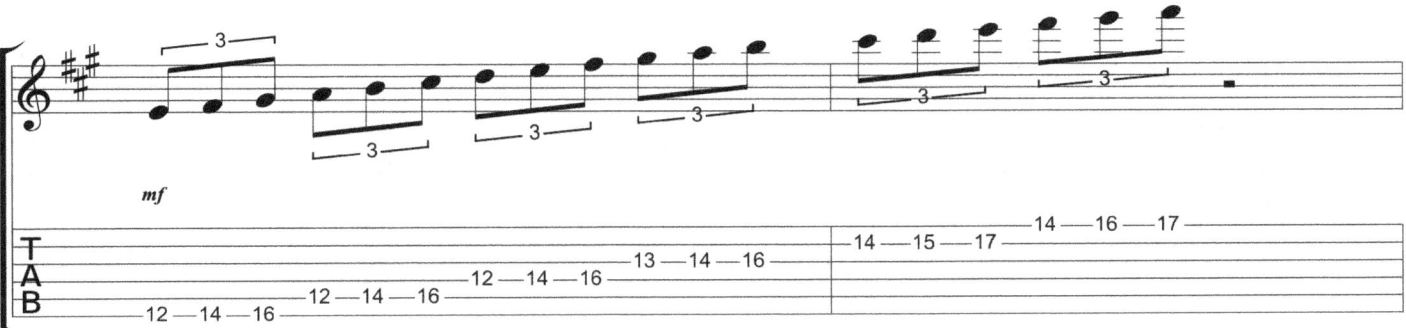

When playing in Mixolydian I like to highlight the major 3rd (G# in the key of E Mixolydian) to convey its happy, positive aspect, and its b7 (D) which is its most flavoursome note. The b7 brings the bluesy-yet-rocky feel to the scale and accentuates the stadium rock sound (as well as the more Celtic hobbit-like sound).

Pentatonics

Let's talk about pentatonics. You may or may not have heard the term "relative minor scale" before, so let's do a quick explanation without boring you to tears. Relative keys are major and minor scales with the same key signatures. The relative minor scale of G Major is E Minor (you can always locate the relative minor by descending three semitones from the root of your major scale on guitar). Many players opt to do this so they can play in the comfortable box of the minor pentatonic. We can apply this same concept to the Mixolydian too. Descending three semitones from the root (E) we arrive at the C# Minor pentatonic.

Example 5h:

The sexiest notes to highlight when using this pentatonic scale shape are the E (the root of E Mixolydian), G# (the major 3rd) and B (the 5th). But you can also add in the blue note G (the b5), as an erotic, outside passing tone.

This next scale shape is my favourite way to solo over a Mixolydian chord progression (or a V chord in an Ionian context). I call it the "Mixolydian pentatonic" because it uses the 1st, 3rd, 4th, 5th and 7th note of the Mixolydian scale. Let's compare the E Minor Pentatonic (E, G, A, B and D) and the E Mixolydian pentatonic (E, G#, A, B and D) side by side.

Example 5i:

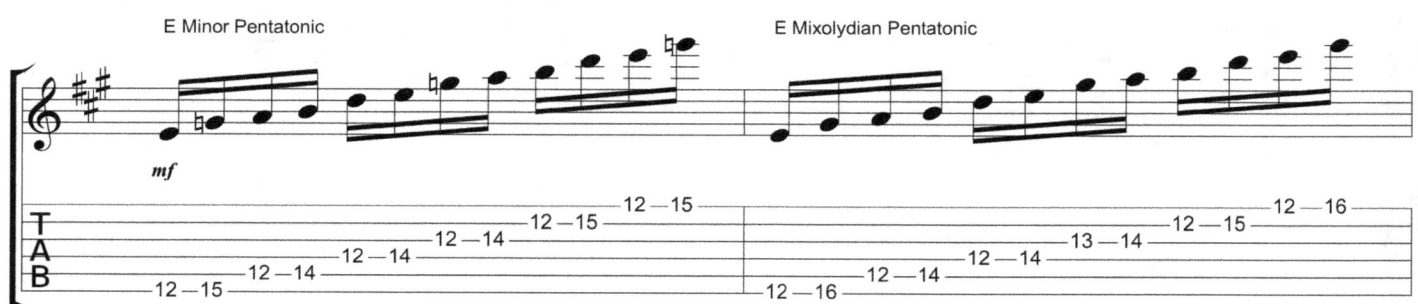

The only difference between the two scales is that E Minor Pentatonic has a minor 3rd interval, while E Mixolydian pentatonic has a major 3rd. Using this scale shape, we can highlight both the major 3rd and the b7, which gives the Mixolydian its bluesy yet fist-raising sound. Then we can transfer this idea to the other positions of the minor pentatonic, *Mixolydianizing* them in the process ... and yes, I just made that word up. Let's compare the scales using those remaining positions.

Example 5j:

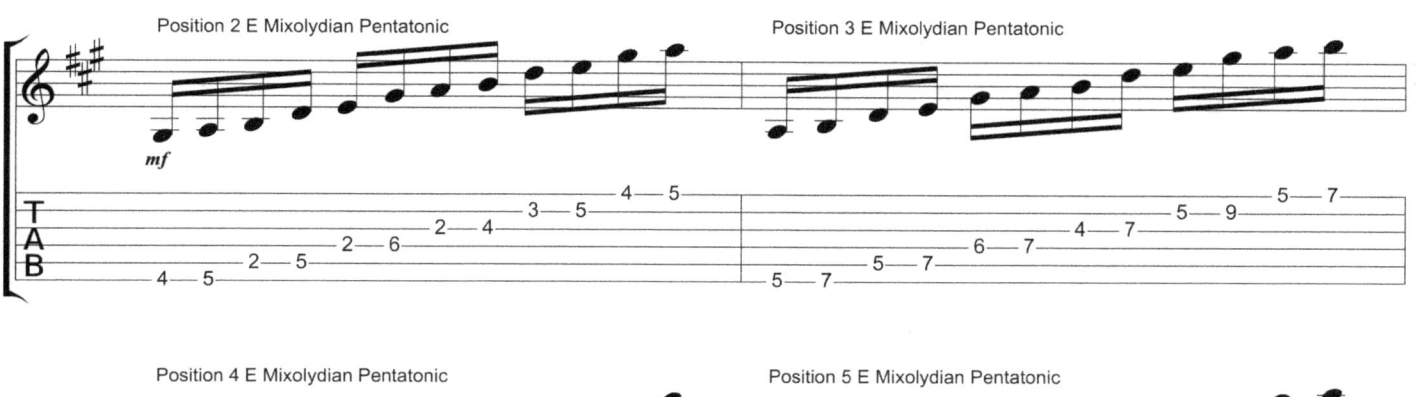

Arpeggios

Now let's talk about the sexiest musical term of them all: *arpeggios!* In the case of the Mixolydian, I only want to focus on dominant arpeggios. An E7 arpeggio is made up of the first note of the scale (E), the major 3rd (G#), 5th (B) and b7 (D). The D is our Mixolydian "flavour" note, so this arpeggio perfectly complements the Mixolydian sound. Let's look at three different ways to play an E7 arpeggio.

The first arpeggio uses the most common five-string major triad shape and adds the b7. Let's compare the basic triad and the dominant 7 arpeggio side by side.

Example 5k:

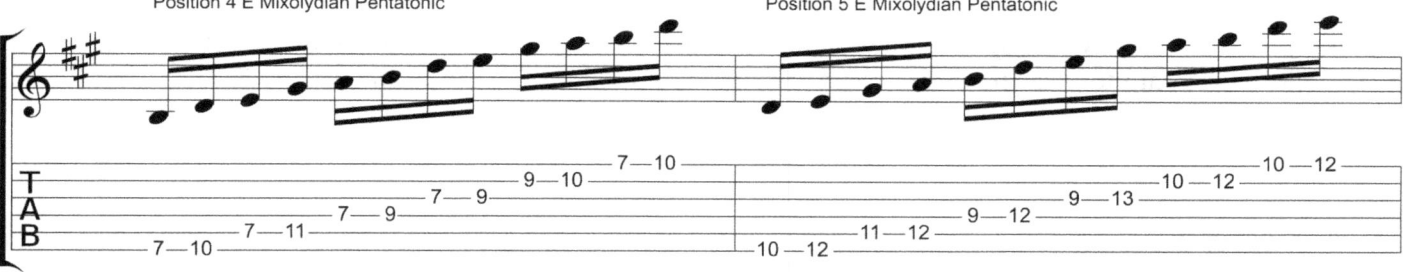

The next arpeggio is based on a less common five-string major triad shape. Once again, we'll look at the arpeggio as a regular triad and dominant 7 arpeggio side by side.

177

Example 5l:

The final shape is an E7 arpeggio spanning all six strings covering three and a bit octaves. Let's compare it to the straight triad again to hear the different flavour the dominant note brings to the arpeggio.

Example 5m:

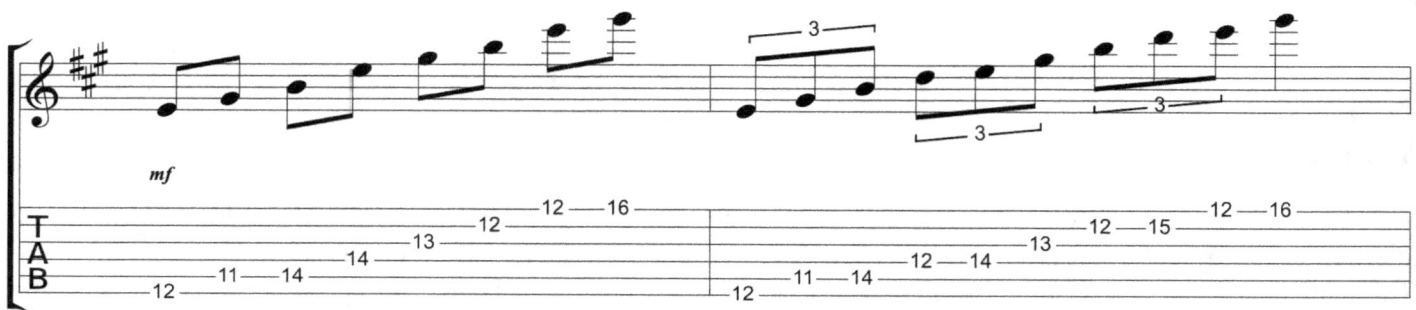

Keep in mind that these arpeggio shapes are moveable into other Mixolydian keys. They are useable in any mode over diatonic and non-diatonic dominant chords!

Part 4: Mixolydian licks to help you get creative!

Here are some licks and concepts to get you using the Mixolydian mode in creative, musical way. In the first lick we'll use the Mixolydian pentatonic scale shape to create a 1/16th note lick with a five-note grouping pulse.

Example 5n: E Mixolydian pentatonic lick with descending fives

I like to use legato technique in five-note pulse licks to add speed and a fluent flurry of notes. The odd number pulse over an even 16th note passage means that the notes appear less "on the beat" and more unpredictable. If you get a taste for interesting patterns with odd pulses, this concept works with regular pentatonics too and also sounds interesting and less predictable if you use seven-note patterns.

Example 5o is based on the Mixolydian pentatonic, but I've changed the note order from the usual 1, 3, 4, 5, 7 pattern (E G# A B D) to 3, 4, 5, 7, 1, 7 (G# A B D E D E). This lick is more fun to play than your usual two-note-per-string pentatonic box shape. It crawls diagonally across the fretboard instead of vertically.

This lick is a cool way to cover a vast melodic range on the guitar, but also calls for position shifts at each octave. Notice the cool sound created by using a seven-note pattern with a triplet feel.

Example 5o: Crawling diagonal Mixolydian pentatonic lick

The next idea uses a simple three-note-per-string diatonic scale shape in E Mixolydian and adds a smooth legato technique with a seven-note pulse.

Example 5p: E Mixolydian rolling legato in sevens with cheeky outside bend

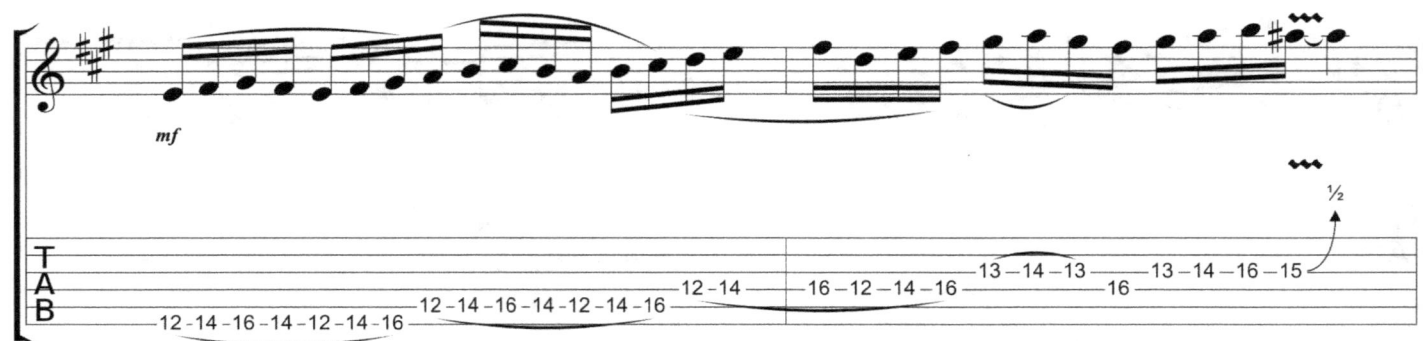

Rolling legato is a great way to create a different kind of speed to normal shred speed. Legato licks like this are particularly interesting because they juxtapose a smooth relaxed vibe with somehow sounding chaotic. I resolved the lick above by bending from an outside note to a scale note. It's a sound I've grown fond of due to growing up listening to and loving Marty Friedman and Cacophony! Bear in mind, this kind of legato playing can be used on any three-note-per-string scale shape.

Example 5q combines an E7 arpeggio with a diatonic descending scale pattern using straight 16th notes. I've included a slide to make the position shift more manageable and seamless.

Notice that the E7 arpeggio starts on a D note – the b7 of the arpeggio, highlighting the b7 Mixolydian sound. The arpeggio also slides into a D note before descending a relatively predictable scale pattern.

Keep in mind that arpeggios are like chord inversions. We don't have to start and finish on the root note. The most important thing to concern yourself with is the notes of the arpeggio. I'll often say to my students, "It's the sum of the parts, not the order of the notes that make the chord." Which is also true of arpeggios. Try mixing different arpeggio shapes with different diatonic scale descents. It will create more interesting intervals, as well as highlighting different aspects of the mode you're working with.

Example 5q: Five-string E7 arpeggio with slide into sixteenths descending pattern

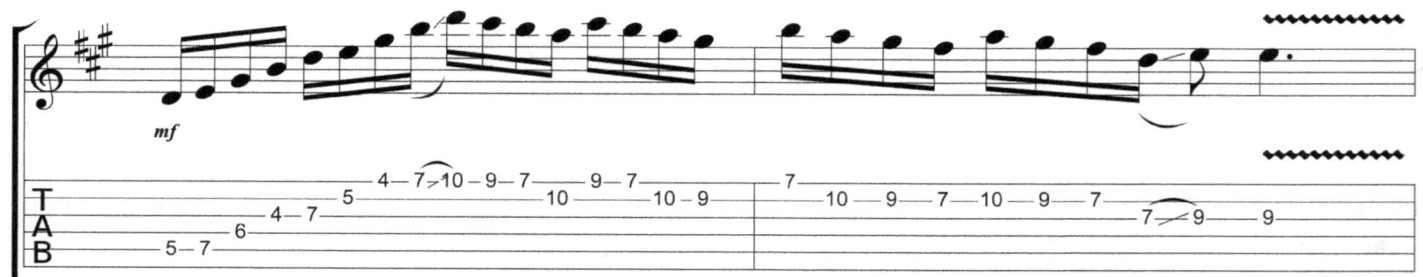

This next lick combines the third position of the E Mixolydian Pentatonic with the second position of the C# Minor Pentatonic. I've added in some legato technique to add smoothness, as well as the occasional triplet and some slides to help with position shifts.

Bear in mind that each of these pentatonic scales brings something different to the table. E Mixolydian Pentatonic has a semitone interval (G# to A) which creates tension and wants to resolve. C# Minor Pentatonic has no semitones and is a bit more predictable, with a straight rocky-blues sound. Blending different sounding scales together is a great way to keep your licks and solos sounding fresh!

Example 5r: E Mixolydian Pentatonic legato lick with slide transition into C# Minor Pentatonic descent

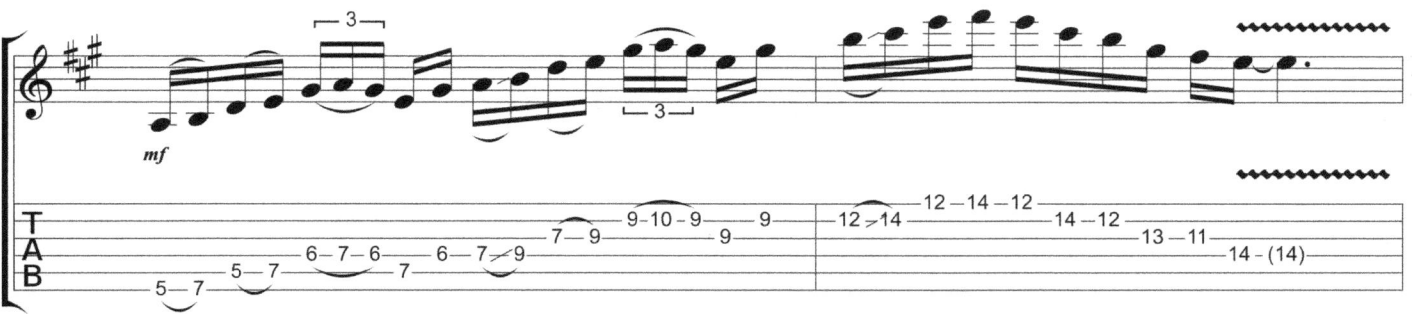

Here is a lick that uses pedal notes from E Mixolydian to drift into a "meat and veg" C# Minor Pentatonic run. It builds slowly by ascending the notes of E Mixolydian, then the pedal note changes from an E to a G#. Then we bring it home with the semiquaver speed of the C# Minor Pentatonic lick.

Example 5s: Mid-register E Mixolydian pedal lick with slide into C# Minor Pentatonic

Try experimenting with changing timing mid-lick. Too many 1/16th notes or triplets in a row can become tiresome and predictable.

Example 5t is based on a six-string E7 arpeggio that uses hammer-ons and slides to make it sound less robotic. It transitions into C# Minor Pentatonic and highlights the "blue" b5 note (G) on the third string 12th fret. Using the relative minor scale like this is a great option, because it produces a happy-yet-bluesy sound that works perfectly over Mixolydian progressions.

Example 5t: Six-string E7 arpeggio lick with slide transition into C# Minor Pentatonic

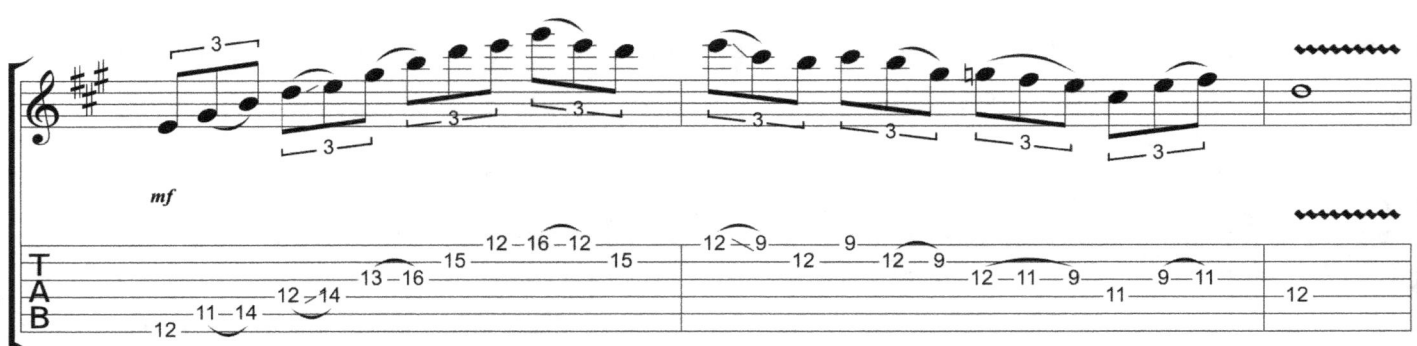

Next, try this descending legato version of the E Mixolydian three-note-per-string shape. I've included a few taps to introduce an element of surprise along the way. The taps also make the legato rolls on each string last a bit longer.

Example 5u: E Mixolydian three-note-per-string legato lick with taps and slides

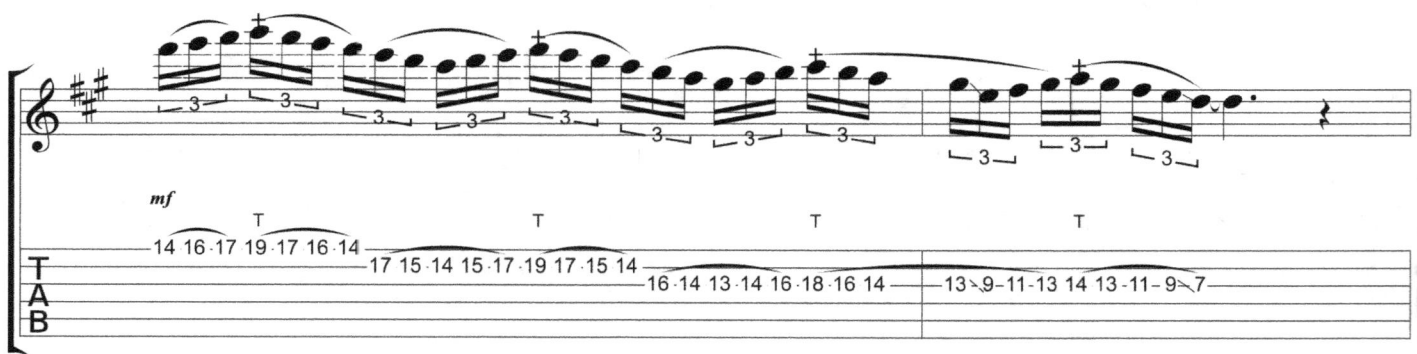

The next lick uses the open first string to create a droning E pedal note. Such opportunities aren't available in every key, so when they are, it's good to capitalise on them.

Example 5v: Open E string pedal ascending Mixolydian lick

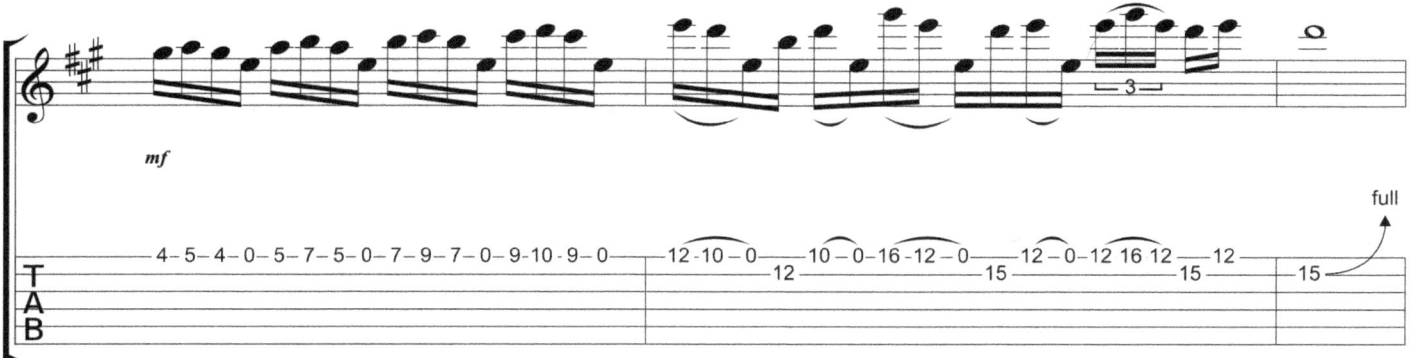

The final lick uses multiple positions of the A Major scale, which shares the same notes as E Mixolydian. It sneakily introduces fragments of G# Locrian, A Ionian and B Dorian three-note-per-string scale shapes. I started on a G# note because I wanted to highlight the third degree of E Mixolydian. The Locrian mode just happened to correspond with this particular note and key signature. This lick uses a relatively simple legato approach, but includes a few slides to create subtle position shifts.

Example 5w: G# Locrian three-note-per-string legato lick with sliding position shift

Go and seek out some Mixolydian jam tracks and jam along until you unlock the fist-raising, glam rock, Celtic beast you never knew existed inside you!

Chapter 6: Astonishing Aeolian

The Aeolian mode is the sixth of our seven diatonic modes and is more commonly known as the Natural Minor scale. The Aeolian is the most used of all the minor modes and can be heard in 99% of all the sad songs ever written.

The Aeolian is the most obviously sad and "minor sounding" of the modes. Most ballads and broken-hearted love songs use the Aeolian mode to create the melodies and chord progressions that tug at our heartstrings.

The one exception to the *Aeolian mode = sad song* rule is the use of the Ionian mode in the classic song *On Top of Spaghetti* – an unforgettable ballad about sneezing, and the mourning of a man who has recently become separated from his poor meatball.

The Aeolian is often referred to as the *relative minor* scale. The boring theory rule is that building a scale on the sixth degree of any major scale forms the relative minor, which functions as the "sad mommy" counterpart to the "happy daddy" major scale.

To find the relative minor of any major scale, you just need to count up six notes from the root of the major scale and start a new scale from there. For example, G Major's relative minor is E Minor and D Major's relative minor is B Minor etc.

Remember, modes contain exactly the same notes as their parent scale, so A Aeolian contains exactly the same notes as the C Major scale, but begins and ends on the note A. Beginning on the sixth note of the major scale creates a new pattern of tones that sound very different from pattern of notes in the major scale.

Check out the pattern of tones and semitones below, and compare the formulas of Aeolian and Ionian:

Aeolian: T St T T St T T (Formula 1 2 b3 4 5 b6 b7)

A Aeolian = A B C D E F G

Ionian T T St T T T St (Formula 1 2 3 4 5 6 7)

C Ionian = C D E F G A B C

You can immediately see from the b3 that the Aeolian is a minor mode.

When I think of the Aeolian mode I see a deep well of sadness. I think of every slow, emotional song Tori Amos and Evanescence have ever written. I think of an emo kid's poem, written on the back of a black and white photo of a tortured willow tree!

But the most Aeolian thing I can think of is the hypothetical situation where I have put bread in my toaster, only to realise there's no margarine in the house! As a result, I have a very difficult choice to make…

1. Eat the toast dry.

2. Feed it to the local gang of pigeon street toughs (who would most likely take it by force anyway).

Either way, I find myself overcome with a deep wave of sadness, loss and disappointment. I feel my eyes well up and hear the sound of violins in the distance. I run to the park near my childhood home with tears streaming down my face, thinking, "Why did this happen to me?!"

I run till I'm out of breath and collapse by a small playground. I am alone next to a creaky swing seat that hasn't been used in years. There was a time where you'd come to this park and find laughing children playing here every day. Now this once happy place is riddled with bird poop and graffitied obscenities. The grey skies rumble and, within a few short moments, I'm drenched in rain, mud swirling at my feet, as though Zeus himself has taken it upon himself to punish me. I can almost hear him bellowing from the highest peak of Mount Olympus,

"Nobody likes you!"

At this moment I am fully immersed in the emotive force that is the Aeolian mode. I think you get the picture…

Part 1: Finding the Aeolian sound

In this chapter we'll use the E Aeolian scale (AKA The E Natural Minor) for our examples. The notes in E Aeolian are E F# G A B C D

Let's play the E Aeolian scale in one octave.

Example 6a:

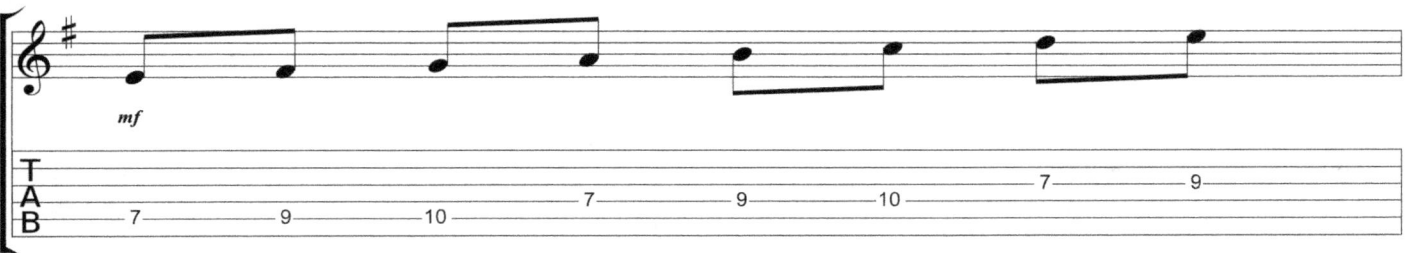

Scale intervals: T St T T St T W

Scale formula: 1 2 b3 4 5 b6 b7

Aeolian will probably sound familiar to you, as it's the most commonly used of the minor modes (modes that contain a b3). The b3, b6 and b7 are where this mode gets all its sadness from. When you turn on the radio and hear a sad song, it's probably because the Aeolian/Natural Minor scale was used to write the chord progression and an array of upsetting melodies.

As you've seen in earlier chapters, we use the "common" sounding Ionian and Aeolian mode formulas as a point of reference when we learn more daunting and interesting modes. Examining how other minor modes – such as the Dorian and Phrygian – are constructed compared to the Aeolian will help you identify the nuances and characteristics that make them different.

When we played through the Ionian mode in the first chapter, it was obvious that it was just the common, well-known major scale. As you play through the Aeolian, you may say, "Hey, hang on! Isn't this just the Natural Minor scale? Why, like the Ionian, does it have a weird/bogus name?"

It's important to identify the fact that we are using the Aeolian mode because the term "minor scale" is very broad and could refer to several scales (Dorian and Phrygian are minor scales, as are the Melodic, Harmonic and Hungarian minor scales). Being specific is incredibly important.

The standout characteristics of the Aeolian mode are its natural 2nd and b6th – in the case of E Aeolian, F# and C respectively. The combination of these two intervals are what separates the Aeolian from the Dorian and Phrygian modes.

We can hear these characteristic notes and their functions more clearly in the simple chord progression in the diagram below. Play through the four-chord progression and then play the ascending and descending variations of the one octave Aeolian scale.

Example 6b: E Aeolian chord progression w/scale ascend & descend

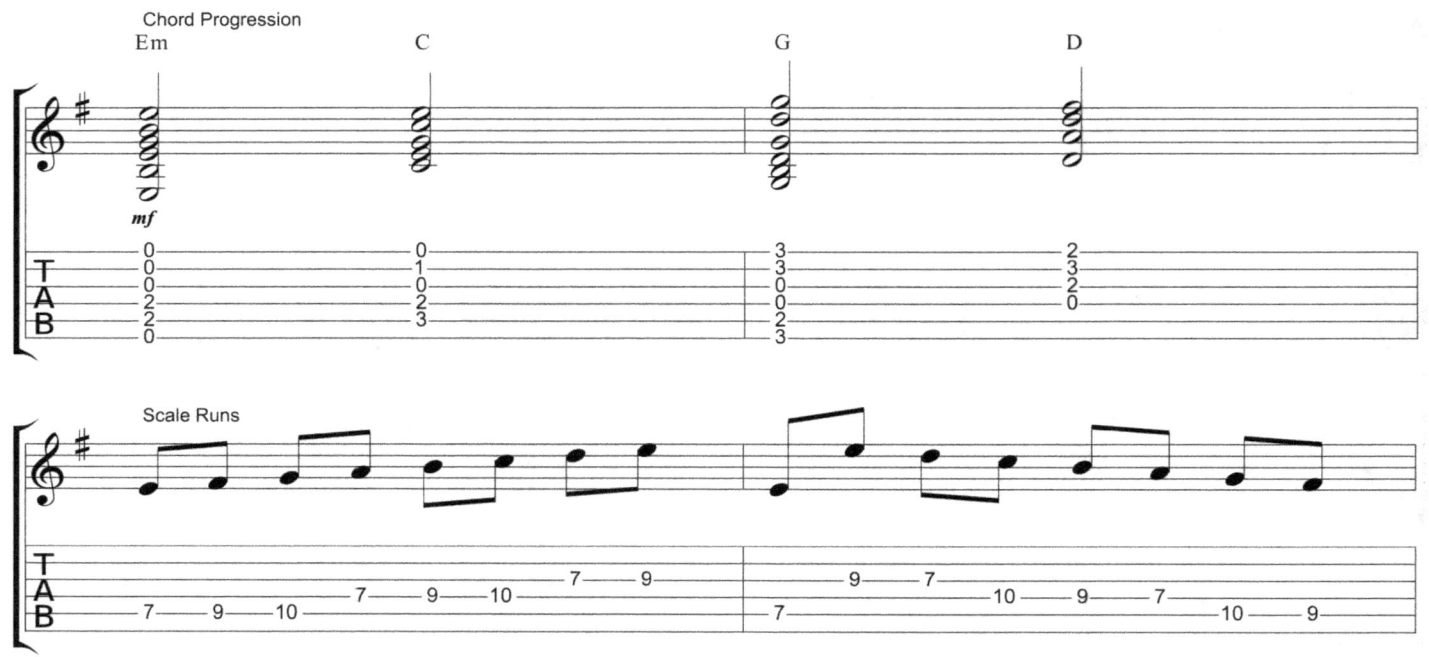

We can hear the natural 2nd (F#) note in the VII (D Major chord), and the b6th (C) note is present in the bVI (C Major chord). The overall sound of the chords and scale together is the characteristically sombre sound that makes the Aeolian mode the first point of call for composing songs about break-ups, loss and especially mourning. It is used frequently in film and television scores to emphasise moments of sadness and trauma.

As you continue to build your knowledge of theory and scales, and grow more confident in your mastery of the fretboard, it's important to remember that nothing compares to having a sound and feeling with which to associate these modes. Here are some Aeolian-based songs to listen to. As previously, seek out and add other songs to the list.

- Save Tonight – Eagle Eye Cherry

- Nothing Else Matters – Metallica

- Polly – Nirvana

- Kryptonite – 3 Doors Down
- Zombie – The Cranberries

Part 2: The Aeolian diatonic chords

In every chapter of this book, I have underlined the importance of knowing the diatonic chords of a key or mode. This knowledge will help you to determine the colours and emotions you may wish to highlight. In the Aeolian mode the most important chord is the i – a minor chord – which is also the vi chord in Ionian progressions. It sets the scene for sad things to come and works particularly well when paired with the bVI or iv chord. The interplay between these three chords are crucial to convey Aeolian's signature melancholy sound.

Let's look at the diatonic chords of the Aeolian mode compared to the Ionian:

Diatonic chords in Ionian:

maj	min	min	maj	maj	min	min7b5 (or 1/2 diminished)
I	ii	iii	IV	V	vi	vii

Diatonic chords in Aeolian:

min	min7b5	maj	min	min	maj	maj
i	ii	bIII	iv	v	bVI	bVII

Now we can take the notes of the E Aeolian scale (E F# G A B C D) and use them to form the following chords.

Example 6c:

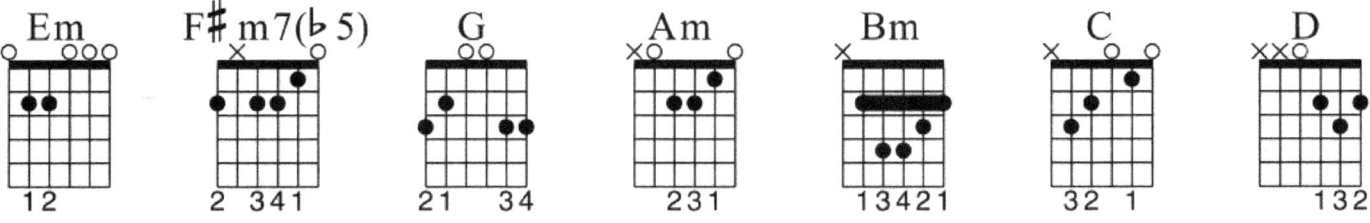

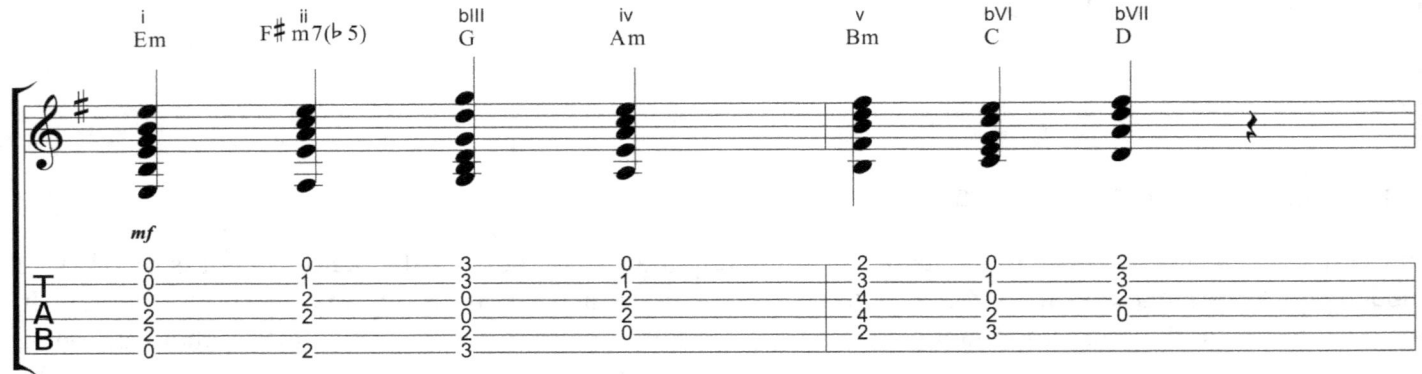

Like the Ionian mode, the characteristics of Aeolian are not as poignant as some other modes. But we can highlight the Aeolian sound and differentiate it from other modes by using chords that contain the b6. In the Aeolian, this interval is more helpless and sombre sounding than the Dorian's natural 6th. The Aeolian's major 2nd is also more subtle and less grating than the Phrygian's b2.

If we begin a progression with the tonic chord (Em), we could follow it with the bVI chord (C Major), as it obviously contains a C note (the b6). We could also use the v or ii chords, as both contain an F# (the Aeolian major 2nd).

C Major (bVI chord) = C E G

B Minor (v chord) = B D F#

F#m7b5 (ii chord) = F# A C E

Try writing a few chord progressions using these chords and try to begin and end on an E Minor chord to get a feel for the Aeolian chord progression. Here are a couple of quick ideas.

Example 6d – Progression 1:

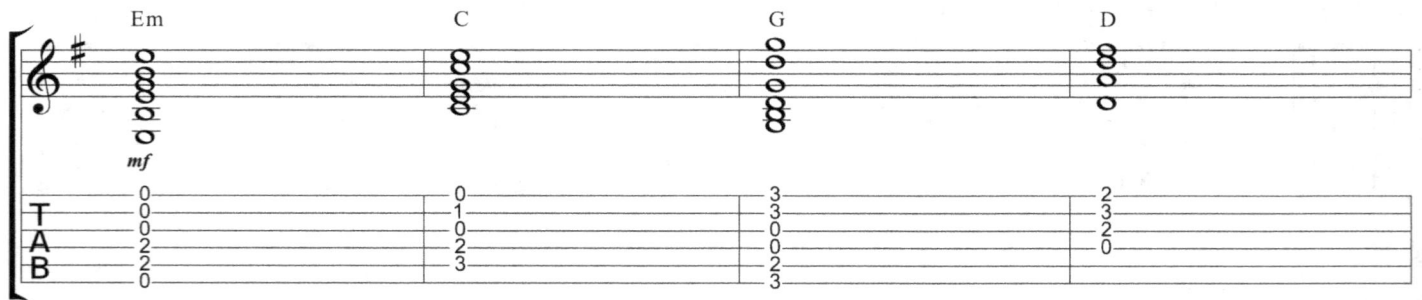

Example 6e – Progression 2:

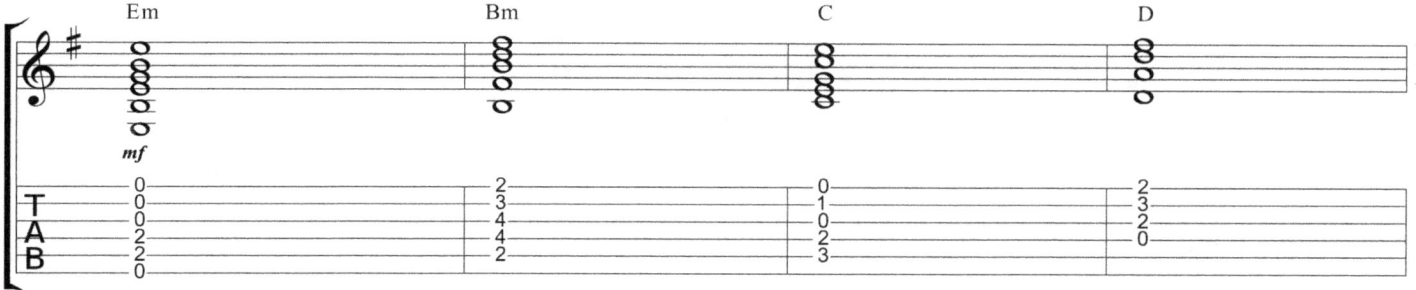

Part 3: Soloing in Aeolian using scales and arpeggios

I've mentioned this five times now! Let's put together a soloing checklist for Aeolian and ask ourselves the three big questions:

1. What is a three-note-per-string version of the scale from the root?

2. What kind of pentatonics can I use e.g. regular, custom or relative minor?

3. What kinds of arpeggios will bring out the flavour of the mode?

Here is the diatonic Aeolian scale spanning six strings with a three-note-per-string pattern.

Example 6f:

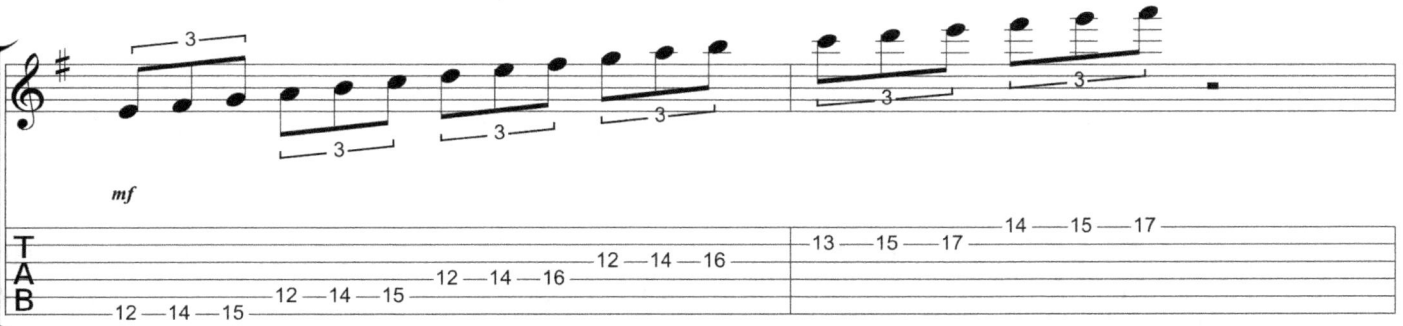

This is great way to hear the mode across the neck and an excellent tool for improvisation and composition.

Pentatonics

Next, I want to talk about the trusty pentatonic, which is a great friend of the Aeolian. Let's have a look at the E Minor Pentatonic scale, which is made from the 1st, 3rd, 4th, 5th and 7th intervals of the Aeolian scale (E G A B D).

Example 6g:

This is a cool scale, but often overused, thus it can sound amateurish. When used sparingly and with attitude, however, the pentatonic can sound brutal, even erotic! We can add further *zazz* to the pentatonic by adding a "blue" note – the b5 from the Aeolian scale – which in this case is Bb.

Example 6h:

When used with taste, this subtle outside note can add attitude and quirky tension to an otherwise simple scale.

Arpeggios

Let's talk arpeggios. We can use a simple E Minor triad arpeggio made from the 1st, 3rd and 5th of the Aeolian scale, but this can sound dull and routine. We can make things more sonically colourful by using an Em7 arpeggio (E G B D). Here are Em and Em7 arpeggios side by side.

Example 6i:

Here is an alternative way to play these arpeggios, using the same notes but with a different shape.

Example 6j:

The final arpeggios are six string shapes that cover three octaves. These are a fun way to cover the neck in a diagonal fashion and an excellent way to create drastic intervals and position shifts in improvisation.

Example 6k:

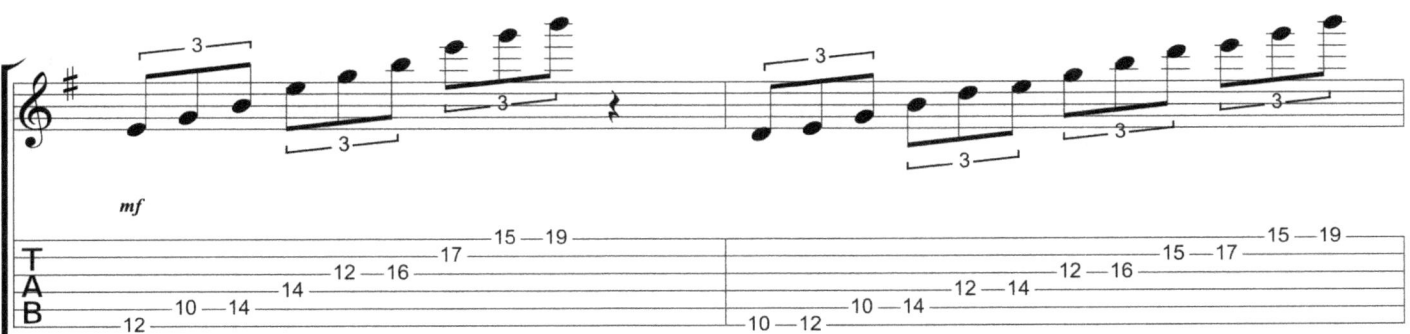

Having alternate shapes of the "same" arpeggio may seem superfluous, but the fact of playing in a different region of the neck often leads to different soloing ideas. It's important to learn multiple different ways to play similar groups of notes. More options mean less restriction and this opens up the fretboard. This in turn will give you limitless freedom that will ultimately lead to further creativity.

Part 4: Aeolian licks to help you get creative

Now let's look at how these ideas can come together in an expressive, musical context.

Example 61 uses the basic E Minor Pentatonic with a classic Chuck Berry entry. The use of bends, legato and slides will make any "meat and veg" blues lick sound instantly more expressive.

Notice that this lick also includes a Bb note (AKA the b5 or devil's tritone). This is the famous "blue" note which creates a moment of sexy blues tension. It is, of course, outside the key signature, so it will sound abrasive and horrendous if you hold it for too long. I tend to play outside notes with slides and quick legato to avoid any sustained, sonic repugnance.

Example 61: E Minor Chuck Berry lick with b5 pull-off roll

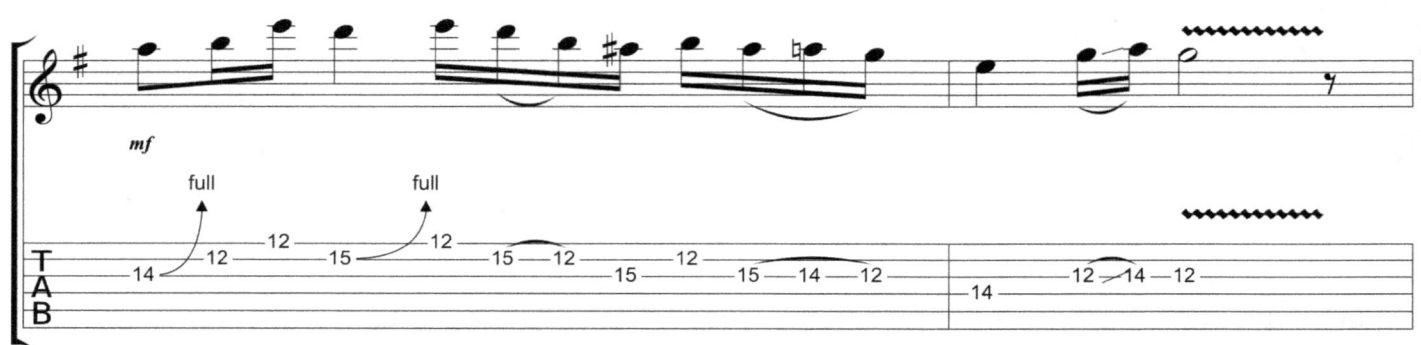

This next idea uses a common three-note-per-string E Aeolian scale shape, but I've added in a few legato notes and bends to avoid the monotony of an ascending diatonic scale run.

One of the first things you'll notice about this lick is the massive bend position shifts in the second bar. I've seen Guthrie Govan execute bends like this to quickly jump to a new position on the neck. If you're attempting to create your own licks like this, you can either return to your original position, like I did, or continue playing from the new position established by your second bend. There are no rules! You could even add a third bend if it's in key!

Example 6m: E Aeolian three-note-per-string lick with hammer-ons and shifting position bends

The next lick combines E Minor Pentatonic with a few notes of the E Aeolian diatonic scale. You'll have noticed that blending pentatonic and diatonic scales is a concept I use frequently. I like that you can quickly shift gears from rocky, bluesy good times, to a more emotive diatonic sound. In the example below, this is achieved simply by introducing the second and b6 of the Aeolian scale to create the emotive semitone intervals that the pentatonic cannot.

Example 6n: Ascending E Minor Pentatonic legato lick with descending Aeolian diatonic notes

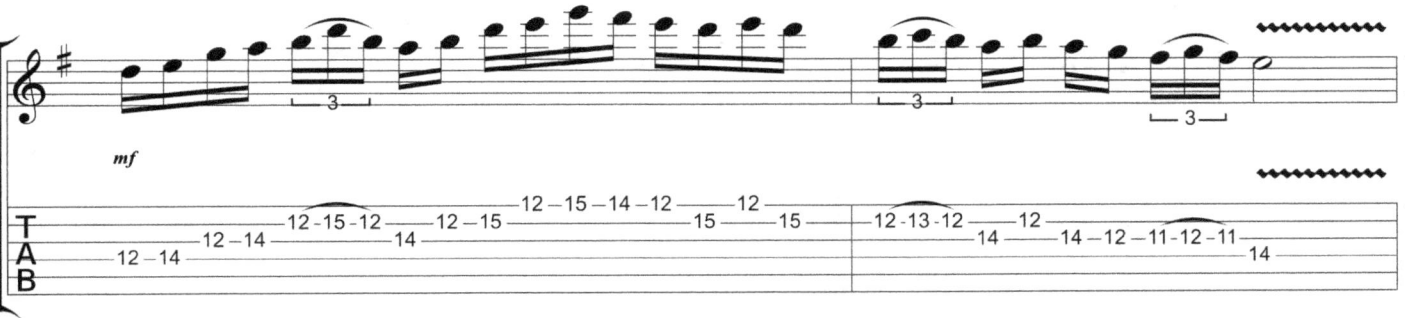

I'll often use legato and triplets to avoid having a lick only made up of 1/16th notes. You can use this concept in other modal contexts too – just make sure the notes you choose from the diatonic scale are ones that express the flavour of the mode (e.g. the Phrygian's b2 or the Dorian's natural 6th).

This next lick combines a simple ascending E Minor triad arpeggio with an Aeolian diatonic scale descent. I've heard Alexi Laiho and Alex Skolnick use this concept extremely well in a few solos. It adds a nice entry to a descending shred passage. The arpeggio can be slowly picked or hastily swept, depending on your preference. This kind of lick could also be reworked with major, diminished or even augmented arpeggios. Just remain aware of the key signature when playing the diatonic descending part of the lick.

Example 6o: E Minor five-string arpeggio with triplet Aeolian diatonic descent

A few years ago I was listening to a progressive metal band called Scar Symmetry and instantly grew fond of Per Nilsson's playing. There was an amazing arpeggio in one of their songs that blew me away and I've since used it when improvising, not only in metal, but in jazz and blues contexts too. Example 6p combines Per's signature minor eleventh arpeggio shape with some cheeky jazz chromatics and grace notes.

Example 6p: Em11 sliding lick with chromatic notes

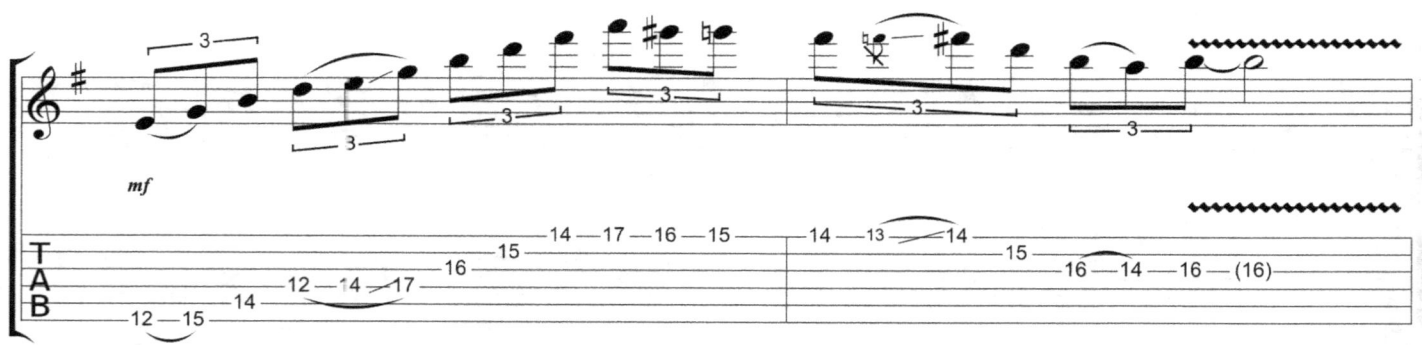

This is the kind of lick that sounds great whether played fast or slow. The arpeggio has lots of melodic colour as it covers the 1st, 3rd, 5th, 7th, 9th and 11th intervals of the Em11 chord. The chromatic notes add a quirky, outside sound, and the grace note slide from the "outside" F adds a smooth jazzy flavour to the phrase.

If you get bored of bland arpeggio triads, the addition of the 7th or 9th is a game changer. However, be sparing with the use of chromatics in your playing, as this trick can be easily overused and things will end up sounding too much like *Flight of the Bumblebee*.

Example 6q is another pedal tone idea, using B as our pedal and the notes of E Aeolian. It leads into an E Minor Pentatonic.

Example 6q: Pedal tone E Aeolian lick

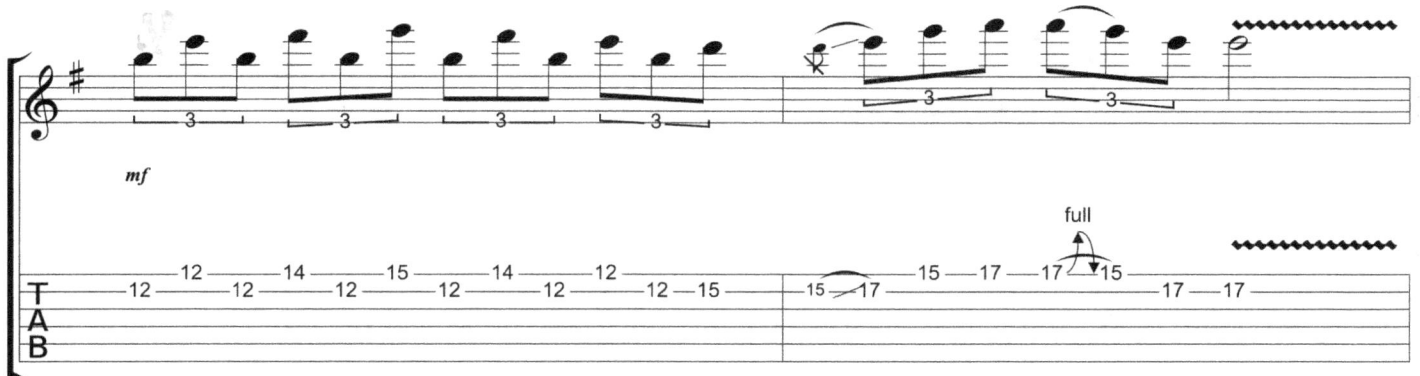

Depending on what chords you're playing over, the notes you play against your pedal tone can change according to the progression. You can also vary where you play the pentatonic part of the lick, if a chord change leads you to a different part of the neck. The more you experiment with this lick, the more you'll discover how to apply it. There are no rules other than staying in key and finding a sound you like.

The next example utilises the E Minor Pentatonic scale again and ascends using legato and five-note groupings. It has a sliding note that transitions into a three-string descending Em7 arpeggio.

Example 6r: E Minor Pentatonic third position in fives with three-string Em7 arpeggio

Blending pentatonics and minor arpeggios is an interesting way to bring together bluesy and jazzy sounds. The reason they work together so well is that the pentatonic scale uses the 1st, 3rd, 4th, 5th and 7th intervals of the minor scale; the minor 7th arpeggio uses the same notes but omits the 4th, so they're one note away from having exactly the same notes, while maintaining their own different vibe and flavour.

Example 6s uses two different E Minor Pentatonic positions for its picked and tapped notes. It descends in quick triplets, then ascends in sixteenths through the scale. It ends with an outside bend from D# to E.

You'll notice I'm pretty obsessed with outside bends and I love ending licks with them. Players like Marty Friedman, Nick Johnston and Guthrie Govan use this technique frequently. It's one way of playing technical, exciting phrases but still adding an element of tension and emotion.

Example 6s: E Minor Pentatonic with taps and sliding position shift

The next lick uses a pretty basic five-string E Minor triad arpeggio, but changes the note order to create a more interesting pattern. This is a quick way to make the arpeggio sound more like a phrase than a linear "textbook" arpeggio.

You'll also notice I've added in some legato and slides, just to force position shifts. Often, playing a passage of notes on just one string using slides is a great "storytelling" technique to add to your lead playing. There's a small lead line in the Iron Maiden epic *Fear of the Dark* that occurs just before the main solos that perfectly illustrates the art of storytelling on guitar.

Example 6t: Skipping interval E Minor arpeggio lick with slides

The final lick in this chapter is a G Ionian string skip lick. Because we are operating in the same key signature as E Aeolian, I promise it's safe to use! The lick shifts between 1/8th note and 1/16th note triplets to add speed and an element of surprise. The use of string skips creates more interesting intervals and at times can sound a bit like an arpeggio.

Example 6u: G Ionian string skip legato lick

Everything you've learned to play in E Aeolian can be modulated to other Aeolian (Natural Minor) keys. As ever, seek out some backing tracks to jam to and keep in mind that Aeolian is the saddest mode of all. Keep a box of tissues handy in case your emotions get out of hand!

Chapter 7: Elusive Locrian

The final chapter of our modal journey is a scary and elusive one. We'll end our adventure by plunging into a dark, mysterious, murky forest. It's likely that the forest is riddled with ghouls and hobgoblins (I probably should've warned you about that). There is an ice-cream truck that only sells liquorice and orange flavours and has an iPod playlist consisting solely of Black Sabbath, Diamond Head and Slayer playing on repeat over a loud speaker. Now you are fully immersed in the mystery and tension that is the Locrian mode.

For many years I was fearful and dismissive of this scary, elusive mode. On many occasions I said to my students, "Don't worry about the Locrian, it's awful. It's almost IMPOSSIBLE to make it sound good." Until very recently I would have stood by those words, but now, as an older, wiser man of thirty-one and a half, I'm here to tell you that the Locrian is a super-interesting mode with tension, allure and subtlety.

The thing that fascinates me the most about the Locrian is that it can sound so poignantly evil. So evil that it has the potential to conjure demons faster than a common household Ouija board (yes, we all have one in the attic). Yet, it also has a tense, jazz-fusion sound to it, which makes it the well-kept secret that most players don't know about.

The Locrian mode is, of course, the last of our seven diatonic modes, which to refresh your memory are: Ionian, Dorian, Phrygian, Lydian, Mixolydian, Aeolian and Locrian – the most evil of all modes.

Part 1: Finding the Locrian sound

In this chapter we will use A Locrian for all our examples. Let's look at the A Locrian scale in one octave.

Example 7a:

Locrian has a dark and dangerous vibe, and of course should be learn as an isolated sound. However, once again, it's useful to have other perspectives in the back of our mind.

Locrian is...

1. The seventh mode of the major scale.

2. An Aeolian (Natural Minor) scale with a b2 and b5 (the latter is often referred to as the diminished 5th).

Let's take a look at A Aeolian and A Locrian side by side:

A Aeolian = A B C D E F G A

A Locrian = A Bb C D Eb F G A

Example 7b:

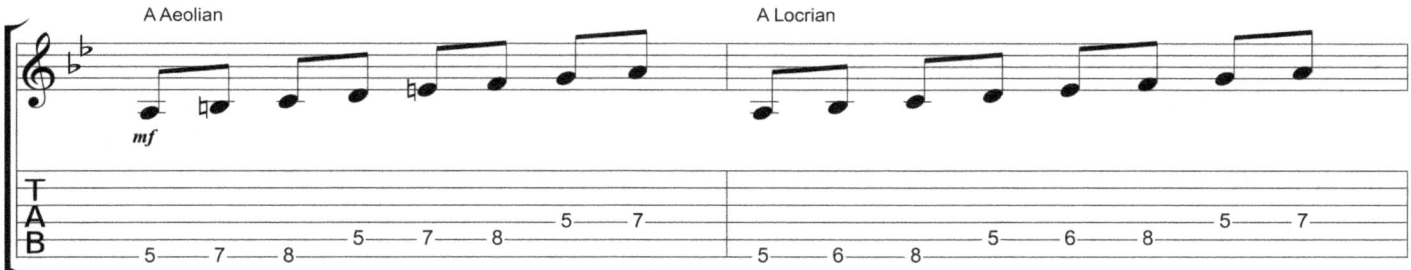

Aeolian scale formula = 1 2 b3 4 5 b6 b7

Locrian scale formula = 1 b2 b3 4 b5 b6 b7

When displayed side by side, you can see there are two notes in the Locrian mode that stand out like a gangsta rapper in a kilt shop. It's the b2 (Bb) and b5 (Eb) that make the Locrian sound more nasty and gross than the inoffensive Aeolian mode.

It's crucial that we highlight these two important notes to bring out the full flavour of the Locrian.

The harsh intervals of the b2 and b5 can be heard in the chord progression example below. Play through the chords and the ascending and descending Locrian scale variations straight after to hear the unsettling, abrasive nature of this scale in a melodic and musical context.

Example 7c: A Locrian chord progression with scale ascend & descend

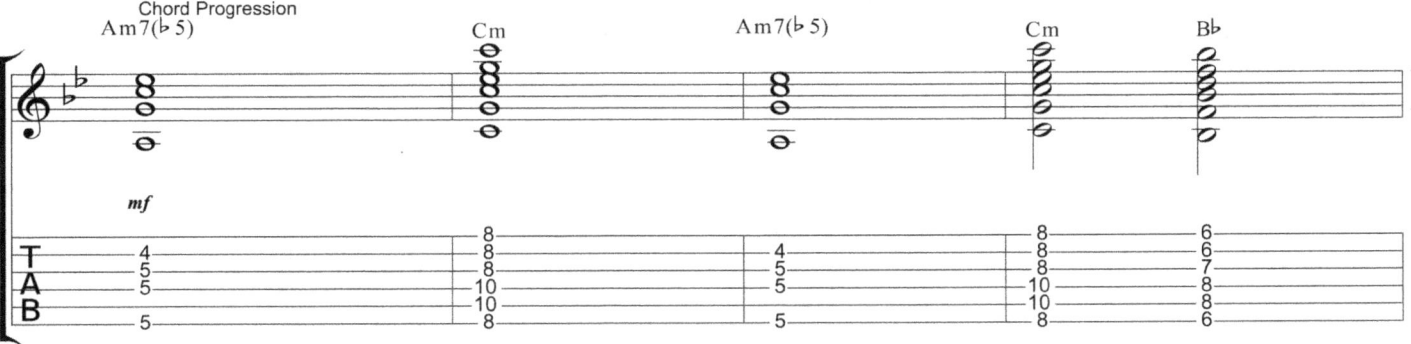

The characteristic b2, Bb note is present in the Bb Major chord, which is quite similar to the tense nature of the b2 we previously saw in Phrygian mode, especially when you hear its interplay with the chords. The other Locrian characteristic note is the b5, Eb note, which can be heard in the Am7b5, C Minor and Bb Major chord. It has a tense, devil-summoning sound that we hear a lot in evilest of heavy metal songs.

As I've mentioned in previous chapters, scale theory and interval knowledge will only take you so far. To further understand the Locrian mode, here's few Locrian songs for you to check out:

- Painkiller – Judas Priest
- Juicebox – The Strokes
- Blackened – Metallica
- Raining Blood (chorus section 1:39) – Slayer

Part 2: The Locrian diatonic chords

Throughout this book I have REPEATEDLY discussed the importance of knowing the diatonic chords within a key or mode. I'm sorry for sounding like such a broken record. Believe me, I get it! Personally, nothing makes me more infuriated than having to sit through one of my dad's stories that he told me only three days ago (though he thinks it's the first time). More so having to pretend that it's just as funny as the first time (breathes heavily into paper bag). Sorry, I had to get that out of my system. I still get night terrors from time to time from all the fake smiles and forced laughter.

That said, understanding the diatonic chords and their function will help you determine how to bring out each mode's unique flavour. The relationship between the i chord and bII chord creates the characteristic semitone tension of the Locrian, while the i and bV chord have the tritone tension. When these tense chord relationships are used in a chord progression, the signature Locrian sound comes out. Let's look at the Locrian diatonic chords compared to that of the Ionian mode.

Diatonic chords starting from chord 1 (Ionian)

maj	min	min	maj	maj	min	min7b5 (or 1/2 diminished)
I	ii	iii	IV	V	vi	vii

Diatonic chords starting from chord 7 (Locrian)

min7b5	maj	min	min	maj	maj	min
i	bII	biii	iv	bV	bVI	bvii

A Locrian is the 7th mode of Bb Major as both scales share the same number of flats. This means we can simply reorder the diatonic chords of Bb Ionian starting from the vii chord to give us the A Locrian chord structure.

Example 7d:

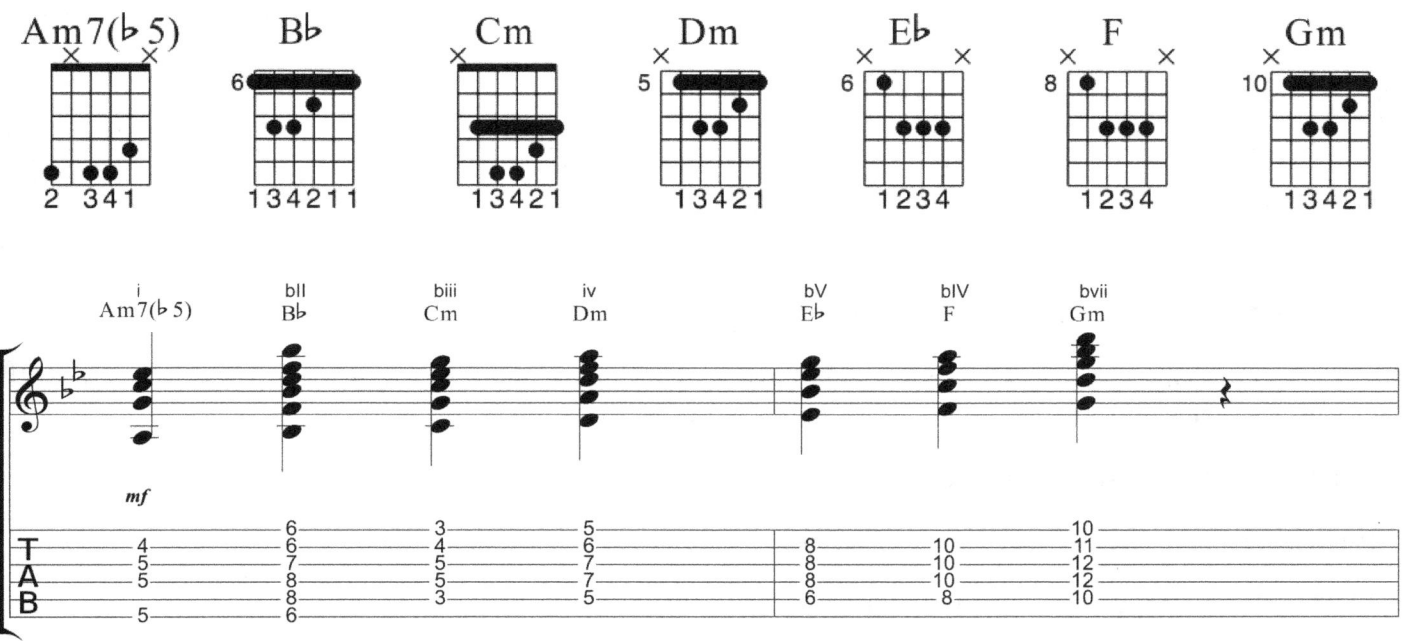

To highlight the unique Locrian sound in a chord progression we will want to focus on the b2 and b5 notes of the mode. The combination of the i and bII chord gives us the *Jaws* sound (similar to the Phrygian). Introducing the bV chord gives us the tritone tension that is also found in the Lydian mode. The bII and bV chords have the root notes Bb and Eb respectively – both Locrian character notes.

Bb Major (bII chord) = Bb D F

Eb Major (bV chord) = Eb G Bb

Try writing a few chord progressions with the Locrian chords, preferably starting and ending on the Am7b5 chord. Here are two ideas to start you off:

Example 7e – Progression 1:

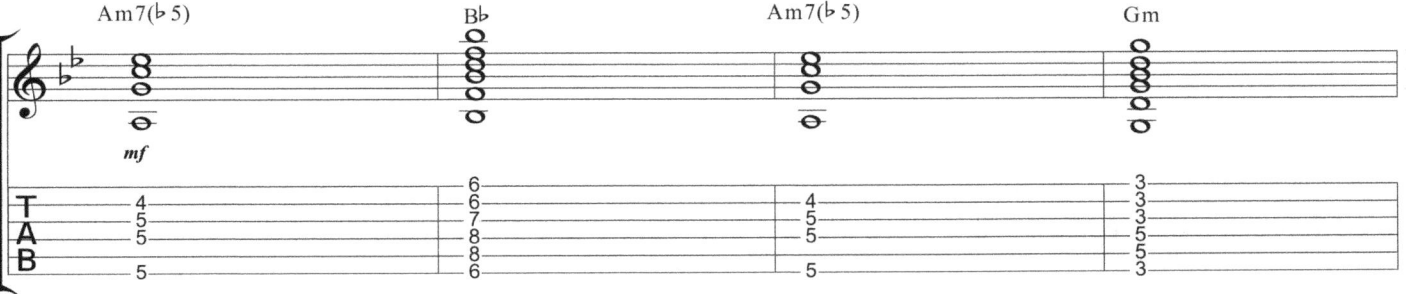

Example 7f – Progression 2:

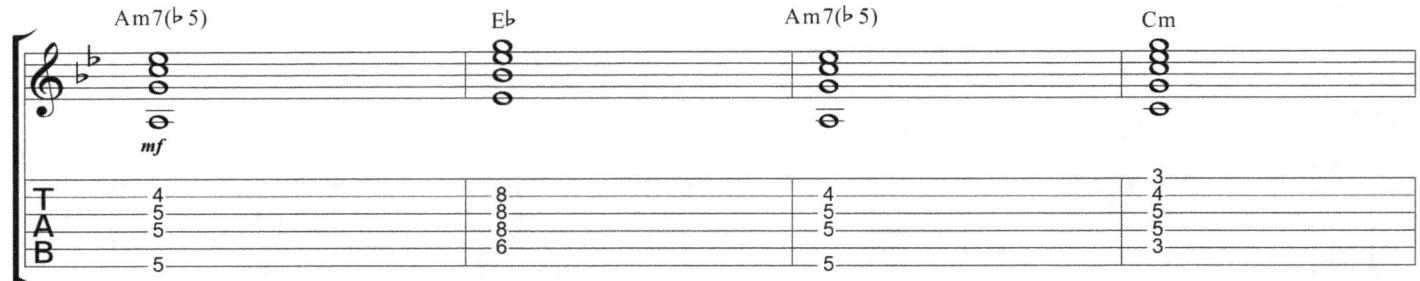

Part 3: Soloing in Locrian with scales and arpeggios

When I solo modally, I feel more confident if I have a wide range of options. In the case of the Locrian, we'll approach it in the same way as the previous modes, with the three big questions:

1. What is a three-note-per-string version of the scale from the root?

2. What kind of pentatonics can I use e.g. regular, custom or relative minor?

3. What kind of arpeggios will bring out the flavour of the mode?

With the Locrian, bear in mind that the b2 and b5 are somewhat problematic intervals. In other words, you'll see some weird scale shapes you may not have seen before!

Let's look at the A Locrian three-note-per-string scale shape. This is the fastest, most effective way to hear the Locrian mode spanning two and a bit octaves. It's also super easy to use in a shred or legato context!

Example 7g:

Pentatonics

The next scale we'll look at is a pentatonic specially designed to deal with the pesky Locrian mode. I call it "pesky" because the Locrian mode it is completely devoid of a natural 5th.

The scale formula for a regular minor pentatonic is 1, b3, 4, 5 and b7, but this doesn't work for the Locrian. If we want to use pentatonic ideas for the Locrian we will have to use the 1 b3, 4, b5 and b7 to cooperate with the chords and key signature. A Locrian's "custom pentatonic" notes are therefore A, C, D, Eb and G.

Let's have a look at the A Minor Pentatonic scale (1 b3 4 5 b7) and an A Locrian pentatonic scale (1 b3 4 b5 b7) side by side:

Example 7h:

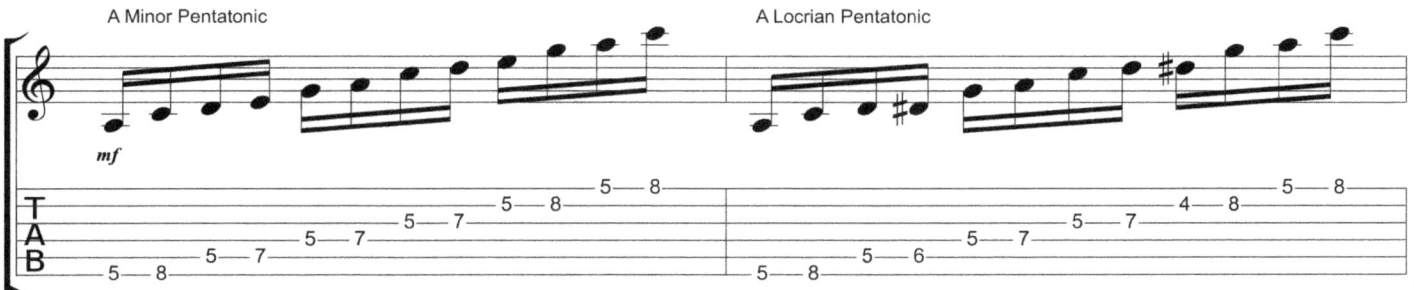

Now let's view these scales in multiple positions across the fretboard. In effect we are playing all the remaining A Minor Pentatonic shapes and flattening the 5th (E to Eb).

Example 7i:

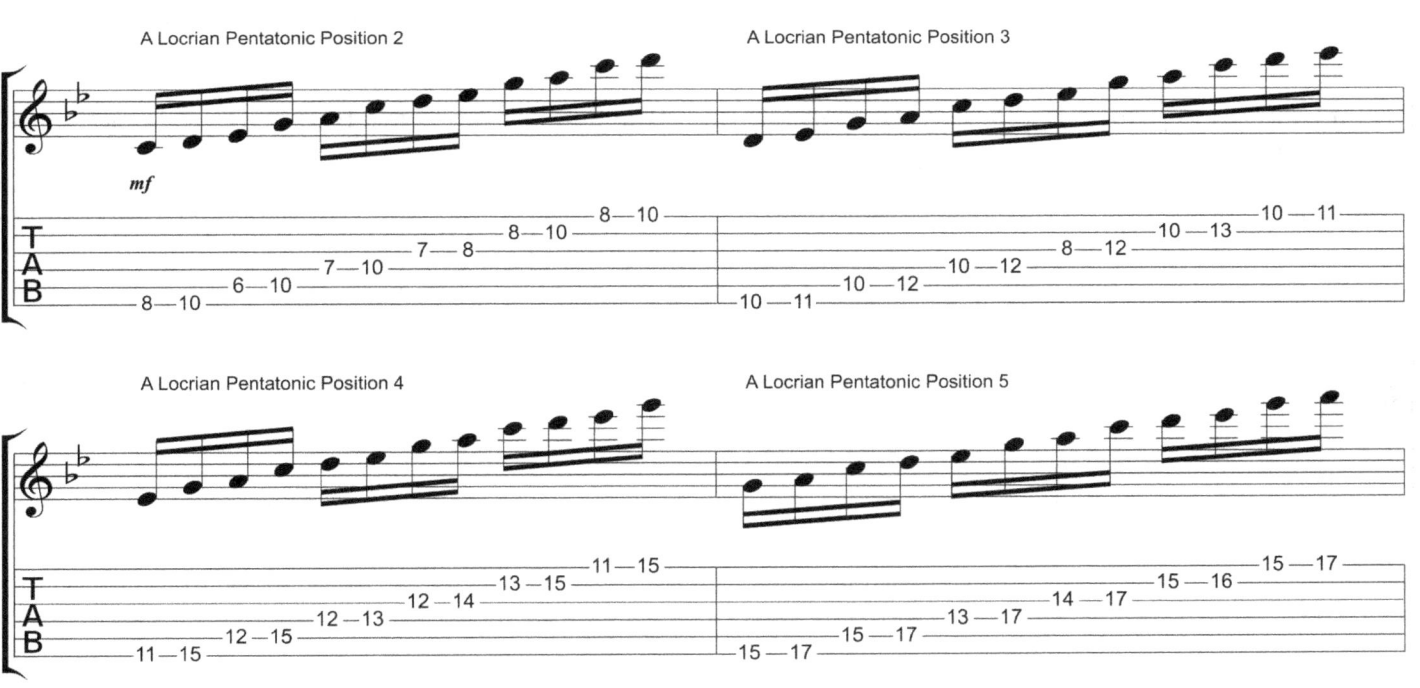

Arpeggios

Finally, let's look at our arpeggio soloing options. Due to the fact that the Locrian mode is so heavily rooted in the minor7b5 chord, we're going to look at multiple sexy ways to play this arpeggio with A Locrian.

The first arpeggio we'll look at is two variations of a five-string Am7b5 arpeggio (A C Eb G). If you wish, you can add hammer-ons on any of the strings that have two notes.

Example 7j:

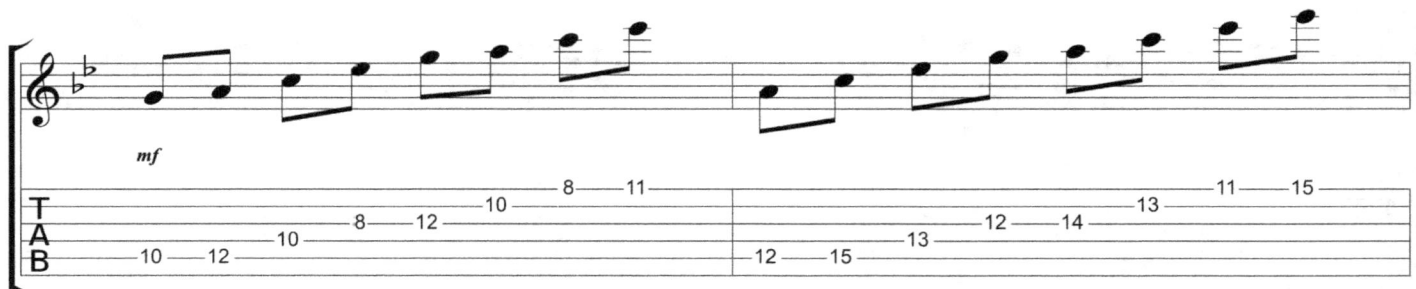

You'll notice that on the first Am7b5 arpeggio shape, the order of the notes has been rearranged to G A C and Eb. We're essentially leading the arpeggio from the seventh instead of the root.

I also use this "leading seventh" approach when playing major, minor and dominant arpeggios. Beginning on the seventh then playing the root soon after creates a nice moment of tension. It's not a rule – just something I'm partial to. You may find you like this approach too. To quote the 80s rock powerhouse Roxette, "Listen to your heart"!

The final arpeggio shape we'll look at is a six-string Am7b5 arpeggio that spans three octaves. Once again we will lead from the seventh of the arpeggio in each octave.

Example 7k:

Keep in mind that these m7b5 arpeggio shapes can be used in any Locrian key, provided you move the root note to correctly modulate to the desired key. You can also try these shapes over the vii chord in any Ionian progression or any time a m7b5 chord comes up.

Another fact of great interest (to me at least – yes, I am a massive nerd!) is that m7b5 arpeggios can be superimposed over ii and V chords in major keys. For example, in the key of G Major, we can play an F#m7b5 arpeggio (F# A C E) over an Am or Am7 ii chord, as it has exactly the same notes as the triad, plus the major 6th, thus bringing out a momentary Dorian inference, and also suggesting an Am6 chord. We can also play an F#m7b5 arpeggio over a D7 V chord (D F# A C). Over this latter chord, it has the effect of creating a dominant ninth sound.

Part 4: Locrian licks to help you get creative

If you've got this far, you've done really well. You know by now that in part four of a chapter we take all the scale shapes and arpeggios from part three and turn them into an array of sexy licks and useable melodic ideas. This chapter is no exception, but I must warn you … some of these licks are pretty *redonkulous*!

This first lick uses the first position of the A Locrian pentatonic. We'll be highlighting the b5 (because we have to!) which will result in a familiar bluesy sound.

Example 7l: A Locrian pentatonic position 1 bluesy lick

The next lick uses the three-note-per-string A Locrian shape. We ascend the scale and add in a few hammer-ons for effect and to vary the timing. This lick ends with an outside-to-inside bend.

Example 7m: A Locrian three-note-per-string ascending shred lick with legato and outside-inside bend

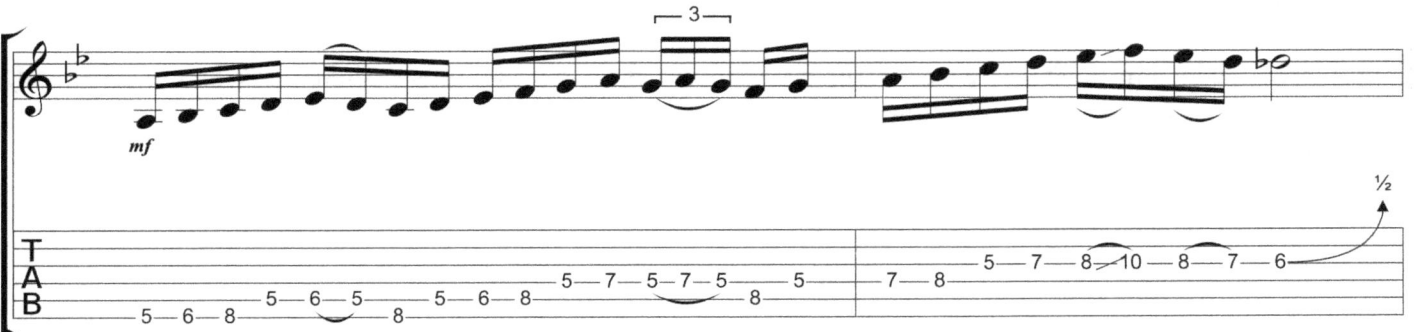

The next example uses the second position of A Locrian pentatonic. We'll ascend using multiple hammer-ons and strange note groupings, but keep to a consistent 1/16th note pulse. The lick resolves with a slide into a descending Am7b5 arpeggio.

Example 7n: A Locrian pentatonic position two with m7b5 arpeggio descent

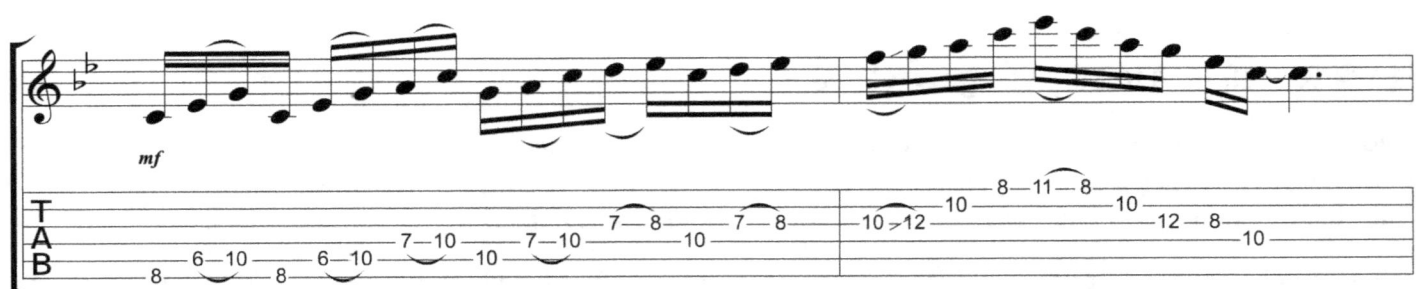

Example 7o uses the combination of an Am7b5 arpeggio and an Eb Major arpeggio with a perfect 4th across two octaves. Each arpeggio is played in an ascending manner with taps.

This lick is an interesting alternative to a linear, one-string tap lick, or a standard ascending triad arpeggio, or swept arpeggio. As you've probably guessed, this concept is not limited to this mode. If you swap around the notes to suit the key you're in, the possibilities are limitless, so get experimenting!

Example 7o: A Locrian two octave tap lick

Example 7p ascends through a five string Am7b5 arpeggio using a triplet pulse. Then it descends through a D Phrygian three-note-per-string scale shape. Pay close attention to the hammer-on placement and cheeky slide at the end of the lick

Example 7p: Five-string Am7b5 arpeggio with D Phrygian diatonic descent

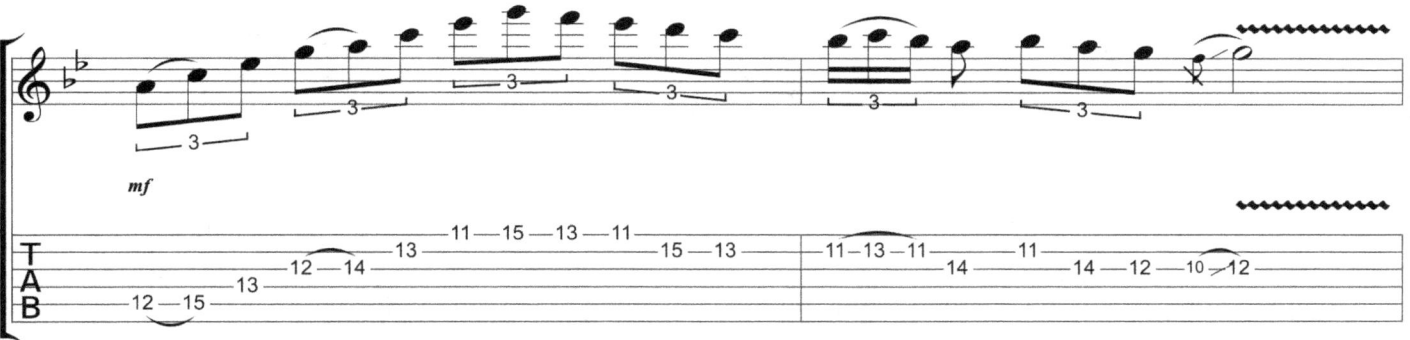

The next lick uses the diatonic A Locrian scale in an ascending manner, but I've mixed up the order of the notes to keep things interesting. The note order in the lick is 1st, 3rd, 2nd, 5th, 7th and 6th, and this repeats over two octaves. I've also used dotted 1/8th notes and regular 1/16th notes to make the timing more interesting and less predictable.

Example 7q: Diagonal 1 3 2 5 7 6 Locrian crawling lick

Here is an idea based on moving swept three-string diminished arpeggios. The idea of moving the same lick up the fretboard in minor 3rds (three semitones) has been done to death. If possible, it's even more offensive when performed with diminished harmony! But, due to the fact that we're not in a harmonic minor key, we can use multiple Am7b5 arpeggio shapes that change in every position!

Example 7r: Three-string multiple position Am7b5 arpeggio

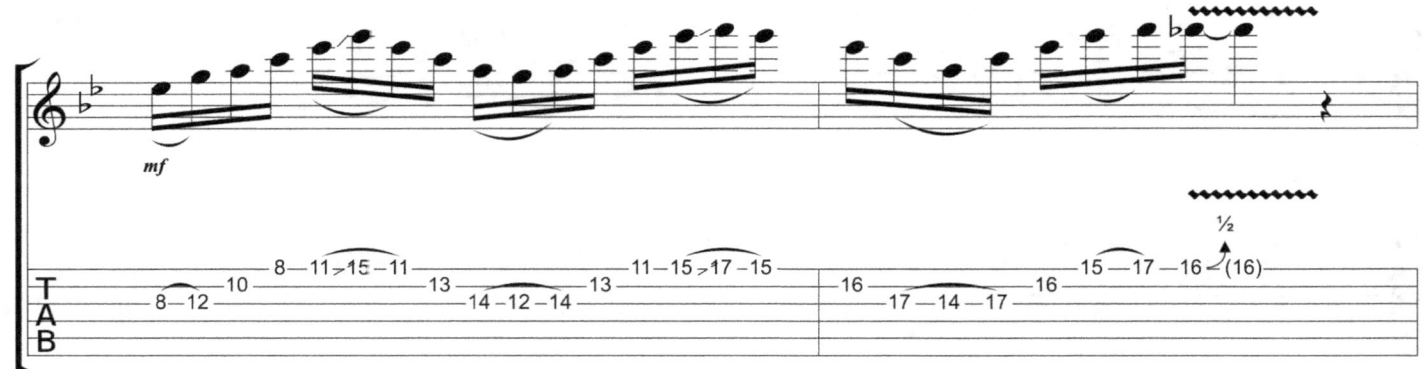

You will notice that once again, I ended this lick with an outside note, bent a semitone to a scale note. I know, I have a problem, but I'm going to get help.

Here is the A Locrian pentatonic ascending in five-note groupings. This lick is played with lots of legato to make it smoother and more "loosey goosey"!

Example 7s: A Locrian pentatonic position three with five-note groupings lick

Now we come to another pedal tone idea – this time using a mid-register "A" note against which we ascend the notes of the A Locrian scale. The lick has a triplet pulse and moves into an ascending Am7b5 arpeggio.

Example 7t: Pedal A Locrian lick with Am7b5 arpeggio

The final example uses two octaves of the six-string Am7b5 shape illustrated in part three. It consists mostly of 1/16th notes with the occasional legato triplet to mix up the rhythm. It ends by descending an A Locrian pentatonic box pattern.

Example 7u: Am7b5 two octave arpeggio with Locrian pentatonic descent

As you know, everything in this chapter can be transferred to other Locrian keys or used in passing over any m7b5 chord that presents itself in a chord progression.

Epilogue & Acknowledgements

I would like to thank the many students I've had over the years, who were with me during my studies and musical journey. You all pushed me to be the best musical version of myself and I'm eternally grateful.

Thanks to the friends I've made in the Melbourne music scene and through YouTube – you have all been an enormous support and have inspired me in my writing and performance. Most importantly, you've helped get me out of my horrendous and often inescapable introvert bubble.

Finally, I want to thank my beautiful wife, Lucie, my son, Alexi, and my cat, Andrew P. Rodriguez. You are the lights in my life. You all manage to make me smile every day, and everything I achieve is with your help, encouragement and love.

SHRED GUITAR IMPROVISATION

The Creative Guide to Rock & Shred Metal Guitar Improvisation

CHRIS ZOUPA

FUNDAMENTAL CHANGES

Introduction

You might have had that dream where you're standing at the front of a classroom. You're making a speech, or maybe doing a "show and tell" of your favourite toy or comic book. Suddenly, you become aware that you are, in fact, naked and everyone in the class is laughing at you.

I still regularly have dreams like this, despite being 32 and having not entered a classroom for nearly 14 years. I'm hoping to use the proceeds of this book to get extensive therapy regarding why these dreams keep happening!

Many guitarists feel "naked" or put on the spot when called upon to spontaneously improvise a solo and experiences the same classroom terror described above. Here are some things I've heard guitarists say out loud hundreds of times:

"What if I screw up?"

"What if I lose my place?"

"Isn't it easier if I just write something."

If this sounds like you, you're in the right place. In this book I'm going to show you that improvisation can be super fun. It's just a matter of doing the preparation beforehand.

One of the biggest perceived obstacles guitarists have is knowing enough theory and having an awareness of how chords work. I know, yawn-fest! But doing some work on this aspect of playing is the launchpad from which magical, spur of the moment creativity and uninhibited stream of consciousness playing can take off!

In this book I'll show you how to play over chords, target certain chord tones to outline the changes, create memorable phrases without resorting to clichés, make scales sound less linear, and add general flair and pizazz to your playing.

Are you pumped? You should be!

Let's dive into the deep end together. Don't worry, I'll be with you whole time.

As Bud, the wise golden retriever once taught me, "Believe in yourself. The magic has been in you all along" – and he played Basketball and Soccer … with *humans*! Amazing right?!

Have fun!

Zoups

Get the Audio

The audio files for this book are available to download for free from **www.fundamental-changes.com.** The link is in the top right-hand corner. Simply select this book title from the drop-down menu and follow the instructions to get the audio.

We recommend that you download the files directly to your computer, not to your tablet, and extract them there before adding them to your media library. You can then put them on your tablet, iPod or burn them to CD. On the download page there is a help PDF and we also provide technical support via the contact form.

For over 350 Free Guitar Lessons with Videos Check out:

www.fundamental-changes.com

Over 10,000 fans on Facebook: **FundamentalChangesInGuitar**

Tag us for a share on Instagram: **FundamentalChanges**

Chapter 1 – Chord Tones and Chord Numbers

"But, Chris…!" I hear you cry, confronted with a diagram at the beginning of Chapter One, "…where are all the sexy licks?"

We'll get to that very soon Mindless atonal shred can be fun and is an excellent way to annoy your loved ones and neighbours, but in order to make great music there are some basic principles you need to know.

A bit of Roman history

A basic understanding of major scale harmony goes a long way when it comes to improvising over a set of chord changes. If you know all this stuff inside out, feel free to skip ahead to the licks – but a theory refresher never hurt anyone.

Let's take the C Major scale for example. The scale is made up of the notes C D E F G A and B. Taking the first note of the scale, skipping the next one, and the one after that gives us our first three-note chord, called a triad: C E G it spells a basic C Major chord.

If we move to the second note in the scale (D) and repeat the process, we get D F A which spells a basic D minor chord. This is called harmonising the scale – in other words, turning it into chords.

Each chord in the harmonised scale is assigned a Roman numeral for shorthand. C Major is the I chord. D minor is the ii chord, and so on. (Major and dominant chords have upper case numbers and minor chords have lower case numbers – blame history!)

The table shows all the chords in the key of C Major. The Roman numeral system comes in handy later when you want to explain a chord progression to someone and make it understandable regardless of what key it will be played in. For example, your basic three-chord blues in C Major is a I IV V progression (C Major, F Major, G Major).

Roman Numeral shorthand	Chord Name
I	C Major
ii	D minor
iii	E minor
IV	F Major
V	G Major
vi	A minor
vii	B minor

Example 1a shows a very common classic rock chord progression (if you use your imagination, it sounds not unlike *Since You've Been Gone* by Rainbow).

The chords are C Major – G Major – A minor – F Major. The sequence in Roman numerals is I V vi IV.

Example 1a:

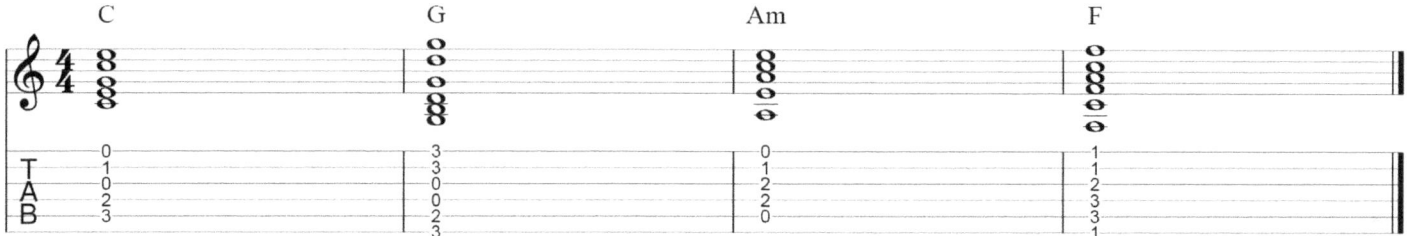

Now look at the triads that created these chords. The notes contained in each is as follows:

C Major = C E G

G Major = G B D

A minor = A C E

F Major = F A C

A triad contains the note intervals that are most important in identifying its flavour:

- The *root* note of the chord (C in the C Major chord)
- The *third* (E in C Major)
- The *fifth* (G in C Major)

Note: the third interval is a *major third* for major chords or a *minor third* for minor chords. "Minor third" just means the note is lowered a half step.

Why am I telling you this?

Well, if you want to play a super strong *articulate* solo when confronted with a set of chord changes, and you're unsure what to play, your first port of call is to *target* those strong notes that outline the chord changes. Once you become adept at this process, you can use tons of other creative ideas in between those chord tones, and your ideas will still sound strong and well defined.

Let me show you how it works in practice…

Targeting the root

Targeting the root note is as simple as playing the C note when a C Major chord is being played.

You might think, "But that's boring… *and* that's the bass player's job!" and there's a degree of truth to this. In a moment we'll be targeting the third and the fifth, but it's important to know where your root is at all times!

Let's get playing and begin simple. Don't worry, simple is good. If you're concerned the material here is beneath you, skip forward to the last chapter and see what you're letting yourself in for!

Begin by learning where the root notes are on each chord of the previous example: C, G, A and F.

Example 1b:

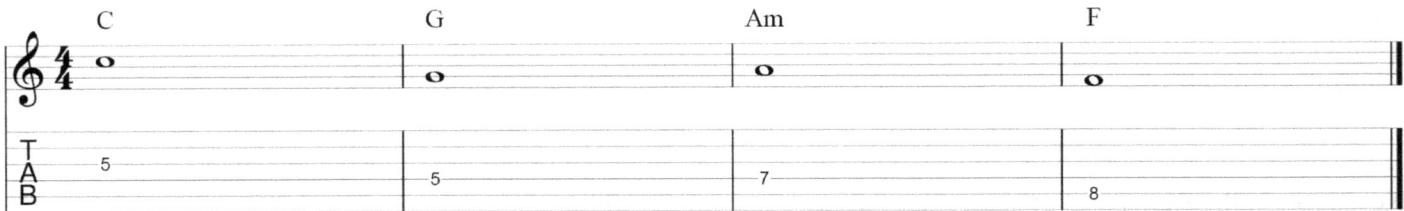

In a moment I'll show you a melodic lick that strongly follows these chord changes by targeting the root notes above. To do this I'll use two scales that sound great played over a chord progression in the key of C Major, and which fall easily on the guitar neck.

The A Minor Pentatonic and A Aeolian scales are built from the sixth note of the C Major scale. Play both scales over backing track one.

Example 1c:

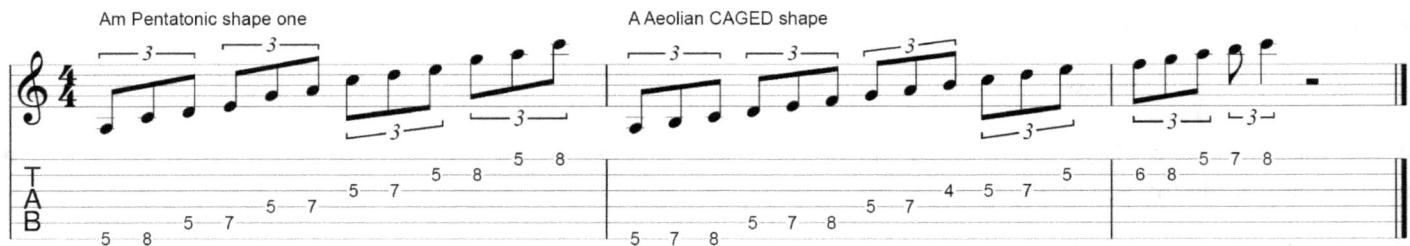

Example 1d targets the root notes of each chord using licks built from the two scales above. The strong scale choice, combined with triad note targeting creates a significant emphasis on chord changes, as well as filling out the bars with interesting hooks and melodies.

Example 1d:

Focusing on the root like this creates a strong foundation for your melodic ideas. Players who have little awareness of the chord changes tend to have a "meandering" sound to their solos and don't often play memorable lines. Targeting the root and other triad notes will help keep your listeners engaged.

Targeting the 3rd

Next, we'll target the third interval of each chord in our progression. Once again, this might seem like a boring bassline to begin with, but the more you practice this the more the sound of each interval will become embedded, and you'll find yourself playing stronger melodic ideas.

The third interval emphasises the *emotional* major or minor quality of each chord and its happy or sad feeling. Notice how targeting the third sounds less "resolved" than targeting the root.

Example 1e:

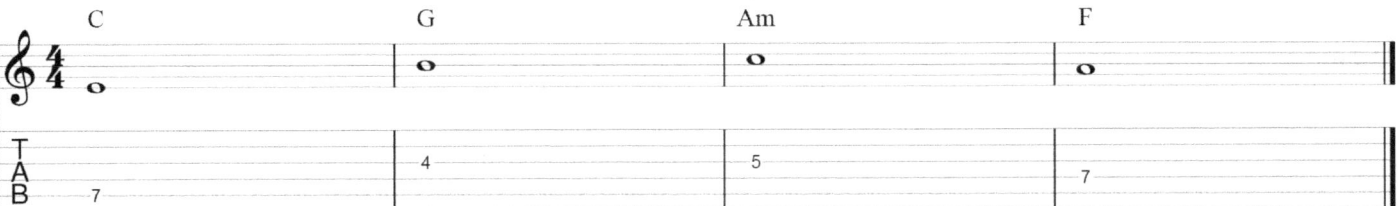

Example 1f targets the thirds on the chord changes and fills out the bars with notes from the A Minor Pentatonic and A Aeolian scale shape to outline the sequence while building a meaningful solo.

Example 1f:

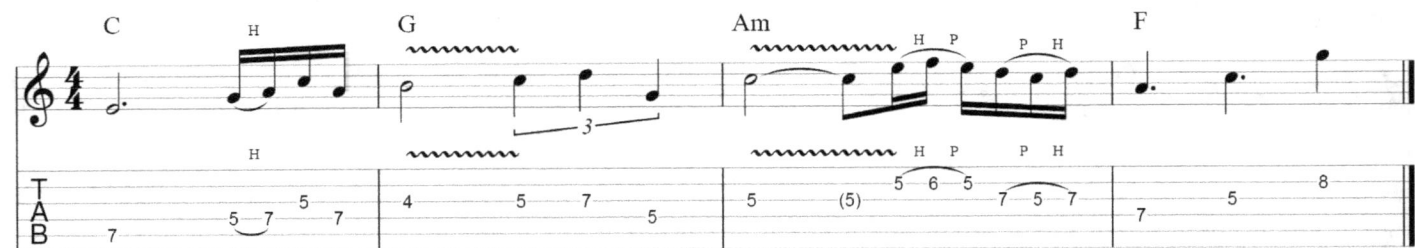

Targeting the 5th

Finally, let's learn to target the fifth interval of each chord.

On their own, these notes form a dull, uninspiring melody, but they do sound *stable*.

Example 1g:

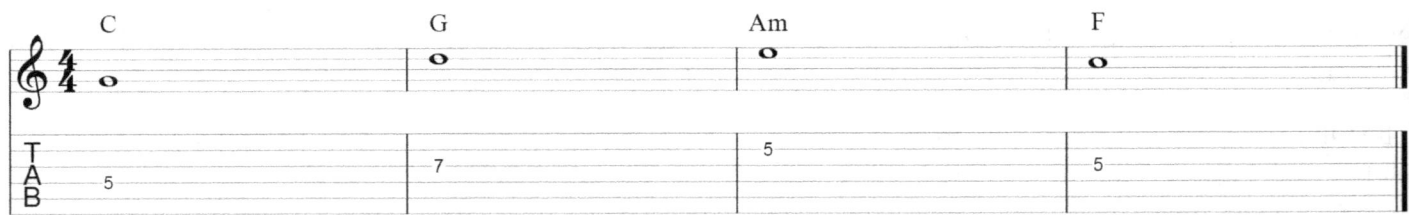

Example 1h uses the A Minor Pentatonic and Aeolian scales again, while targeting the fifths.

Example 1h:

Targeting all three notes of the triad

Once you've practised targeting root, third and fifth separately, it's time to mix things up and target all three triad notes. You can be as organised as you like when practicing this technique, but we have to start somewhere so let's begin by targeting the following chord tones:

Over C Major we'll target the root (C)

Over G Major we'll target the major 3rd (B)

Over A minor we'll target the 5th (E)

Over F Major we'll target the major 3rd again (A)

Here is how that sounds:

Example 1i:

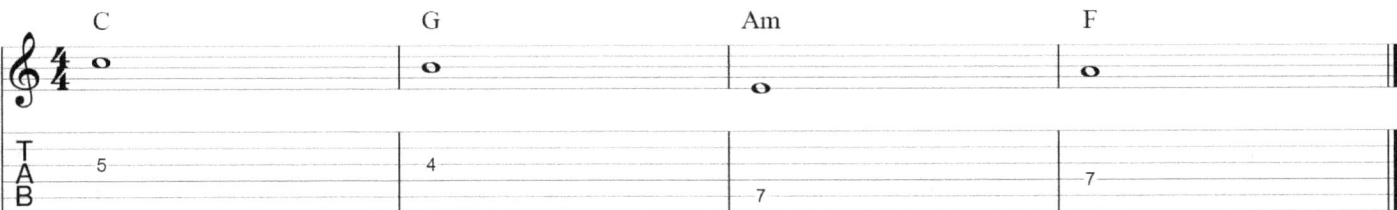

Example 1j combines these target notes with the A Minor Pentatonic and A Aeolian scales. You'll hear different the *colours* of each chord being highlighted.

Example 1j:

Now we've worked on targeting any triad note in each chord in the progression, practise this technique as follows:

1. Go back to the beginning and play through the progression using only root notes.

2. Compose a melodic line of your own that contains the root note of each chord falling on beat 1 when that chord is played in the backing track.

3. Now play through the progression highlighting only the third of each chord.

4. Compose a melodic line that highlights the third on each chord change.

5. Play through the progression highlighting only the fifth.

6. Compose a line highlighting the fifth on each change.

7. Finally, choose a target note "route" through the changes (i.e. third of C Major, root of G Major, fifth of A minor, root of F Major) and compose a melodic line that fits around it.

It's important to say at this point that a small percentage of improvisation occurs due to a happy accident. The more preparation you've done, the more likely it is that a beautiful line will come out of you by "accident". So, it's fine to write lines and build your vocabulary until you can play without really thinking about it.

In the initial stages, the things you play may sound stale and robotic, but rest assured that after enough experimentation you'll begin to find the phrasing and embellishments that bring out *your* voice as a musician. This is a journey of self-discovery. Yes, I'm aware that I sound like a pretentious douchebag writing a self-help book, but trust me, there's nothing less authentic than a mediocre regurgitation of stolen licks from your favourite players. We've all seen *that* guy at the guitar store, playing the same two SRV licks over and over. Never be the "rip off lick guy" – learn to kick the most ass you can with your own personality!

In the next chapter you're going to take the number system to the next level and there will be plenty of cool licks to learn too.

Chapter 2 – The I Chord (G Major)

Next level Roman history

As we've seen, the harmonised major scale and the Roman numeral chord system helps us to understand how chords are formed, and how progressions are constructed. In Chapter 1 we discussed how to target specific chord tones to create lines that strongly outline the changes. Roman numeral chord numbers can also be used to help find specific scale, pentatonic or arpeggio choices that ultimately give each chord number its own "tailored" sound. Over the next few chapters we'll discuss what soloing options are available for each chord in the harmonised major scale.

All the examples are in the key of G Major. This is the parent scale from which all other scale choices are derived. Here are the diatonic chords in the key of G Major with their respective chord numbers.

Chord	G Major	A Minor	B Minor	C Major	D Major	E Minor	F#mb5
Roman Numeral	I	ii	Iii	IV	V	vi	vii

We're going to work through each chord in turn using the same process. You'll learn:

- The scale across all six strings in both three-note-per string and CAGED patterns
- The pentatonic scale relating to each chord
- The chord's triad arranged in three positions across all six strings
- The chord's seventh arpeggio (e.g. Gmaj7, Am7 etc) in three positions across all six strings
- A tasty lick for each of the above to show how you can use them in a musical context

I chord: G Major

To begin mastering the I chord, play through Example 2a. This is a G Major scale (also known as the G Ionian mode) spanning all six strings. Bar 1 is a useful three-note-per-string pattern. Bar 2 is a CAGED system scale shape.

Important disclaimer! *There is much debate about whether it's better to use three-note-per-string or CAGED shapes. It doesn't matter. Get used to both and use what works for you when improvising. Steer clear of internet arguments pertaining to this subject. It could be time better spent watching old seasons of Gilmore Girls. #teamlogan*

Example 2a:

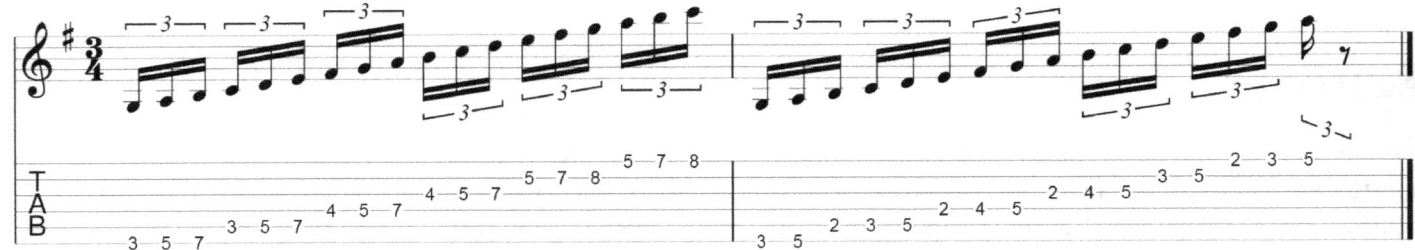

Example 2b uses the three-note-per-string pattern but includes expressive techniques and varying subdivisions to create an interesting and musical lick.

Example 2b:

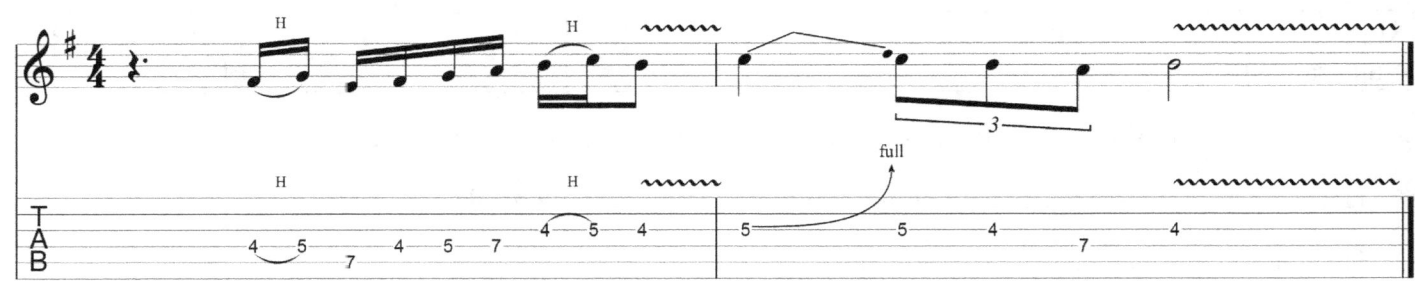

Next, I use the G Major CAGED shape, but vary the timing.

Example 2c:

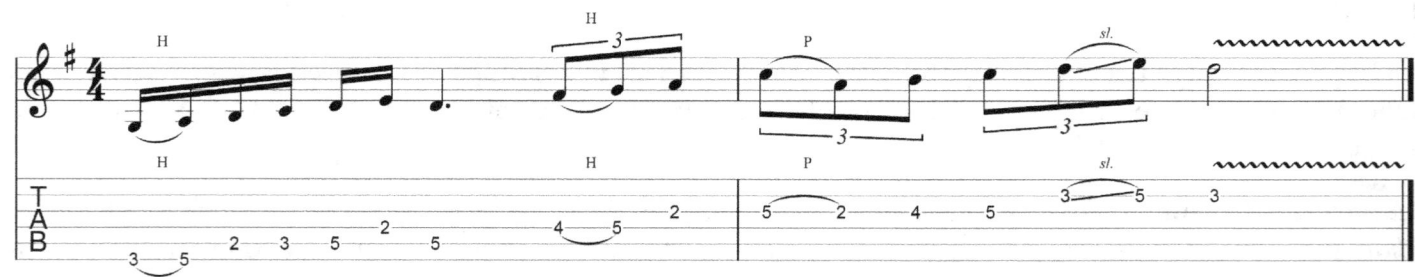

The G Major Pentatonic scale is made up from five sweet G Major scale notes: G, A, B, D and E (intervals 1, 2, 3, 5 and 6). Play through the G Major Pentatonic scale in the box and horizontal shapes.

Example 2d:

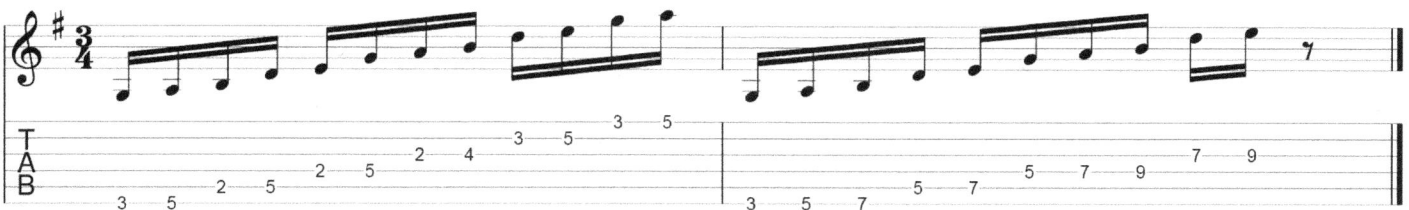

The lick in Example 2e is created from the major pentatonic box shape. You'll notice at the end of the lick there's a double stop. Don't be afraid to experiment with these mini chords in your solos!

Example 2e:

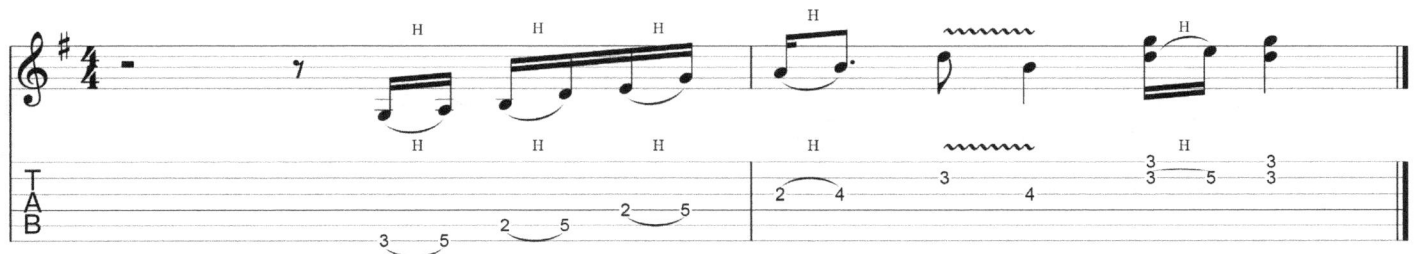

Example 2f comes from the crawling pentatonic shape, played using predominantly 1/8 triplet notes.

Example 2f:

The 1, 3 and 5 intervals of the G Major scale (G, B and D) create a G Major triad. Example 2g shows how to play the triad in six- and five-string variations.

Example 2g:

Here's a lick based on the six-string triad shape. I've used multiple varying triplet subdivisions and a few diatonic notes to stop this arpeggio lick from sounding too bland.

Example 2h:

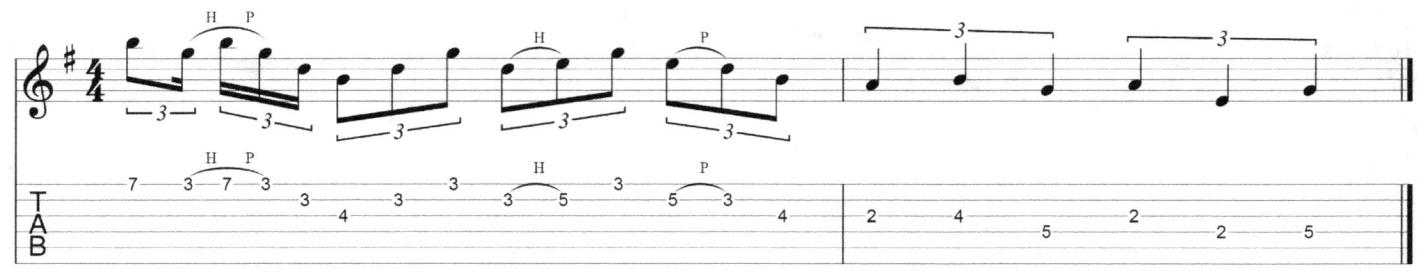

Now play through Example 2i, a lick based around the second G major triad arpeggio.

Example 2i:

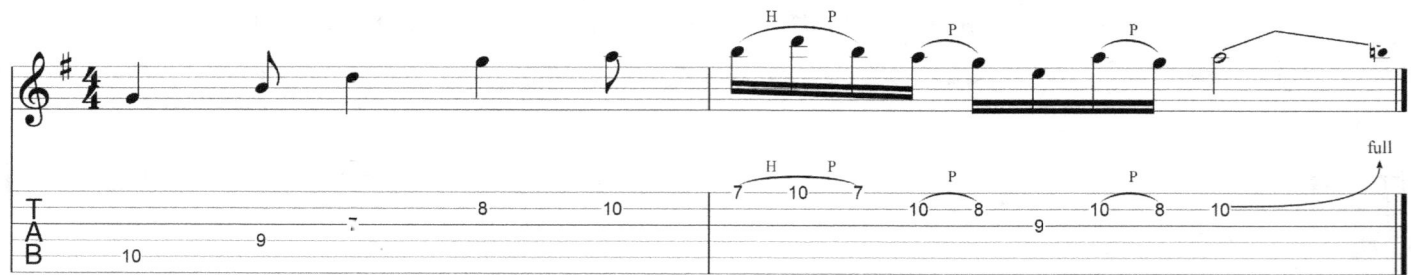

Now, here's a lick that uses the third triad shape. The lick resolves to an E minor pentatonic shape reminiscent of Marty Friedman and The Scorpions.

Example 2j:

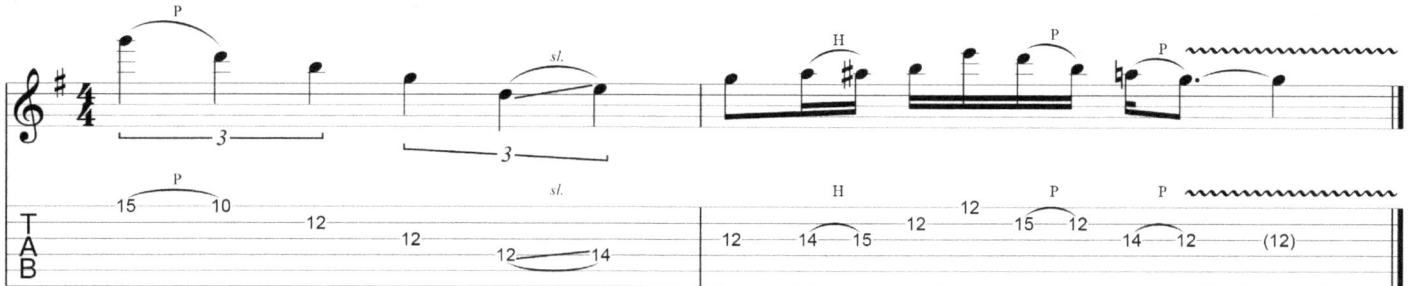

We can turn simple triads into extended arpeggios by adding the 7th interval, immediately making them more sophisticated. The G Major triad becomes a Gmaj7 arpeggio (G, B, D and F#). First play through the three maj7th arpeggios shown below.

Example 2k:

Here is a lick based on the first Gmaj7 arpeggio shape above, which also include notes from G Major Pentatonic.

Example 2l:

The second Gmaj7 lick uses 1/8 note triplets and dotted 1/8 note double-stops.

Example 2m:

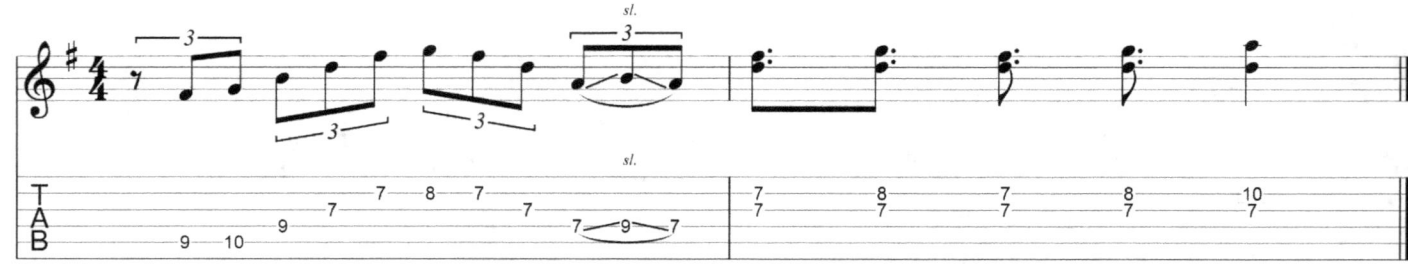

Finally, here's a lick that uses varying subdivisions and a quick position shift to keep things interesting.

Example 2n:

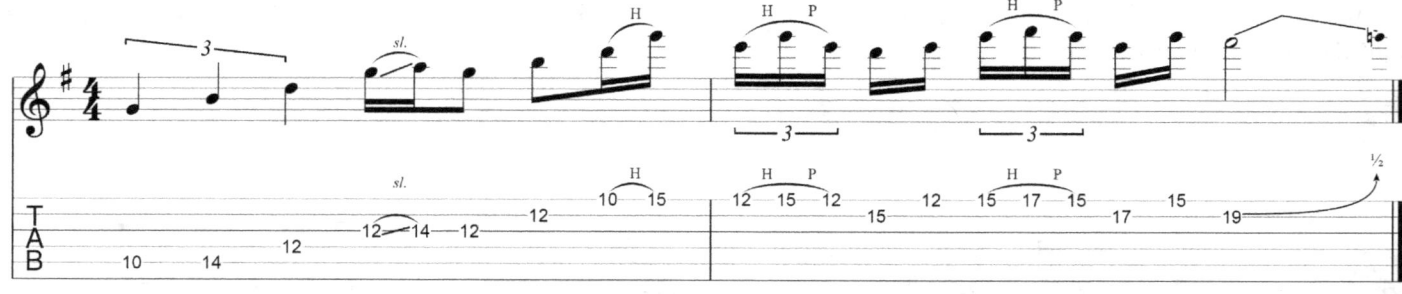

Chapter 3 – The ii chord (A minor)

To solo over chord ii in the harmonised major scale (A minor), we play a G Major scale that begins and ends on the note A. It has all the notes of G Major, but now our focus has shifted to A minor (AKA the A Dorian mode). Example 3a shows the G Major scale starting from an A note, spanning all six strings in three-note-per-string and CAGED patterns.

Example 3a:

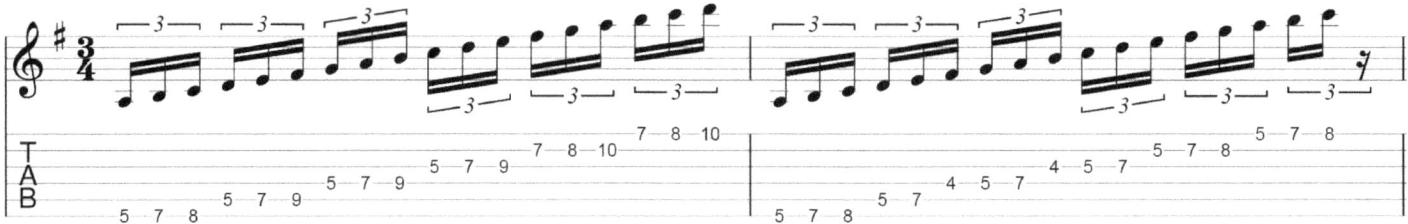

Example 3b shows how the three-note-per string shape translates into a lick with added legato and a final bend.

Example 3b:

In the next example, the A Dorian CAGED shape switches between 1/8 and 1/16 notes to keep timing of the lick varied and less predictable.

Example 3c:

Next, play through the box and horizontal versions of the G Major Pentatonic scale beginning from an A note to target the ii chord.

Example 3d:

Here's a lick I've created using the box shape, with varied timing and hammer-ons.

Example 3e:

Here's an example using the crawling scale shape, played with predominantly 1/8 triplet notes and resolving on a bend.

Example 3f:

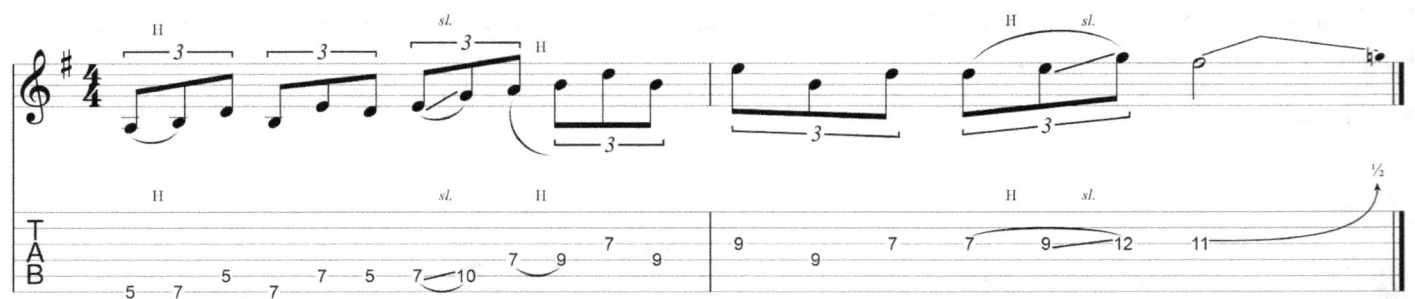

The A minor chord triad consists of the notes A, C and E. Here are the six- and five-string triad patterns.

Example 3g:

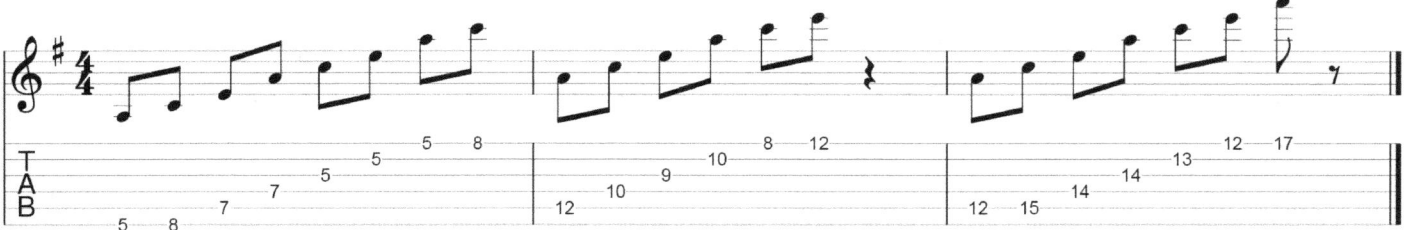

Example 3h, based on the six-string shape, features a few moments of legato to add smoothness and speed.

Example 3h:

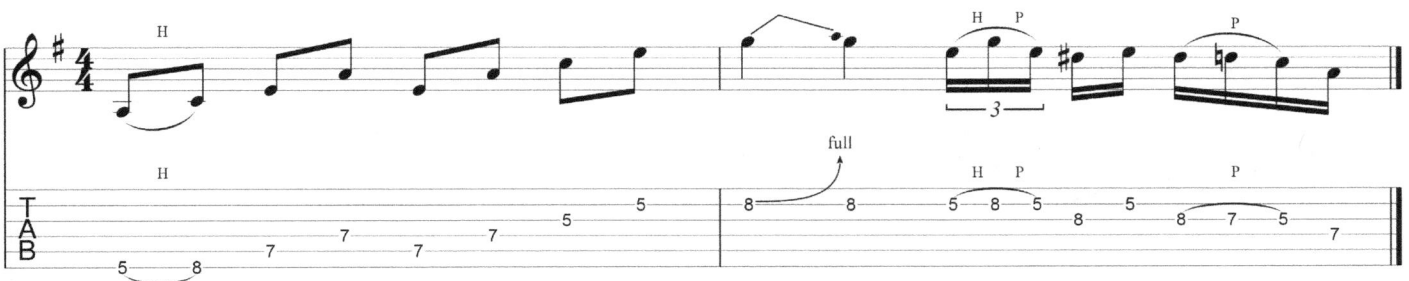

In Example 3i, legato technique is used again and is great for adding a surprise burst of speed.

Example 3i:

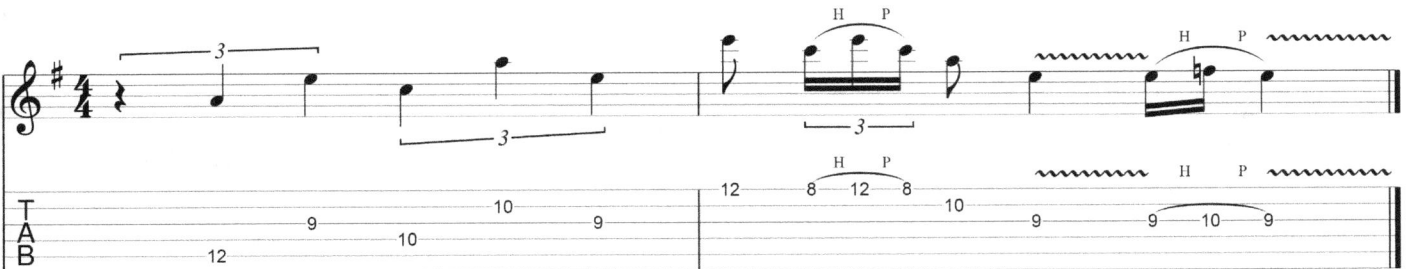

Here's an idea using the third triad shape played almost exclusively in 1/8 note triplets.

Example 3j:

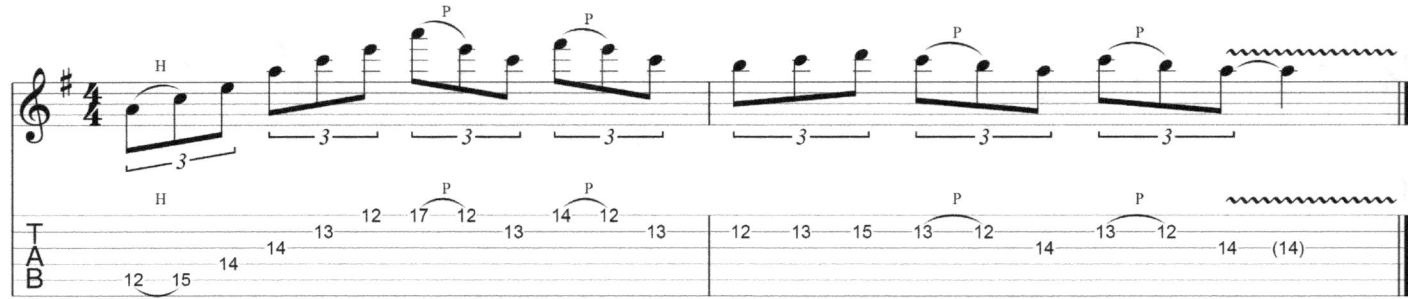

Now we'll extend our triad to include the 7th interval to spell an Am7 arpeggio (A, C, E and G). First play through all three arpeggio shapes below.

Example 3k:

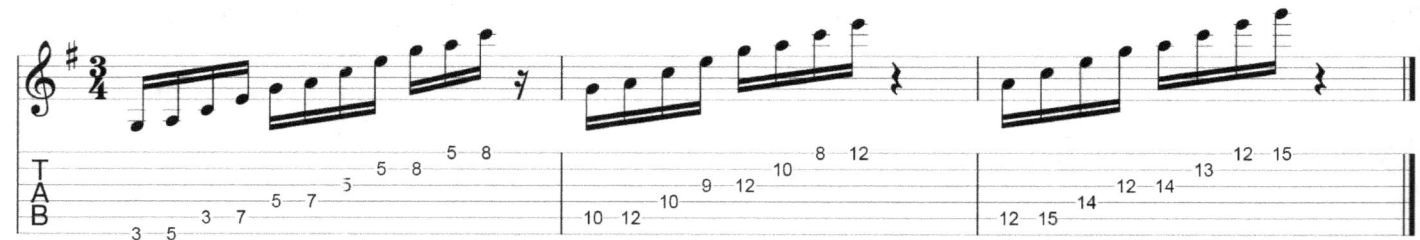

Here is a melodic line based on the first Am7 arpeggio shape.

Example 3l:

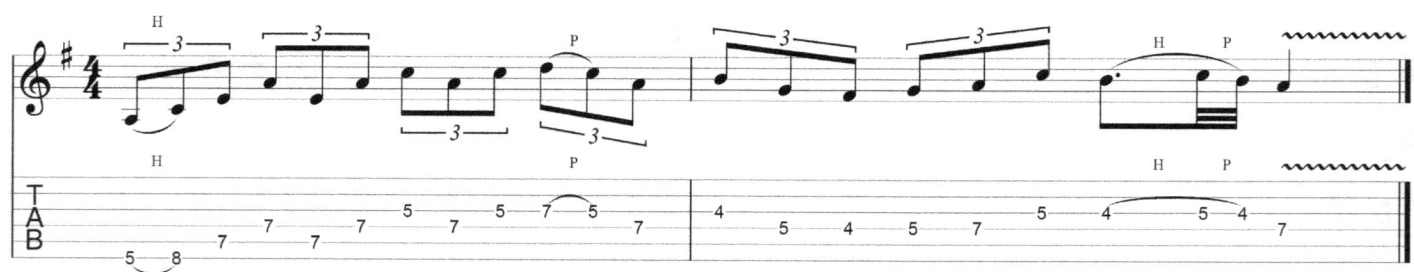

Example 3m uses the second arpeggio shape and combines 1/8 note triplets with moments of legato.

Example 3m:

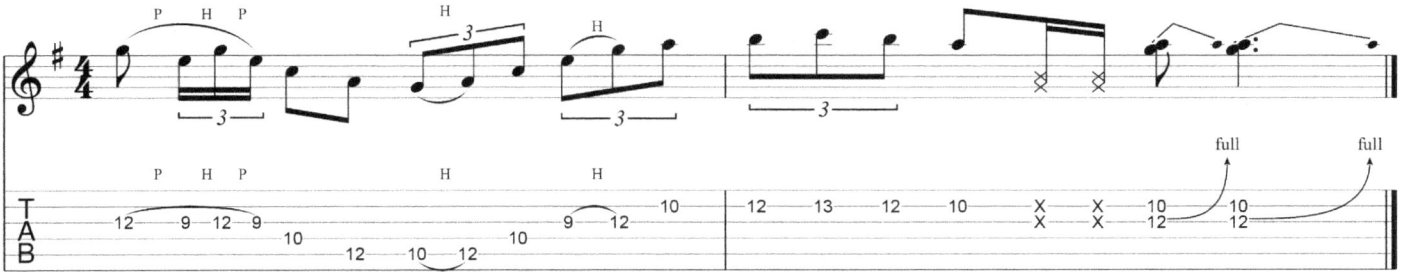

Here's an idea that uses string skips to create interesting intervals and legato to create bursts of speed.

Example 3n:

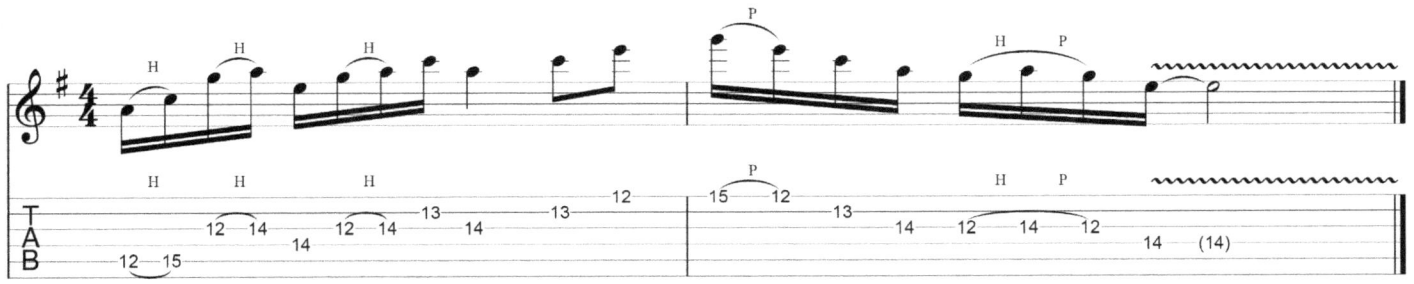

Chapter 4 – The iii chord (B minor)

To solo over chord iii in the harmonised major scale (B minor), we play a G Major scale that begins and ends on the note B. It has all the notes of G Major, but now our focus has shifted to B minor (AKA the B Phrygian mode). Example 4a shows the G Major scale starting from B, spanning all six strings in three-note-per-string and CAGED patterns.

Example 4a:

The first example is based on the three-note-per-string pattern and ends with a full tone bend.

Example 4b:

This lick uses the CAGED shape, varying the timing to give the line more expression.

Example 4c:

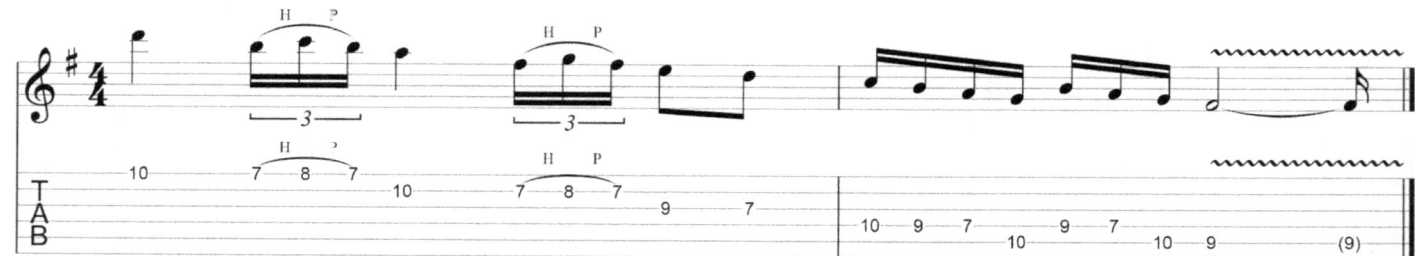

Now we move on to the box and horizontal versions of the G Major Pentatonic scale, leading from a B note to target the iii chord (B minor).

Example 4d:

The use of 4th intervals and 1/8 note triplets help make this lick more interesting.

Example 4e:

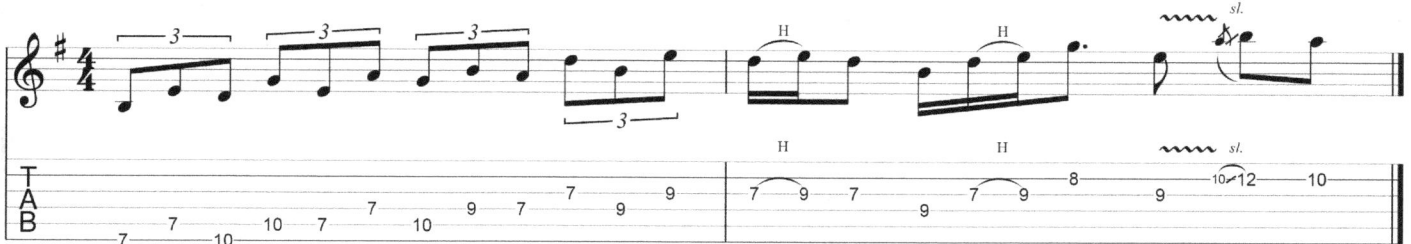

Example 4f employs the crawling pentatonic shape with a combination of 1/16 notes and 1/4 note triplets. It concludes with a brief B minor triad arpeggio.

Example 4f:

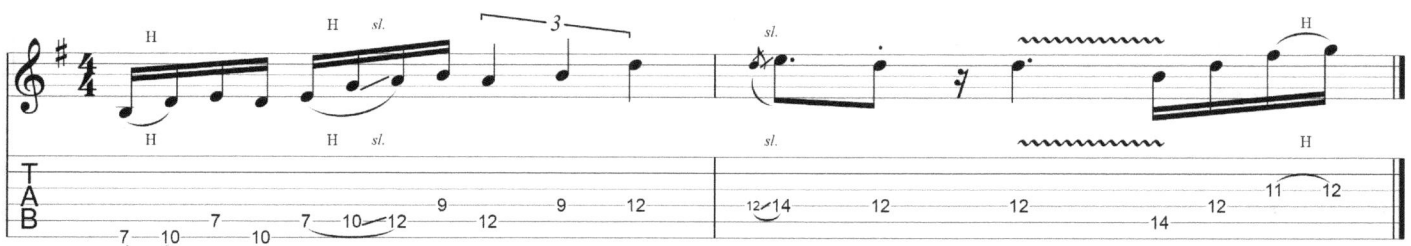

The B minor chord triad is constructed from the notes B, D and F#. Play through the six- and five-string variations of this arpeggio.

Example 4g:

Example 4h begins with a slower 1/8 note descending arpeggio and resolves with some faster ascending 1/16 notes to add some speed and excitement.

Example 4h:

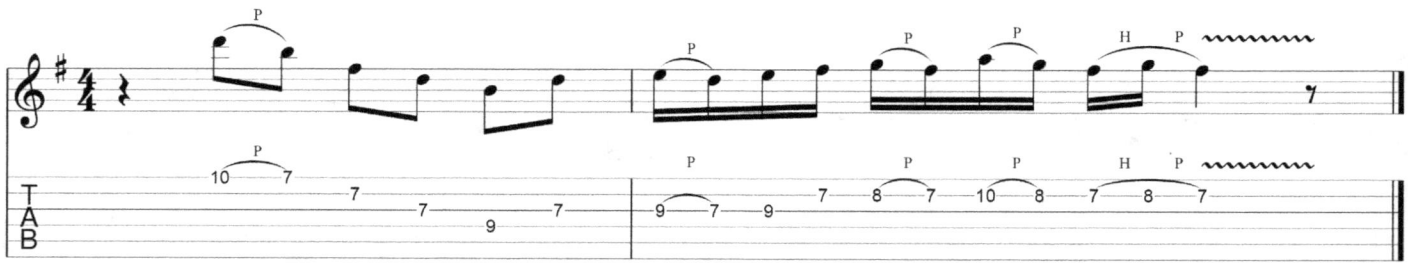

This lick based around the second B minor triad shape uses a simple descending idea with even 1/8 note timing.

Example 4i:

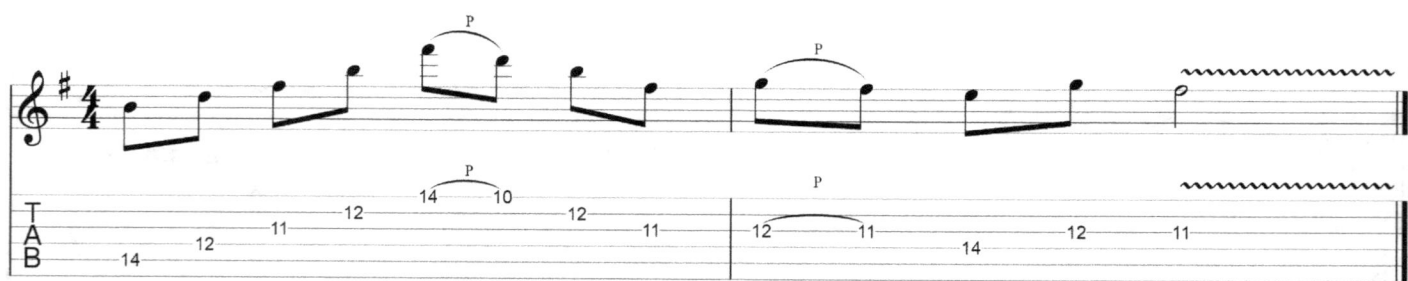

The lick uses varying subdivisions, slides and legato to keep things interesting.

Example 4j:

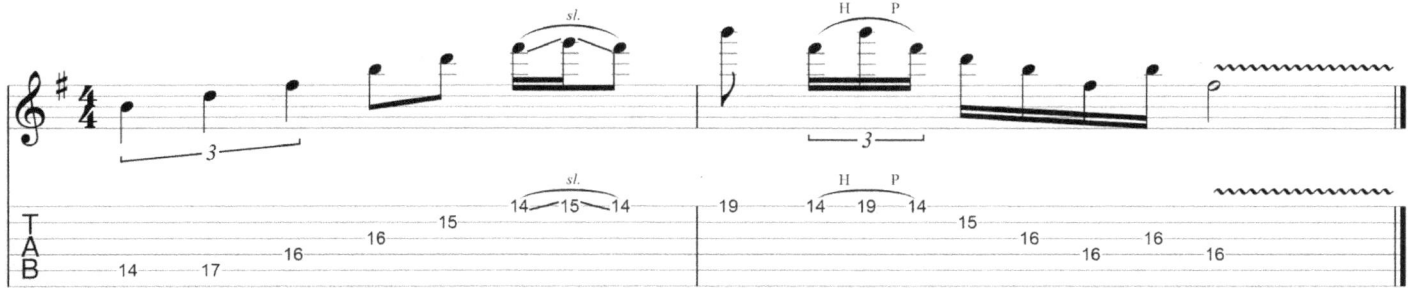

Now we extend our triad to become a 7th arpeggio (B, D, F# and A). Play through the three Bm7 arpeggios shown below.

Example 4k:

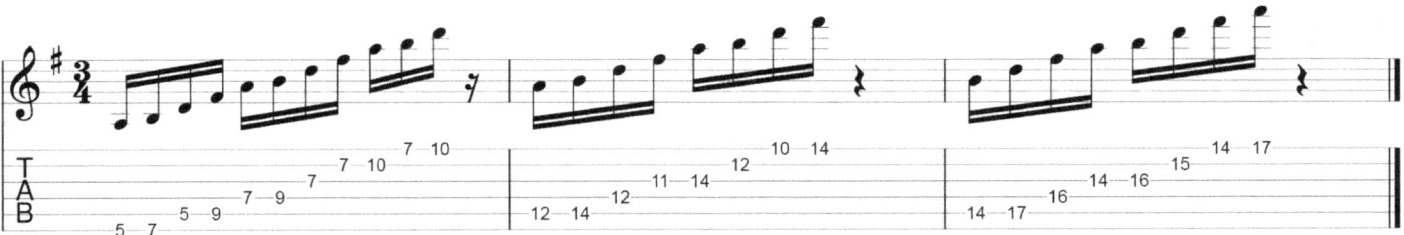

The first idea here uses repetitive building 1/16 notes to ramp up the tension ready for the release in bar two.

Example 4l:

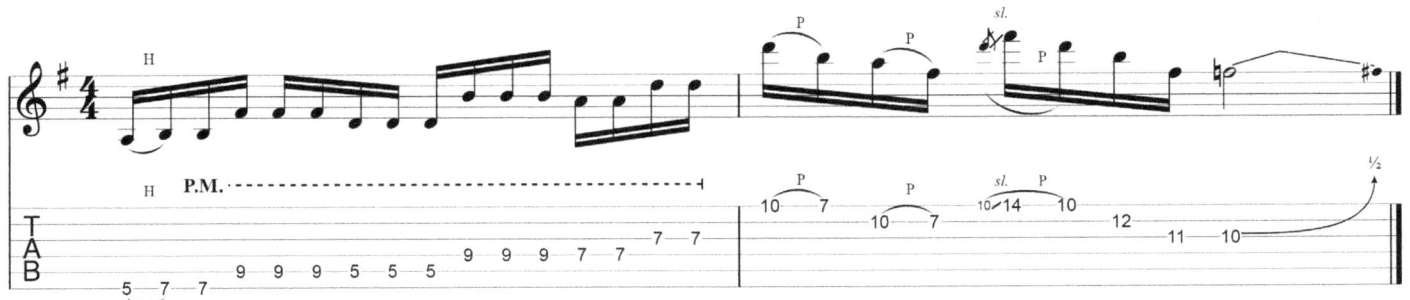

This lick features plenty of bends to achieve its distinctive rocky edge.

Example 4m:

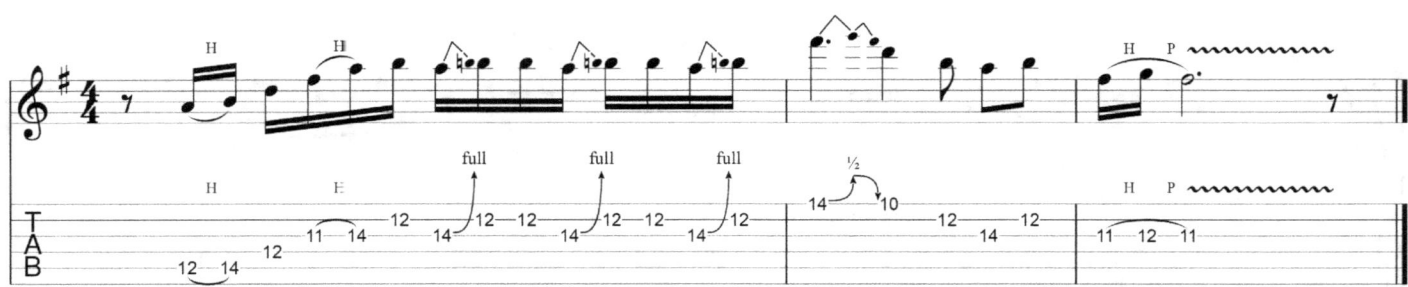

The final lick, based on the third Bm7 arpeggio shape, ascends using 1/8 note triplets and some quick legato.

Example 4n:

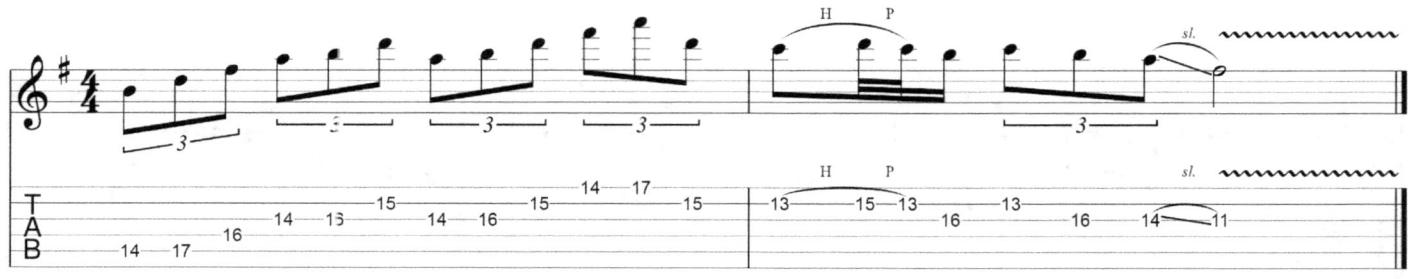

Chapter 5 – IV chord (C Major)

To solo over chord IV in the harmonised major scale (C Major), we play a G Major scale that begins and ends on the note C. It has all the notes of G Major, but now our focus has shifted to C Major (AKA the C Lydian mode). Example 5a shows the G Major scale starting from C, spanning all six strings in three-note-per-string and CAGED patterns.

Example 5a:

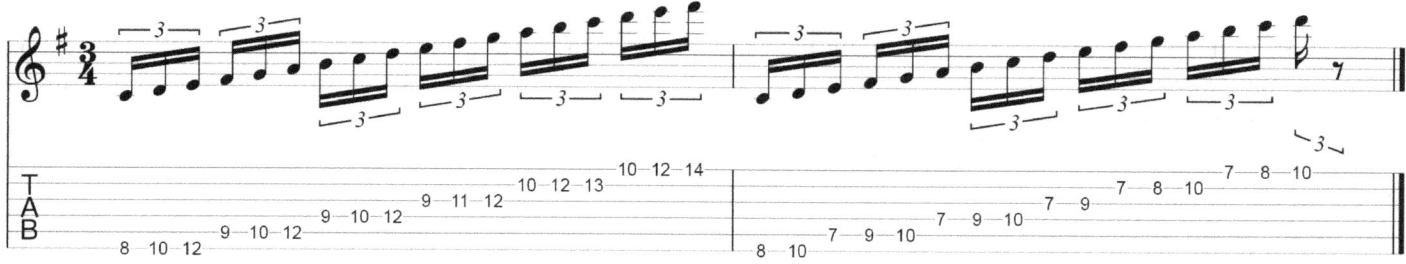

Example 5b features a 1/16 note line with an interesting pattern to turn an otherwise linear scale shape into something more exciting.

Example 5b:

When faced with a potentially dull scale, you can also create an interesting combination of rhythms to keep things fresh. This idea has a combination of 1/8 notes, 1/8 note triplets and 1/16th notes.

Example 5c:

Curve ball alert! For the pentatonic scale choice over the IV chord, I'm going to deviate from the pattern I've followed thus far and make an outlandish suggestion! The E Hirajoshi scale is a great pentatonic scale choice here. The notes of this Japanese pentatonic scale are E, F#, G, B and C, but when they're rearranged to start from a C note, the scale has an oriental, perhaps galactic, Lydian sound that targets the root, 3rd, #4, 5th and 7th of the IV chord.

Example 5d:

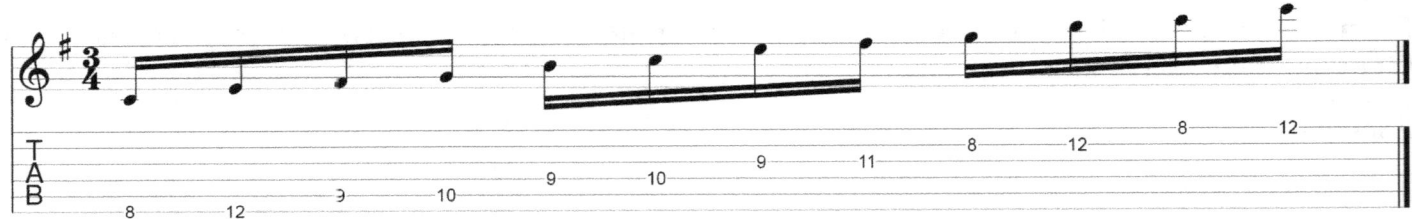

Side note: If you want to learn more about Hirajoshi and Lydian scales, you may wish to check out my second book *Rock Guitar Mode Mastery*.

Example 5e:

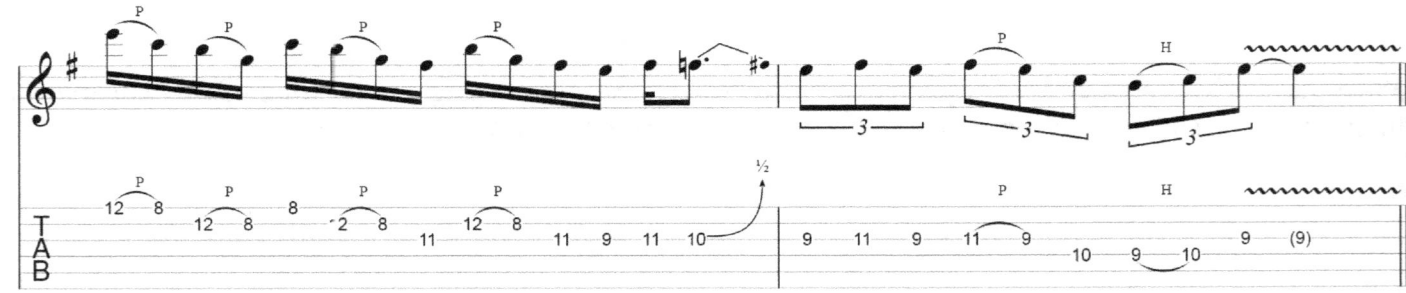

The C Major chord triad is constructed from the notes C, E and G. Play through the six- and five-string variations in Example 5f.

Example 5f:

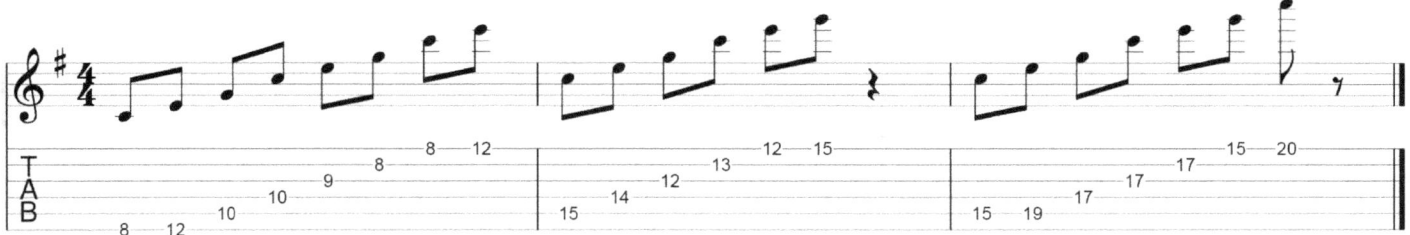

In Example 5g I have juxtaposed 1/4 notes with 1/16 notes add a big variance in speed.

Example 5g:

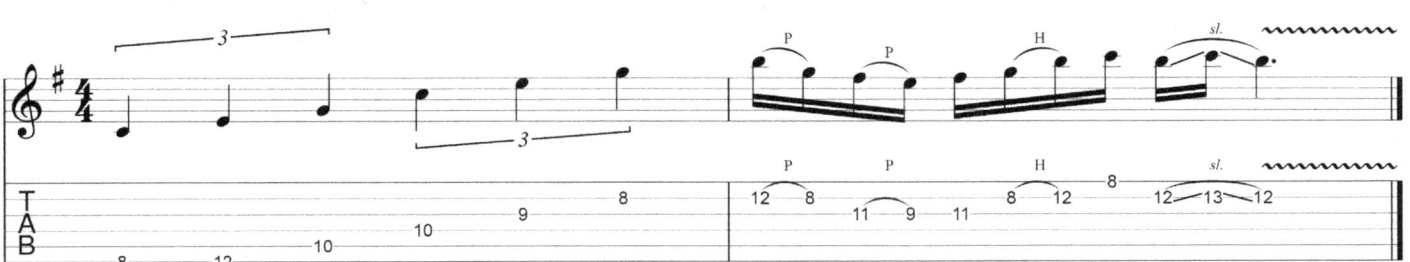

The next example includes a brief motif from E minor Pentatonic box shape one.

Example 5h:

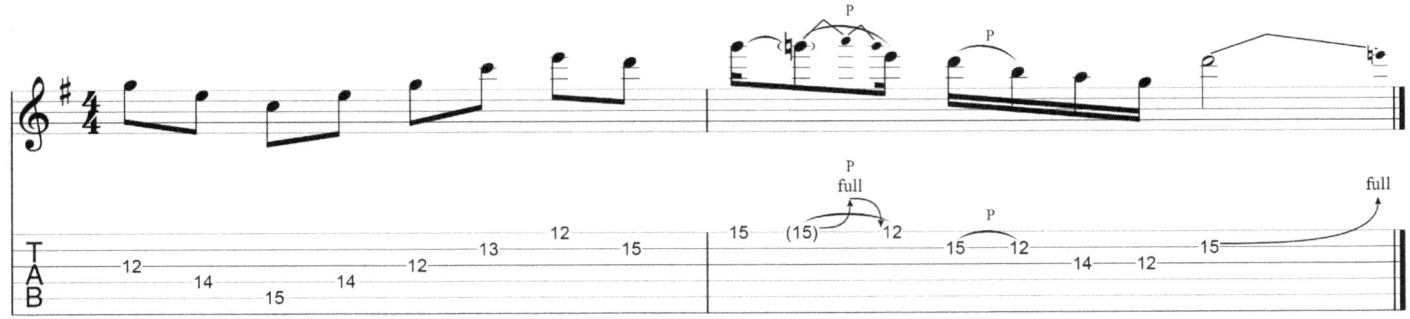

The lick is played using one bar of 1/4 note triplets, then a bar of 1/8 triplets, which gives the lick a progression in speed.

Example 5i:

Now we'll turn our attention to the IV chord's 7th arpeggio. Cmaj7 is constructed from the notes C, E, G and B. Play through the three major 7th arpeggios shown here.

Example 5j:

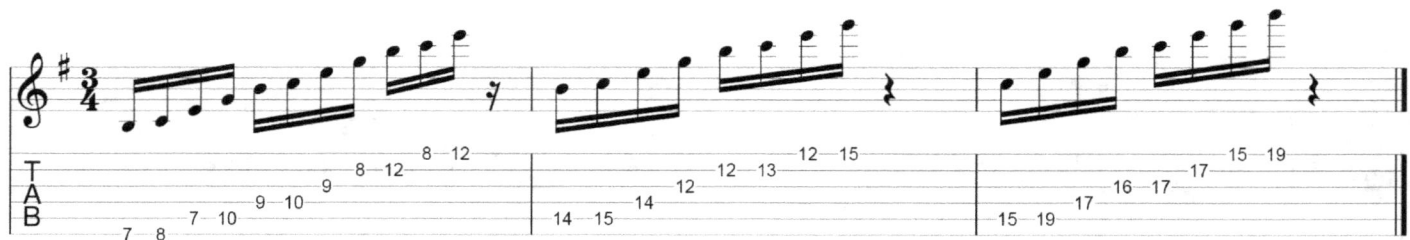

Based on the six-string arpeggio shape, this lick has several changes of direction, keeping the listener guessing about whether it's ascending or descending.

Example 5k:

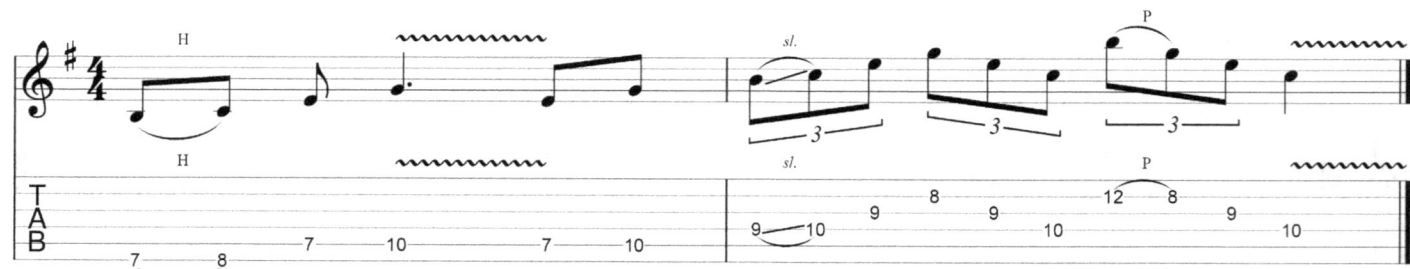

This line has descending 1/16 note triplets and some slow sexy slides, with massive intervals.

Example 5l:

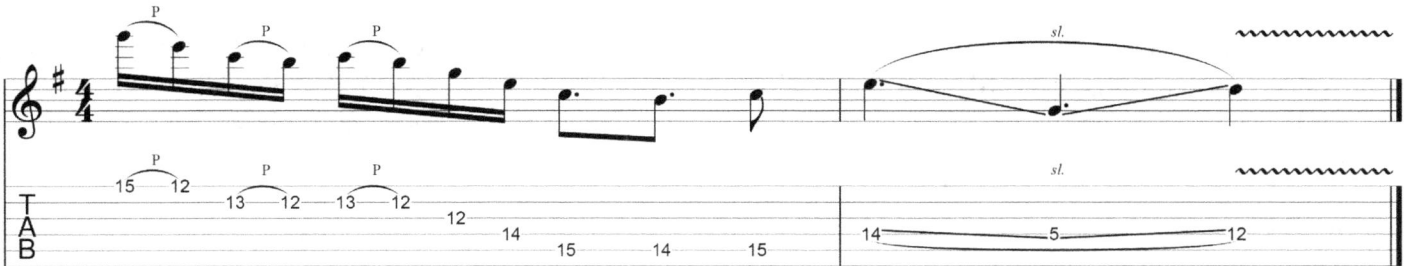

Finally, I use string skips in Example 5m to produce some surprising intervals, and vary between 1/16 and 1/8 note triplets to create a gradual decline in speed as the lick progresses.

Example 5m:

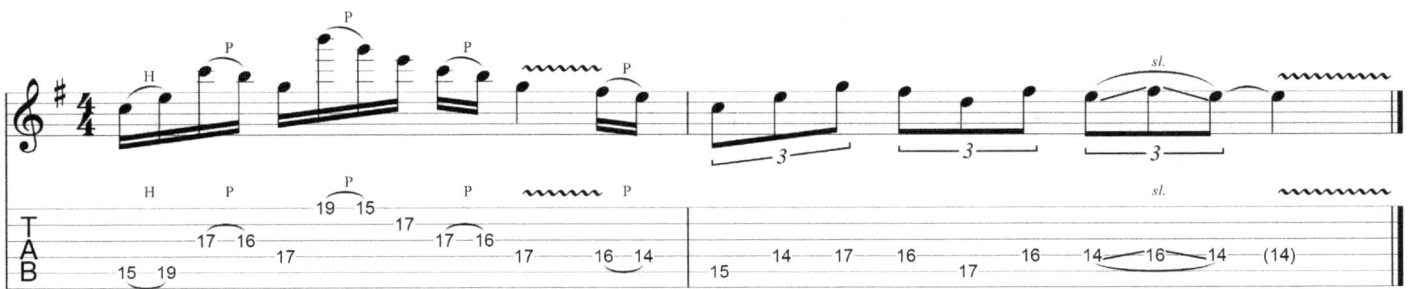

Chapter 6 – The V chord (D Major)

Chord V in the harmonised major scale is D Major. To improvise over it we can play a G Major scale that begins and end on the note D. It's still a G Major scale, but our focus has shifted to D Major (AKA the D Mixolydian mode). Example 6a shows the G Major scale starting from D, spanning all six strings in three-note-per-string and CAGED patterns.

Example 6a:

In Example 6b I use the three-note-per-string shape above, but include a few expressive techniques, with varying subdivisions to create an interesting and musical lick.

Example 6b:

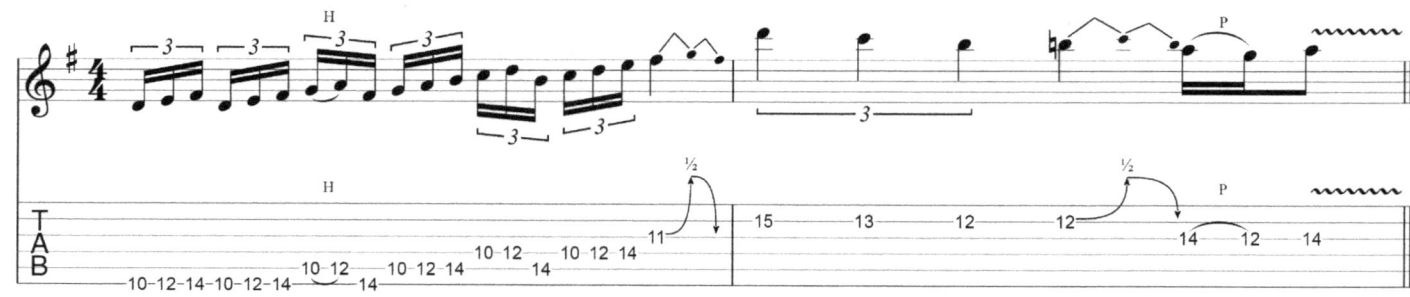

In the next example, using the CAGED shape, the use of 1/16 notes adds an element of speed and the bend at the end of lick gives it a sense of resolution.

Example 6c:

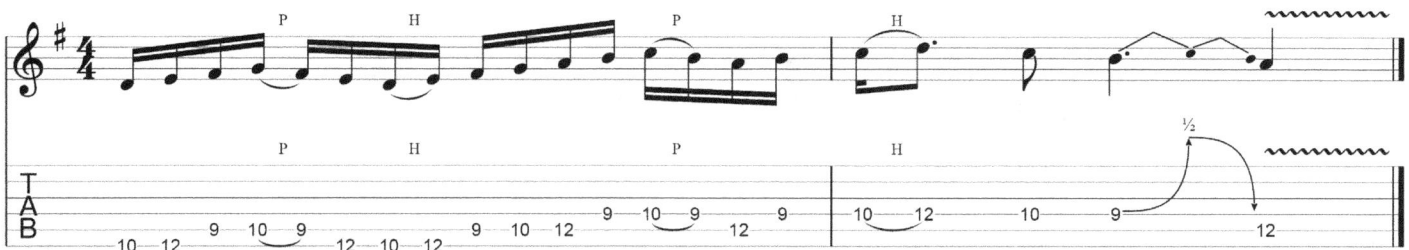

Now play through the box and horizontal versions of the G Major Pentatonic scale, leading from the D note to targets the root of the V chord.

Example 6d:

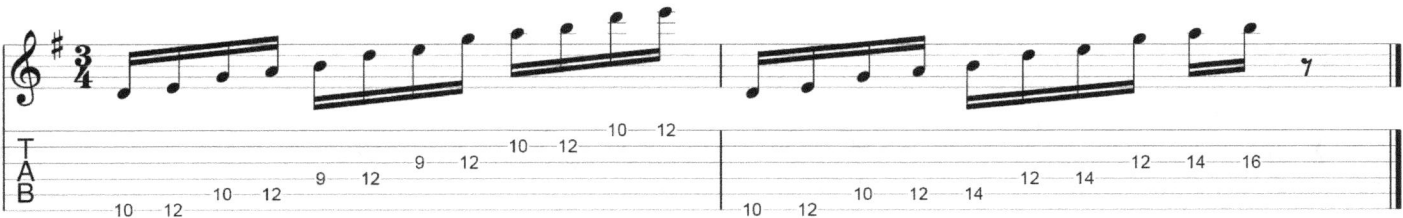

This lick resolves on some repeating 1/8 note triplets. It's a quick reminder that you're allowed to play the same note, two or more times in a row in your solos! (Check out the solo in Motley Crue's song *Dr Feelgood*, to hear this concept executed perfectly.

Example 6e:

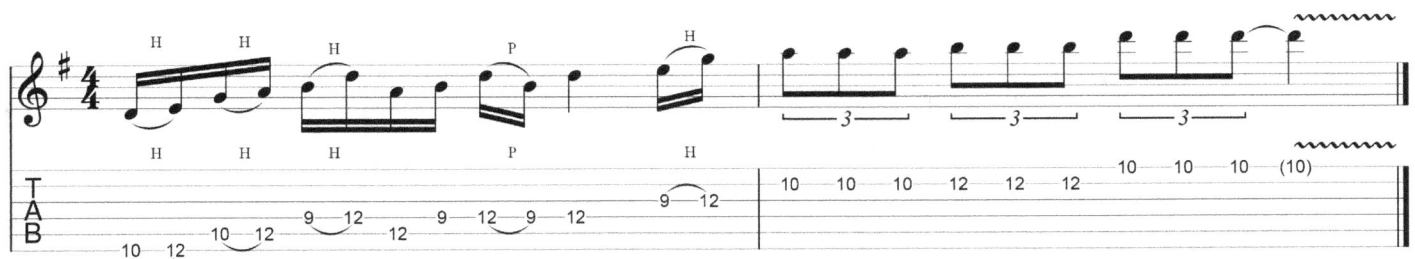

Example 6f uses the G major crawling pentatonic shape and a brief 1/4 note triplet D major arpeggio.

Example 6f:

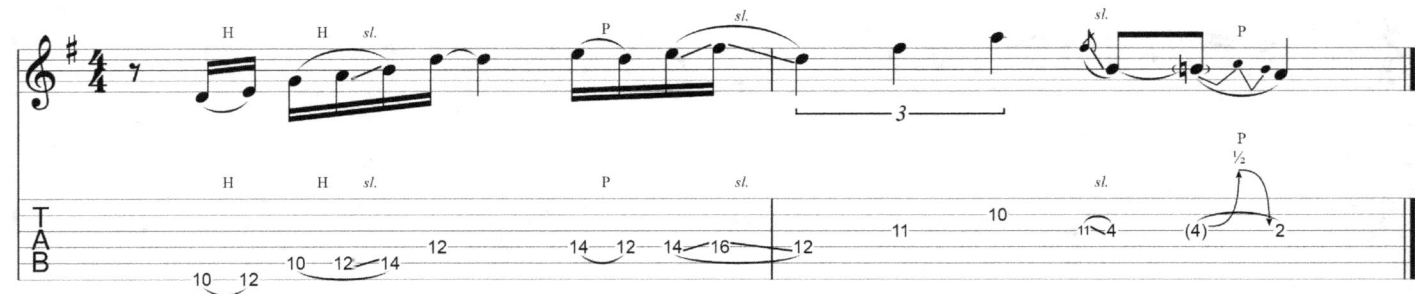

For the pentatonic element in this chapter, I'm going to focus exclusively on the D Mixolydian Pentatonic scale. It has a scale formula of 1, 3, 4, 5 and b7 (D, F#, G, A and C). This scale highlights all the crucial aspects of the V chord.

Example 6g:

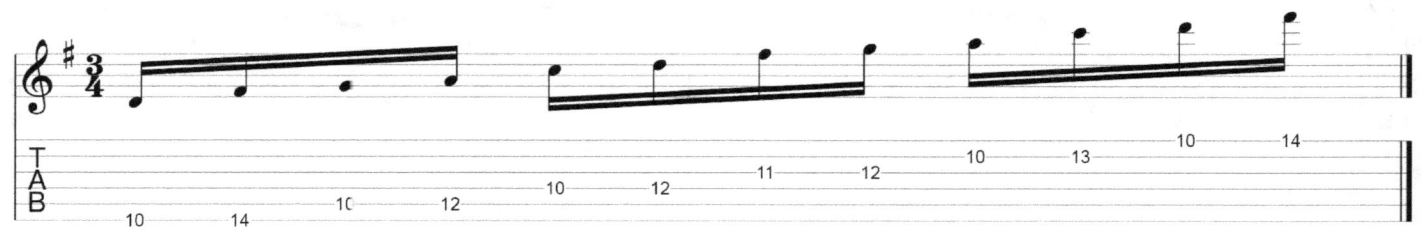

To demonstrate this scale, I'm playing a fast descending lick using legato and slides.

Example 6h:

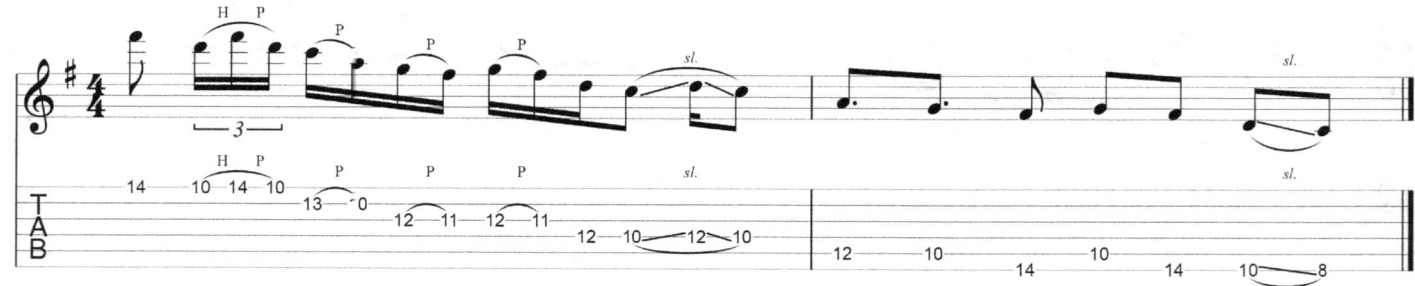

The V chord (D Major) is built from the notes D, F# and A to form a D Major triad. Play through the six- and five-string variations of this arpeggio.

Example 6i:

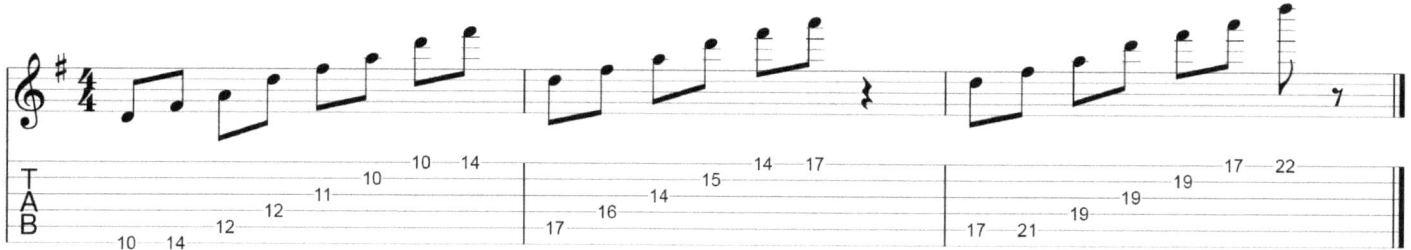

Example 6j is a lick built from the first triad shape. It uses varying triplet subdivisions and a few diatonic notes to keep the lick fresh and sassy.

Example 6j:

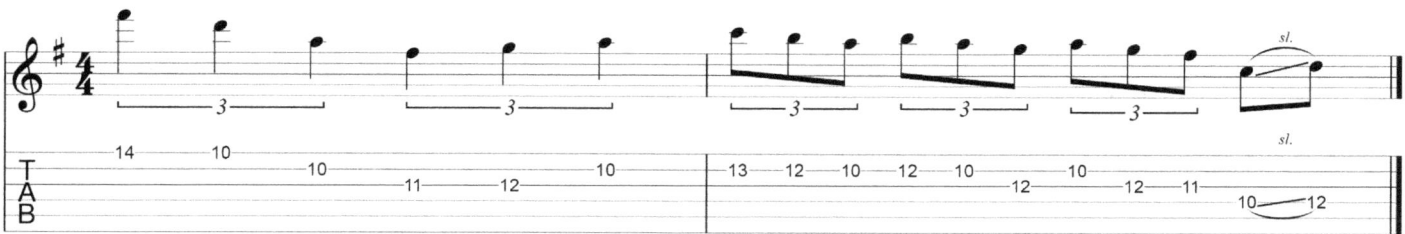

The next example includes a few notes from G Major Pentatonic to resolve the lick.

Example 6k:

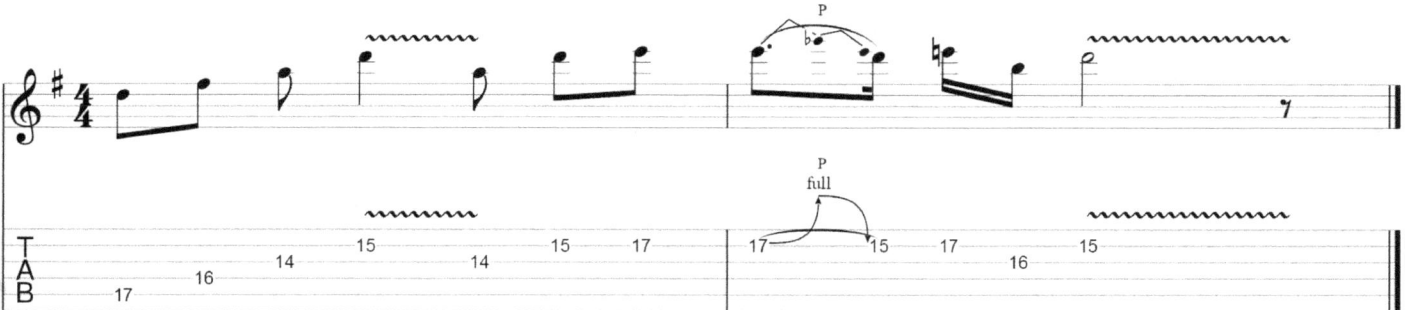

Here is a similar approach, borrowing a few notes from G Major Pentatonic.

Example 6l:

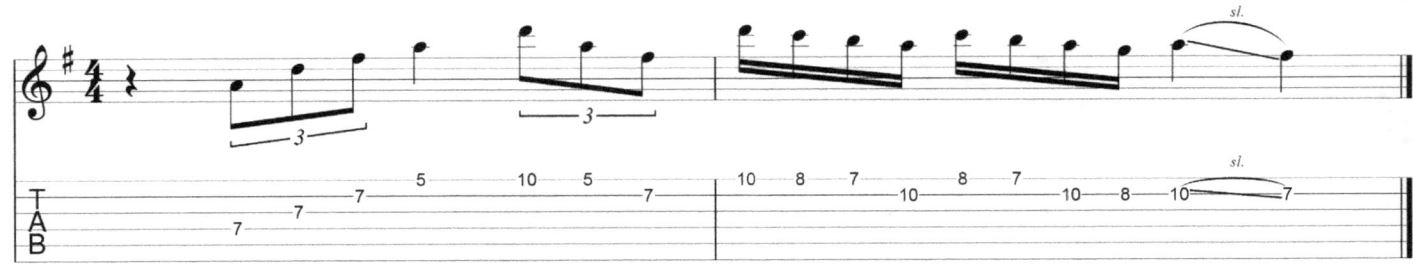

As before, we'll turn our triad into a 7th arpeggio to make the V chord a D7 (D, F#, A and C). Play through the three dominant 7th arpeggios shown below.

Example 6m:

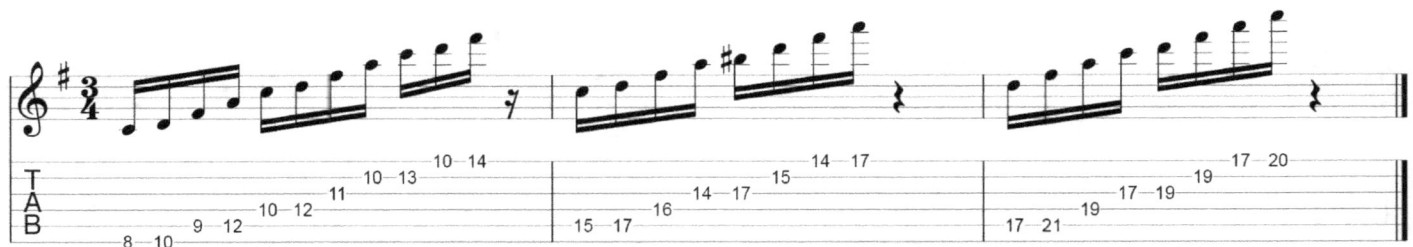

Example 6n is based predominantly on 1/8 note triplets and includes some cool bends.

Example 6n:

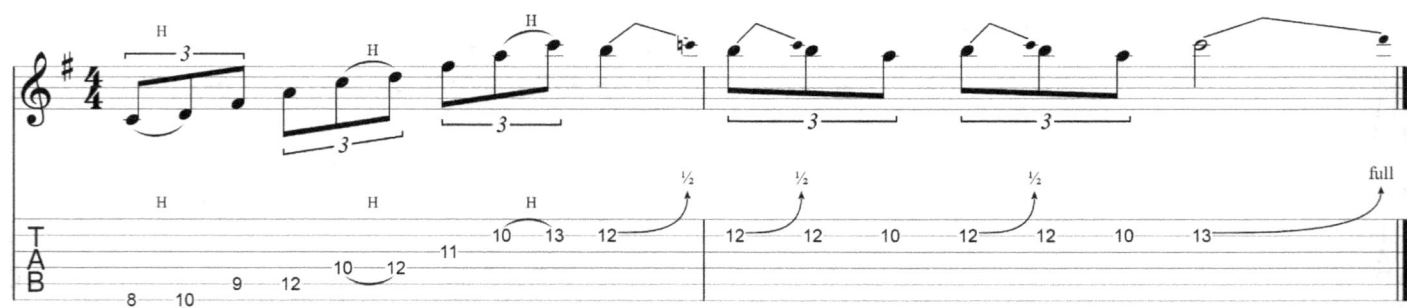

Example 6o features a line based on the second D dominant 7th arpeggio shape and drifts between ascending and descending notes.

Example 6o:

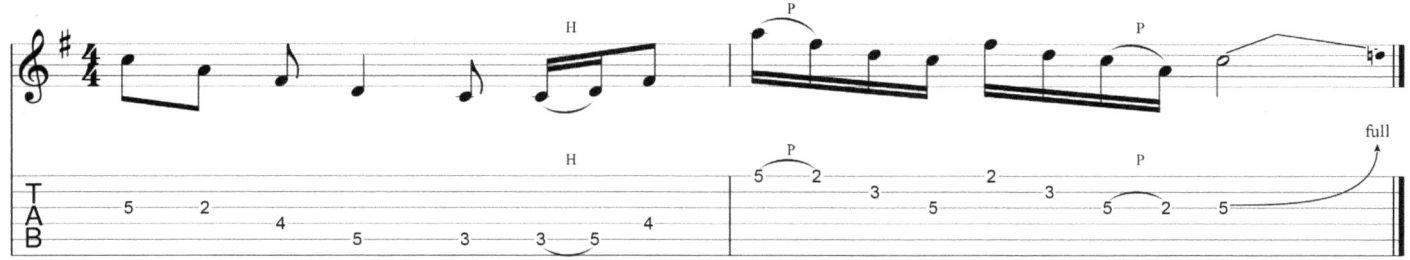

The final example uses legato and 1/16 notes to deliver a fast 'n' fresh lick.

Example 6p:

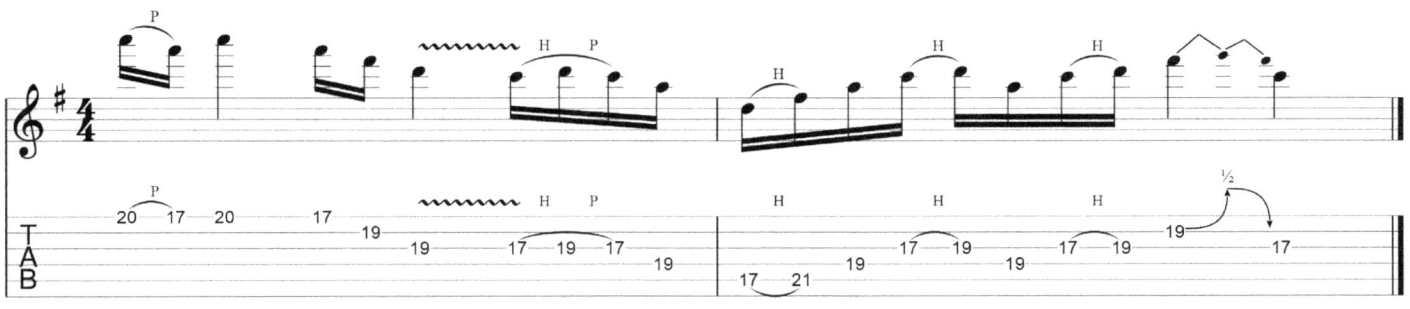

Chapter 7 – The vi chord (E minor)

Chord vi in the harmonised major scale is E minor. To improvise over it we can play a G Major scale that begins and end on the note E. It's still a G Major scale, but our focus has shifted to E major (AKA the E Aeolian mode or E Natural minor scale). Example 7a shows the G Major scale starting from E, spanning all six strings in three-note-per-string and CAGED patterns.

Example 7a:

The first example has string skips and slow moving 1/4 note triplets to make the intervals sound less predictable.

Example 7b:

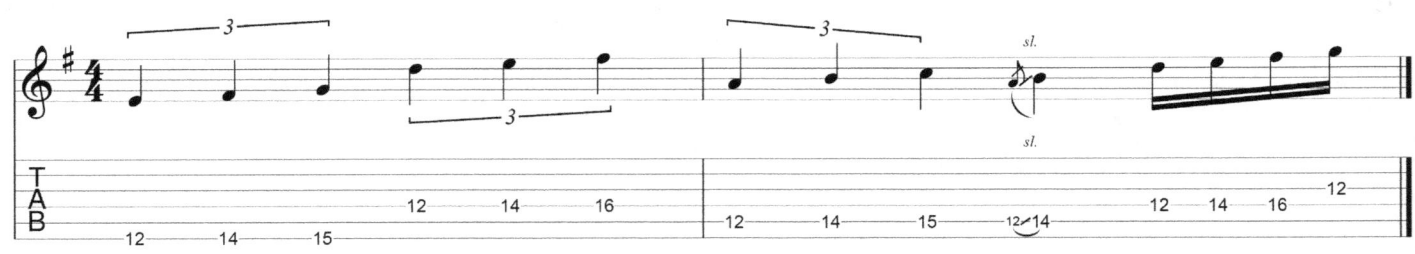

You can always use a combination of expressive techniques and varied timing to create a musical sounding lick from a simple scale.

Example 7c:

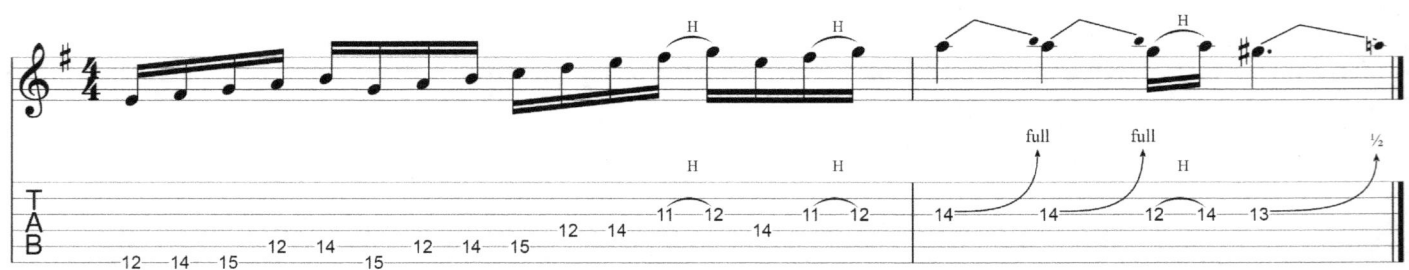

Here are the box and horizontal versions of the E Minor Pentatonic scale. It targets the root, b3rd, 5th and b7 of the E minor chord.

Example 7d:

Here's a lick using the box shape. When writing this lick I had in mind Angus Young's speed and sometimes chaotic playing style and Marty Friedman's use of tense sounding outside note. Who doesn't love an outside to inside note bend?!

Example 7e:

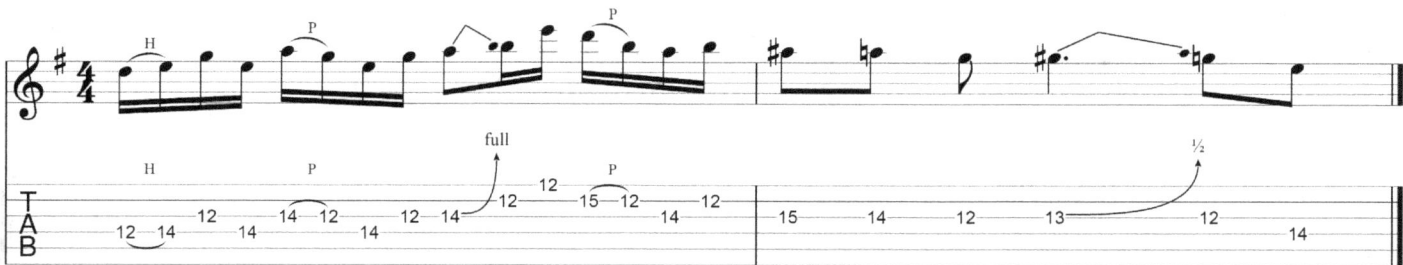

This example uses the crawling pentatonic shape. Be wary of the tricky hammer-ons and slides in the second bar.

Example 7f:

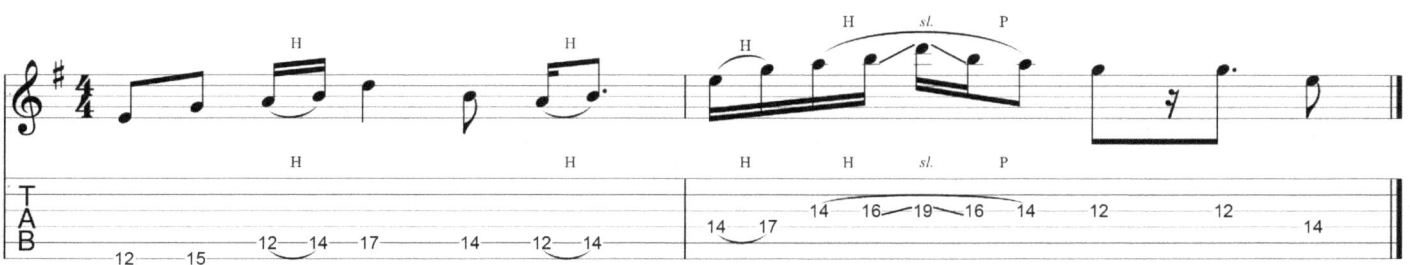

Let's return briefly to the Hirajoshi pentatonic scale! Here the scale formula for E Hirajoshi is 1, 2, b3, 5 and b6 (E, F#, G, B and C). This scale sounds great over a vi chord if you want to add some oriental spice to your soloing ... and who doesn't? Example 7g illustrates box and horizontal versions of this scale.

Example 7g:

Here's a medium paced lick using 1/8 and 1/8 note triplets, with a few expressive techniques to add some musicality.

Example 7h:

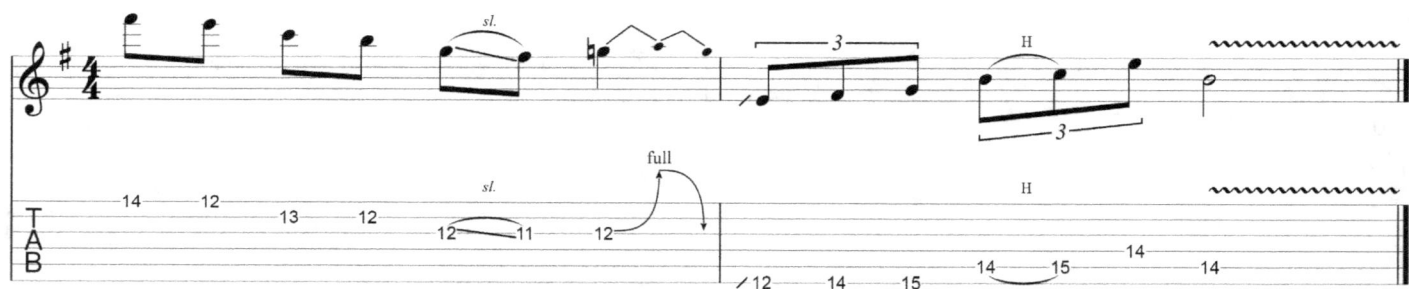

This next idea is played almost entirely in 1/8 note triplets and combines legato and slides to add a sexy-smoothness to its delivery.

Example 7i:

Chord vi is built from the notes E, G and B, forming an E minor triad. Play through the six- and five-string variations of this arpeggio.

Example 7j:

For the first triad example lick, I decided to use dotted 1/4 notes and a 1/2 note to make this lick a pleasantly slow one. It's good to have a few licks up you sleeve for the "calm after the storm" moments in your improvised solos.

Example 7k:

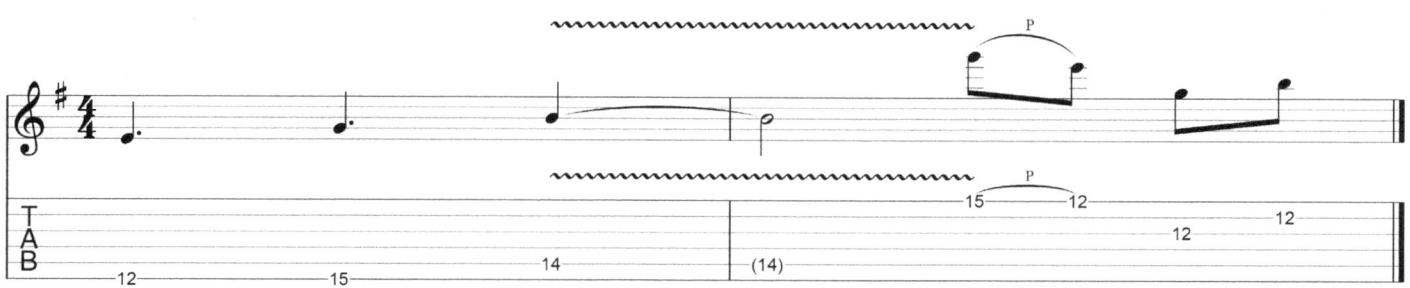

Here, however, I play predominantly 1/16 notes, because sometimes, you just gotta play fast!

Example 7l:

Example 7m mixes things up speed-wise.

Example 7m:

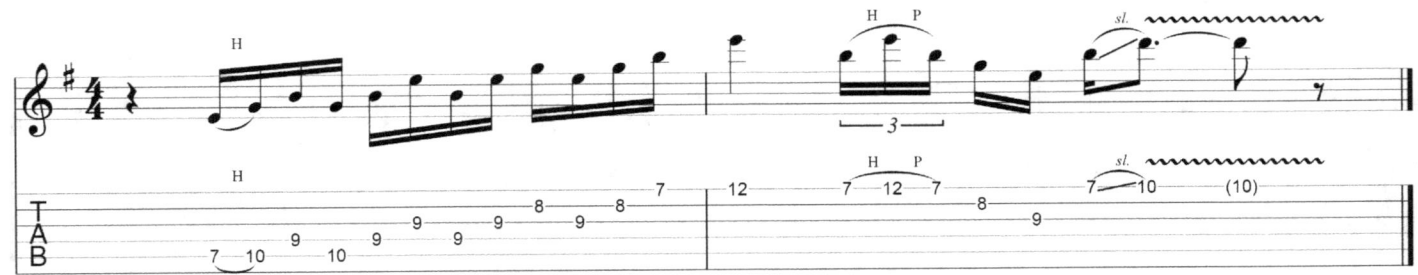

Now we'll turn our E minor chord into Em7 (E, G, B and D). Play through the three minor 7th arpeggios below.

Example 7n:

I've used legato here to add smoothness, as well as an inside to outside bend to give the lick a funky resolution.

Example 7o:

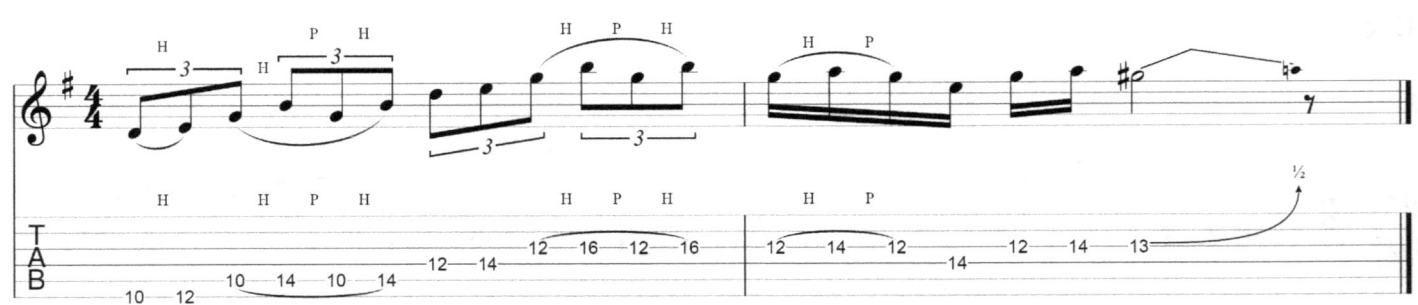

This next idea is relatively simple, drifting between 1/8 and 1/8 note triplets, with a few moments of cheeky legato.

Example 7p:

Lastly, a combination of 1/16 notes, legato and slides to give this lick speed and aggression.

Example 7q:

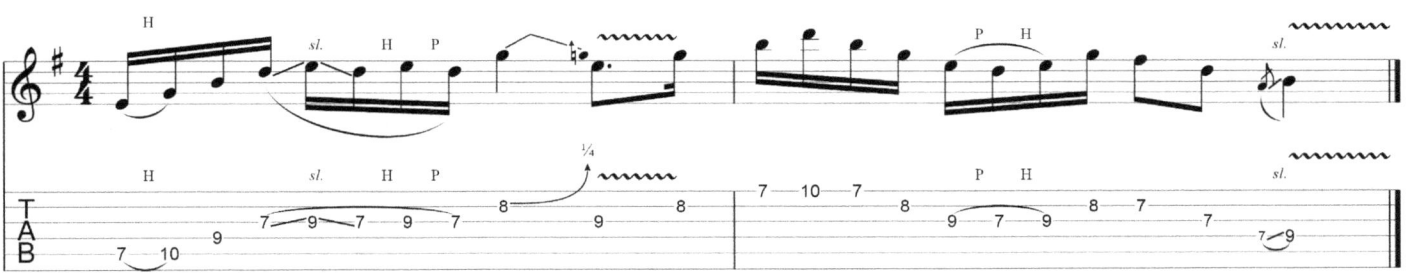

Chapter 8 – The vii chord (F#m7b5)

Chord vii in the harmonised major scale is F#m7b5. To improvise over it we can play a G Major scale that begins and end on the note F#. It's still a G Major scale, but our focus has shifted to F# minor (AKA the F# Locrian mode). Example 8a shows the G Major scale starting from F#, spanning all six strings in three-note-per-string and CAGED patterns.

Example 8a:

Our first example uses the three-note-per-string F# Locrian pattern and ends with a cheeky unison bend.

Example 8b:

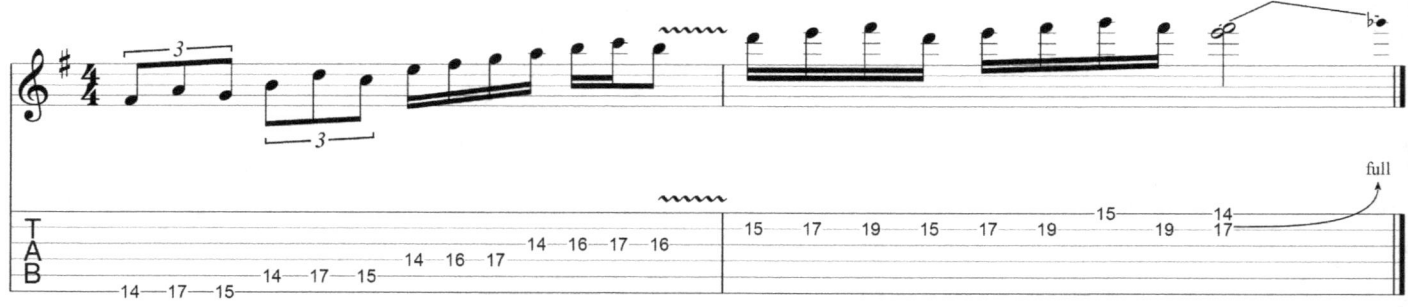

As seen in previous examples, here I vary the timing and expression to create an interesting musical lick.

Example 8c:

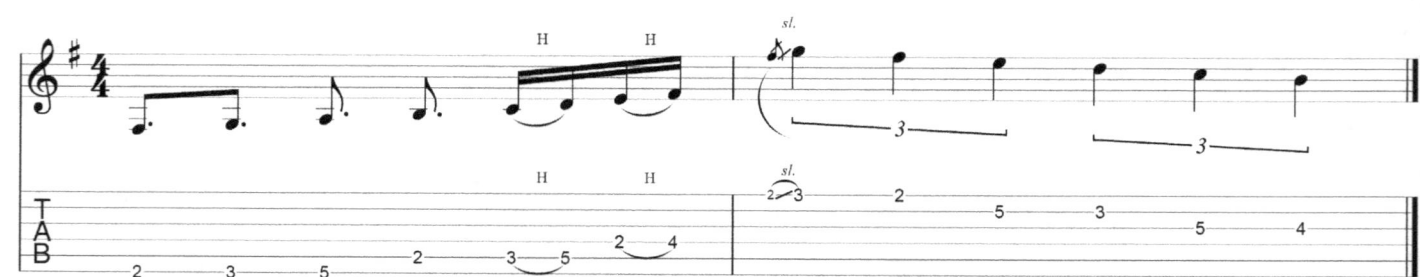

Now we'll use the F# Locrian Pentatonic scale as our main weapon of choice. The scale formula is 1 b3 4 b5 b7 (F#, A, B, C and E). It could also be described as the F# Minor Pentatonic scale with a flattened 5th, and it works perfectly over a vii chord.

Example 8d:

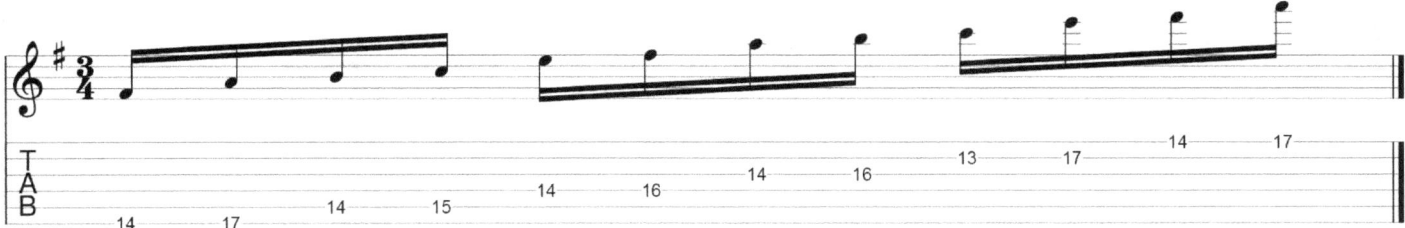

This crazy lick combines legato and 1/16th notes to keep it fast and exciting.

Example 8e:

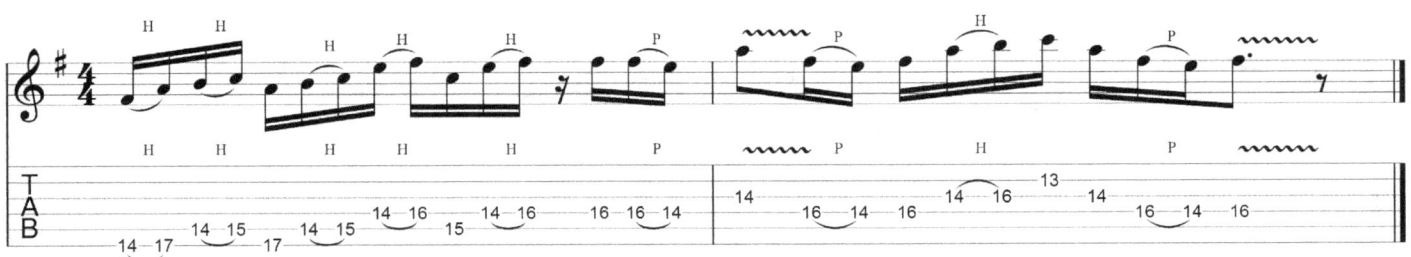

Side Note! If you want to learn more about the Locrian Pentatonic in multiple position, get hold of my book *Rock Guitar Mode Mastery*.

The vii chord triad is built from the notes F#, A and C (intervals 1, 3 and b5). Play through the six- and five-string variations of this arpeggio.

Example 8f:

The first triad lick is played in a descending manner with a cheeky outside bend.

Example 8g:

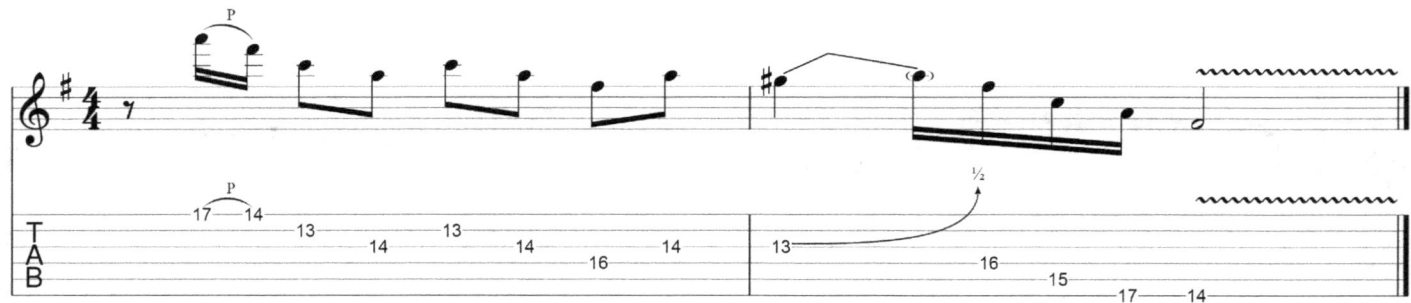

Example 8h uses 1/16th notes with an emphasis on groups of three.

Example 8h:

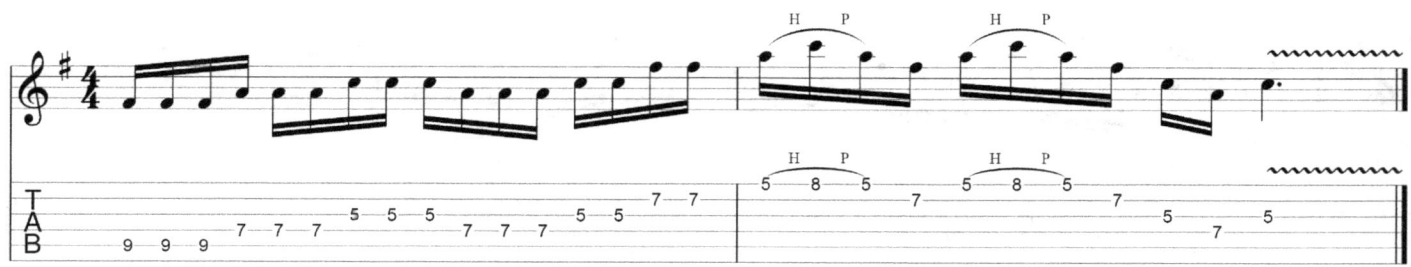

Here's a relatively slow lick, delivered in 1/4 note triplets for a slow, staggered effect.

Example 8i:

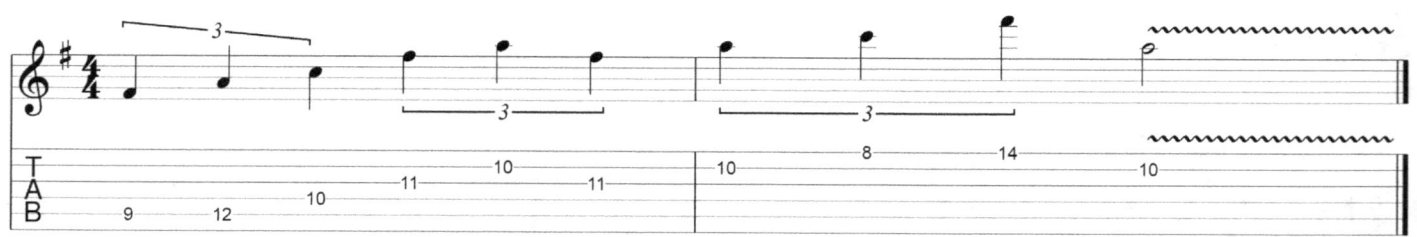

Our vii arpeggio is built from the notes F#, A, C and E to form an F#m7b5. Play through the three m7b5 arpeggios shown below.

Example 8j:

Example 8k begins with straight 1/16 notes, but uses many varying subdivisions in the second bar to throw the listener.

Example 8k:

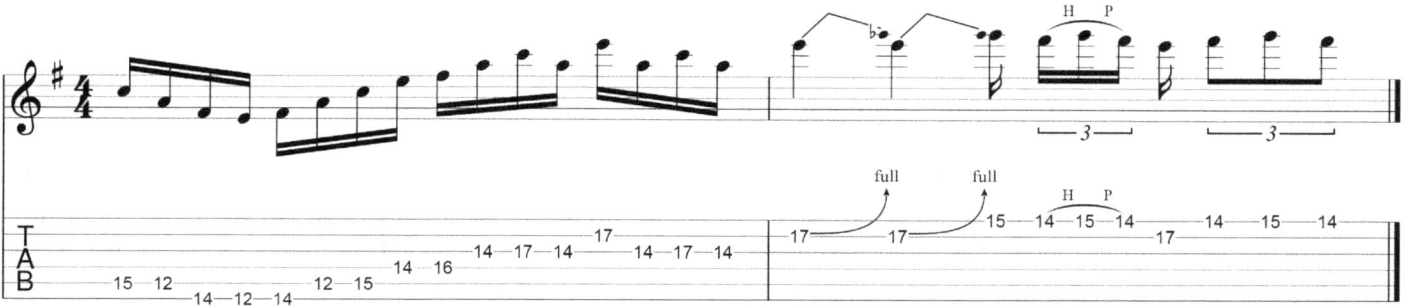

This lick uses a lot of 1/8 notes to keep the speed manageable, and throws in a few legato notes for smoothness and speed.

Example 8l:

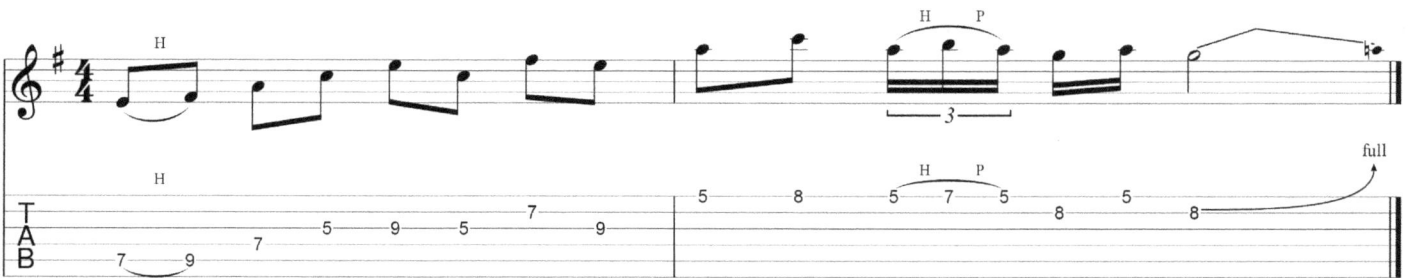

Lastly, here is a slow-moving 1/4 note triplet lick.

Example 8m:

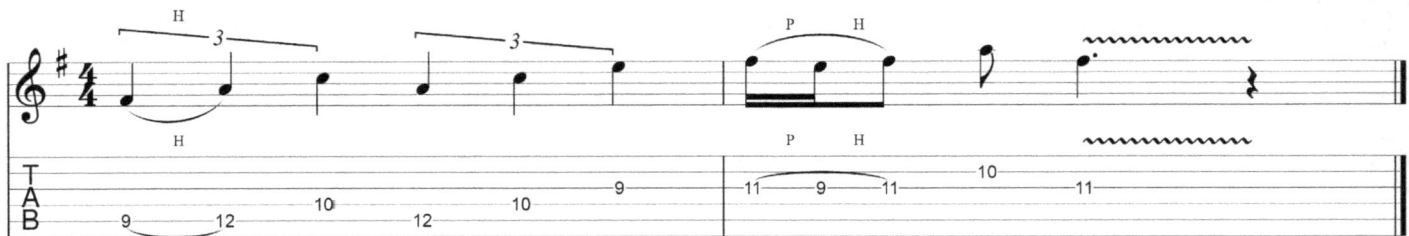

Keep in mind that all of these targeted chord options are easy to modulate. They can all be moved around from key to key and are also relative in modal chord progressions too. For example. if an A Mixolydian chord progression has the chords I, bVII, IV and I those chords will be A, G, D and A, but that will also work in a theoretical sense with V, IV, I and V chord from D major as both share the same notes and chords. This means all your target chord number options will be the same, after you have done the math!

Using chord numbers together in a progression

We've worked through every chord in the harmonised major scale and learnt tons of licks, to close out this chapter I've included a couple examples of how you can apply these ideas over popular chord progressions. This is just a small taste of what is possible and you should go and practise all the ideas covered so far over some jam tracks.

First, let's look at a I V vi IV progression in G Major (G Major – D Major – E minor – C Major)

Below is a mini-solo over this progression. Here's a breakdown of melodic ideas I chose to use for each chord:

Gmaj (I): G Major triad five-string arpeggio

Dmaj (V): G Major Pentatonic scale from D (D, E, G, A and B)

Em (vi): E Aeolian mode

Cmaj (IV): Cmaj7 six-string arpeggio

Example 8n:

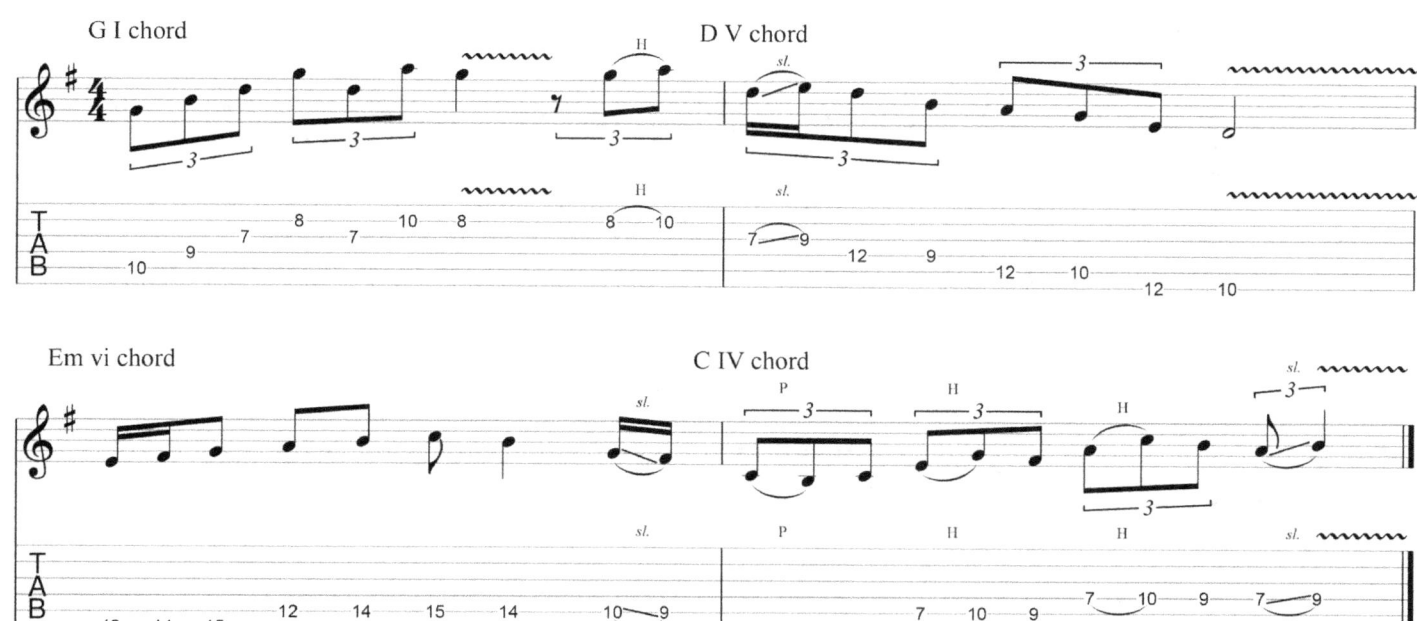

The next example progression is a I vii ii IV progression in G Major (G Major – F#m7b5 – Am – C Major). Here's the breakdown of my melodic choices:

Gmaj (I): G Major diatonic CAGED shape

F#m7b5 (vii): F#m7b5 arpeggio, two octaves, leading from F#

Am (ii): G Major Pentatonic scale from A (A, B, D, E and G)

Cmaj (IV): C Lydian/E Hirajoshi pentatonic box

Example 80:

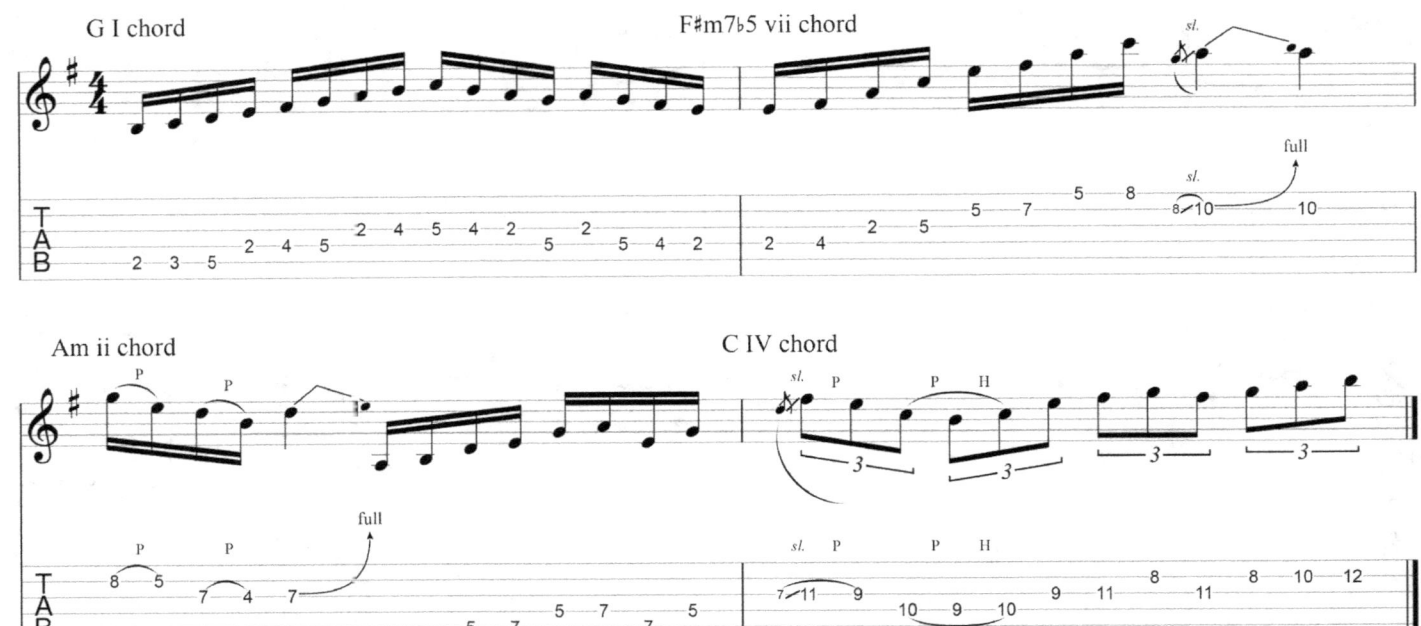

One final example: a vi iii IV V progression in G Major. The result of not including a G Major chord here will give the progression more of an E minor sound. Play through the example and listen to the interplay between the chords and the lead lines. Here's a breakdown of my scale choices:

Em (vi): Em7 five-string arpeggio shape

Bm (iii): B Phrygian CAGED shape

Cmaj (IV): C Major six-string triad arpeggio

Dmaj (V): D Mixolydian three-note-per-string scale shape

Example 8p:

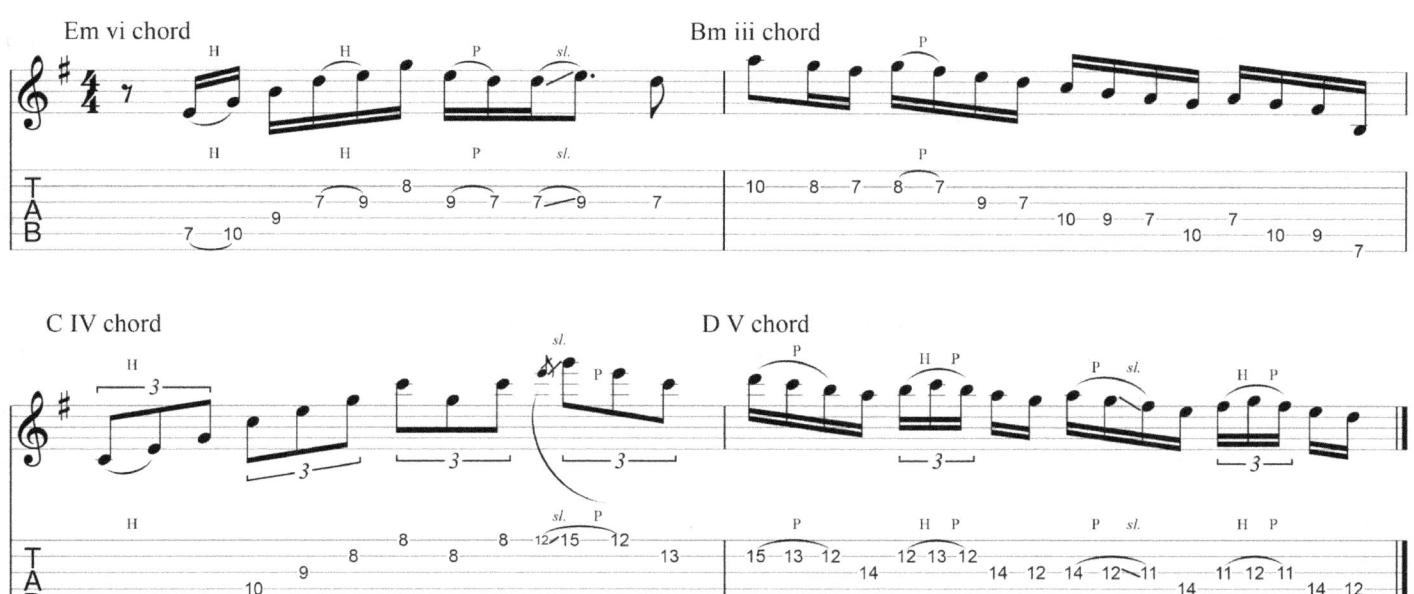

Now that you've seen how these concepts can be applied to three common chord sequences, it's time to write some progressions of your own and to practise soloing over them. I suggest you start in the key of G Major and use your favourite licks so far. When you start to feel comfortable applying these ideas in G Major, transpose your progressions/licks to other keys.

Chapter 9 – Handling Non-Diatonic Chords

In the previous chapters we worked systematically through the diatonic chords in the harmonised G Major scale and learnt how to solo over each. Hopefully, everything made sense to you and felt "Hunky Dory" (which in Latin, I believe, means *hunky dory*).

However, many chord progressions don't contain solely diatonic chords. Chords outside of the diatonic harmony will come to visit and we'll need to adjust the way we solo over them accordingly. It's important we make these "visiting" chords welcome and ourselves sound awesome.

Non-diatonic chords can create all sorts of problems when it comes to improvisation. The sudden curveball chord can leave players puzzled and flustered. Fear not though, by the end of this chapter you'll be able to tackle them confidently.

Now, I know what you're thinking…

"This sounds like silly bogus jazz business, Christopher. I like Blues, Rock and Metal! I don't even listen to music with OUTSIDE or VISITING chords!"

I assure you that lots of the music you listen to features non-diatonic chords. They're often used to create an element of surprise to grab the listener's attention. Since the Beatles rise to fame, non-diatonic chords have been widely accepted in contemporary pop music. Let's look at an example.

The progression is Example 9a is the same as the first four bars of *Creep* by Radiohead. The chords are G Major, B Major, C Major and C minor. The G Major and C Major chords are diatonic to G Major; the B Major and C minor chords are non-diatonic. In Roman numerals we'd write the progression like this: I III IV ivm.

In G Major, the iii chord is B minor. Here it has been changed to B Major, so is designated III rather than iii in numerals to indicate it's a major chord type. B Major has a D# note in it, which is non-diatonic to the key of G major.

The IV chord in G Major is C Major, but in the last bar has been changed to C minor, so is designated iv (sometimes written ivm) rather than IV to indicate it's a minor chord type. C minor has a D#/Eb note in it, which is non-diatonic to the key of G Major.

Example 9a:

"Well, what do we do now, Christopher?" I hear you ask. We ADAPT! For the rest of this chapter we're going to look at common non-diatonic chords that frequently pop up in the key of G Major (including the two pesky examples we've just discussed) and discover what we can play over them.

III/III7 chord: B major/B7

In the key of G Major, the non-diatonic III chord is a major chord (B Major) but is also frequently played as a dominant chord (B7).

B Major has just one note different to B minor. This is useful to know because we want to focus on any notes that fall outside our original key signature.

B minor (iii chord) = B D F#

B Major (III chord) = B D# F#

The key of G Major has only one sharp (F#), so it's the D# note that will cause us grief if we're not prepared. What scale can we play to take account of this non-diatonic note? The B Phrygian Dominant and B Mixolydian Pentatonic scales are both great choices.

B Phrygian Dominant = B C D# E F# G A

B Mixolydian Pentatonic = B D# E F# A

Play a B Major or B7 chord, then play through the B Phrygian Dominant scale below. I've arranged it across all six strings in a three-note-per-string shape.

Example 9b:

Let's hear how we can use this in a creative lick:

263

Example 9c:

Play a B Major or B7 chord again, then play through the B Mixolydian Pentatonic scale below.

Example 9d:

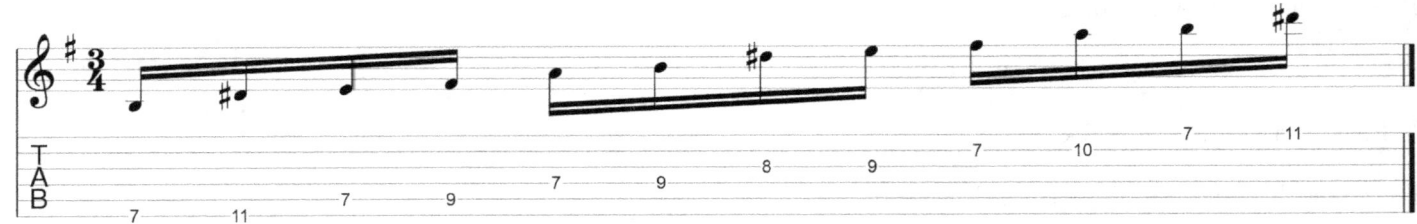

Here's a lick using this idea which includes an expressive bend.

Example 9e:

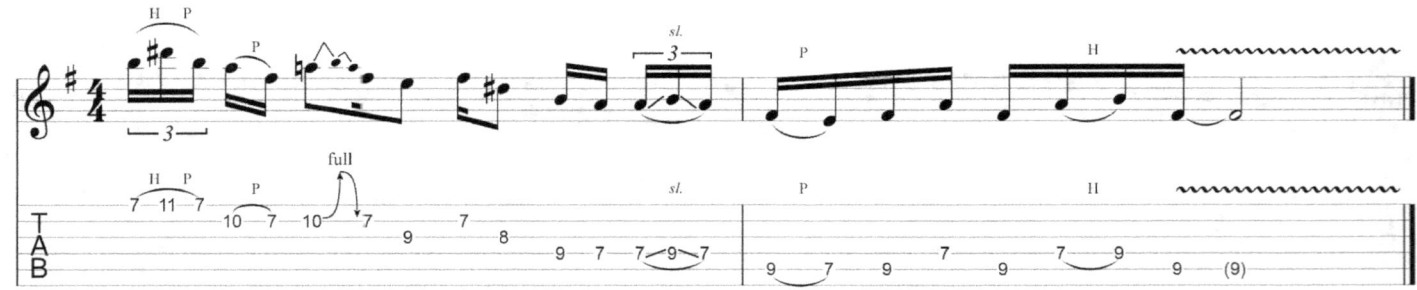

B Phrygian Dominant is the fifth mode of E Harmonic minor (i.e. if you take the E Harmonic minor scale and harmonise it like we did the major scale, the scale built from the *fifth* degree is B Phrygian Dominant. It's just like playing an E Harmonic minor scale beginning and ending on the note B).

It's a common technique to superimpose different scales over a chord to achieve a specific effect. Because of the B Major chord's relationship to E Harmonic minor, we can play a custom Harmonic minor pentatonic scale over it as illustrated in Example 9d. I like to call it a Pentamonic!

The scale formula is 1 b3 4 5 7 (E, G, A, B and D#).

If we play these notes beginning and ending on B, we get the pentatonic shape below, which works perfectly over the III chord.

Example 9f:

Here's a lick that uses the scale to double back on itself as it crosses the fretboard.

Example 9g:

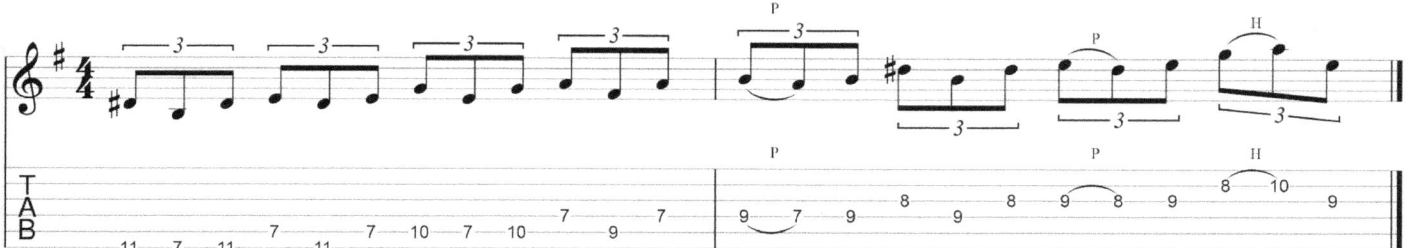

The next most obvious way to deal with the major III chord is to use dominant arpeggios. Played over a regular V chord, dominant arpeggios will sound very safe. Played over the major III chord, however, they suddenly take on an exotic, almost Flamenco/Egyptian-like sound (apologies for mashing together two distinct cultures there without so much as a by your leave!)

Play through the three B7 arpeggios shapes shown below. Each will work well over the III chord.

Example 9h:

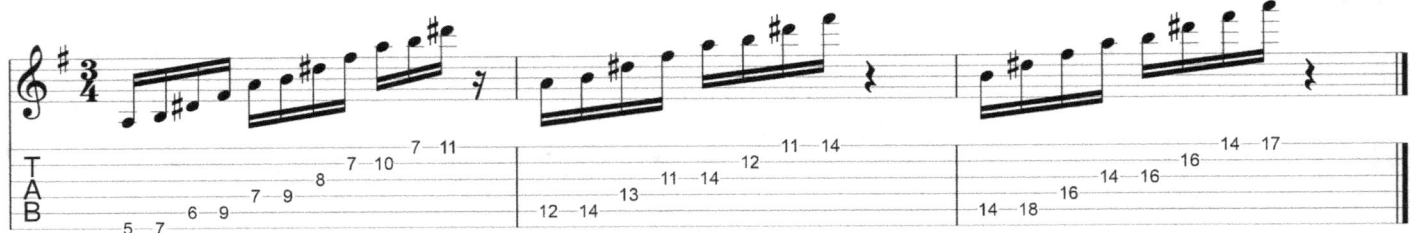

Here's a lick that illustrates a cool arpeggio-based line. Work through each of these three shapes and invent your own.

Example 9i:

The B Augmented arpeggio is also a good choice because it contains the notes B, D# and G. These notes correspond with the 1st, 3rd and 6th notes of the B Phrygian Dominant scale. Augmented arpeggios are moveable shapes, so you can in fact play a B Augmented, D# Augmented or G Augmented arpeggio and they'll all achieve the same effect – they all contain the same three notes, and they all sound great over a B7 chord.

Example 9j:

The augmented arpeggio is ideal for creating angular-sounding ideas like this one.

Example 9k:

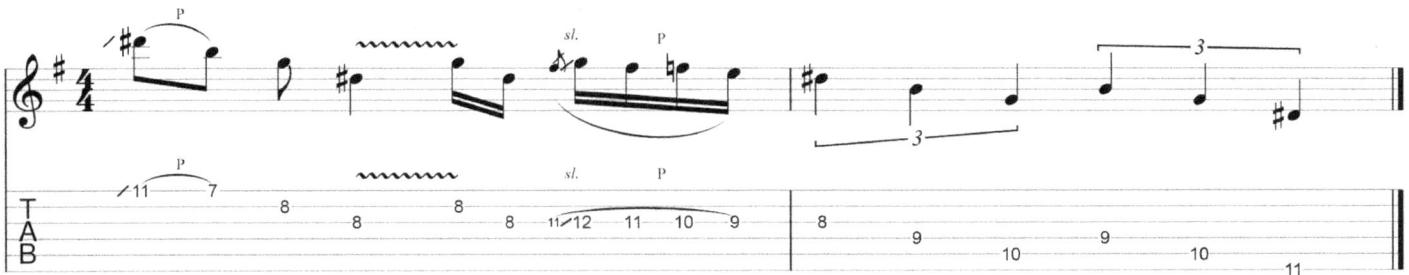

Side Note: Give some time to experimenting with augmented arpeggios – they are dreadfully underrated compared to diminished arpeggios (which are used frequently in metal – core, tech, death, thrash, power etc) – neo-classical shred and flamenco). The great thing about augmented arpeggios is that they create an element of surprise to the listener – a bit of Gypsy Jazz flavour for your rock/metal playing!

Below is a mini-solo that shows how you can handle the III chord in musical context. Example 9l is a vi V IV III progression in the key of G Major/E minor. Pay close attention to the III chord. Here's a summary of what I decided to play over each chord:

Em (vi): E minor triad arpeggio

D (V): D7 arpeggio paired with a tiny section of the G Major three-note-per-string scale shape

C (IV): C Lydian three-note-per-string scale shape

B7 (III): B Phrygian Dominant three-note-per-string shape

Example 91:

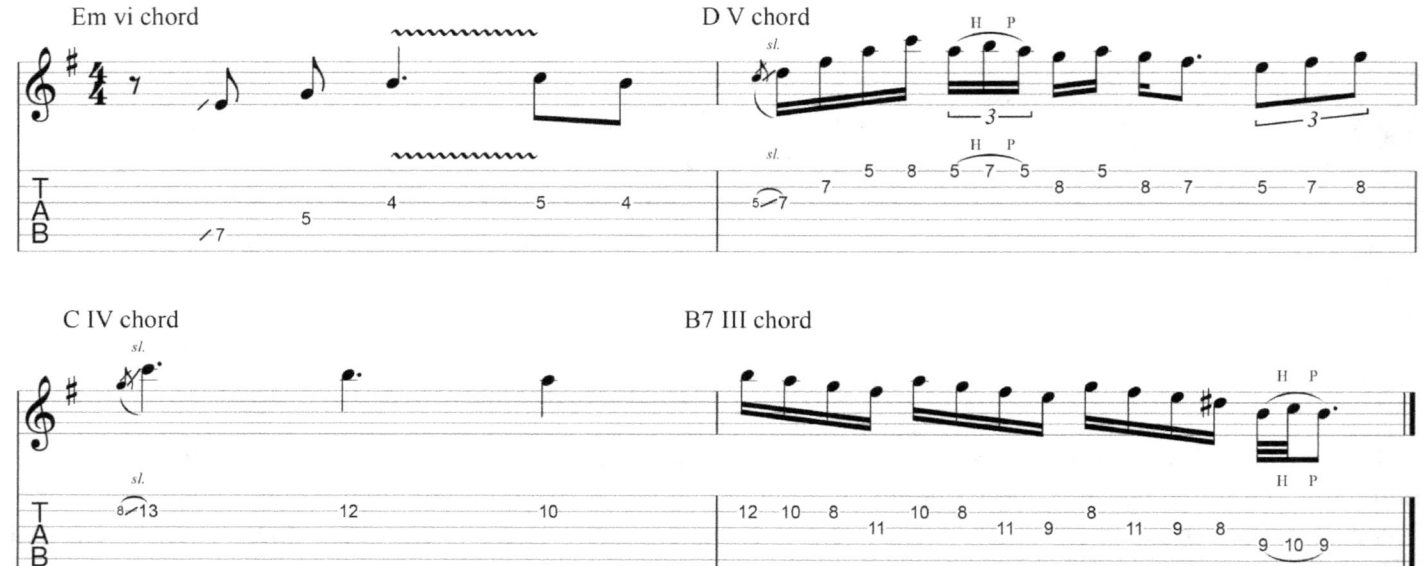

iv chord: C minor

In the key of G Major, the iv chord is usually C Major. The common non-diatonic alternative is to change this to a C minor. The iv minor chord appears in many popular songs (that usually play the C Major first, then change it to a C minor), such as *When September Ends* by Green Day and *In My Life* by The Beatles.

Let's compare the iv minor to the standard IV chord:

C Major (IV) = C E G

C minor (iv) = C Eb G

The Eb (or D#) in the C minor chord is the note to look out for.

The perfect scale to accommodate this chord is C Dorian.

C Dorian = C D Eb F G A Bb

The scale has three notes that don't appear in the key of G Major (so don't go playing it over a G chord!). However, over C minor it sounds great.

Here's C Dorian arranged in as a three-note-per-string scale.

Example 9m:

Now here is how you can apply this scale in a lick over C minor.

Example 9n:

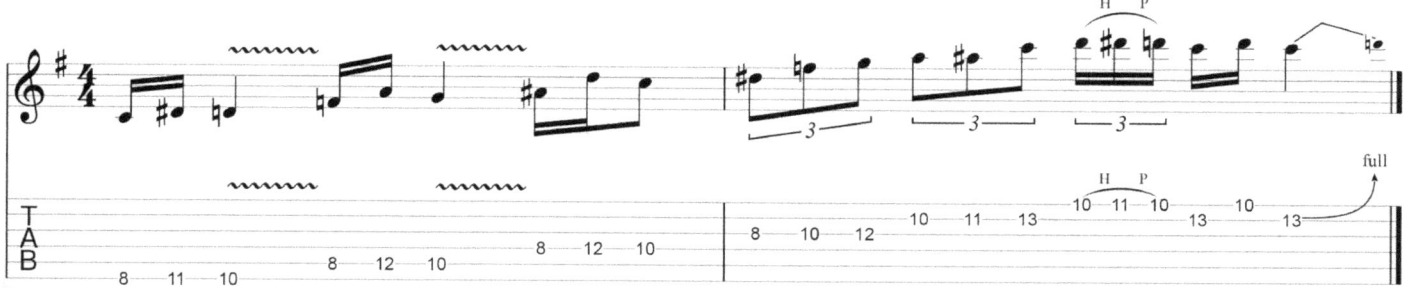

Example 9o shows the box and vertical shapes of the C minor Pentatonic scale, which of course will work swimmingly over our C minor chord. Remember you can use any of the five minor pentatonic shapes, so go and experiment.

Example 9o:

Here's an idea that makes great use of hammer-ons / pull-offs.

Example 9p:

As we've done with every other chord so far, we can attack the iv minor chord with straight-up minor triad arpeggios. Play through the three shapes below.

Example 9q:

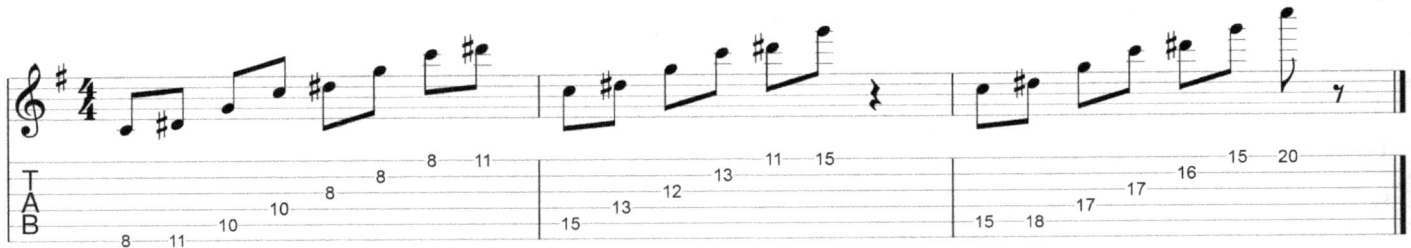

Now here's a lick that puts these ideas to work.

Example 9r:

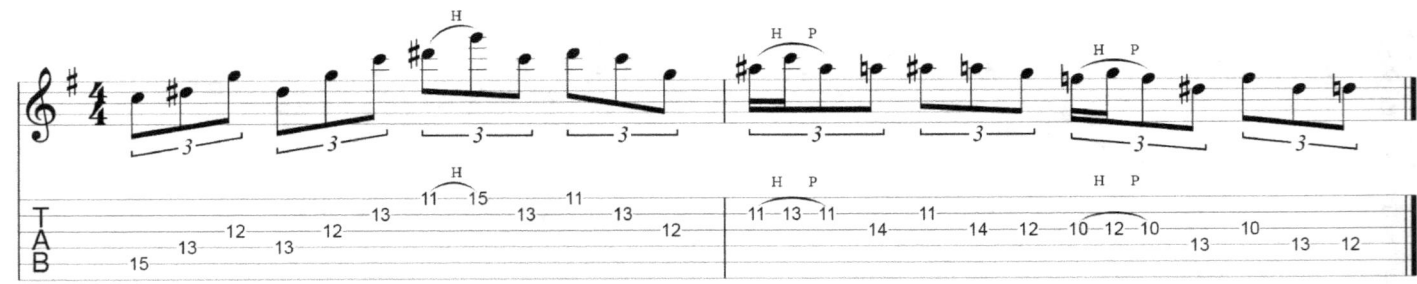

Let's add the 7th interval to turn the triads into minor 7th arpeggios.

Example 9s:

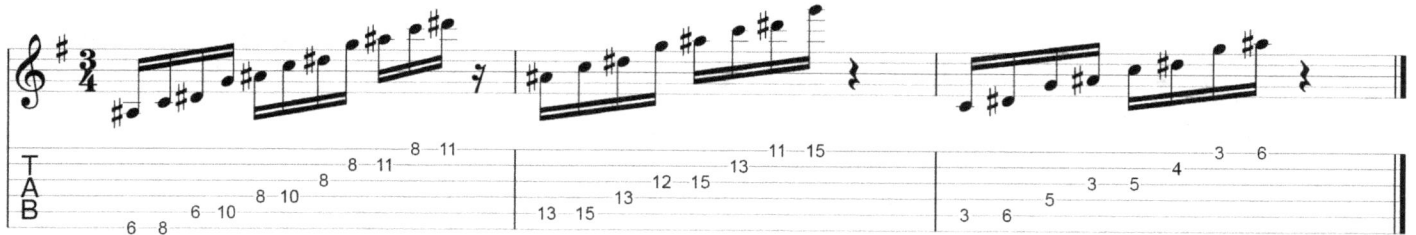

Example 9t uses the third arpeggio shape.

Example 9t:

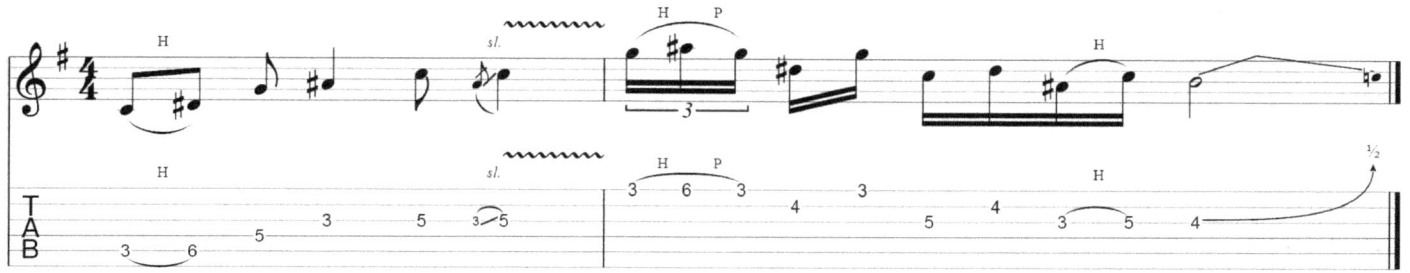

Now let's see how these ideas work in a mini-solo over a I iii IV iv progression in the key of G Major. Pay close attention to the iv chord. Here's breakdown of the ideas I used:

G (I): G Major Pentatonic scale (high octave)

Bm (iii): B minor five-string arpeggio shape

C (IV): C Lydian three-note-per-string scale shape

Cm (iv): C minor descending six-string arpeggio

Example 9u:

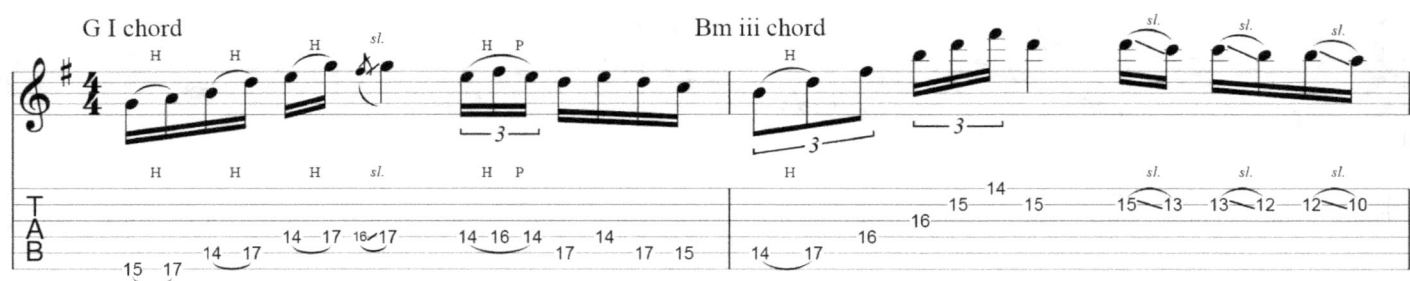

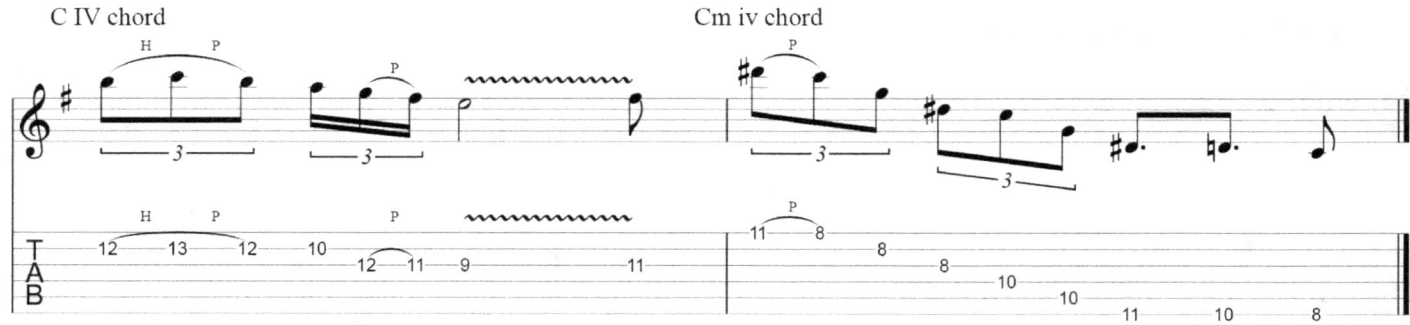

VI/VI7 chord: E Major/E7

There are two more non-diatonic chords that crop up in the key of G Major. Here's the first! We would expect the vi chord in G Major to be an E minor. This frequently gets turned into an E Major or E7 chord. The VI7 chord is commonly found in jazz, but can work in any genre. Here's how the diatonic/non-diatonic chords compare:

E minor (vi): E G B

E Major (VI): E G# B

This time we've got a G# note to contend with, so our licks will sound particularly heinous if we take this next idea anywhere near a G Major chord. You have been warned!

Brace yourself. A great scale choice to play over the VI/VI7 chord is the E Hindu Mixolydian scale. "What the crap is that, Chris?!" I hear you cry. Trust me, you'll love it. What has been coined the "Hindu Mixolydian" is the fifth mode of the Melodic Minor scale. Its scale formula is 1 2 3 4 5 b6 b7. It is also sometimes known as the Mixolydian b6 scale and sounds excellent over the non-diatonic VI chord.

Example 9v:

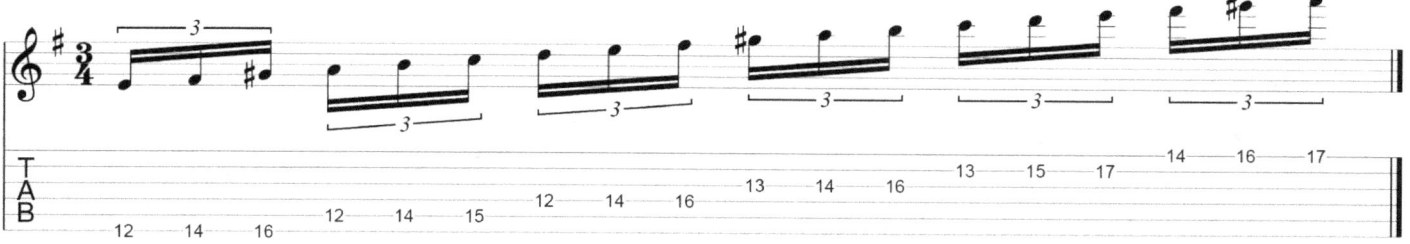

How might this exotic scale sound in lick form? Here's an example.

Example 9w:

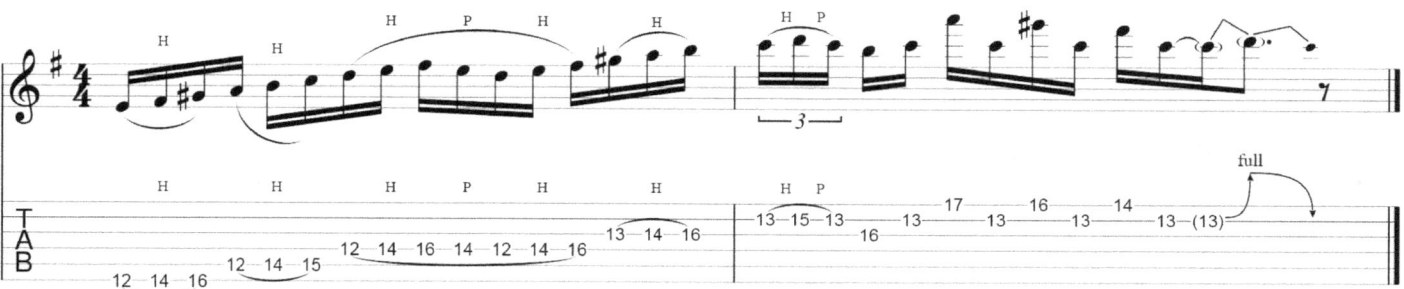

"How come this works, Chris?" I hear you ask. E Major/E7 is the V chord in the key of A Major. Viewing the VI7 chord as the V chord from A Major means we can play the mode associated with it – E Mixolydian. Here's a useful shape that maps out an E Mixolydian Pentatonic scale.

Example 9x:

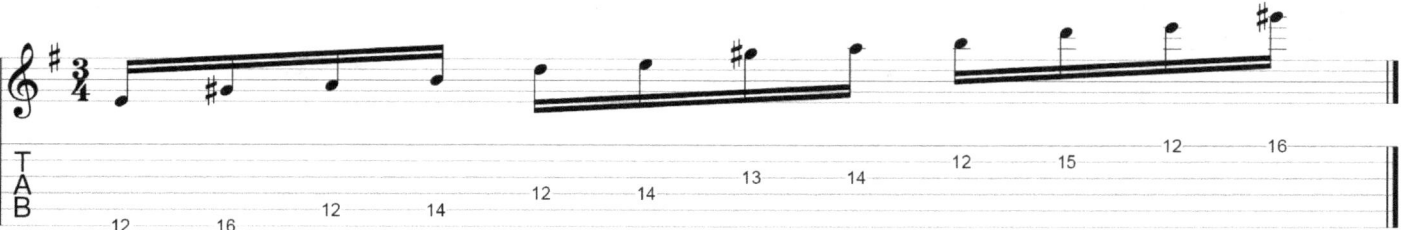

And here's a lick that puts it to work over the E Major/E7 chord.

Example 9y:

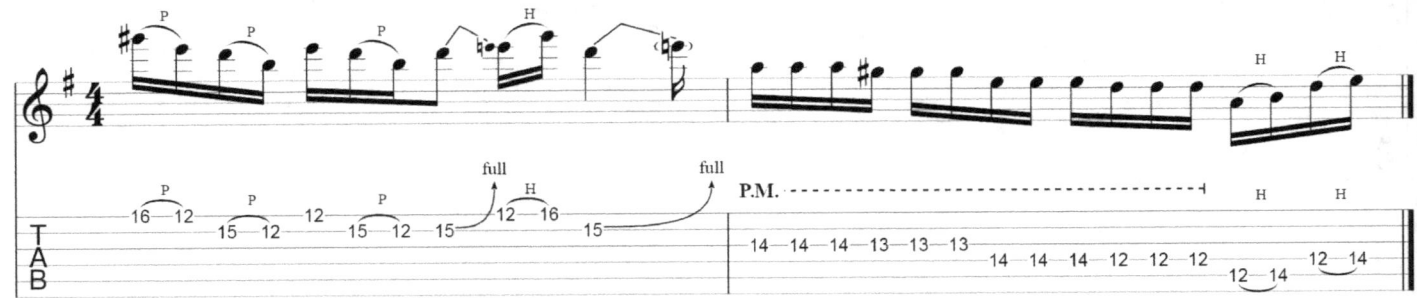

Now let's approach the V7 chord with E7 arpeggios as shown in Example 9z.

Example 9z:

Here's a lick that uses these arpeggios over an E7 chord.

Example 9z1:

What other scale choices might sound cool over this chord? In Example 9z2 I use the whole tone scale (which contains the notes E, F#, G#, A#, C and D). It's got the all-important G# note we need to accommodate, but the other intervals help produce a cartoon-like effect – that thing they do in movies where someone is being hypnotised, falling asleep or entering a dream sequence. It's the fact that all the notes are a tone apart that give it its spacey effect.

The whole tone scale can create outside quirkiness on any dominant 7th chord, but I think it sounds particularly cool on VI7 chords. Check out the solo in the song *Silent Wars* by Arch Enemy. There's a whole tone run of death at 2:50. Enjoy!

Example 9z2:

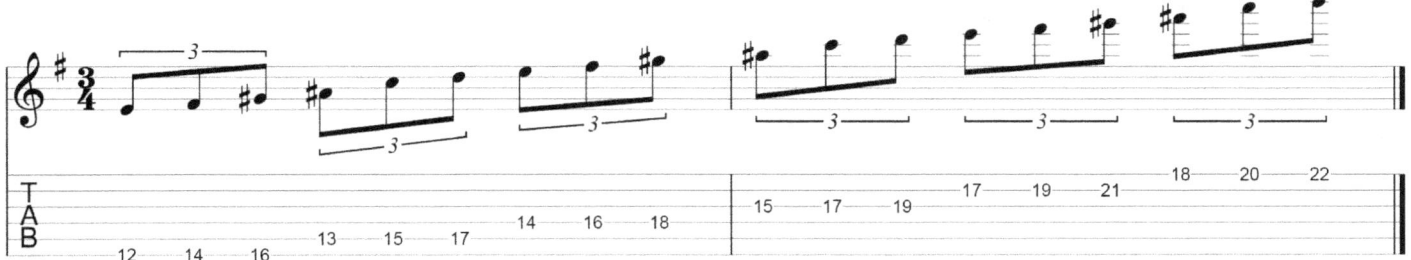

Here's just one example of how you might use the scale in a real-life situation.

Example 9z3:

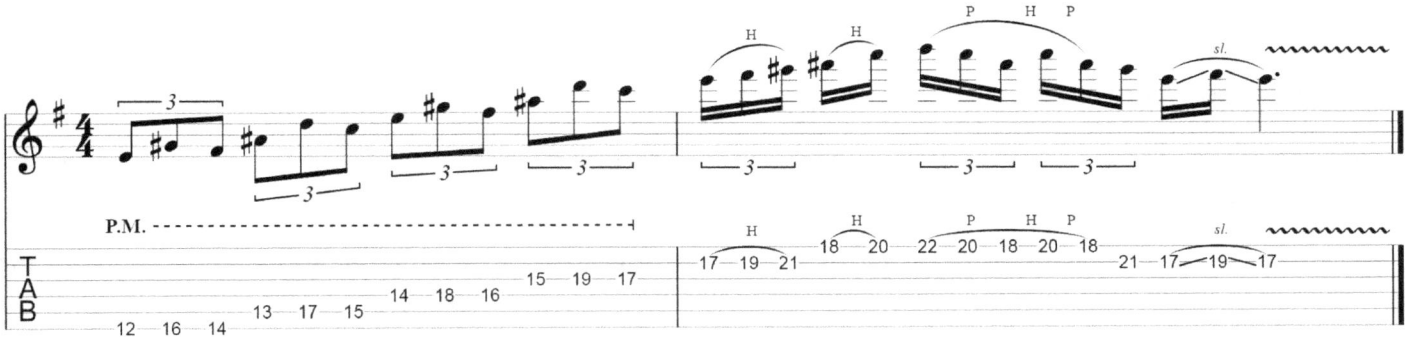

Now let's put some of these ideas into a mini-solo. Example 9z4 is a ii V I VI7 progression in the key of G Major. Here's a summary of what I played over it.

Am (ii): G Major Pentatonic scale shape two

D (V): D7 arpeggio

G (I): G Major three-note-per-string scale shape

E7 (VI7): Descending E Augmented arpeggio

Example 9z4:

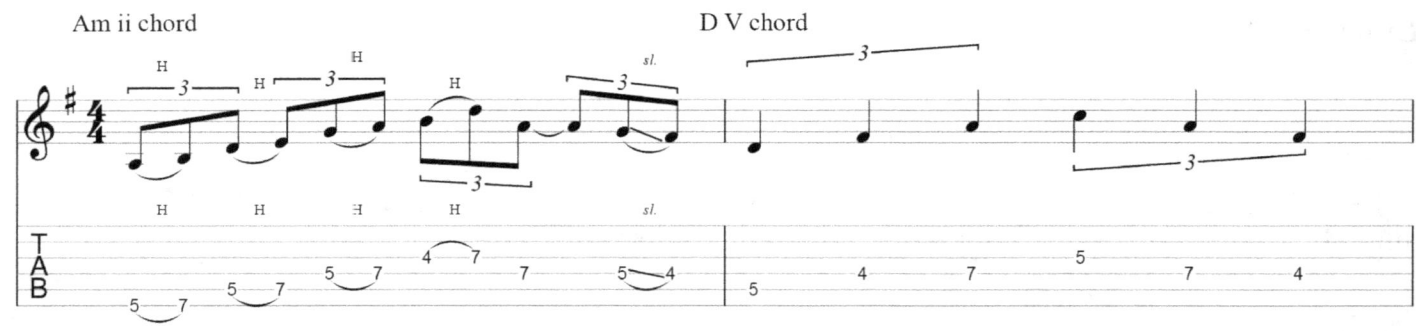

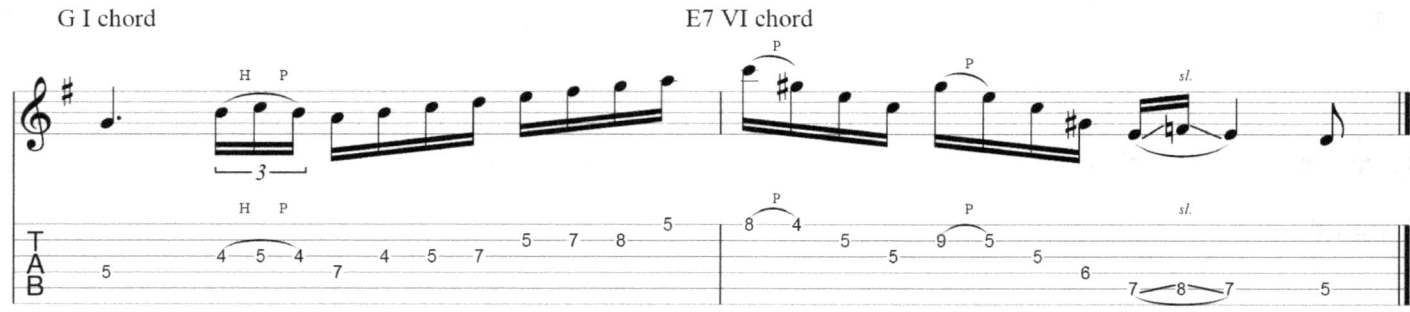

vii Diminished 7 chord: F#dim7

Lastly, the non-diatonic viidim7 chord can easily be mistaken for the diatonic vii chord – but the non-diatonic chord is diminished, whereas the diatonic chord is a m7b5.

In other words, in the context of the key of G Major, the non-diatonic viidim7 chord is F#dim7 and not the expected F#m7b5. The F#dim7 chord contains one outside note. Let's compare the two:

F#m7b5 (vii): F# A C E

F#dim7 (viidim7): F# A C D#

F#dim7 contains a D# note which is not in the key of G Major. The quickest way to deal with this chord is simply by playing an F#dim7 arpeggio. Here are two useful shapes for this in five- and six-string patterns.

Example 9z5:

Here's an idea based on these shapes.

Example 9z6:

What makes diminished 7th chords special is that the notes they contain are all spaced a minor third apart. This means that can easily be inverted and moved around. All the notes are the same, just in a different order. All the arpeggios below will therefore work over the viidim7 chord. (D#dim7, F#dim7, Adim7 and Cdim7).

In Example 9z7 the same five-string arpeggio shape is played in four different positions to achieve this effect.

Example 9z7:

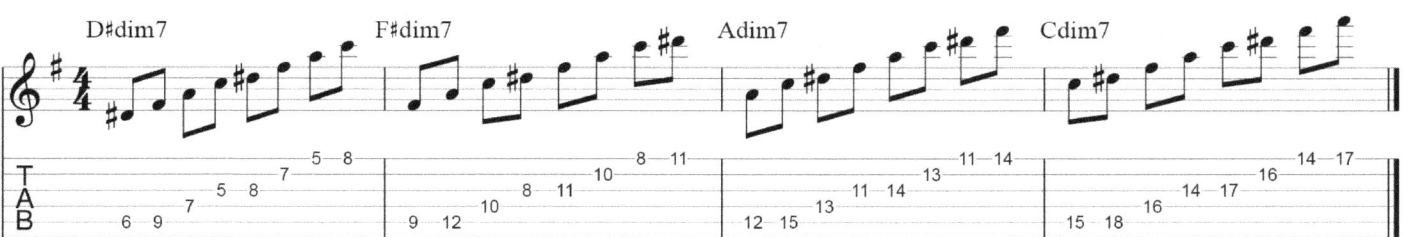

Here's a lick that combines some of these shapes.

Example 9z8:

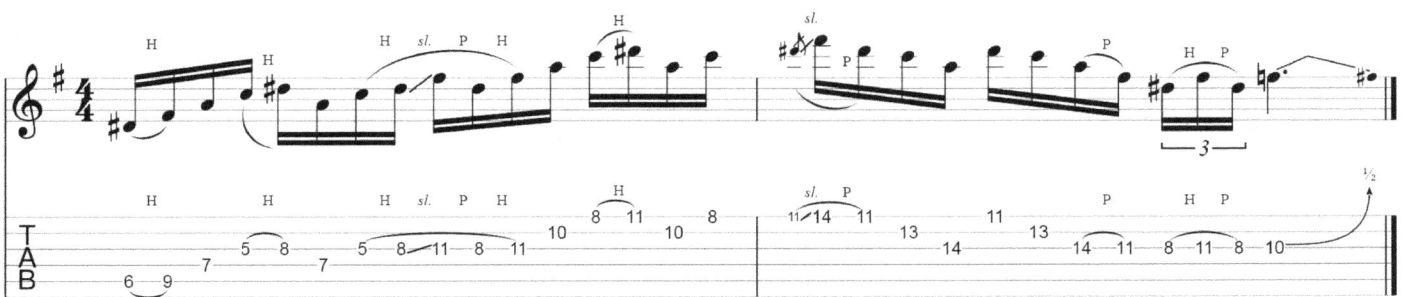

Alternatively, we can use the Diminished Scale over the viidim7 chord. This is sometimes called the half-whole or whole-half scale. The intervals are played as a whole step followed by a half step in a repeating pattern or vice versa. Play through both variations of the F# Diminished Scale below as a three-note-per-string pattern, spanning five strings.

Example 9z9:

Here's a creative lick that moves freely through the two patterns.

Example 9z10:

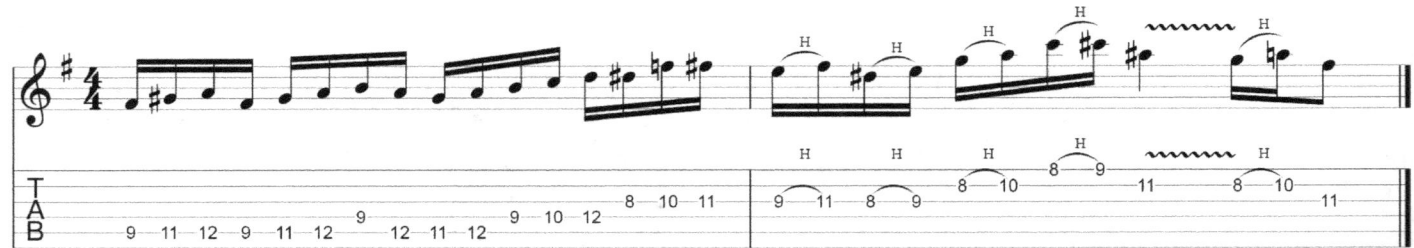

A final scale choice is the F# Locrian Natural 6th Scale. OK, that's a lot of information right there. The Locrian mode is the seventh mode of the major scale and designed to fit over m7b5 chords. Since our viidim7 chord has one note different to the m7b5 chord, we're adjusting one note. It's a Locrian scale with a natural 6th instead of a b6.

Example 9z11:

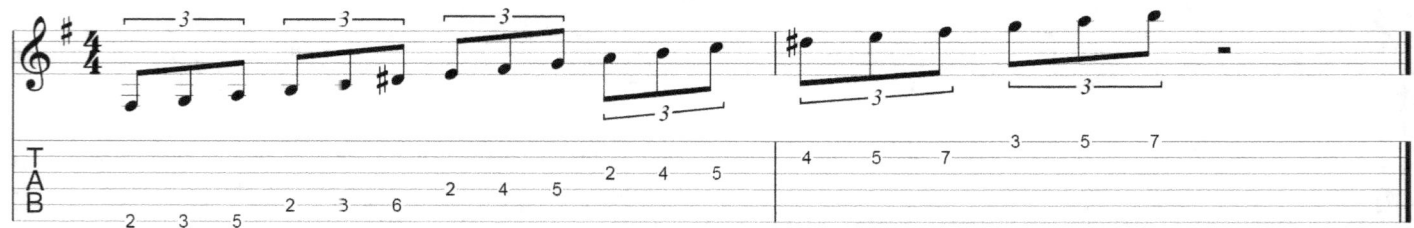

Here's a cool, angular-sounding lick using the scale.

Example 9z12:

Here's a I IV vi viidim7 progression in the key of G Major and an accompanying mini-solo. Here's the usual breakdown of what I decided to play:

G (I): G Major Pentatonic scale in a horizontal crawling shape

C (IV): Cmaj7 arpeggio plus E Hirajoshi scale fragment

Em (vi): E Minor Pentatonic

F#dim7 (viidim7): F#dim7 arpeggio and a descending diminished scale

Example 9z13:

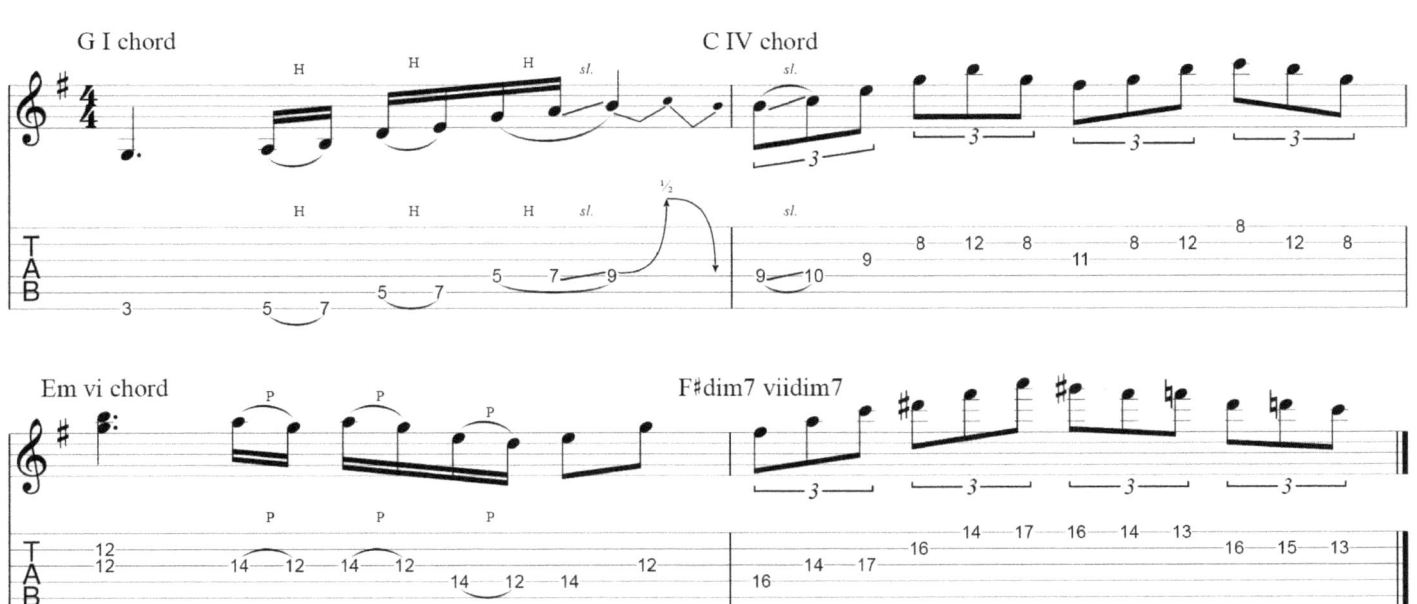

I thought I'd end this viidim7 section in Jerry Springer style, like a *Jerry's final thoughts* reflection. Diminished chords are tricky things, but as you've seen, there are more creative ways to play over them than sweeping a diminished arpeggio. Keep things interesting with multiple approaches. Then, and only then, will you be the coolest kid in the playground… it's never too late to prove those jerks wrong!

Chapter 10 – Soloing Using Chords & Breaking Out of the Single Note Box

So far, you've encountered a huge number of licks that can be played over diatonic and non-diatonic chords. But single line solos and motifs should not be the only weapon in your melodic improvisation arsenal. "What else is there besides cool single note licks, Christopher?" I hear you ask.

That's the subject matter and rabbit hole we'll concern ourselves with next. In this chapter you'll learn how to use chordal concepts and combine them to great effect with your single line soloing. We'll cover major and minor 3rds, 4ths, 5ths, 6ths and "bleeding note" arpeggiated chords.

This chapter also heralds a change of key and all the examples will be based around the G Dorian mode.

Thirds

The G Dorian scale is built from the notes G A Bb C D E F. It is the second mode of the key of F Major (like playing an F Major scale, beginning and ending on the note G).

For starters, we're going to take the G Dorian scale (or mode if you prefer) and play through the scale using major and minor thirds. This is the simplest, most rudimentary introduction to using chords (chord fragments in this case) in your solos. But, when used tastefully, 3rd-based chords can create some cheeky motifs in your lead playing.

Play through the following example.

Example 10a:

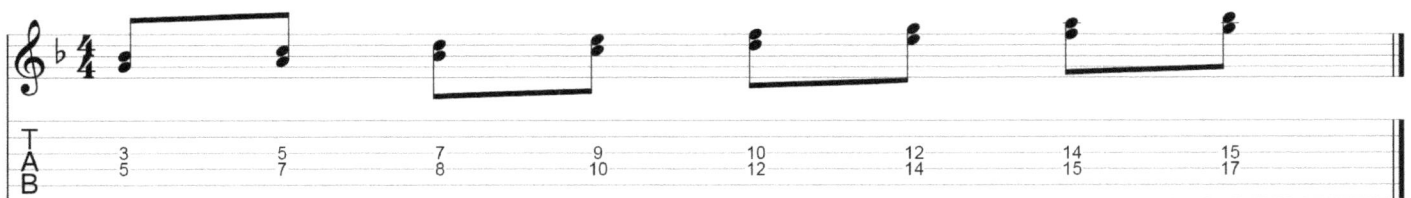

If we were to harmonise the G Dorian scale like we did the major scale, we'd get the following chords:

Gm7 – Am7 – Bbmaj7 – C7 – Dm7 – Ebm7b5 – Fmaj7

In Example 10a, the lower pitched note is the root note of these chords. The higher pitched note is either a minor or major third, accordingly:

Root note:	G	A	Bb	C	D	E	F
3rd above:	Bb	C	D	E	F	G	A
Interval:	b3	b3	3	3	b3	b3	3

Here's how chord fragments like this can work used as part of a lick.

Example 10b:

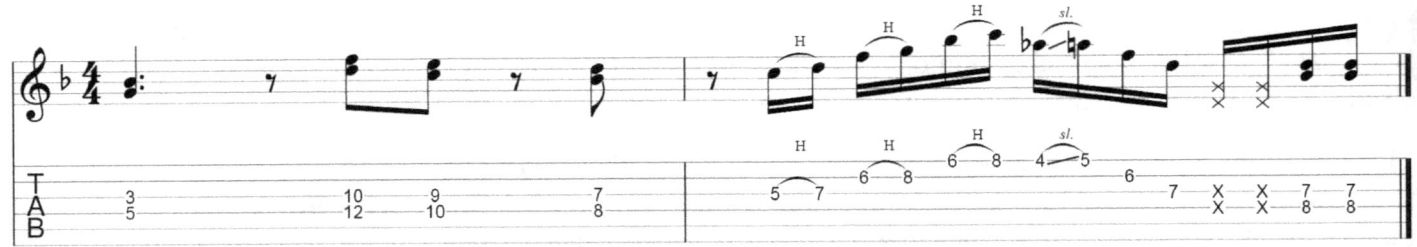

Fourths

Compared with the mellow sounding thirds, fourths have a harder-edged, more powerful sound. Play through the G Dorian scale with these 4th interval chords.

Example 10c:

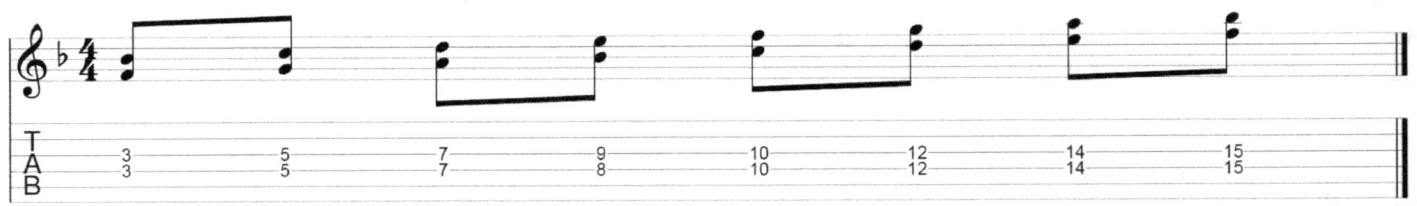

Let's look at the root note/interval relationship again:

Root note:	F	G	A	Bb	C	D	E
4th above:	Bb	C	D	E	F	G	A
Interval:	4	4	4	#4	4	4	4

With the exception of the #4 interval between Bb and E, the rest of this diatonic chord 4th scale is in perfect 4th intervals.

The first bar of Example 10d uses 4ths in a sliding, riff-like motif, then works its way into a lick based around a Gm7add13 arpeggio.

Example 10d:

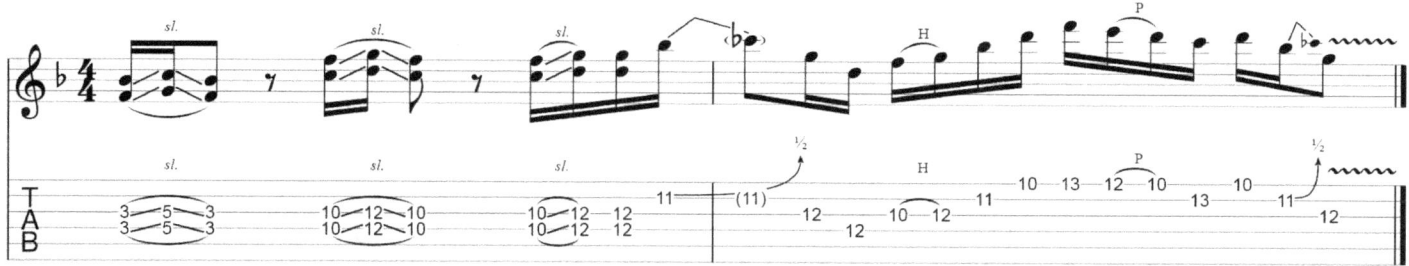

The 4th interval itself is not as emotionally driven as the major/minor 3rd sound, so you won't likely use it as a means to accentuate joy or sadness. I mostly use it as testosterone driven, Rock n' Roll garnish.

Plenty of great riffs have been written using 4ths (*Money For Nothing* by Dire Straits and *Smoke on the Water* by Deep Purple spring to mind). Their purpose is usually to establish a rockin' vibe.

The perfect 4th chord can all be used to get a Hendrixian or Steve Vai-esque sound. There's quite a number of sexy 4th chords in the emotive Steve Vai ballad, *Sisters*.

Fifths

One might wonder, "Why in the name of the Holy Honey Badger would I play power chords in my solo?". And in most instances, you'd have received a round of applause and a signed glossy of Argentinian-born, NBA superstar Manu Ginobli. However, today we're going to explore the 5th interval (AKA power chord) as a tool for lead guitar playing.

Here's the G Dorian scale played with 5th interval chords.

Example 10e:

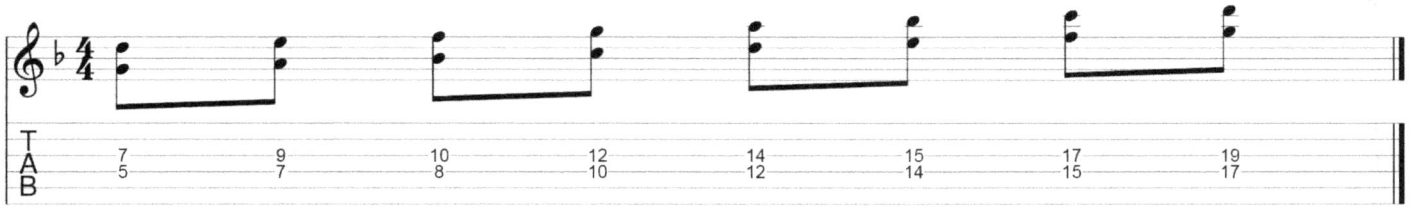

Root note:	G	A	Bb	C	D	E	F
5th above:	D	E	F	G	A	Bb	C
Interval:	5	5	5	5	5	b5	5

As an ascending scale, 5ths leave little to the imagination. It reminds me of one of my least favourite INXS songs, *Don't Change*. But we're going to use it in more of a soloing manner. In the first bar of the example lick below, I use building 5th interval chords to transition into an Em7b5 arpeggio. The coarse and unmelodic nature of the 5ths is immediately juxtaposed by the melodic and jazzy arpeggio.

Example 10f:

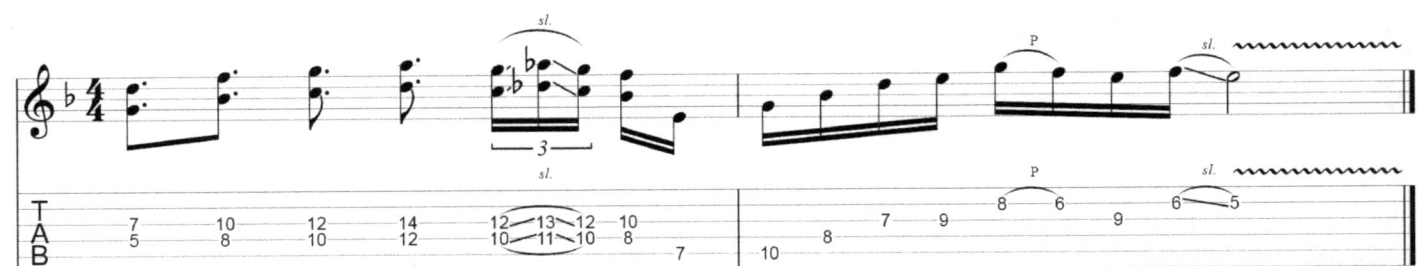

Like 4ths, 5th chords do not yield instantaneous emotion. Quite the opposite. They can sound robotic unless used in the right place – the right place being the introduction to Jimi Hendrix's *Castles Made of Sand*, for instance, or even *CAFO* by Animals As Leaders. 5ths can add a layer mystique and awesomeness, so don't be shy. Get the 5th chord involved in your soloing but use wisely!

Sixths

Like 3rds, 6ths will be major or minor, depending on the chord. This means that we can use these chords as a means to highlight the joyous and more melancholy sounds of a chord progression.

Play though the G Dorian scale with major and minor 6ths.

Example 10g:

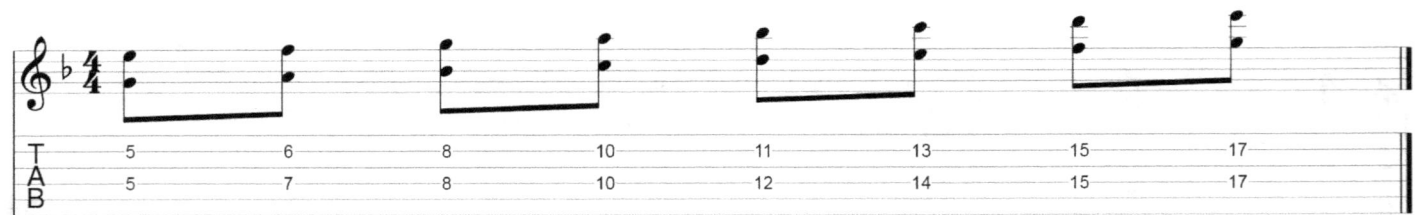

Root note:	G	A	Bb	C	D	E	F
6th above:	E	F	G	A	Bb	C	D
Interval:	6	b6	6	6	b6	b6	6

You can hear 6th chords like these in twelve bar blues turnarounds, as well as the delightful intro to *Wanted Dead Or Alive* by Bon Jovi.

You can hear the signature Slash 6th chords, similar to those in Example 10h, in songs like *Night Train* and *Welcome To The Jungle*.

Example 10h:

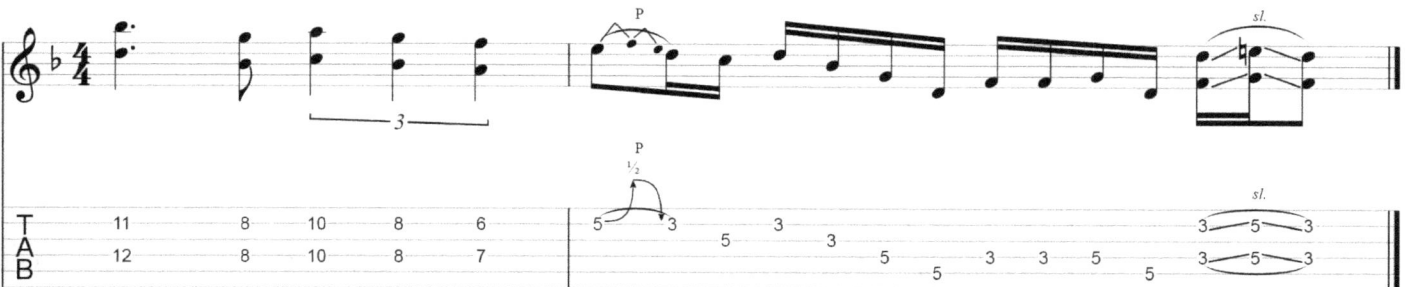

Octaves

If you ever watch me improvise on any of my YouTube videos, you'll notice I use octave chords quite a lot. They sound great in a funky George Benson context, a mystical Steve Vai context, or even a fist-raising Smashing Pumpkins rock context. The great thing about an octave chord is that you're playing the same note twice in different registers, making any melody you're playing sound twice as significant.

Example 10i shows all the octave chords in G Dorian to one octave starting on a Bb. In the song *Killing in the Name* by Rage Against The Machine, the build-up and climax into the timeless "F*** you, I won't do what you tell me!" section is created by ascending octave chords. You can also hear the building octave, climax effect in the Foo Fighters songs *Best of You*, *My Hero*, *Everlong* and *The Pretender*.

Example 10i:

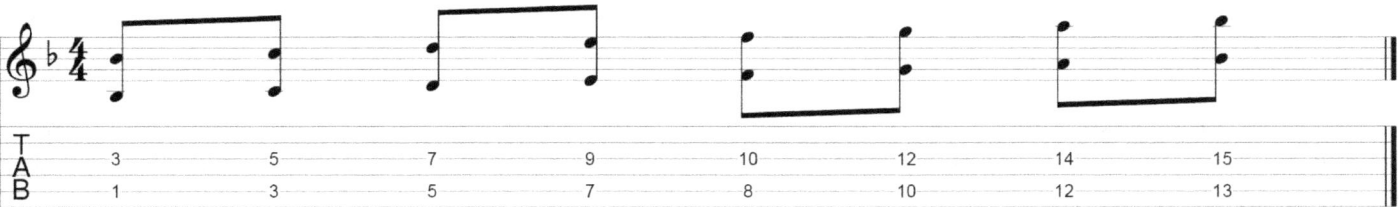

In Example 10j, I play octave chords from the 1st string to the 5th and blend it with a fragment of a Gm7add13 arpeggio.

Example 10j:

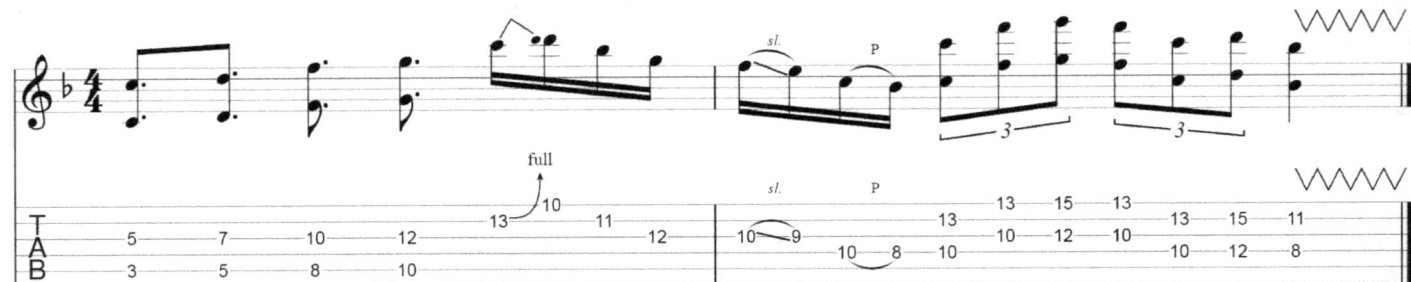

Unison bends

Connected to this idea of doubling up notes, unison bends can really cement a melodic idea. A unison bend begins with two notes a tone apart played simultaneously. The lower of the two is then bent until both notes are the same.

In Example 10k I begin with E and D notes. The D is bent a full tone and we end up with two E notes in the same register, creating a slightly wobbly chorus effect.

Play through this G Dorian scale to one octave, using unison bends, starting and ending on an E note.

Example 10k:

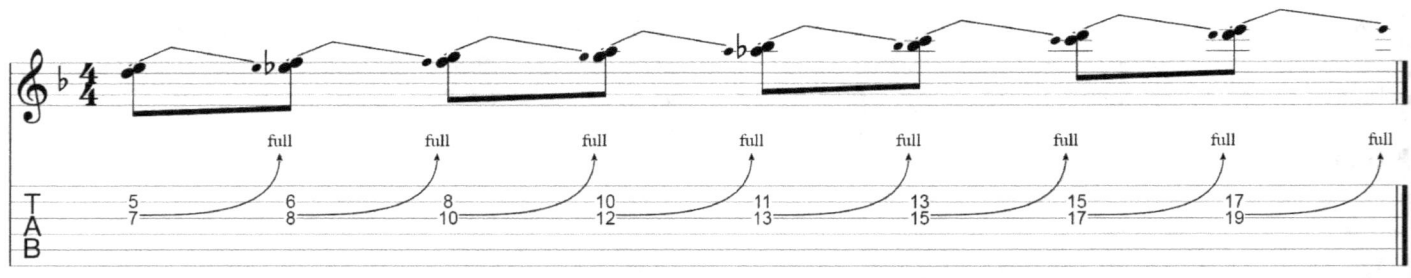

In Example 10l, I've used unison bends to highlight D, F and E (the 5th, minor 7th and major 6th of the G Dorian scale). The line resolves on a triplet run using the 1st and 2nd strings from the G Dorian three-note-per-string shape.

Example 10l:

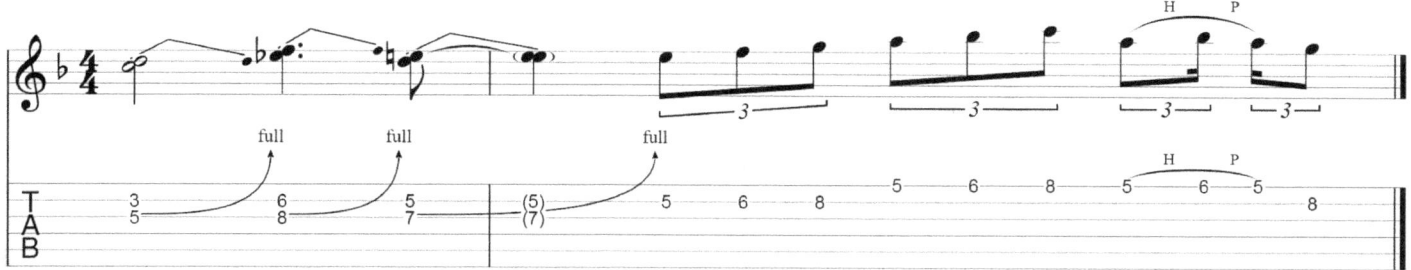

You can hear the excellent use of unison bends by Jimmy Page in the outro to *Stairway To Heaven* by Led Zeppelin. The slow ascending bends create a brooding tension and build up to the song's final climax.

Josh Homme from Queens of The Stone Age and Kyuss has been using unison bends his whole career, as a staple of his lead guitar approach. He often uses them in a fast, abrasive, staccato manner in order to somewhat attack the listener.

I've always loved how much impact a unison bend can have when played slowly. It can sound abrasive and huge! They will also encourage you, the player, to slow down and not constantly fill your phrases with a bajillion notes.

Sustained (or bleeding) arpeggiated chords

Another great chordal technique can be achieved through the use of arpeggios. Rather than play a "clean" arpeggio, we can hold the notes and allow them to "bleed" into each other. Jerry Cantrell uses this concept in several Alice in Chains solos and some of his solo projects. The solo in *Anger Rising* has some great sustained chord arpeggiations.

Josh Middleton from Sylosis uses this concept in countless solos. There's a few beautiful examples of sustained chord arpeggiations at the beginning of the solo in *Eclipsed*.

Example 10m has a chord progression of Gm, F and C. Here I play sustained arpeggio triads over each chord change.

Example 10m:

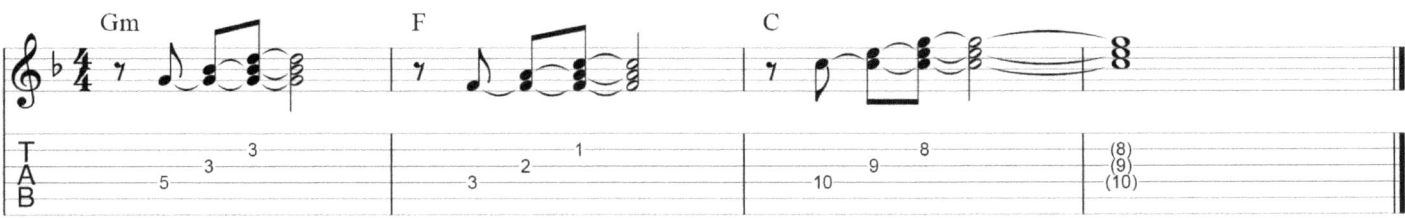

We can take this idea further by using slightly more complex arpeggiated chord voicings. In Example 10n, instead of basic triads, I play a Gm7, Fmaj9 and C7.

Example 10n:

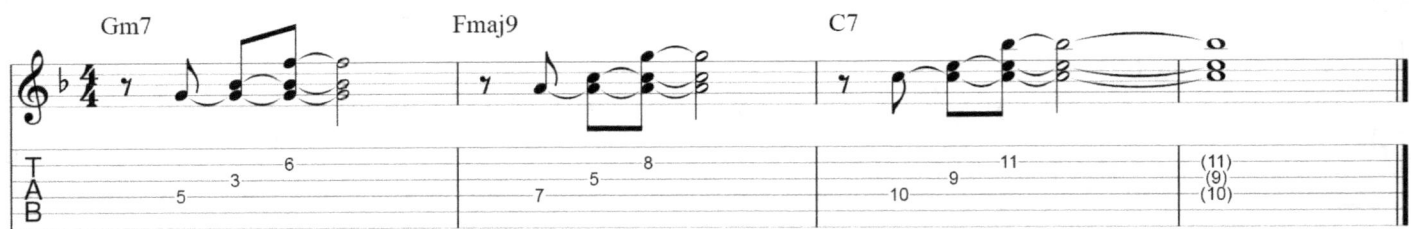

One of the coolest things about playing lead guitar with chords and arpeggiations is that it prevents us from stuffing our solos with wild shredding, sweeping and crazy legato… well, most of the time. Holding rigid chord shapes to play arpeggiated ideas slows us down and forces us to be more measured. This is effective when juxtaposed against a climatic 1/16th triplet shred-passage-of-destiny. Played one after the other you get the excitement of chaos followed by the calm after the storm.

There are so many places where you can use chords in your soloing. The key is experimentation. Work on adding more dynamics into your solos and figuring out ways to make chordal concepts part of your lead guitar tool kit.

Chapter 11 – Varying Scales & Shred Sequences

So far, we have covered a lot of sonic territory together. You've learnt how to analyse and play over the common diatonic chords that will frequently occur in songs, plus how to tackle the non-diatonic ones. You've also learnt how to mix things up with chordal ideas. Of course, you've learnt lots of cool lick ideas along the way, but all that groundwork has been *preparation for improvisation*.

Sometimes players think that to improvise means that ideas will suddenly appears from nowhere, falling out of the sky. The truth is, all the hard work that goes into preparation is what gives you the ability to be spontaneous.

But still, the threat remains, with the scale and arpeggio knowledge you've gained, that your melodic ideas can sound clichéd. When I first plunged into the world of improvisation, I found myself constantly falling into the robotic delivery of scales, arpeggios and shred sequences. Everything I played sounded "up and down". It was hardly memorable. My improvisation lacked *pizazz*.

From one gangsta to another, there's nothing more offensive than hearing a guitarist trying to find their own expressive voice, playing solos that sound like exercises straight out of a scale book.

This chapter, then, is solely devoted to teaching you different approaches to soloing with common scales, so that they sound sexy, less linear. This will lead you into a truer expression of your personality as musician.

All the examples in this chapter are demonstrated in the key of B minor. You can also jam to your heart's content over the B minor backing track included in the free download.

Pentatonic Sequences

The pentatonic scale is definitely the most popular in the world of guitar soloing. As a result, it's also the most likely to sound scale and predictable in the wrong hands. However, in the hands of a musician who has exciting tools and approaches at their disposal it can sound super interesting and sexy.

Let's begin by playing B Minor Pentatonic in its simplest ascending form.

Example 11a:

To help avoid sounding routine, we could first add some rhythm and play with a triplet pulse. You may have heard pentatonic sequences like this being played by Kirk Hammett and Ace Frehley. This is a common way to add speed and variance to the pentatonic shape.

Example 11b:

We can also use B minor Pentatonic in four-note groupings with a 1/16th note pulse. This approach is used by blues guitar greats like Eric Johnson and Joe Bonamassa.

Example 11c:

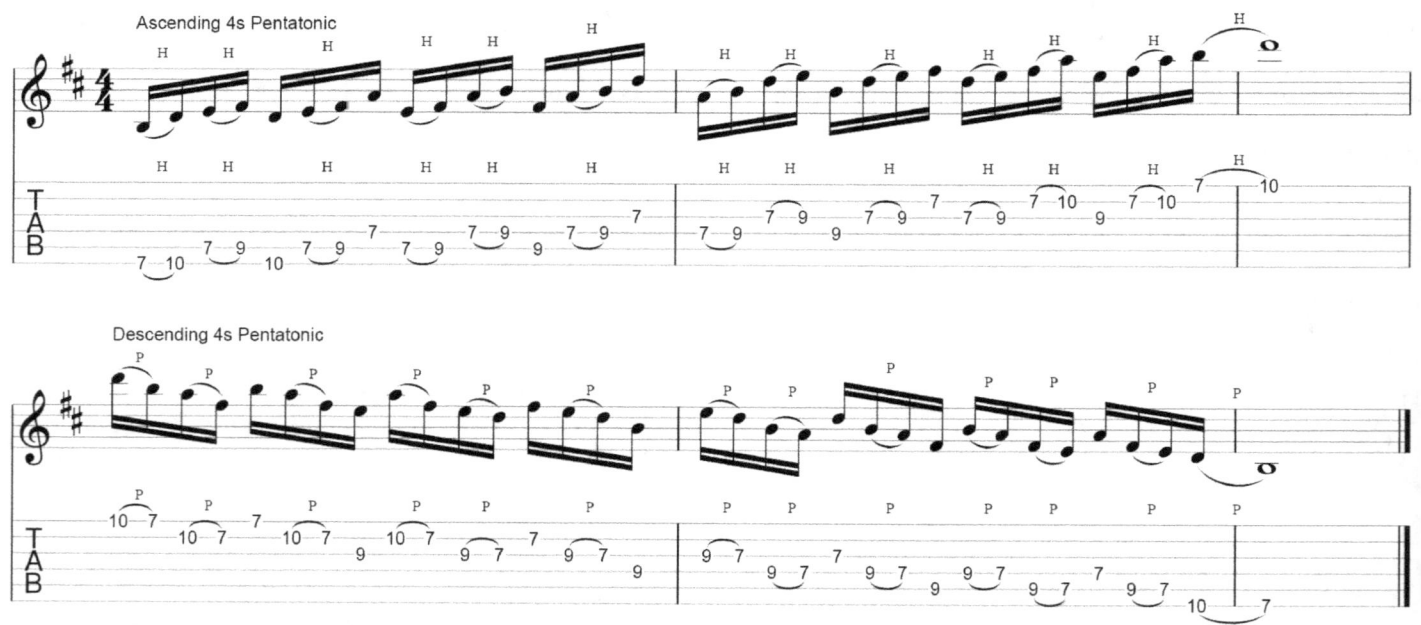

Now here's something a little different. B minor Pentatonic played in five-note groupings and with a 1/16th note pulse. When played with a backing track, you'll hear that the phrasing of the scale lands in some pretty interesting places, making it less predictable to the listener. This approach to pentatonic playing is reminiscent of virtuosic players like Guthrie Govan and Shawn Lane.

Example 11d:

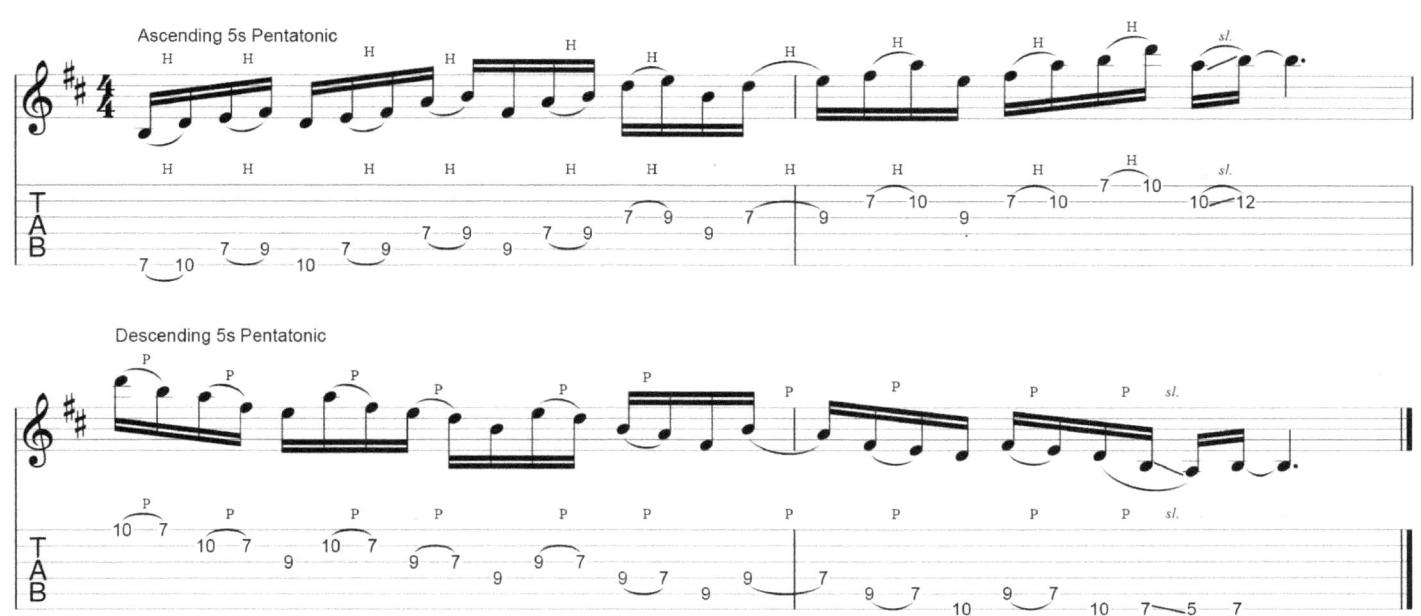

The next example breaks up the pentatonic scale into jumps of predominantly 4ths, with an occasional major 3rd interval thrown in for good measure. This intervallic approach to playing the pentatonic scale creates a very different sound to the pentatonic clichés one might expect.

Example 11e:

The following pentatonic line uses predominantly 5th and some minor 6th intervals. Stacking multiple 5th intervals on top of each other can create a galactic, space adventure vibe, reminiscent of virtuoso Steve Vai. A perfect example of this is the bridge section of his song *Die to Live*.

Example 11f:

Example 11g has an ascending idea with string skips. This is a simple way to create large intervallic jumps and create an element of surprise for the listener.

Example 11g:

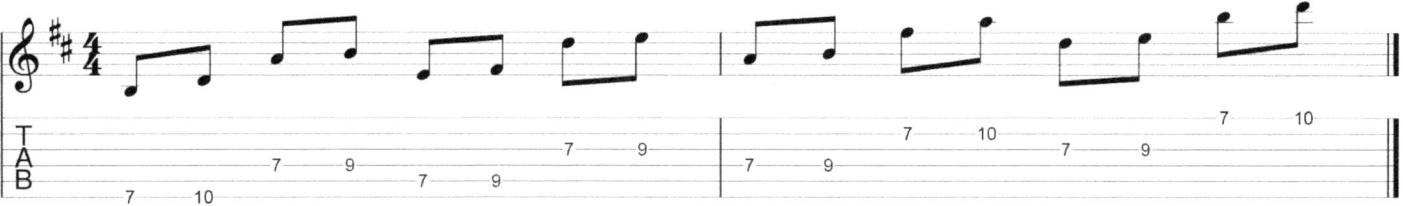

Here's another descending triplet pentatonic idea, but this time it includes string skips!

Example 11h:

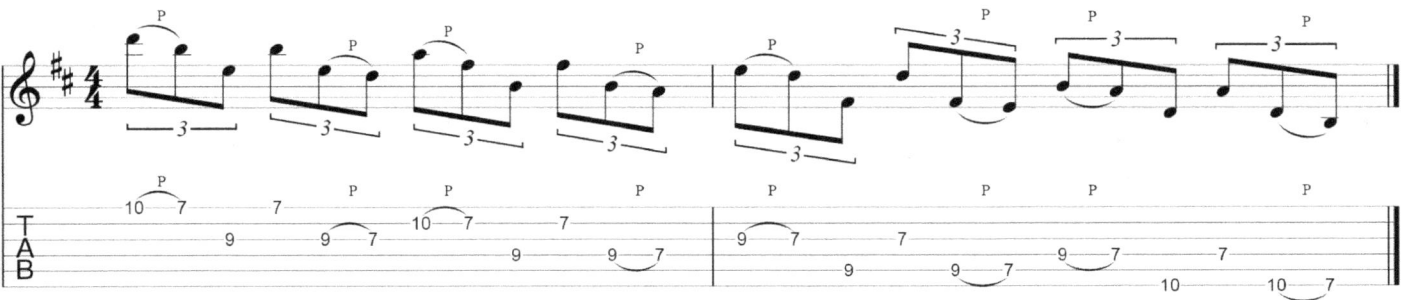

You could use the string skip idea with *any* of the concepts we've discussed in this book, to vary how they are played and avoid sounding like you're running up and down scales.

Try each of these pentatonic ideas in all five positions of the pentatonic scale in various keys.

Diatonic Shred and Legato Sequences

Diatonic, three-note-per-string scales can sound incredibly dull and robotic if applied without creativity. This section is devoted to making these scale shapes sound interesting and less predictable. We'll use the B Aeolian (AKA B Natural Minor) scale throughout, but you should practise these ideas with different scales, shapes and keys.

Here's a three-note-per-string B Aeolian scale shape covering all six strings.

Example 11i:

An easy way to break up the linear nature of the scale is to play it in intervals. Here it is arranged with 3rd interval jumps.

Example 11j:

If you come up with a great idea, always play it ascending and descending.

Example 11k:

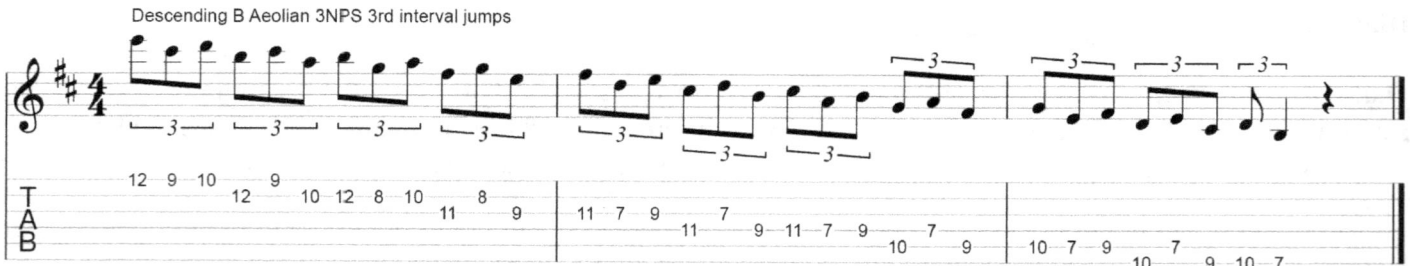

The next idea has the B Aeolian scale arranged in groups of four notes ascending and descending. This approach to shredding can be heard in Alex Skolnick's solo in the Testament masterpiece *Apocalyptic City*.

The descending version of this idea has more of a hair metal sound to it. Players like Satchel (Steel Panther) and CC Deville (Poison) use this pattern in countless solos.

Example 11l:

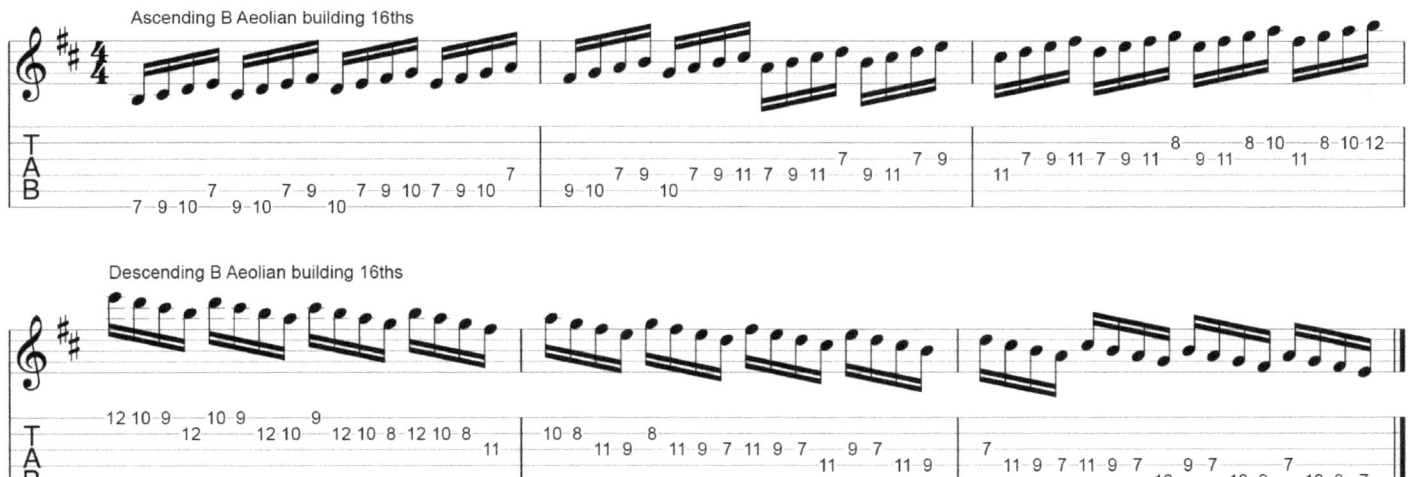

Here is a B Aeolian "double triplet" shred idea. Matt Heafy and Corey Beaulieu from Trivium use this approach in the solos on *Into The Mouth Of Hell We March* and *In The Fire*.

Example 11m:

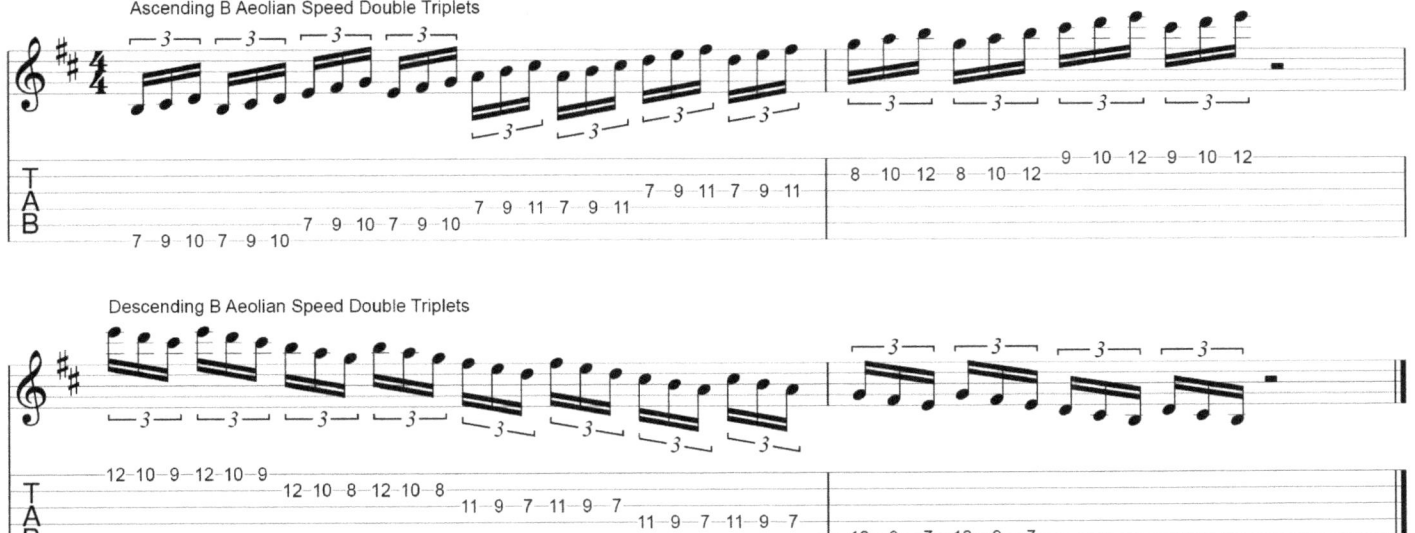

Here's an interesting B Aeolian three-note-per-string shape that uses legato and a five-note pulse. Unpredictable pulses and note groupings are a great way of keeping shred and legato passages unpredictable.

Example 11n:

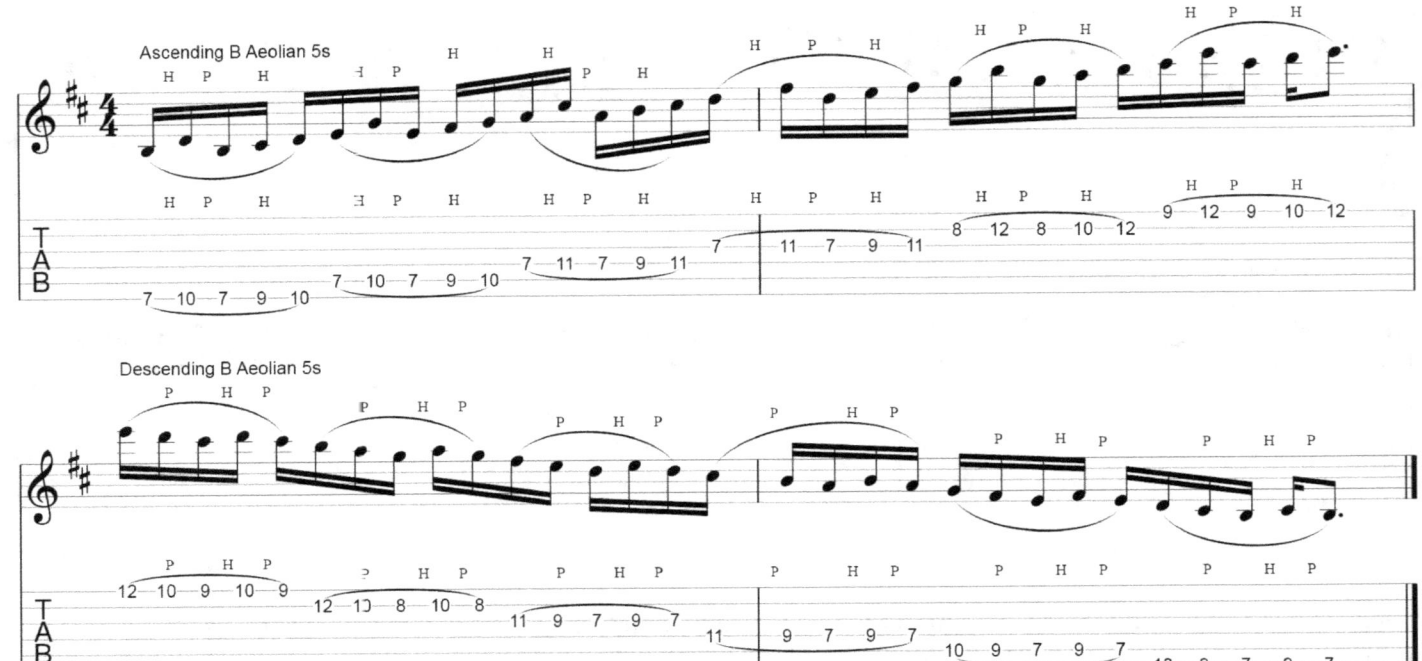

Here's a similar legato idea, but this time the notes are grouped in sevens. Rolling in triplets with a sevens pulse is pretty weird, so be patient if you're trying to lock in with music or a metronome.

Example 11o:

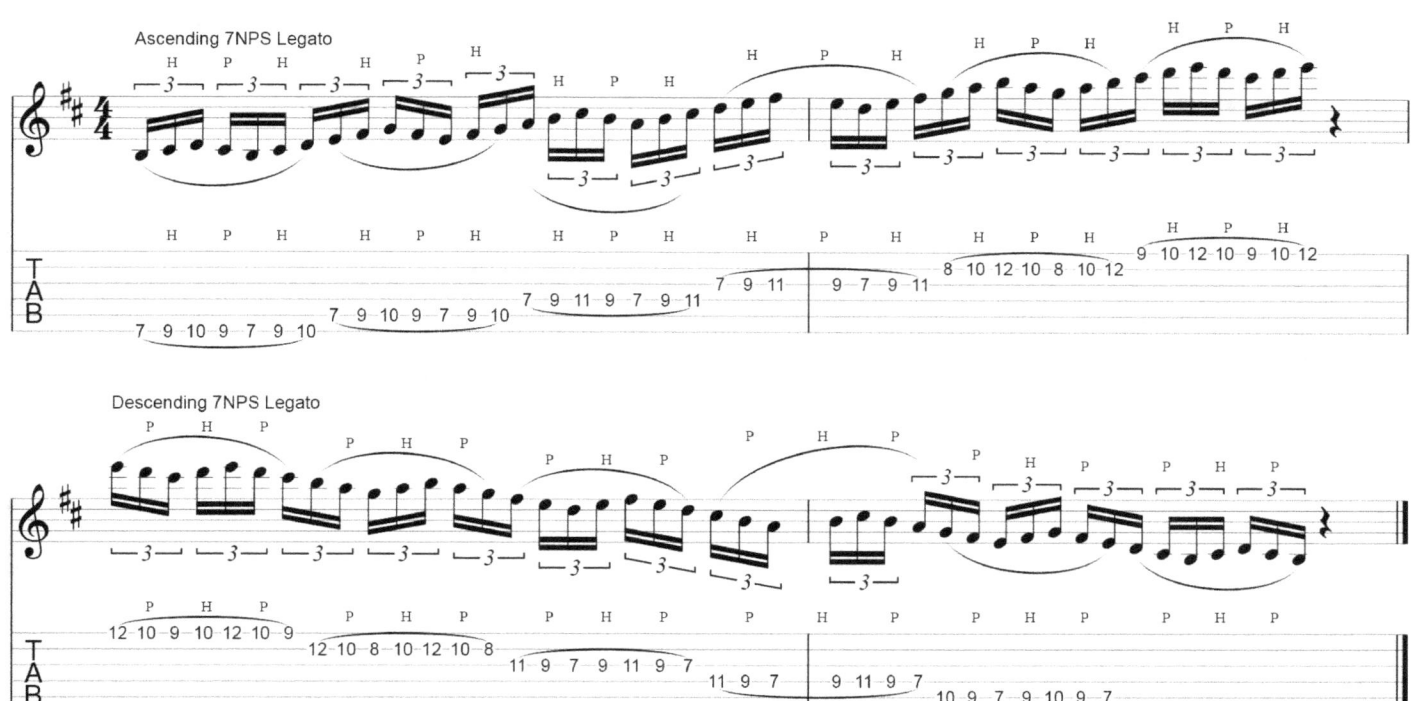

The next creative idea is a Neoclassical three-note-per-string concept that's used by players like Yngwie Malmsteen, Jason Becker and Michael Romeo. It gives these shapes a violin-esque sound, reminiscent of the playing style and compositions of Paganini and Vivaldi.

Each string has four picked notes which allows you to keep your picking consistent across all six strings. This makes the picking pattern less confusing, as string changes and 1/16th note playing on three-note-per-string patterns can be quite difficult.

Example 11p:

The next idea is formed from a three-note triad built on each note of the scale. This means that every three notes form the triads of Bm, C#m7b5, D Major, Em, F#m, G Major and A Major in sequence. It's a powerful approach and shows that triads don't just have to be used for chord targeting.

Example 11q:

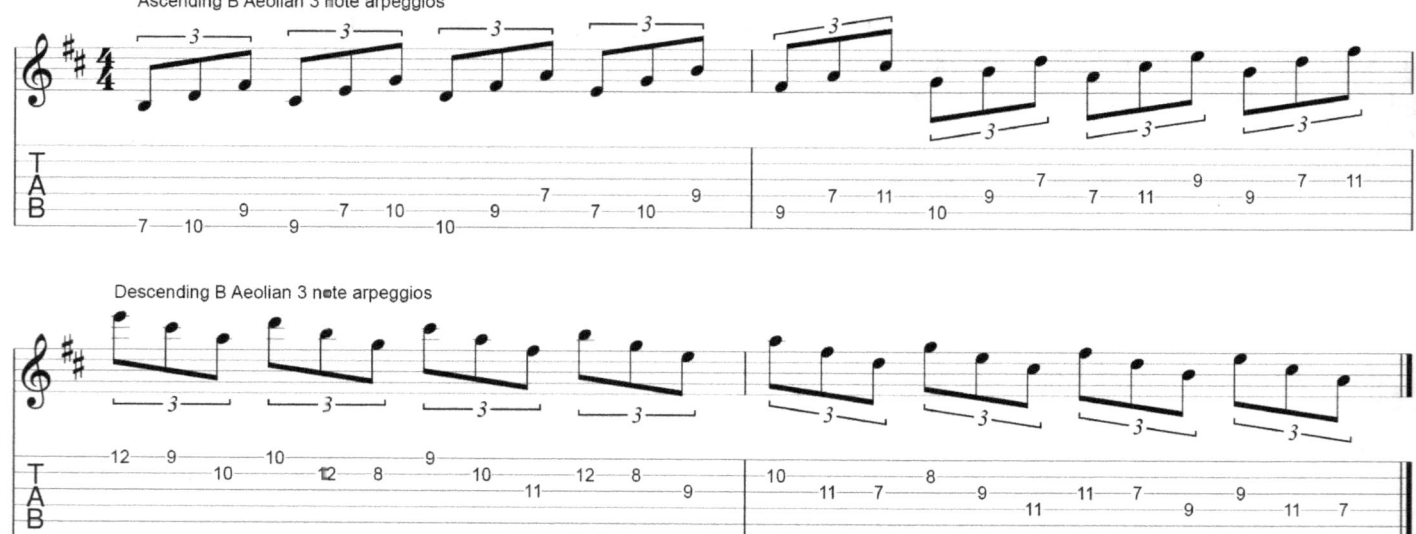

Now play through this B Aeolian three-note-per-string shape with added string skips. This is not only fun to play creates some interesting intervallic jumps.

Example 11r:

In Example 11s I demonstrate a combination of the string skipped legato and the five-note-per-string rolling legato from earlier examples.

Example 11s:

Remember that everything discussed in this section can be transferred to any key, and any three-note-per-string scale. You can transfer these ideas to G Lydian, F Dorian or even an E Hungarian Minor three-note-per-string scale shape! Get creative and try them out in a few different contexts.

More Interesting Arpeggio Sequences

In the final section of this chapter, we'll look at the two most common, five-string arpeggio shapes and how to rearrange them to sound more interesting. All examples use a B minor / D Major triad pattern. First, learn then both in their simplest ascending form.

Example 11t:

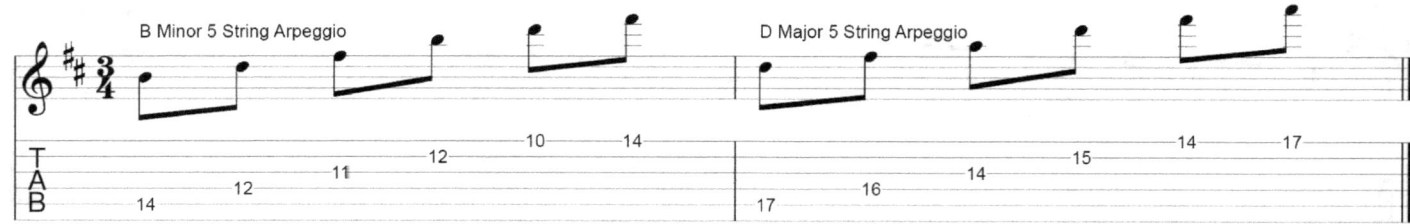

In the first example, both arpeggios are made more interesting by skipping every second note to create a less linear sequential line.

Example 11u:

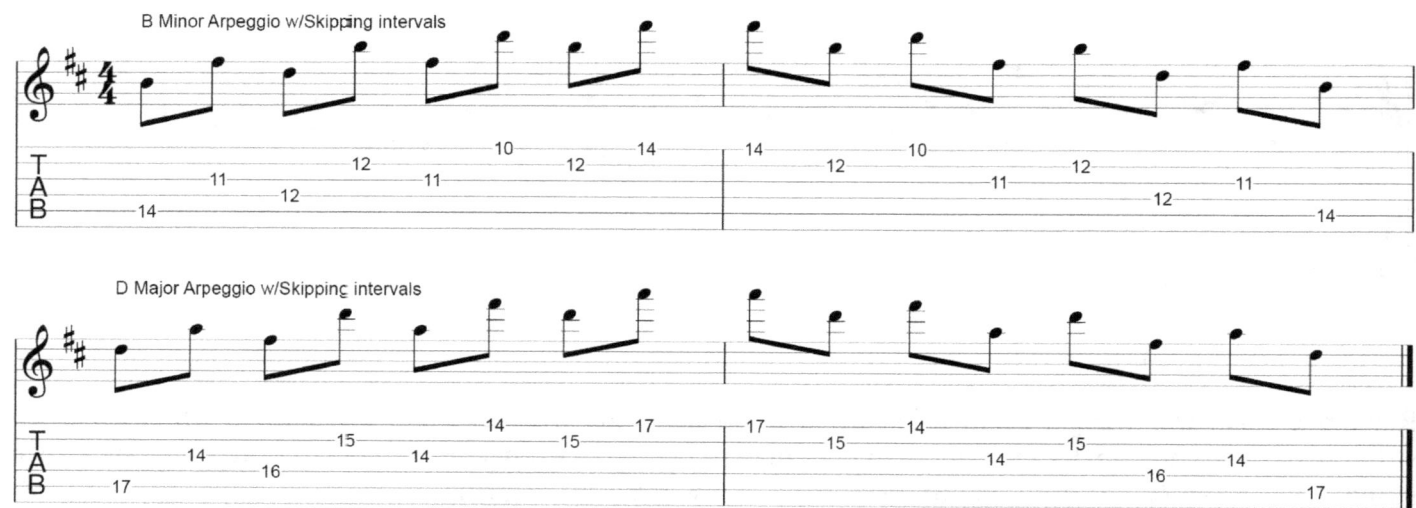

Now try playing the B minor and D Major arpeggio with gradually ascending 1/8th note triplets. This simple approach makes a six-note, two-octave arpeggio, that is twelve notes in length.

Example 11v:

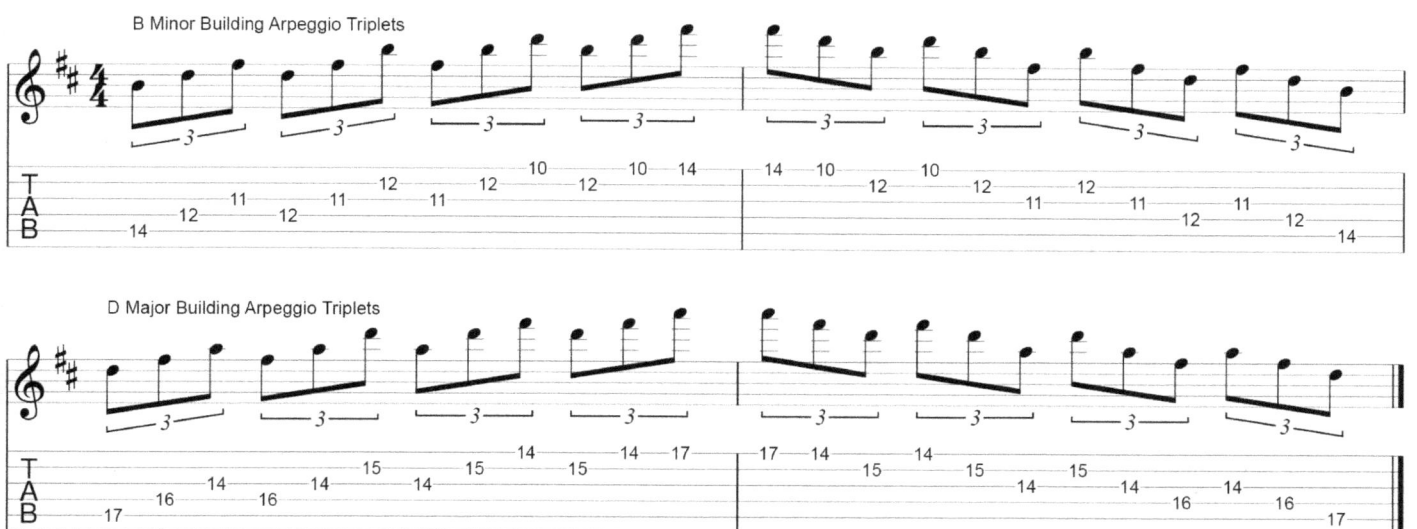

In this final example, each note of the arpeggio is followed by a 5th interval to create a less predictable melody with a futuristic, power chord-esque vibe.

Example 11w:

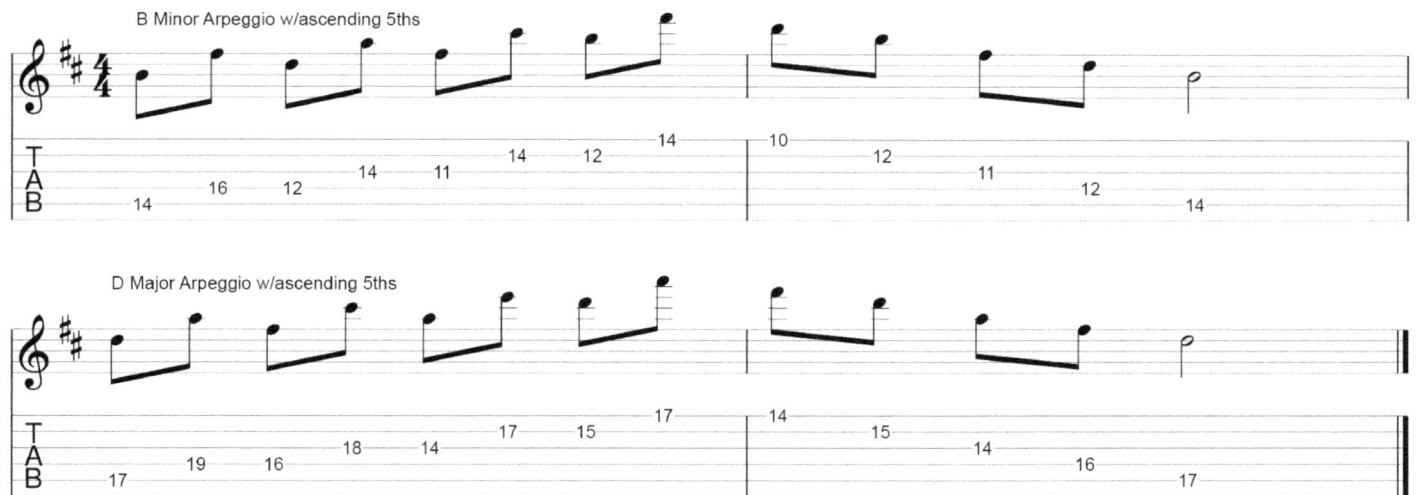

Remember that any of these arpeggio concepts can be used on any triad and any major 7th, minor 7th, dominant 7th, diminished or augmented arpeggio.

This book isn't designed to be a thesaurus of arpeggio shapes, but merely to plant the seed of creative approaches you can use on any arpeggio in an improvised or written solo.

Chapter 12 – Adding Even More Flair, Sass & Pizazz

What makes Slash, Hugh Jackman and Shania Twain infinitely cooler than all of us? Well I guess I could narrow it down to three things: *flair, sass* and *pizazz!*

I bet you're thinking, "Those are dumb buzz words, Chris! What am I going to do with that?" and you'd be right.

Let's put it a different way. How can you add cool techniques to your playing that make it more exciting? That give it a creative edge? In this chapter we'll add the icing on the cake and discuss how to achieve this by using bends, slides and legato. I'm also going to throw in some cheeky grace notes and the odd "outside" note. All of which will add up to make you stand out from the crowd as a player.

Add Flair with Bends

One of the things that really sets the guitar apart as an instrument is the ability to bend notes in order to create emotion and expression. How we bend notes and add vibrato to them is so personal that many players can immediately be identified just by playing a couple of notes. Here are a few cool bending ideas you should incorporate into your playing right away.

In Example 12a I use three bends to transition from shape three to shape one of the E Minor Pentatonic scale. This concept is not limited to pentatonic scales, of course, and can be used to shift to different positions of any scale or arpeggio.

Example 12a:

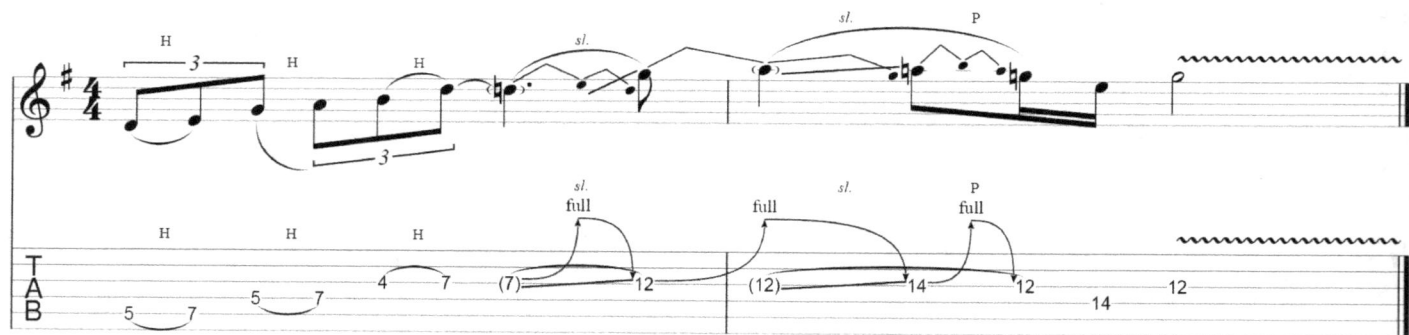

The next idea uses a five-string E minor triad arpeggio with a tense, outside bend from the b5 (Bb) to 5 (B). What's not to love about an outside-to-inside bend?

Example 12b:

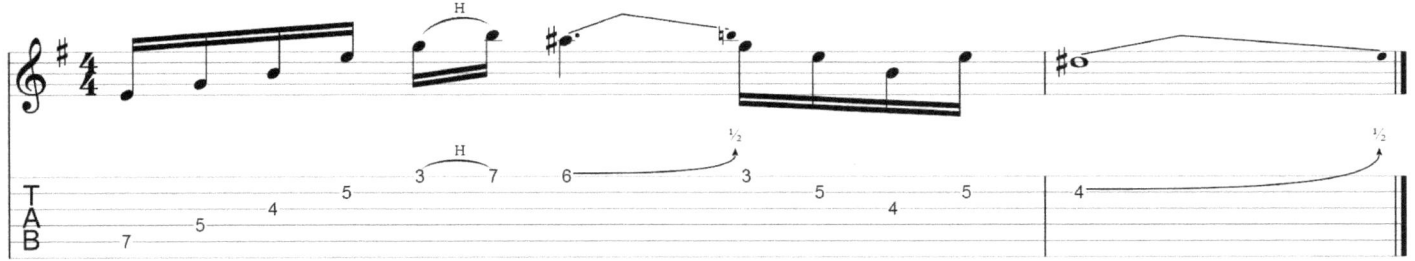

Here's an E Hirajoshi lick with an outside bend from an F (b2) to F# (natural 2). The b2 has a tense Phrygian sound until it resolves into the bent natural 2nd. The release bend in the second bar helps the lick resolve in a pleasing manner.

Example 12c:

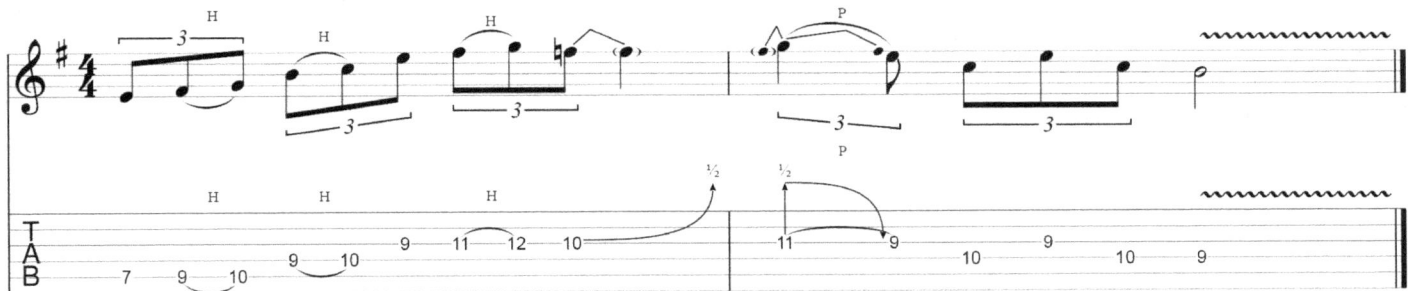

Here's an E minor Pentatonic lick using shapes one and two. It capitalises on a tense outside bend from a major 3rd to perfect 4th in two octaves. You can always milk a bend by playing it slowly!

Example 12d:

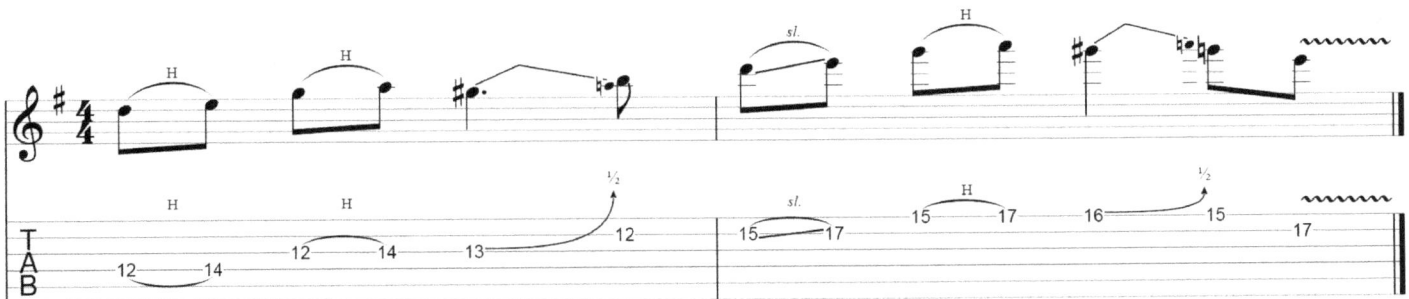

In the final example I use bends to descend the fretboard through multiple shapes of E minor Pentatonic. The large interval jumps and position shifts are not only impressive to watch, but add a bonus of 40% to your total flair score from the Norwegian judge.

Example 12e:

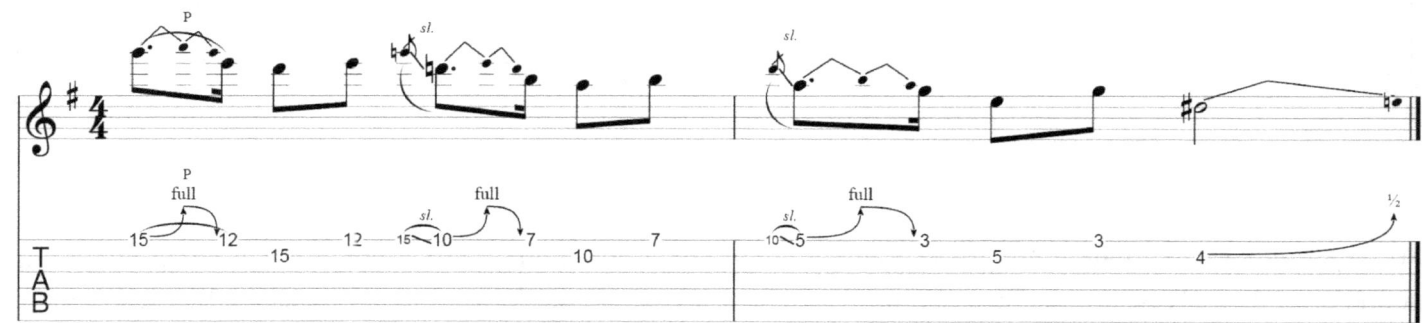

Add Sass with Slides

Like bends, you can also use slides as a means of creating tension. They are ideal to help you shift position and, of course, the old Zoupa favourite – to add interesting outside notes.

Here's an E minor Pentatonic idea with two slides from the b5 to perfect 5th, played on the B string.

Example 12f:

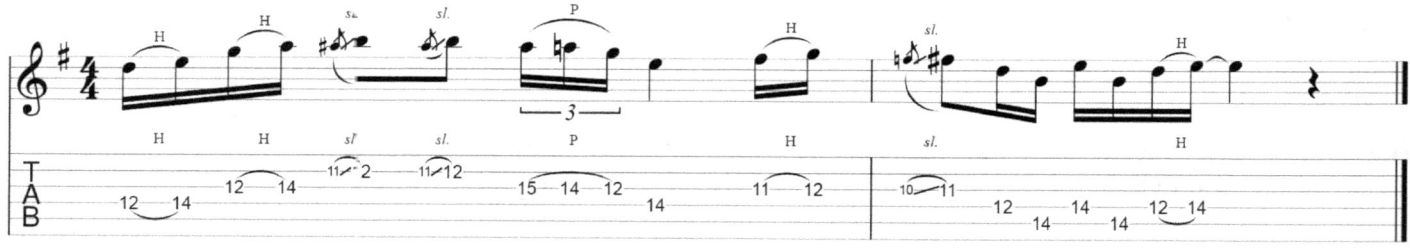

Example 12g has a two octave E minor triad arpeggio with a slide from the major 7th to root, and the b5 to perfect 5th. This approach adds tension to any arpeggio at the entry point, midway, or at the end. You should also experiment with this concept on major, augmented and diminished arpeggios.

Example 12g:

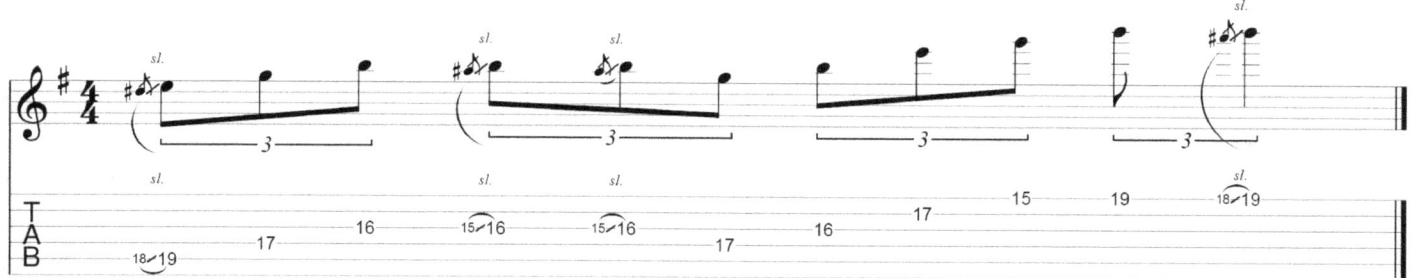

This next idea uses a six-note A Dorian shape ascending three octaves. This lick includes slides from an outside F note (b2) into an inside F# note (2). This approach works well on any six-note scale shape.

Example 12h:

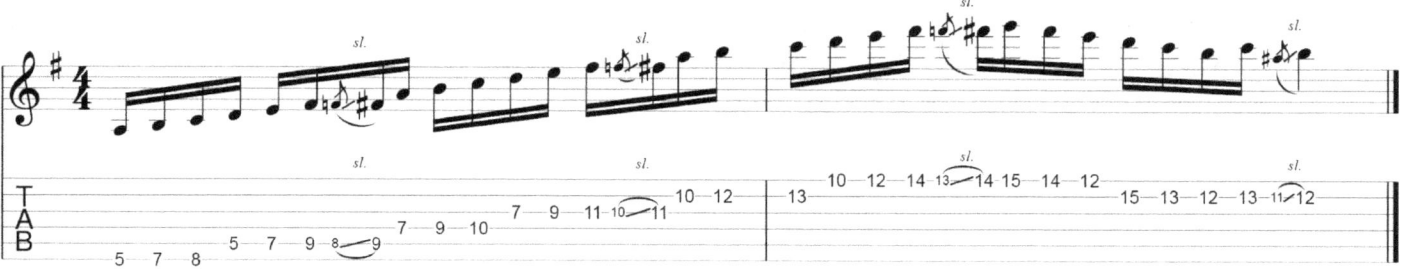

The next example features a variation on a standard jazzy chromatic run, commonly referred to as "the lick". The outside slides create a tension between the b2 and the regular 2nd and also between the b5 and perfect 5th. Well placed chromaticism is a great way to add quintessentially jazzy flair to metal and rock soloing.

Example 12i:

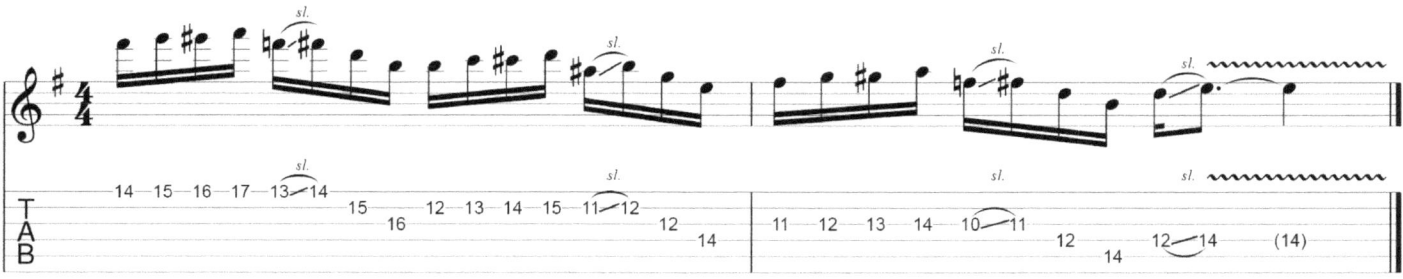

Next is an E minor Pentatonic played across two strings with outside note slides to create multiple position shifts. The horizontal slides add visual flair, but also have a less linear melodic delivery.

Example 12j:

Cheeky Outside Legato Pizazz

A sprinkle of well-placed legato will always create tension, unexpected bursts of speed, interesting outside note usage and, most importantly, *pizazz*.

Play through this E minor Pentatonic fragment that descends through shape three. Speed is created with the placement of legato 1/16th triplets while the lick also highlights the tense, outside b5 note.

Example 12k:

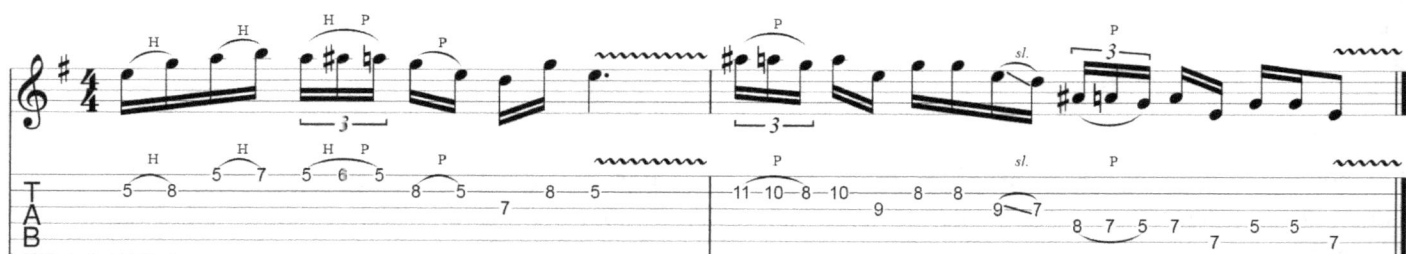

Here's another take on this idea that includes the outside sounding b5.

Example 12l:

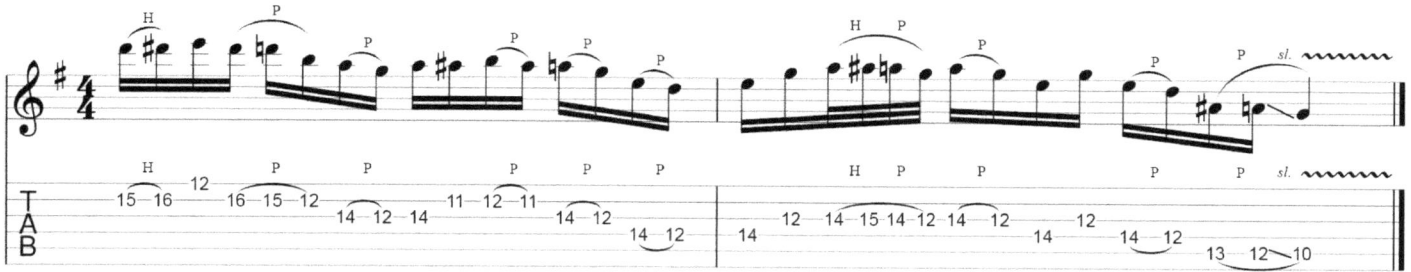

Example 12m features a G Major idea, similar to the previous example, that highlights the b5 and major 7th for another morsel of "outside note goodness".

Side Note: I just coined that term… still not sure if I'm fond of it.

Example 12m:

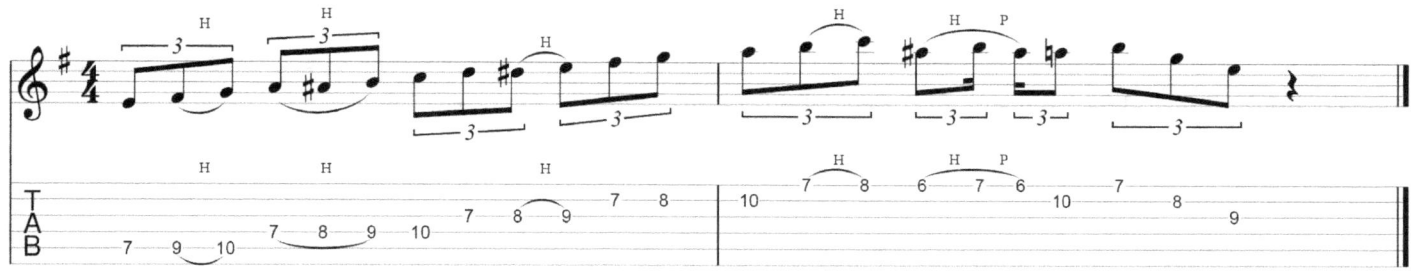

Next is a five-string E minor triad arpeggio with triplet 1/16ths and grace notes to create tension on the b5 and the major 7th. This approach adds an element of Gypsy Jazz to the sound of an otherwise overused, meat and veg arpeggio shape.

Example 12n:

In the next example I demonstrate a pentatonic idea that moves horizontally over three octaves. The outside legato is played as a grace note to create a burst of tension and resolve between the b5 and the perfect 5th. There's also a major 7th interval played with grace notes on the final octave (because when in Rome, right girlfriends?)

Example 12o:

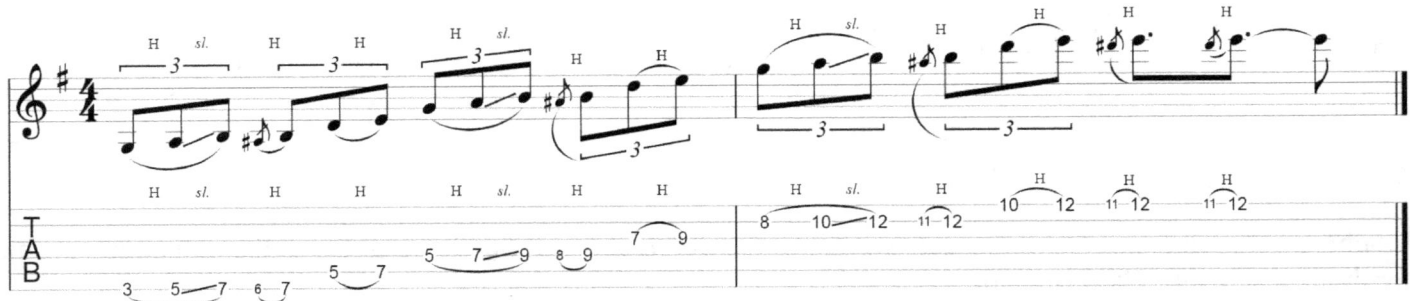

Hopefully, this chapter has stimulated some creative ideas you can apply right away to the licks you know. It's amazing what mileage you can get out of a pretty standard lick by adding a healthy dose of flair, sass and pizazz.

Remember, these ideas are not key specific. Try them in other keys and intertwine the different techniques to create your own individual, unique flair, sass and pizazz to your improvisations.

Chapter 13 – Writing a Solo and Bringing it all Together

We've covered so much territory in this book that it's impossible to pack all of those ideas into ONE solo. I had to be selective – and yet, this is what I'll attempt to do now!

In order to get better at improvisation, in the beginning it's fine to have a plan – even a rough map of the territory you intend to cover. Learning how to structure and a solo with your composition head on will not only aid your song writing, but also your improvisation.

In this last chapter I'm going to give you a run down on how to structure a guitar solo help you think about how you can write your own. I'll include as many elements as possible from the previous chapters.

If you think of some of the greatest solos of all time, whether they were composed or improvised, they all have a *storytelling* element to them that makes them memorable and takes the listener on a journey. What does storytelling have to do with guitar solos? Let's take look at the tale of *Little Red Riding Hood* in the most concise manner possible. Bear with me…

Beginning: Little girl decides to venture into the woods to visit Grandma.

Middle Part 1: Girl encounters wolf; politely sidesteps being eaten and continues on her way.

Middle Part 2: Wolf goes to Grandma's house and eats her, then poorly disguises himself in her bed to ready himself for a second helping of person.

Ending: Girl finds out Granny had been eaten, yells "Wolf!" till woodsman comes and slays the wolf.

This story has a beginning, and end, and a two-part double-jeopardy middle section. This exactly how I try to write my guitar solos. An obvious beginning, an interesting dual-faceted middle and a climatic or resolved ending. With that thought process in mind, have a look at the solo I've created for you to learn.

I have used the key of F# minor as the backing to the solo.

Beginning: The First Four Bars

The beginning of a solo should set the tone for things to come without giving away too much too soon.

I use 1/4 notes and dotted 1/4 notes in the first two bars to keep the melody slow and simple as well as highlighting the chord tones of the F#m. In the third bar I use 1/4 note triplets to superimpose a Dmaj7 arpeggio over the Bm chord, then I build speed using F# minor Pentatonic shape five with 1/16th notes and hammer-ons.

Example 13a:

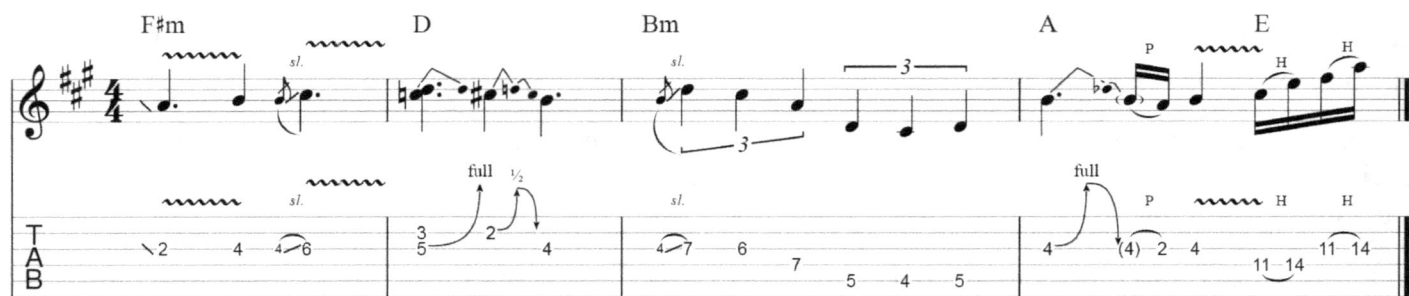

Middle Part 1: Bars 5-8

In this section of the solo, I want the story to progress a bit further and add some tension to keep the story exciting and the listener engaged.

Using the momentum built from bar four, I continue the F# minor Pentatonic run through bars five and six, nearly playing in strict 1/16th notes with an initial triplet and a few 1/8th notes.

In bar seven, I use an outside to inside bend to target the root note of the Bm chord. I also use some double-stop chords as a contrast to all the single note lines that have been played so far. I resolve the final bar on some slow notes from F# minor Pentatonic shape three.

Example 13b:

Middle Part 2: Bars 9-12

In the majority of my solos, this is the point at which I'll bring the most chaos and aim for a climactic peak. You'll notice that these next four bars have more notes than any of the other sections.

The ninth bar begins with a 1/16th rest, then works into a combination of an F#m7 arpeggio with a superimposed Amaj7 arpeggio. This bar is made entirely of 1/16th notes and heads towards a tapped pentatonic on bar ten. This is played with 1/16th triplets to create another shift in gear.

Example 13c:

Ending: The Last Four Bars

To end this solo, I decided to pull back from the chaos a little to give the solo dynamics and varying moments of intensity.

In the first bar, over the F#m chord, I play a simple F# minor Pentatonic lick beginning with an outside grace note. I then work into a simple octave chord melody using 1/4 note triplets to add a staggered, minimalist sound.

In bar 15, over the Bm chord, I leave ample space at the beginning of the bar, then pick up with a lick based around F# minor Pentatonic shape three.

Over the A chord in bar 16 I use the A Ionian three-note-per-string shape with a neoclassical picking pattern. I then turn the lick into a mixture of legato and shred, increasing the speed by using 1/16th and 1/32 triplets.

Example 13d:

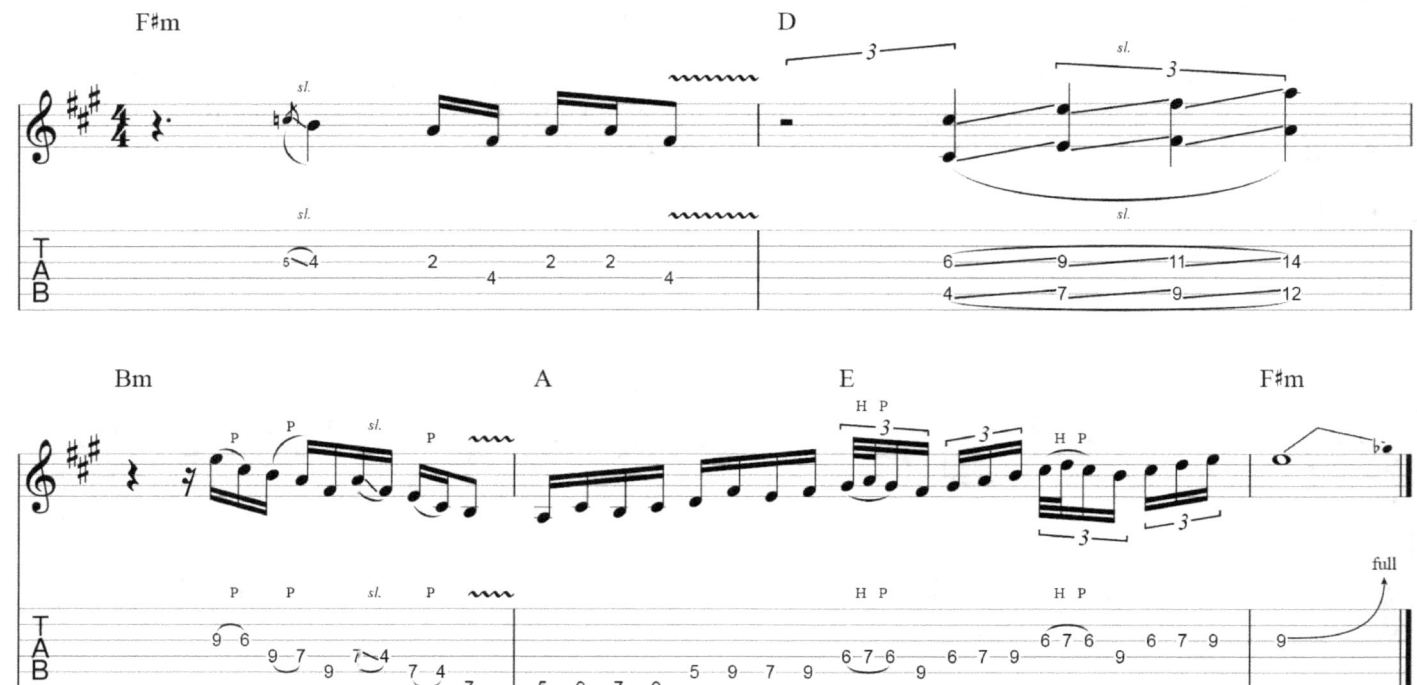

Listen to the backing track provided and try to create your own solo. You can use my soloing guide as a structure to create your own, but experimentation is the name of the game. Break all the rules and do whatever you want to do! Try drawing at least one idea from every chapter in your solo composition!

The following pages feature the notation/TAB for the entire solo. You can listen to it on audio Example 13e included with the free download.

Full Solo

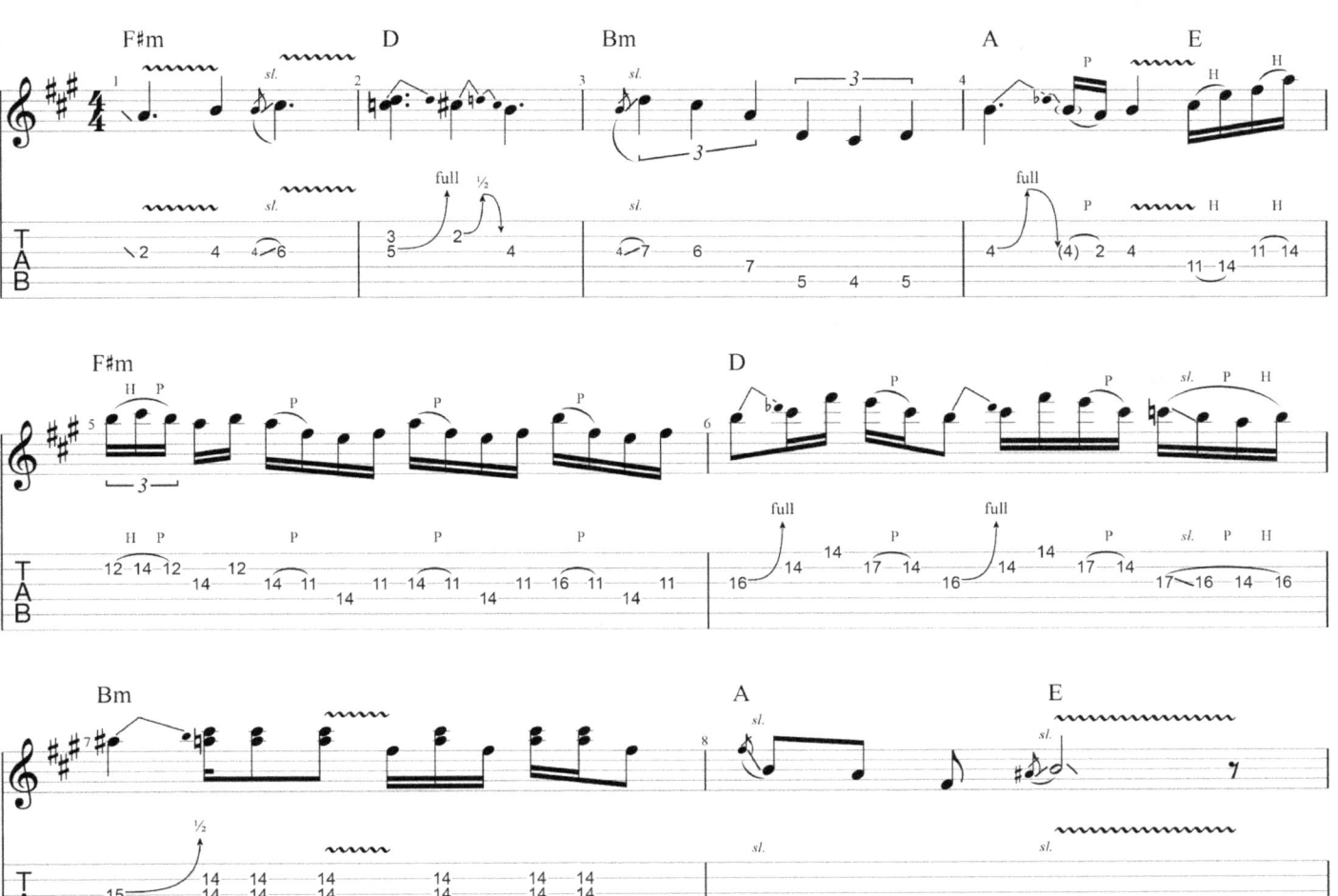

A Gentleman's Conclusion

Congratulations! You've made it to the end of this book! Now you should have many approaches, sequences, licks and ideas to add to your improvised (and even composed) solos.

More important than just "doing what Chris said in his book" I have to stress the importance of finding *the thing* (or things) that make *your* playing personal and identifiable.

The journey of self-discovery is a long, harrowing and ever-changing one, and it is my hope that my learning, note choices and taste continues to evolve throughout my life. I wish all of my students and readers of this book to keep a similar, open mind. It all comes down to experimentation and finding your unique voice.

Keep shreddin', improving and composing those solos. Take some risks, get uncomfortable and discover some new and crazy ways to express yourself on the guitar.

Chris

www.ingramcontent.com/pod-product-compliance
Lightning Source LLC
Chambersburg PA
CBHW051147290426
44108CB00019B/2634